Daily Lives, Miracles, and Wisdom of the Saints & Fasting Calendar 2020

∞

Front Cover: St. Mary of Egypt receiving the Holy Eucharist from St. Zosimas Icon courtesy of St. Nektarios Orthodox Church, Lenoir City, TN

ST. MARY OF EGYPT (April 1). The priest-monk St. Zosimas went into the deep wilderness during Lent to pray when he happened upon Mary, who fled when she saw him. She was naked with dark skin and white hair. She called him by name and asked for his cloak and a blessing and told him of her life. She had been a prostitute in Alexandria for seventeen years until an invisible force prevented her from entering the church to venerate the Life-giving Cross. Mary wept bitterly and confessed her sins before an icon of the Mother of God. Then an unseen force parted the crowd, and she venerated the Cross. Mary heard a voice from the icon telling her that she would find peace across the Jordan River. She lived as an ascetic in the wilderness for forty-six years, eating plants and battling the passions and elements. Zosimas saw Mary suspended in midair when she prayed. She asked him to return a year later to the bank of the Jordan River to give her the Holy Eucharist which he did. He watched her make the Sign of the Cross and quickly pass over the water. Again, she asked him to return the following year, which he did. He found her body with a message traced in the sand, saying that she had reposed immediately after receiving the Holy Eucharist. With the assistance of a lion, Sozimas buried St. Mary.

RESEARCHED AND WRITTEN BY TOM AND GEORGIA MITRAKOS

ORTHODOX CALENDAR COMPANY ☦ PITTSBURGH, PENNSYLVANIA

This calendar follows the Revised Julian Calendar (New Calendar). All listed commemorations and Scripture readings are according to the Greek Orthodox Church liturgical calendar.

The fasting guidelines are those prescribed by the Church. Fasting is a spiritual discipline and it is recommended that each Orthodox Christian consult with their spiritual father.

Fast-free - All foods allowed.

Strict Fast - Abstain from meat products, dairy products, fish, oil, and wine.

Copyright © 2019 Orthodox Calendar Company
All rights reserved.

Orthodox Calendar Company
P. O. Box 11331, Pittsburgh, PA 15238
Tel: 412-736-7840
Email: OrthodoxCalendarCompany@gmail.com
Facebook.com/OrthodoxCalendarCompany

ISBN-13: 978-0-9980817-3-1
ISBN-10: 0-9980817-3-6

Printed in the United States of America.

WEDNESDAY

JANUARY 1

Circumcision of Christ
Fast-free
Colossians 2:8-12; Luke 2:20-21, 40-52

Alleluia! Let us praise God, brethren, with our life, with our lips, with our heart, with our mouth, with our voice, with our example. God wants us to sing the *Alleluia* without any inconsistency in us. Let us then align our life with our lips, with our mouth, with our conscience. Let us take care that our life agrees with our voice, because otherwise the *Alleluia* will be to our condemnation.

St. Augustine of Hippo

THE CIRCUMCISION OF OUR LORD AND SAVIOR JESUS CHRIST. The Circumcision of Christ took place on the eighth day after His Nativity, according to the Old Testament Law of the Covenant of God with the Forefather Abraham and his descendants. The ritual of circumcision prefigured the sacrament of Holy Baptism. On the day that Jesus was circumcised, He received the name Jesus, which means "salvation," to announce the coming of our own salvation. St. John of the Ladder says, "Flog the adversaries incessantly with the name of Jesus; there is no weapon more powerful in heaven or on earth."

COMMEMORATIONS: The Circumcision according to the Flesh of Our Lord and God and Savior Jesus Christ; Basil the Great, Archbishop of Caesarea; Gregory, Bishop of Nazianzus; Theodosius of Tryglia; Fulgentius, Bishop of Ruspe; Basil of Ancyra; Peter of the Peloponnesus; Platon of Revel, with Michael, Nicholas, and Alexander; Theodotos and Telemachos; Emilia, mother of St. Basil the Great; Athanasius, Bishop of Mogilev; New Hieromartyr Jeremiah; Clarus of Vienne; Fanchea of Killeany; Eugendus, abbot of Condat.

Thursday   **Fast-free**

January 2

Hebrews 5:4-10; John 3:1-15

Do not reproach anyone for their sins, but consider yourself responsible for everything, even for your neighbor's sins.
+Elder Justin Parvu of Romania

MARTYR SERGIOS OF CAESAREA IN CAPPADOCIA. During the third- and fourth-century persecutions of Emperor Diocletian, Governor Sapritius traveled through Caesarea in Cappadocia and imprisoned the few Christians there, as most had fled to the mountains. None of those arrested denied their faith despite cruel tortures. Sergios, who was once a judge, was now an older man and a monk living in the wilderness, but no one knew about him. However, on the day of the Christian arrests, he felt an inner turmoil and went to the town square in Caesarea, where the annual sacrifice to the pagan god Zeus was celebrated. The pagan priest told the people that the gods refused the sacrifice because the Christians refused to participate. Filled with zeal, Sergios ascended the temple steps and gave a fiery sermon rebuking the worship and sacrifice to idols, and by his prayers, the sacrificial fires were extinguished. The enraged governor gave orders to behead St. Sergios and all the Christian prisoners.

COMMEMORATIONS: Cosmas I, Patriarch of Constantinople; Sylvester, Pope of Rome; Theogenes, Bishop of Parium; Gerasimus II, Patriarch of Alexandria; Theodota, mother of the first Cosmas and Damian; Sergios of Caesarea; Ammon of Tabennisi; Mark the Deaf; Righteous Theopemptos; Sylvester of the Kiev Caves; Juliana of Lazarevo; Martyr Theopistos; George (Zorzes) the Georgian; Nilos the Sanctified; Basil of Ancyra; Smaragda, abbess of Nezhinsk (Ukraine); Schottin, hermit of Ireland; 1,000 Martyrs of Lichfield; Repose and second finding of the relics of St. Seraphim of Sarov.

FRIDAY

JANUARY 3

Malachi the Prophet
Fast-free
Acts 10:44-11:10; John 1:18-28

If you will pray for your enemies, peace will come to you!
St. Silouan the Athonite

ST. THOMAIS OF LESVOS. Thomais was from the tenth-century island of Lesvos. Her parents, Michael and Kali, were childless but through the intercessions of the Panagia, who appeared to Kali, Thomais was born. When she was 24 years old, her parents pressured her to marry a barbaric man named Stephen, who beat her every day for thirteen years. She was kicked, slapped, berated, and burned, among other torments. Still, she prayed, gave alms, had patience, and gave thanksgiving. Thomais and Stephen moved to Constantinople, and her mother became a nun and later abbess at the Mikra Romaiou Convent. The abuse continued, but Thomais received comfort by doing good for others and attending church services where she prayed for the salvation of the world, even though Stephen often prevented her. Thomais died at the age of 38 and was buried in her mother's convent. Forty days after her burial, the incorrupt relic of St. Thomais was uncovered and placed it in a reliquary inside the church. Her hands still bore the wounds inflicted by her husband. After her death, Stephen became demon-possessed, but they led him in chains to her tomb and he was healed. Many other miracles were wrought at the saint's grave, including the healing of the demon-possessed, epilepsy, paralysis, and those suffering from terrible stomach and head pains. Her relic was lost, most likely during the sack of Constantinople in the early thirteenth century.

COMMEMORATIONS: Prophet Malachi; Genevieve of Paris; Peter of Atroa; Gordius at Caesarea; Euthymius, the Man of God of Tbilisi; Abelard of Belgium; Titus, Bishop of Tomis; Thomais of Lesvos; Findlugan of Islay; Three martyrs, a mother and her two children slain by fire; Finding of the relics of New Monk-martyr St. Ephraim of Nea Makri.

Saturday

January 4

Saturday before Holy Theophany
Fast-free
1 Timothy 3:13-4:5; Matthew 3:1-6

*D*o not ask for anything worldly, but everything spiritual, and you shall receive for sure.

St. John Chrysostom

ST. DAFROSA OF ROME. Dafrosa was married to Flavian, the fourth-century prefect of Rome, during the reign of Emperor Julian the Apostate. When it was discovered that Flavian was a Christian, he was removed from office, branded on the forehead as a slave, and exiled to a village in Tuscany, Italy, where he was tortured and died. Dafrosa was sent to the house of a certain Faustus, who wanted to marry her. She refused and instead converted him to Christianity. After his baptism, he was executed, and Dafrosa secretly buried his body at night. After five days, while in prayer, she departed to heaven. Another account says she was taken outside the city and beheaded. Dafrosa and Flavian had two daughters, Bibiana and Demetria, who were stripped of their possessions and left to suffer in poverty. However, they were unaffected, passing their time in fasting and prayer. When the prefect Apronianus saw this, he summoned them. Demetria confessed her faith and fell dead at his feet. Bibiana was subjected to beatings and persuasion, but she remained faithful. Finally, she was tied to a pillar and flogged with scourges laden with lead pieces. Bibiana endured this with joy and died under the blows. She was left to wild animals, but none would touch her. After two days, she was buried. A church was built over the site of her martyrdom, and the Basilica of St. Bibiana still exists.

COMMEMORATIONS: Synaxis of the 70 Apostles; Eustathios I of Serbia; 13 Syrian Fathers of Georgia; Gregory, Bishop of Langres; Theoctistus of Cucomo; Euthymios the New of Thessalonica; Zosimas the Hermit and Athanasios the Commentarius; Aquila of the Kiev Caves; Euthymios and 12 monks of Vatopedi; Dafrosa of Rome; Symeon of Smolensk; Holy 6 Martyrs; Apollinaria of Egypt; Chrysanthos and Euphemia in Constantinople; Timothy the Stylite of Kakhshata; Nikephoros the Leper; Onuphrius of Gabrovo; Mark of Sergievsk; Ethiopian Eunuch of Queen Candace.

Sunday

January 5

Sunday before Holy Theophany
Abstain from meat and dairy products, and fish.
2 Timothy 4:5-8; Mark 1:1-8

Let not one think, my fellow Christians, that only priests and monks need to pray without ceasing and not laymen... No, no! every Christian without exception ought to dwell always in prayer.
St. Gregory Palamas

ST. MENAS OF SINAI. Menas lived at a monastery in Sinai for 59 years. Once, the abbot wanted to test his patience, so when Menas went to the abbot's cell as usual in the evening, he prostrated himself before the abbot to get his instruction. However, the abbot left him lying on the ground for many hours. Finally, he blessed Menas and rebuked him for being fond of self-display and for being impatient, and he ordered him to get up. The abbot did this for the edification of the monks because he knew Menas would bear it courageously. A disciple of St. Menas asked him if he fell asleep while laying prostrate before the abbot, and he replied that while lying on the ground, he recited by heart the whole Psalter. Menas died peacefully in the sixth century. Three days after he died, they had performed the customary rites over him, when suddenly the whole place filled with a fragrance. They uncovered his coffin and saw myrrh was flowing from his feet like two fountains. St. John Climacus speaks of St. Menas in the book, *The Ladder of Divine Ascent*, where he is portrayed as a model of obedience.

COMMEMORATIONS: Syncletike of Alexandria; Phosterios and Menas of Sinai; Gregory at Akrita; Martyr Sais; Theopemptos of Nicomedia and Theonas; Martyr Theoeidos; Righteous Domnina; Righteous Tatiana; Romanos of Carpenision; Talida, abbess of Antinoe, and Taora; Theophan of the Rykhlovsk Monastery (Ukraine); Symeon of the Pskov Caves; Niphon, Bishop of Cyprus; Cera (Kiara) of Ireland.

Monday

January 6

Holy Theophany
Fast-free

Titus 2:11-14, 3:4-7; Matthew 3:13-17

Moses baptized but it was in water ... John also baptized ... not only in water, but also "unto repentance." Still it was not wholly spiritual, for he does not add "And in the Spirit." Jesus also baptized, but in the Spirit. This is the perfect Baptism.

St. Gregory the Theologian

THE HOLY THEOPHANY OF OUR LORD AND SAVIOR JESUS CHRIST. From the Biblical Greek, "Epiphany" means "Manifest upon," and "Theophany" means the "Manifestation of God." Theophany is considered one of the great feasts of the Orthodox Church. It commemorates the Baptism of Jesus in the Jordan River by St. John the Baptist. St. Cyril states that the beginning of the world was water, and the beginning of the Gospel was the Jordan when the Holy Trinity was revealed to the senses. Jesus allowed Himself to be baptized with the sinners even though he had no sin, showing that he accepts His calling as the "Lamb of God Who takes away the sins of the world (John 1:29)." The Holy Spirit was seen in the form of a dove, and St. John the Baptist bore witness. "He saw the Spirit of God descending like a dove and alighting upon Him (Mt 3:16.) The Father spoke, saying, "This is My beloved Son, in Whom I am well pleased (Matthew 3:17)."

COMMEMORATIONS: Holy Theophany of Our Lord Jesus Christ; New Martyrs Priest Andrew Zimin, his wife Lydia, their three daughters, and Domnica, of Russia; New Martyr Romanus of Lacedemonia, at Constantinople; Laurence of Chernigov; Repose of St. Theophan the Recluse.

Tuesday

January 7

Synaxis of St. John the Forerunner
Fast-free
Acts 19:1-8; John 1:29-34

If you take little account of yourself, you will have peace, wherever you live.

St. Poemen the Great

SYNAXIS OF THE HOLY GLORIOUS PROPHET AND FORERUNNER ST. JOHN THE BAPTIST. The Synaxis is the gathering of God's people to listen to John preaching repentance for the forgiveness of sins. He was the last of the Old Testament prophets and the only one able to point to Jesus of Whom some had prophesied saying, "Behold, the Lamb of God." John's ministry began about two years before Jesus began His. The icon portraying him is always next to the icon of Jesus on the icon screen in Orthodox churches. John's finger is portrayed unusually long in Byzantine icons to express that his primary purpose was to point to Jesus as the Messiah. The highest moment of his ministry was Theophany. After he was beheaded in the dungeons of Machaerus, his head was buried deep in a dishonorable place, and then quickly reburied respectfully by a pious woman at the Mount of Olives. His body was buried where he had died in Sebaste. St. Luke the Evangelist succeeded in taking John's hand to Antioch, where a small chapel was built. Crowds of people came to venerate and experience miraculous cures as well. It remained there for eight hundred years until the emperor transferred it to Constantinople. It was said that on every anniversary of St. John's feastday, the holy hand would either be open, meaning it would be a fertile year, or closed, predicting a year of famine.

COMMEMORATIONS: Synaxis of St. John the Forerunner; Miracle of St. John the Baptist in Chios; Translation of the right hand of St. John the Baptist; New Martyr Athanasios of Attalia and Smyrna; Cedd, Bishop of Lastingham; Brannock (Brynach) of Braunton (England); Kentigerna of Loch Lomond; Paphnutius (Kostin) of Optina Monastery; Nicholas (Parfenov), Bishop of Atkarsk.

WEDNESDAY

Strict Fast

JANUARY 8

Romans 6:3-11; John 3:22-33

We must never believe that our sinful state is beyond repair. We must be confident that there is always forgiveness for us. All we need to do to be forgiven is to ask.

+Elder Sergei of Vanves

ST. THEODORE OF CONSTANTINOPLE. Theodore was the uncle of Empress Theodora, wife of Emperor Justinian, in fifth-century Constantinople. He became an anchorite and lived in a small hut near Antioch and was known as a holy man. Justinian had recalled him to help the Church fight against the heresy of the Theopaschites, who claimed that Christ had only one nature, the divine, and that this nature suffered at the Crucifixion. Afterward, Theodore decided to settle in a small cell in northwest Constantinople that had water and a small garden nearby. About a dozen able ascetics gathered around him who were educated in the study of scripture and psalmody, and soon the number of monks grew to 100. Because of the financial assistance from Justinian, the Monastery of Chora was established. They offered a guest house for the sick, the poor, and the blind. It was said that Theodore oversaw this community for almost 60 years, running it as a private foundation. It prospered primarily as a result of his energy, strong will, and talents, with the help of a few close advisors. The monastery was destroyed in the middle of the sixth century and was rebuilt by Justinian.

COMMEMORATIONS: Carterios of Caesarea; Dominica of Carthage; Atticus and Cyrus, Patriarchs of Constantinople; George the Chozevite; Agathon of Egypt; Abo the Perfumer; Elias of Egypt; Julian, Basilissa, Marcionilla, Celsus, Anthony, Anastasius, 7 children, and 20 soldiers at Antinoe; Theophilus and Helladius in Libya; Gregory of Ochrid; Gregory of the Kiev Caves, wonderworker; Gregory of the Kiev Caves, recluse; Paisius of Uglich; Macarius (Macres) of Vatopedi; Isidore and 72 companions at Yuriev; Severinus of Austria; Theodore of Constantinople; Pega of Peakirk; Wulsin of Sherborne; Erhard of Regensburg; Gudula of Brussels; Nathalan of Aberdeenshire; Severin of Cologne.

Thursday   **Fast-free**

January 9

2 Timothy 2:1-10; Mark 1:9-15

If there is a chance I will be saved, it will be through the prayers of mothers. Do you know how many moving letters I get where they thank me for having convinced their children to cut their hair and take out their earrings?

— St. Paisios the Athonite

MARTYR POLYEUKTOS AT MELITENE. Polyeuktos was a pagan and the first martyr in the town of Melitene, Armenia in the third century. Emperor Valerian posted a royal decree that all Christians were to be killed. Nearchos was a Christian and friend of Polyeuktos, and he began to prepare for his death. When Polyeuktos heard about his friend's plight, he promised to become a Christian. That night he saw Jesus in a dream, Who clothed him in a bright garment and placed him on a winged horse. The next day Polyeuktos tore up the royal decree and went about smashing idols. He was arrested, tortured, and condemned to death. In route to his execution, he saw Nearchos, and he called to him, saying, "Save your soul my dear soul friend!" Nearchos later was martyred by fire.

COMMEMORATIONS: Peter, Bishop of Sebaste, brother of Basil the Great and Gregory of Nyssa; Polyeuktos of Melitene in Armenia; Eustratios of Tarsus; Philip, Metropolitan of Moscow; Jonah, founder of Holy Trinity Monastery in Kiev; Adrian of Canterbury; Parthena of Edessa; Finian, Bishop of Lindisfarne; Prophet Shemaiah (Sameas); Berhtwald, Archbishop of Canterbury; Fillan, abbot of Strathfillan; Translation of the relics of St. Judoc, hermit of Ponthie.

FRIDAY

St. Gregory of Nyssa
Strict Fast

JANUARY 10

Ephesians 4:7-13; Matthew 4:25-5:12

*C*ourage and confidence are our weapons to deflect the enemy's surprise attacks. Hope and patience are the staffs to lean on when we are worn out by worldly trials. And we must stock up on sorrow and be ready to apply it, if need be, when we repent of our sins. At the same time, we must believe that it is only useful for serving our repentance. Righteousness will be our straight-edge ruler, guarding us from stumbling in word or action, guiding us how to use our spiritual abilities, and teaching us to be considerate towards everyone we meet.

St. Gregory of Nyssa

ST. GREGORY, BISHOP OF NYSSA. Gregory was a force for Orthodoxy in the fourth century. He was part of the triumvirate, including his brother St. Basil the Great and St. Gregory the Theologian, which helped to defeat Arianism and other heresies of the time. Arians believed that God created Jesus, and therefore not equal to God, and this distorted the truth of the Holy Trinity. Gregory was a translator of Holy Scripture, as well as a priest. Together with his wife, he traveled the empire teaching Christianity. After her death, St. Basil ordained Gregory bishop of Nyssa. Following a trip to Constantinople, where he spoke against the Arians before the Arian Emperor Valerian, Gregory was exiled for several years. He returned when Valerian and his army were killed in battle. St. Gregory participated in the Second Ecumenical Council. He is credited with writing the section of the Creed that includes the Holy Spirit.

COMMEMORATIONS: Gregory, Bishop of Nyssa; Theophan the Recluse; Theosebia the Deaconess, sister of Basil the Great and Gregory of Nyssa; Marcian of Constantinople; Dometian, Bishop of Melitene; Ammon of Nitria; Paul of Obnora; Ephraim and six incorrupt monks of Obnora; Macarius of Pisemsk and Kostroma; Peter Uspensky of Radushino; Antipas of Romania; Macarius of Pisma Monastery; Miltiades, Pope of Rome; Antipas of Valaam; Anatole of Odessa; Arsenia, abbess in Shuisk.

SATURDAY

JANUARY 11

Saturday after Holy Theophany
Fast-free
Hebrews 13:7-16; Matthew 4:1-11

*D*o not search for exalted experiences in prayer—they are not proper to a sinner. Even the desire of a sinner to feel exalted is already delusion. Seek instead the resurrection of your dead, petrified heart, that it may become open to the knowledge of its own sinfulness and the depth of its fall and its insignificance, to see it and to admit it with self-denial. Then you will find within yourself the true fruit of prayer—sincere repentance.

St. Ignatius Brianchaninov

NEW MARTYR NIKEPHOROS OF CRETE. Nikephoros was a Christian from the early nineteenth-century village of Kritsa in Crete. He married a Muslim woman and had two sons. During this time, he changed his faith and became a Muslim. Later, he repented and lived the Christian faith and life. His wife denounced him to the authorities, and he was arrested and taken before the judge in Heraklion. The case was referred to the religious court, and when Nikephoros confessed his faith, he was hanged, at the age of thirty.

COMMEMORATIONS: Theodosios the Great, the Cenobiarch; Theodosios, Metropolitan of Trebizond; Theodosios of Antioch; Stephen of Placidian; Agapius of Apamea; Romilos the Hermit of Veddin; Vitalis of Abba Serid at Gaza; Michael of Klops Monastery; Joseph of Cappadocia; Nikephoros of Crete; Martyr Mairus; Hyginus, Pope of Rome; Vladimir the Confessor of Minsk; New Martyrs Nicholas, Theodore and Vladimir; "Chernigov-Eletskaya" Icon of the Mother of God.

SUNDAY

Sunday after Holy Theophany
Fast-free

January 12

Ephesians 4:7-13; Matthew 4:12-17

*F*aith and love which are gifts of the Holy Spirit are such great and powerful means that a person who has them can easily, and with joy and consolation, go the way Jesus Christ went. Besides this, the Holy Spirit gives man the power to resist the delusions of the world so that although he makes use of earthly good, yet he uses them as a temporary visitor, without attaching his heart to them. But a man who has not got the Holy Spirit, despite all his learning and prudence, is always more or less a slave and worshipper of the world.

St. Innocent of Irkutsk

ST. ELIAS THE WONDERWORKER OF EGYPT. Elias remained in the desolate desert and mountain of Antinoe for 70 years. He lived to be about 110 years old. The monks used to say that the spirit of the Prophet Elias rested upon him. He never went down to Shaina, but there was a difficult and narrow path that pilgrims could traverse to get to his dwelling under a rock in a cave. Elias had a condition that caused him to tremble, but he would work miracles daily and healed the sick. When he grew old, he would eat three ounces of bread and three olives every evening. However, as a young man, Elias would eat only once a week. He said that he feared three things: the moment his soul would leave his body, when he would appear before God, and when his sentence would be given.

COMMEMORATIONS: Tatiana of Rome; Peter Absalom in Palestine; 8 Martyrs of Nicaea; Philotheus of Antioch; Mertius of Mauretania; Theodora of Alexandria; Eupraxia of Tabenna in Egypt; Elias the Wonderworker, of *The Paradise*; John of Tula, fool-for-Christ; Galacteon and Martinian of White Lake; Martyr Euthasia; Benedict Biscop, abbot of Wearmouth; "The Milk-giver" and Hilander "Of the Akathist" Icons of the Mother of God; "Popska" and "Mesopanditissa" Icons of the Mother of God; (1st Sunday after Theophany: Neollina, Domnina, and Parthena of Edessa; Joseph the New of Cappadocia.

Monday

Fast-free

January 13

Galatians 3:23-4:5; Luke 20:1-8

*W*hat should be our main interest: how others see us, or how Christ sees us? Will others be our driving force, or will Christ? You are a serious person; do not become light-headed. Even serious people praise me many times, and this just makes me feel sick. I laugh inside and merely dismiss their words. You too should dismiss such words of praise at once. They are useless! What shall we gain if others are admiring us — that the little devils will admire us in the future? Whoever rejoices when others admire him is being mocked by the demons.

St. Paisios the Athonite

MARTYRS HERMILOS AND STRATONIKOS THE MARTYRS. These saints were Christians in the fourth century during the persecutions of Emperor Licinius. Hermilos was a deacon, and Stratonikos was his friend. Hermilos was arrested and brought before Licinius, where he confessed his belief in Jesus Christ. He was beaten for this with copper rods and then his body was torn with thorny sticks. Hermilos turned to Stratonikos during the torments and invited him to speak out and confess his faith. Seeing his friend's belly and chest completely torn, Stratonikos sympathized with Hermilos, and he immediately confessed to the king that he was also a Christian. He was also beaten, and the two martyrs were thrown into the Danube River, where they gave up their souls.

COMMEMORATIONS: James, Bishop of Nisibis; Hermilos and Stratonikos at Belgrade; Hilary, Bishop of Poitiers; Maximos of Kapsokalyvia, Mt. Athos; Peter of Anium; Irenarchus of Rostov; Martyr Athanasios; Martyrs Pachomius and Papyrinos in Greece; Remigius of Rheims; Eleazar of Anzersk Island at Solovki.

TUESDAY

Leavetaking of Holy Theophany
Fast-free

JANUARY 14

Acts 2:38-43; Luke 12:32-40

No one heals himself by wounding another.
St. Ambrose of Milan

ST. NINA, EQUAL-TO-THE-APOSTLES AND ENLIGHTENER OF GEORGIA. Nina was a well-educated Christian girl living in third-century Cappadocia. One day she began to wonder what happened to the Lord's robe woven by the Theotokos. She was told how the robe came to be buried in a grave in the town of Mtskheta, Georgia. Nina prayed to the Theotokos that she be allowed to acquire the robe. The Theotokos appeared to her in her sleep and told her to go to Georgia to preach the Gospel. In route to Georgia, an angel of the Lord appeared to her in a dream holding a scroll that contained ten quotes from Scripture, and she was told to go to the city of Mtskheta to deliver it to the pagan king. When Nina arrived there, she happened upon a pagan festival and the worship of a brass statue of a man with a sword. Anyone who touched it would die. Nina raised her arms to God and prayed that these people be brought to His true knowledge. A storm formed suddenly, and lightning struck the idol and the temple, hurling them down. The priests and the royal family fled in terror. Nina spent nine months in prayer and fasting in a shack given to her by a devout barren woman. She converted the family, and by a miracle caused them to have a child. The people began to bring their sick, and Nina healed them. She reached all layers of Georgian society and baptized them all. Nina finally converted the king after she restored his vision. St. Nina died peacefully.

COMMEMORATIONS: Sava I, first Archbishop of Serbia; Nina (Nino) of Georgia; Holy Fathers slain at Sinai and Raithu: Isaiah, Sabbas, Moses, Moses, Jeremiah, Paul, Adam, Sergius, Domnus, Proclus, Hypatius, Isaac, Macarius, Mark, Benjamin, Eusebius, Elias, and others; Theodoulos of Sinai; Acacius of Tver; Macrina, grandmother of St. Basil the Great; Ambrose (Gudko) and others martyred at Sinai; John of Verkhoturye; Martyr Agnes; Meletius of Ryazan; Stephen of Chenolakkos; Joseph Analytinus of Raithu; Felix of Nola; Kentigern of Glasgow.

WEDNESDAY

JANUARY 15

St. John the Hut-Dweller
Strict Fast
Galatians 5:22-6:2; Luke 12:32-40

*W*hen you read the Gospels, Christ speaks to you; when you pray, you are speaking to Him. The Bible should be read not just for analysis, but as an immediate dialogue with the living Word Himself—to feed our love for Christ, to kindle our hearts with prayer and to provide us with guidance in our personal life.

St. Tikhon of Zadonsk

HOLY VIRGINS MAURA AND BRITTA OF TOURAINE. There was a small hill in Tours covered with briers and wild vines. It was rumored that two virgins dedicated to God were buried there. During the vigils before festival days, believers saw a light burning there by the power of God. One man went and saw a candle shining with marvelous brightness, and he returned to tell of it. The virgins appeared in a dream to a local inhabitant and said they could not endure any longer without a shelter from the storms. They wanted the thorns cut down and a roof built over their tombs. The man forgot what he had dreamt, and they appeared to him again on another night and threatened him that he would leave the world during that year if he did not cover the place. Terrified, he chopped down the thicket, exposed the tombs, and found large drops of fragrant candle wax, and he built an oratory during the summer. Then he invited Bishop Euphronius of Tours to bless it, but because of his age and the foul weather conditions, he excused himself. However, later the virgins appeared to the bishop and begged him with tears to bless their new dwelling. They told him that their names were Maura and Britta. During the bishop's journey, the rain and wind died down and he blessed the place.

COMMEMORATIONS: Paul of Thebes; John Calabytes of Constantinople; Pansophios of Alexandria; Prochorus of Pshina in Bulgaria; Maurus, disciple of St. Benedict; Maximus, Bishop of Nola; Salome and Perozhavra of Sivnia, Georgia; Ita of Killeedy; Maura and Britta of Touraine; Gabriel, founder of Lesnov Monastery; Gerasimos Palladas, Patriarch of Alexandria; Benjamin, Bishop of Romanov; Nectarius of Tobolsk.

Thursday

January 16

Veneration of Apostle Peter's Precious Chains
Fast-free
Acts 12:1-11; John 21:14-25

At all costs do not allow anxiety in your heart. Mental chaos is a state of fallen spirits.

+Elder Thaddeus of Vitovnica

BLESSED MAXIMUS OF TOTMA, FOOL-FOR-CHRIST. Maximus was a priest for 45 years in the Russian town of Totma, in the early seventeenth century. He led the ascetic life of a fool-for-Christ, with ceaseless prayer, fasting, nakedness, and with total disregard for his body. He possessed grace-filled gifts from God. Maximus died in deep old age in the year 1650. Because of the miraculous healings that came from his grave, it inspired some to compile his life story. However, this work burned in a church fire, so a new one was compiled. In the meantime, the miracles continued at the grave of St. Maximus. These miracles were depicted on the margins of his icons. One man from Totma lay paralyzed for half a year, but as soon as he called on St. Maximus, he received healing. Another could not rise from his bed for nine weeks, but when he called on the saint, his sickness went away. A peasant named Theodore was paralyzed for nine years. In a dream, an old man went to his bed and said, "Theodore, stop your sorrowing." Taking Theodore by the shoulder, he led him to the church to venerate the reliquary of St. Maximus. When Theodore awoke, he felt so healthy that he walked to the Resurrection Church to venerate the grave of St. Maximus.

COMMEMORATIONS: Veneration of the Precious Chains of Apostle Peter; Speusippos, Eleusippos, and Meleusippos, with Neon, Turbo, Leonilla, and Jonilla in Cappadocia; Honoratus, Archbishop of Arles; Danax the Reader in Macedonia; Damascene of Bulgaria; Maximus of Totma; Nicholas of Mytilene; Romilos of Mt. Athos and Ravanica (Serbia), and with him Nestor, Martinius, Daniel, Sisoes, Zosimas, and Gregory; Sigebert, King of the East Angles; Fursey of Burgh Castle; James of Tarentaise.

FRIDAY

JANUARY 17

St. Anthony the Great
Abstain from meat and dairy products, and fish.
Hebrews 13:17-21; Luke 6:17-23

To escape death is impossible. Knowing this, those who are truly intelligent and practiced in virtue and in spiritual thought accept death uncomplainingly, without fear or grief, recognizing that it is inevitable and delivers them from the evils of this life.

St. Anthony the Great

NEW MARTYR GEORGE OF IOANNINA. George was orphaned at eight years of age and was raised by his brother and sisters. He found employment as a stable boy for a Turkish officer and moved to Ioannina with the army. While there, he married a Greek Orthodox girl. The Turks attempted to charge him with treason for leaving their religion, but his employer rescued him, saying that George had never left Christianity. A few years later, and now a father, George had a dream that he would become a martyr. That very day, he was arrested in the city, and false witnesses came forward against him. When he would not deny his Christian faith, he was hanged. The holy relics of St. George are known to produce miracles even to this day.

COMMEMORATIONS: Anthony the Great; Theodosios the Great; George of Ioannina; Anthony the Roman of Novgorod; Macarius (Kalogeras) of Patmos; Achilles of Egypt; Anthony the New of Berea in Macedonia; Anthony of Dymsk Monastery (Novgorod); Anthony of Chermoezersk Monastery; Anthony of Krasnokholmsk Monastery (Tver); Severus the Pious, Bishop of Bourges; Mildgyth of Minster.

SATURDAY

JANUARY 18

Sts. Athanasios and Cyril
Fast-free
Hebrews 13:7-16; Matthew 5:14-19

*E*vils reinforce each other; so do virtues, thus encouraging us to still greater efforts.

St. Mark the Ascetic

ST. ATHANASIUS, FOUNDER OF NOVOLOTSK MONASTERY. At the end of the sixteenth century, Athanasius founded a monastery in Russia, not far from the city of Petrozavodsk. Soon after he accomplished his work, he fell ill and died. After 40 days, Athanasius appeared to four sick people who lived in different locations and healed them. He ordered them to bury his body in the place where it lay. These people buried the holy relic that they found incorrupt and giving off a beautiful fragrance, and they set up a chapel over it. People came from afar, and approaching with faith, they were healed. About 50 years later, in 1647, many priests and peasants gathered at the grave to uncover the saint's relics because of the miracles that took place there. However, when they began the excavation, everyone got sick, and they prayerfully abandoned their plan. About 75 years later, the Holy Synod ordered the relics uncovered, and they were found incorrupt with a beautiful fragrance, even though they were buried in the ground and not in a tomb. Finally, the relics were placed in a clean sheet in a coffin and buried in the chapel.

COMMEMORATIONS: Cyril and Athanasios, Archbishops of Alexandria; Joachim, Patriarch of Turnovo; Maximus, Archbishop of Wallachia; Cyril and Maria, parents of Sergius of Radonezh; Martyr Xenia; Theodula, Helladius, Evagrius, Macarius, and Boethos of Anazarbus; Marcian of Cyrrhus in Syria; Silvanus of Palestine; Ephraim, Bishop of Mylasa in Caria (Asia Minor); Ephraim the Lesser of Georgia; Leobardus of Gaul; Athanasius of Novolotsk Monastery (Karelia); Alexis of Teklati, Georgia; Athanasius of Syadem and Vologda; Ninnidh of Inismacsaint; Vladimir Zubkovich of Smolevichi (Belorussia).

Sunday

January 19

Twelfth Sunday of Luke
Fast-free
Colossians 3:4-11; Luke 17:12-19

*A*lmsgiving above all else requires money, but even this shines with a brighter luster when the alms are given from our poverty. The widow who paid in the two mites was poorer than any human, but she outdid them all.

St. John Chrysostom

ST. MAKARIOS THE GREAT OF EGYPT. The son of a priest, Makarios lived for sixty years in the fourth-century Egyptian desert of Scetis. He married out of obedience to his parents, but when his wife died, he became a monk. As he worked to purify himself, he excelled in many virtues. He answered once that his thinness, whether due to fasting or not, was out of fear of God. Men and demons stood in awe of his humility. He counseled that we should condemn no man in order to be saved. He once saw thieves taking his belongings, and he helped them to get everything he owned, reasoning that we brought nothing into this world. He was granted the gift of working miracles through his prayers and raising the dead. St. Pachomios and St. Anthony the Great also lived during this time. They appeared to Makarios foretelling his death in nine days. The Cherubim came with praises to receive his soul.

COMMEMORATIONS: Makarios the Great of Egypt; Mark Eugenikos, Archbishop of Ephesus; Arsenius, Archbishop of Corfu; Euphrasia of Nicomedia; Macarius of Alexandria; Meletios of Mt. Galesios; Anton the Stylite of Martgopi; Theodore of Novgorod; Macarius the Faster of the Kiev Caves; Macarius, Hierodeacon of the Kiev Caves; Macarius the Roman of Novgorod, and his disciple Chariton; Anthony Rawah the Qoraisite; Branwalader (Breward) of Cornwall; Peter Skipetrov of Petrograd; Translation of the relics of St. Gregory the Theologian; Translation of the relics of St. Peter the Wonderworker from Rome to Argos; Uncovering of the relics of St. Sabbas of Zvenigorod.

MONDAY

JANUARY 20

St. Euthymius the Great
Fast-free
2 Corinthians 4:6-15; Luke 6:17-23

*W*hatever you do, on no account condemn anyone!
St. Ignatius Brianchaninov

ST. PETER OF CONSTANTINOPLE. Peter was a wealthy, powerful tax collector from Constantinople in the sixth century. He did not pity the poor and was known as "the miser." Emperor Justinian appointed him to administer the Roman province of Africa. Once, a poor man made a wager to see if he could get alms from Peter. Finding no stone to throw, Peter grabbed a loaf of bread and threw it at the beggar. Two days later, Peter lay dying, and he saw himself in a vision before the Judge and a pair of scales. The demons were heaping his evil deeds on one side, and two angels were lamenting that they only had a loaf of bread to put on their side, but it seemed to balance the evil deeds. The angels told Peter to add something to the loaf, or the demons would have him. He awoke cured of his illness, with the thought to do good. Walking along, he gave his finest cloak to a shipwrecked man who asked for something to wear. That night in an apparition, Peter saw the cloak on the Lord, Who thanked him for helping Him when he was freezing. Peter awoke and swore he would become one of the poor. He secretly arranged to have himself sold as a slave for 30 pieces of silver he gave to the poor. The emperor and everyone bemoaned Peter's loss. One day, some of Peter's old neighbors recognized him at a gathering, where Peter was working as a servant. In order to escape, Peter commanded a deaf-mute doorman to let him out. Immediately, the doorman regained his hearing and speech and told everyone that he saw a flame come out of Peter's mouth when he spoke. Peter hid until his death.

COMMEMORATIONS: Euthymios the Great; Leo I, Emperor of Byzantium; Inna, Pinna, and Rimma in Scythia; Euthymius Kereselidze of Georgia; Bassos, Eusebius, Eutychios, and Basilides at Nicomedia; Martyrs Thyrsos and Agnes; Peter the Publican; Anna at Rome; Euthymius, Patriarch of Turnovo; Euthymius the Silent; Laurence the Recluse; Zacharias of Patras; Theodore of Tomsk; Euthymius of Syanzhemsk; Euthymius of Archangelsk; Paul of Ryazan.

TUESDAY

JANUARY 21

St. Maximos the Confessor
Fast-free
Philippians 1:12-20; Luke 12:8-12

*W*hatever a man loves he inevitably clings to, and in order not to lose it he rejects everything that keeps him from it. So he who loves God cultivates pure prayer, driving out every passion that keeps him from it.

St. Maximos the Confessor

SYNAXIS OF THE CHURCH OF HOLY PEACE BY THE SEA AT THE PERAMA. The church was built in fifth-century Constantinople by St. Markianos, a presbyter and steward of the church. The site of the church and its dimensions were revealed to him in a divine vision. Markianos died before its completion, and Empress Verina finished it and adorned it with magnificence. Parts of the church were destroyed by fire, but it was restored in the twelfth century by Emperor Manuel I Komnenos. During the original construction of the church, two marble pillars were about to be set before the altar, but a demon sat on the larger of the two, and the builders could not lift it. Markianos prayed and made the Sign of the Cross over it, then rebuked the demon. As he prayed, Markianos helped the builders move the pillar with ease, even though he was old and weak. However, the pillar leaned slightly, and it was left this way as a testimony of this miracle.

COMMEMORATIONS: Maximos the Confessor; Neophytos of Nicaea; Zosimas, Bishop of Syracuse; Agnes of Rome; Maximus the Greek of Russia; Eugene, Candidus, Valerian, and Aquila at Trebizond; Anastasius, disciple of St. Maximos the Confessor; Neophytos of Vatopedi; 4 Martyrs of Tyre; Timon, monk of Kostroma; Fructuosis of Tarragona, Spain; Synaxis of the Church of Holy Peace by the Sea, Constantinople; "Consolation" (Paramythia) and "The Stabbed" Icons of the Mother of God.

Wednesday

January 22

Apostle Timothy of the 70
Abstain from meat and dairy products, and fish.
2 Timothy 1:3-8
Matthew 10:32-33, 37-38, 19:27-30

Humility and fear of God are above all the other virtues.
St. John the Dwarf

ST. JOSEPH SAMAKOS THE SANCTIFIED OF CRETE. Joseph was from a pious family in fifteenth-century Crete. A spiritual father educated him at a monastery in modern-day Heraklion. He fervently read Church books and the writings of the holy Fathers, and through this learning, he developed a desire for the imperishable gifts of heaven. He committed himself to accomplish virtuous deeds. When his parents died, he distributed his inheritance to the poor. He gained self-control by fasting on bread and water, sleeping little, and keeping vigil. He practiced unceasing prayer and prostrations. Joseph was devoted to the priesthood, and he showed love for his neighbor primarily by the giving of alms. Upon the death of his elder, he gave away everything his elder left him. Joseph kept nothing for himself, not even sustenance. At one time, he even gave away the Prosphora that was being kept for the Liturgy, but miraculously a warm loaf was found ready for the service. By night, Joseph would secretly leave bread at the door of the poor. He also helped the sick, those in prison, and the disabled. Joseph died peacefully at the age of seventy-one. Many years later, the faithful learned in a vision that St. Joseph's relics were incorrupt. When they were uncovered, they were found fragrant and healing.

COMMEMORATIONS: Apostle Timothy of the Seventy; Joseph Samakos the Sanctified of Crete; Anastasius the Persian; Manuel, Bishop of Adrianople; Anastasius of the Kiev Caves; Macarius of Zhabynsk; Martyrs Manuel, George, Peter, Leontius, bishops, and Sionius, Gabriel, John, Leontus, and Parodus, presbyters, and 377 companions in Bulgaria; Brithwald of Wilton; Wendreda of March.

THURSDAY

St. Clement, Bishop of Ancyra
Fast-free

JANUARY 23

Philippians 3:20-21, 4:1-3
Mark 2:23-3:5

*B*efore all else, let us list sincere thanksgiving first on the scroll of our prayer. On the second line, we should put confession and heartfelt contrition of soul. Then let us present our petition to the King of all. This is the best way of prayer.

St. John Climacus

ST. ASCHOLIOS, BISHOP OF THESSALONICA. Ascholios was a friend of St. Basil the Great, and they were both from Caesarea. Ascholios was appointed Bishop of Thessalonica by Pope Damasus of Rome in the fourth century when Constantinople was the capital of the Roman Empire. Following his victory over the Goths, Emperor Theodosius hastened to Constantinople by way of Thessalonica. However, he was taken gravely ill and asked for baptism into the true Orthodox faith by Bishop Ascholios. Not many days after his baptism, the emperor recovered from his disease, and he continued to Constantinople. Shortly after that, the Edict of Thessalonica was issued in February 380 by three reigning Roman emperors, making Nicene Christianity the state religion of the Roman Empire. Bishop Ascholios influenced this edict. The emperor suppressed the non-Nicene sects (Arians, Anomoeans, and Macedonians), and they lost the right to meet, ordain priests, or spread their beliefs.

COMMEMORATIONS: Clement, Bishop of Ancyra, and Agathangelos; Salamanes the Silent of the Euphrates; Dionysios of Olympus and Mt. Athos; 2 Martyrs of Parion; Gennadius of Kostroma; Eusebius of Mt. Coryphe; Mausimas the Syrian; Ascholios of Thessalonica; Seraphim (Bulashov), abbot, and Virgin-martyrs Eudokia, Ecaterine, and Militsa, of Moscow; Barlaam of Siberia; Commemoration of the Sixth Ecumenical Council; Translation of the relics of St. Theoctistus of Novgorod; Synaxis of All Saints of Kostroma.

FRIDAY   **Strict Fast**

JANUARY 24

Galatians 5:22-6:2; Mark 12:1-12

*S*in is a deadly sickness of the soul, a sickness which deprives us both of the joys of earth and the joys of heaven. Sin is a most terrible and most lamentable spiritual death, which separates us eternally from the heavenly inhabitants of Paradise and buries us in the darkness of hell.

+Archimandrite Seraphim Aleksiev

HOLY THEOSEMIA—THE MIRACULOUS RESCUE OF ST. NEOPHYTOS THE RECLUSE. The translation of the word Theosemia is "Sign of God." In the late twelfth century, St. Neophytos lived on a cliff, eighteen fathoms high that was difficult to climb or descend. Looking down would cause vertigo. For this reason, Neophytos needed to carve out a path to mitigate the danger of the climb. He did this with great care and success over many days. As he was about to finish the task, a large boulder came crashing down on him and caught him by his garments on his right arm. The boulder was now pushing him down, and if he had fallen off the cliff, it would have been certain death. He called out to the Theotokos and Christ, and immediately a force pushed the boulder in the opposite direction. Another monk arrived with a hammer and broke the boulder into three parts. St. Neophytos immediately lifted his hands glorifying God. Later, the boulder was pushed off the cliff.

COMMEMORATIONS: Babylas, Timothy, and Agapius of Sicily; Philo, Bishop of Carpasia; Zosimas of Cilicia; Gerasimus, Bishop of Perm; John of Kazan; Xenia, deaconess of Rome, and 2 female slaves; Xenia of St. Petersburg; Martyrs Hermogenes and Mamas; Neophytos the Recluse of Cyprus; Philip the presbyter and Barsimus of Syria and his two brothers; Paul, Pausirius, and Theodotian of Egypt; Macedonius of Mt. Silpius, near Antioch; Lupicinus of Gaul; Felician, Bishop of Foligno in Italy; Sophia of Shamordino Convent; Translation of the relics of St. Anastasius the Persian.

SATURDAY

JANUARY 25

St. Gregory the Theologian
Fast-free
Hebrews 7:26-8:2; John 10:9-16

*H*ere is how you should respond to the misfortunes of others: Give something to the needy, even if it is a little; it is not [little] to the one who is utterly destitute, nor to God either, if it is the best in your power. Offer your hearty goodwill, in lieu of a large donation; if you own nothing, shed a tear; compassion, that issues from the heart, is a great balm for the afflicted, and sincere sympathy goes a long way in lightening the burden of misfortune.
St. Gregory the Theologian

ST. MARES THE SINGER OF OMEROS. Mares built a small hut at the village of Omeros, in the region of Cyrrhus, and lived there 37 years. It received much rain from a neighboring mountain. Even in the winter season, it poured out streams of water. Some diseases were produced from this, but not even this would cause Mares to change his cell. Through the labors of reclusion, he preserved the purity of body and soul his whole life. He had a brilliance of voice. He loved the simplicity and abhorred subtlety of character. During his life of ninety years, he wore clothing made of goat's hair. Bread and a little salt supplied his need for food. Mares desired for a long time the offering of Holy Communion. They brought the divine vessels to him, and so he was filled with every spiritual joy. He said he had never experienced such delight.

COMMEMORATIONS: Gregory the Theologian, Archbishop of Constantinople; Moses, Archbishop of Novgorod; Gabriel, Bishop of Imereti; Castinus, Bishop of Byzantium; Apollo of Thebes; Mares the Singer of Syria; Felicitas of Rome and 7 sons; Publius of Syria; Medula and companions; Bretanion of Romania; Demetrios Skevophylax of Constantinople; Anatole I of Optina; Gregory of Golutvin; Vladimir of Kiev; Auxentios of Constantinople; Praejectus, Bishop of Clermont; Dwyn of Llandwyn; Athanasia (Lepeshkin) of Zosima Hermitage; Basil, Bishop of Priluksk; Peter, Archbishop of Voronezh; Margaret (Gunaronulo) of Menzelino; "Assuage My Sorrow" and "Unexpected Joy" Icons of the Mother of God.

Sunday

January 26

Fifteenth Sunday of Luke
Fast-free
1 Timothy 4:9-15; Luke 19:1-10

Christ is wholly love, goodness and consolation, and never suffocates. He has an abundance of spiritual oxygen.

St. Paisios the Athonite

ST. CLEMENT THE STYLITE OF MOUNT SAGMATA. Clement was born into a pious Athenian family in the eleventh century, and he showed religious tendencies from an early age. At the age of 30, he renounced the vanities of the world and entered the Monastery of Myoupolis, founded by St. Meletios. Clement was a model monk by his obedience and humility, and he would withdraw to pray in the solitude of Mount Sagmata. One day a fellow monk caught Clement by surprise, his spirit was in ecstasy, and his body was raised above the ground. Wishing to flee admiration, Clement received the blessing of St. Meletios to live in a cave situated like a column on a promontory of Mount Sagmata. He spent many years there and attracted a growing number of disciples. However, when St. Meletios died, the new abbot excommunicated Clement because he refused to return to the monastery. Not long afterward, the new abbot fell ill and wanted to travel to Clement to ask his forgiveness, but he died. Hearing of the holiness of Clement, Emperor Komnenos gave the monastery a precious fragment of the True Cross. St. Clement died peacefully in the early twelfth century. His holy skull can be venerated today at the Holy Monastery of the Transfiguration of the Lord on Mount Sagmata. Also preserved is the saint's cave.

COMMEMORATIONS: Xenophon, Mary, John and Arcadios of Constantinople; Symeon the Ancient of Mt. Sinai; Ammon of Egypt; Ananias the presbyter, Peter, and 7 soldiers in Phoenicia; Joseph, Bishop of Thessalonica; Clement and Germanos of Mt. Sagmata; David IV the Restorer of Georgia; Gabriel, abbot at Jerusalem; Paula of Rome; 2 Martyrs of Phrygia; Xenophon of Novgorod; Joseph Naniescu of Romania; Cyril, Metropolitan of Kazan; Matushka Maria of Gatchina; Conon, bishop on the Isle of Man; Transfer of the relics of St. Theodore the Confessor, abbot of the Studion.

Monday

Translation of the Relics of St. John Chrysostom
Fast-free

January 27

Hebrews 7:26-8:2; John 10:9-16

Almost all of us at times find ourselves unable to sleep at night. We lie awake during the dark, silent hours. This rarely happens when our hearts and souls are at peace; it usually happens when we are troubled in some way. For this reason, do not curse your lack of sleep. These times of wakefulness have been sent by God as a sign that something is wrong, and as a period for reflection. So when you cannot sleep, allow the thoughts that lie deepest in your heart to rise up to the surface. Often these thoughts are a reproach, telling you of a sin you have committed or an act of charity you failed to perform. If you have already confessed and made amends for these past failures, then you must assure yourself that God has forgiven you, so that you can sleep in peace. But if you have not confessed and made amends, then you must confess at once, admitting to God the precise nature of your sin, and asking forgiveness. Then you must plan how the following day you can put right your wrong.

St. John Chrysostom

NEW MARTYR DEMETRIOS AT CONSTANTINOPLE. Demetrios owned a very successful hotel and restaurant in Constantinople in the eighteenth century. Turkish enterprises continued to fail in competition against him. One day a fight between two Turkish men erupted in front of his hotel, and Demetrios rushed out to stop it, but one of the men was killed. The crowd that had gathered there blamed Demetrios. He was tried and convicted and was offered a full pardon if he would deny his Christian faith and embrace their religion. St. Demetrios was executed for his refusal.

COMMEMORATIONS: Peter of Egypt; Marciana the Empress; Venerable Claudinus; Peter of Russia; Leonty of Ivanovo; Demetrius at Constantinople; Demetrius Klepinine of Paris; Translation of the relics of St. John Chrysostom.

Tuesday

January 28

St. Ephraim the Syrian
Fast-free
Galatians 5:22-6:2; Luke 6:17-23

Anyone who fears sin will not fear Satan. And all who yearn for God's gift will have no dread of temptations. Anyone who believes firmly that the will of the Creator controls his entire creation will not be perturbed by anything.

St. Isaac the Syrian

ST. ISAAC THE SYRIAN, BISHOP OF NINEVEH. Isaac and his brother entered a monastery near Nineveh in the sixth century. Because of Isaac's ascetic life, virtues, and learning, he was asked to become abbot. However, he preferred a life of silence, so he left the monastery to live as a hermit in the desert. Isaac's fame soon spread, and he was elevated to Bishop of Nineveh. However, he became discouraged, as these were unruly, disobedient people. Isaac was once asked to settle a disagreement between two Christians. One owed the other money and had asked for an extension to repay, and the other would not allow it. When Isaac offered that the Gospel tells us to be merciful, the lender snapped at him, saying to leave the Gospel out of it. This time Isaac went to live in the mountains with the hermits, and he attained a high level of spiritual perfection. After more than one thousand years, in the eighteenth and nineteenth centuries, did St. Isaac's life and deeds come to light.

COMMEMORATIONS: Ephraim the Syrian; Isaac the Syrian, Bishop of Nineveh; Ephraim, Bishop of Pereyaslavl (Kiev Caves); Palladius the Hermit of Antioch; James (Jacob) the Ascetic of Porphyreon in Palestine; John of Reomans (Gaul); Theodosius, founder of Totma Monastery (Vologda); Martyr Charitos; Ephraim, founder of Boris and Gleb Monastery (Novotorzhok); Ignatius, Bishop of Skopin, with Vladimir, Bartholomew, and Olga; Leontius (Stasevich) of Jablechna (Poland); Arsenius (Stadnitsky), Metropolitan of Tashkent and Turkestan; "Sumorin Totma" Icon of the Mother of God.

WEDNESDAY

JANUARY 29

Translation of the Relics of St. Ignatius the God-bearer
Strict Fast
Hebrews 10:32-38; Mark 9:33-41

The saints were always concerned with the next life. Remembrance of death is a gift. God protects us from temptation. He doesn't allow us to be tempted beyond our powers. Everything He permits is for our good. Trust in the Lord in all things and He will nourish you in time of famine.

St. Amphilochios Makris

SEVEN MARTYRS AT SAMOSATA: PHILOTHEOS, HYPERECHIOS, HABIB, JULIAN, ROMANOS, JAMES, AND PAREGORIOS. They lived in the third-century city of Samosata during the Christian persecutions of the ruthless Emperor Galerius, a fanatical idolater. Once before a battle against the Persians, Galerius required all the citizens to worship at the Temple of Fortune. However, two Christians, Philotheos and Hyperechios, refused and went instead to worship at a chapel, together with Habib, Julian, Romanos, Iakovos, and Paregorios. While there, soldiers came and arrested the seven. Their arms and thighs were broken with thick rods. Then they were flayed without mercy, bound in heavy chains, and imprisoned. Later again, they were flayed, and their skin scraped. They received their crowns of martyrdom when their heads were nailed to wood. Fifteen years later, the persecutions ended when Emperor Galerius died from a painful and disgusting disease that he believed the God of the Christians inflicted upon him.

COMMEMORATIONS: Silvanus, Bishop of Emesa, Luke the Deacon, and Mocius the Reader; Sarbelos and his sister Bebaia of Edessa; Barsimaeus the Confessor, Bishop of Edessa; Gerasimus, Pitirim, and Jonah, Bishops of Perm; Seven Martyrs of Samosata—Philotheos, Hyperechios, Habib, Julian, Romanos, James, and Parigoreas; Aphrahates of Persia; Laurence of the Kiev Caves, Bishop of Turov; Ignatius of Smolensk; Demetrios of Chios; Ashot Kuropalates of Tao-Klardjeti; Righteous Acepsimas; Gildas the Wise of Brittany; Severus of Gaul; John, Leontius, Constantine, and 5 martyrs with them; Translation of the relics of St. Ignatius the God-bearer.

THURSDAY

JANUARY 30

Synaxis of the Three Hierarchs
Fast-free

Hebrews 13:7-16; Matthew 5:14-19

Every Psalm anticipates the anguish of the night and gives rest after the efforts of the day. It is safety for babes, beauty for the young, comfort for the aged, adornment for women.

St. Basil the Great

COMMEMORATION OF THE MIRACLE OF GREAT MARTYR GEORGE IN ZAKYNTHOS IN 1688. In 1669 an old icon of St. George was brought to Zakynthos from Crete and placed in the Church of St. Demetrios of Kola. In 1688 thieves stole the icon, stripped it of its silver, and threw it in a trough. Two young men happened upon the icon and told the parish priest at St. Demetrios. Many priests went to the spot of discovery with candles and incense and brought the icon to St. Mark Square, where an excommunication was read towards the thieves. Then the icon was returned to the church. Some days later, on November 24th, a plague spread throughout the entire district, which the people considered divine punishment. They fasted and prayed, and by January 30th, they were completely free of the plague. This miracle was attributed to St. George, and a feast was established. Later a church was built in honor of St. George to house the miraculous icon, and it bore the following inscription: "George, by this church in your city, we foreigners entrust to you our salvation."

COMMEMORATIONS: Synaxis of the Three Hierarchs: Basil the Great, Gregory the Theologian, and John Chrysostom; Hippolytus of Rome, and those with him; Zeno of Antioch; Zeno the Faster of the Kiev Caves; Grand Dukes Paul Alexandrovic and Dimitri Konstantinovich, and Eugene Poselianin; Adelgonda, foundress of Maubeuge; Demetrius of Sliven; Peter, King of Bulgaria; Hadji Theodore of Mytilene; Theophilus the New in Cyprus; Theophil, fool-for-Christ; Pelagia of Diveyevo, fool-for-Christ; Bathild, Queen of France; "Panagia Evangelistria" Icon of the Mother of God in Tinos; Commemoration of the Great Martyr George in Zakynthos.

FRIDAY

JANUARY 31

Sts. Cyril and John the Unmercenaries
Strict Fast

1 Corinthians 12:27-13:8
Matthew 10:1, 5-8

You must cross yourself more often because it guards you just like a lock on the door. Save yourselves and defend yourselves with the power of the honorable and Life-giving Cross.

St. Matrona the Blind of Moscow

ST. ARSENIUS THE NEW OF PAROS. After the death of his pious parents, nine-year-old Arsenius made his way from Epirus to Asia Minor where he excelled in his schoolwork. One day Father Daniel of Zagara went to the school to hear confessions, and Arsenius became his disciple. Soon after the two went to Mt. Athos to practice the monastic life, which is called "the art of arts" and "science of sciences." Arsenius learned to cut off his own will, he acquired humility and obedience, and this helped him to make progress in the other virtues. He received the Great Schema and lived six years there with his elder. Later they resettled on the island of Pholegandros. Arsenius lived there for eleven years, instructing the children in the required subjects, in addition to character development and Christianity. After Father Daniel's death, Arsenius providentially went to live at St. George's Monastery on Paros. He was elevated to the priesthood, and each day, he would study the Holy Scripture and the writings of the Fathers. He practiced the Jesus Prayer, known as the prayer of the heart, and developed the gift of tears, like St. Arsenius the Great. He served the liturgies with great compunction, and his face was often radiant. He became known as an excellent spiritual confessor, and multitudes flocked to him for the spiritual medicine needed for the health of their souls.

COMMEMORATIONS: Cyrus and John the Unmercenaries, and with them Martyrs Athanasia and her daughters Theoctiste, Theodota, and Eudoxia, at Canopus in Egypt; Tryphaina at Cyzicus; Victorinus, Victor, Nicephorus, Claudius, Diodorus, Serapion, and Papias of Egypt; Nicetas of the Kiev Caves; Marcella of Rome; Pachomius of Keno Lake; Athanasius of Methone; Arsenius the New of Paros; Elias Ardunis of Mt. Athos.

If you are praised, be silent. If you are scolded, be silent. If you incur losses, be silent. If you receive profit, be silent. If you are satiated, be silent. If you are hungry, also be silent. And do not be afraid that there will be no fruit when all dies down; there will be! Not everything will die down. Energy will appear; and what energy!

    St. Feofil of the Kiev Caves, the Fool-for-Christ

SATURDAY

FEBRUARY 1

Forefeast of the Presentation
Fast-free
Romans 8:28-39; Luke 10:19-21

To have faith in Christ means more than simply despising the delights of this life. It means we should bear all our daily trials that may bring us sorrow, distress, or unhappiness, and bear them patiently for as long as God wishes.

St. Symeon the New Theologian

STS. GEORGE, SYMEON, AND DAVID THE BROTHERS, OF MYTILENE. David was a shepherd, and he had a vision of St. Anthony the Great calling him to the monastic life at Mt. Ida in Asia Minor. He lived there in a cave for thirty years as an ascetic, surviving on wild greens. He had another vision of an angel of God who told him to build a monastery there, where many monks gathered. After ten years, his widowed mother took her eight-year-old son Symeon to be raised by David. He was educated there, tonsured, and ordained. David died a few years later, but before his death, he told Symeon to return to Mytilene, and he obeyed his brother. Desiring to become a stylite, he loaded himself with chains and climbed a pillar, living in extraordinary asceticism. Soon his brother George, who was a monk and priest, joined Symeon. A monastery was built there, and multitudes of Christians gathered, thirsty for spiritual advice and blessings. However, the iconoclast persecution began. Symeon miraculously escaped death and was later exiled to an uninhabited island after a punishment of 150 lashes. When the last iconoclast emperor, Theophilos, died, Symeon and George, along with Patriarch Methodios, were Empress Theodora's most trusted advisors.

COMMEMORATIONS: Perpetua, Felicitas, Saturus, Revocatus, Saturninus, and Secundulus of Carthage; Basil, Archbishop of Thessalonica; Peter of Galatia; Tryphon of Campsada; Brigid of Kildare; Tryphon of Pechenga; Bendimianus of Bithynia; Martyr Carion; Theion with 2 children at Kariona; Elias the New of Damascus; Timothy the Confessor; David, Symeon, and George of Mytilene; Seiriol of Penmon; Tryphon, Bishop of Rostov; Anastasios at Nauplion; Socola Icon of the Mother of God.

Sunday

February 2

Presentation of Our Lord
Fast-free
Hebrews 7:7-17; Luke 2:22-40

Appetite comes from eating and prayer from praying.
Elder Ephraim of Arizona

SYNAXIS OF PANAGIA KOUTSOURIOTISSA IN ERATEINI OF PHOCIS. A seventeenth-century monk of the Archangels Monastery in Aigio would see a light in the same spot in the distance that was unusual in brilliance and vividness. Later this monk saw the Panagia in his dream, and she told him, "At exactly the spot where you see the light is my icon, and I want you to dwell there." He acted quickly and traveled to where he had seen the light. He climbed down a steep, rocky cliff about 800 meters above sea level, near the village of Amygdalia Doridos. There he saw a cave with a tree at its entrance. In the hollow of the tree, was the icon of the Panagia. He built a chapel inside the cave that still exists, and there placed the holy and wonderworking icon. It attracted many pilgrims, and it became known as the Panagia Koutsouriotissa, named after the hollow trunk, where the icon was found. In 1670 a church was built on top of the hill, with cells around it, which later became a monastery. In 1825 it was destroyed by the Turks and was rebuilt ten years later. The people of that area would flee to the monastery for protection from their enemies. An earthquake damaged the monastery in 1995, but a beautiful church was rebuilt. This icon is celebrated on four separate dates in the Church calendar.

COMMEMORATIONS: Presentation of Our Lord and Savior Jesus Christ; Anthimos of Chios; Agathodoros of Tyana; Gabriel at Constantinople; Jordan of Trebizond; Synaxis of Panagia Koutsouriotissa in Erateini of Phocis; Synaxis of Panagia Ypapanti in Kalamata; Synaxis of Panagia Sergena of Santorini; Synaxis of Panagia Chrysaliniotissa in Nicosia of Cyprus; Synaxis of Panagia Goumenissa of Kilkis; Synaxis of Panagia Marouliani in Oia of Santorini; Synaxis of Panagia Thalassitra in Kastro of Milos; Synaxis of Panagia of Holy Obedience in Kostos of Paros; Synaxis of Panagia of the Wicked Bees in Levadi of Kythera.

Monday

February 3

Synaxis of St. Symeon the God-Receiver
and Prophetess Anna
Fast-free
Hebrews 9:11-14; Luke 2:25-38

Once the soul starts to feel its own good health, the images in its dreams are also calm and free from passion.
St. Maximos the Confessor

MARTYR BLAISE OF CAESAREA IN CAPPADOCIA. Blaise tended the cattle for his affluent parents, and as the herds increased, Blaise gave yet more alms to the poor. When persecution began, Blaise heard that he was being hunted, so he willingly turned himself in, and as he stood bound hand and foot before the governor, he was bull whipped. But God eased his pain and healed his wounds as he stood there. The governor perceived this as sorcery, so he ordered that Blaise be boiled in a cauldron. For five days, angels of God encouraged him, and then extinguished the fire. When the governor sent soldiers, they found Blaise in the cauldron chanting hymns with angels, and the soldiers became Christians. More soldiers were sent, and they also were converted. The governor himself went to Blaise and saw the water boiling in the cauldron, and he assumed that it was refreshing. He asked for some of the water to wash his face, and immediately he lost his sight and died. The soldiers that witnessed the miracle were baptized, and Blaise returned home. He instructed his family in the ways of salvation and gave up his soul. A luminous white dove left his body and flew into the heavens. His relics were buried, and an altar built over them. The saint's staff was planted next to the altar, and it grew into an enormous tree.

COMMEMORATIONS: Symeon the God-receiver and Anna the Prophetess; Prophet Azarias; James, Archbishop of Serbia; Nicholas, enlightener of Japan; Symeon, Bishop of Polotsk; Ansgar of Hamburg; Blaise of Caesarea; Papias, Diodorus, and Claudianus at Perga; Adrian and Eubulus at Caesarea; Sabbas of Ioannina; Paul the Syrian; Sviatoslav-Gabriel and Dimitry of Yuriev; Nicholas, Stamatios, and John of Chios; Romanus, Prince of Uglich; New Martyr Alexander, in Russia; Ignatius of Mariupol in Crimea; Ia of St. Ives; Werburga of Chester; Laurence of Canterbury; Vladimir (Zagreba) of Borisoglebsk Monastery.

TUESDAY   **Fast-free**

February 4

Ephesians 2:19-3:7; Mark 6:1-7

*D*o not give vent to your feelings. We must force ourselves to be friendly with those that we don't like.

St. Nikon of Optina

ST. EVAGRIUS, FELLOW-ASCETIC OF ST. SHIO OF MGVIME. Evagrius was raised in the country of Georgia during the sixth century. From a very young age, his parents read him the Holy Gospel. Later he was made the ruler of that area as well as the military leader. While hunting one day, Evagrius saw a bird taking food to the cave of the hermit Shio in the Sarkineti Mountains. When Evagrius found Shio, he was amazed at the monk's strict asceticism, and he committed himself to live that holy life. Shio warned him of the danger of this impulsiveness. He gave Evagrius his staff and told him to return home and put his affairs in order. He also said that the staff would part the river when it touched the water to make the trip easier. However, Shio warned him that if the staff did not part the river on his return, it was not God's will for him to return. In fact, the river parted in both directions. Evagrius gave all his possessions to the poor and was tonsured a monk by Shio. He learned to pray, be vigilant, and patient. As the holiness of these two ascetics became known, many pilgrims journeyed to them for their blessing. Others remained and became monastics. King Parsman traveled to their monastery in an attempt to bring Evagrius back, but the monk said that he was made to serve God and did not want to be a dog returning to his vomit. Upon his death bed, St. Shio appointed the very reluctant St. Evagrius abbot of the monastery.

COMMEMORATIONS: Isidore of Pelusium; Nicholas the Confessor; Abramios of Arbela; Lucius, bishop in Africa; Martyrs Jadorus and Isidore; John of Irenopolis; Martyr Theoktistos; Iasimos, wonderworker; George, Prince of Vladimir; Joseph of Aleppo; Abraham and Coprius of Pechenga; Phileas of Thmuis and Philoromus the Magistrate; Evagrius of Tsikhedidi; Cyril of New Lake; Modan of Stirling; Aldate of Gloucester; Methodius of Petropavlovsk; Theodosios of Chudov, and Nicholas, Boris, Alexander, Alexander, Peter, John, and Nicholas.

WEDNESDAY

Strict Fast

FEBRUARY 5

Ephesians 3:8-21; Mark 6:7-13

If the occasion demands it, a wise man will readily accept bodily infirmity and even offer his whole body up to death for the sake of Christ… This same man is not affected in spirit or broken with bodily pain if his health fails him. He is consoled by his struggle for perfection in the virtues.

St. Ambrose of Milan

ST. SAVVAS THE NEW OF SICILY. Savvas was born in the first half of the tenth century. His father was tonsured a monk, and his mother founded a monastery for women. Savvas and his brother Makarios the Younger, also a monk, retired to a hermitage with their father. In 940-941, because of a famine and the advance of the Arabs in eastern Sicily, the entire family sought refuge in Calabria. Savvas and Makarios established the monastery of the Holy Archangels in northern Calabria. They moved several more times because of Arab attacks, building small churches and monasteries wherever they went. Savvas became known as a great wonder-worker, and the story of his life recounts many miracles. In 982 he enclosed himself in a cave in Atrani on the Amalfi Coast. Later they established the St. Lawrence Monastery in Salerno where Savvas followed his father as abbot. At the end of his life, Savvas was asked by the duke of Amalfi to travel to Rome to help with a political favor from the empress. He became ill and died there.

COMMEMORATIONS: Polyeuctus, Patriarch of Constantinople; Theodosius, Archbishop of Chernigov; Agatha of Palermo; Savvas the New of Sicily; Anthony of Athens; Theodosios of Skopelos; Matushka Agatha, Eugene, and Paramon of Belorussia; Gregory Rosca of Romania; Valeriu Gafencu of Romania; Avitus of Vienne; Martyrs Alexandra and Michael; "In Search of the Perishing," "Eletsk-Chernigov," and "Sicilian" Icons of the Mother of God.

Thursday

February 6

St. Photios the Great
Fast-free
Hebrews 7:26-8:2; John 10:9-16

If you examine your life well, you will find many instances when God showed his unmistakable mercy to you. Trouble was brewing, but it passed you by for some reason. God delivered you. Acknowledge these and thank God, who loves you.

St. Theophan the Recluse

VIRGIN MARTYR DOROTHEA OF CAESAREA. Dorothea was a Christian from Caesarea in Cappadocia. She refused to marry in favor of virginity for Christ. Two pagan women were sent to seduce her, but when Dorothea converted them to Christ, the governor inflicted on her the cruelest torments. As the saint was led to execution, a lawyer named Theophilus, jeered at her, telling her to send him fruits from the garden she expected to see after her death, and she promised to do this. Dorothea knelt and prayed, and an angel of the Lord appeared with a basket of three apples and three roses. She had these sent to Theophilus with a message that she would await him in that garden. When Theophilus tasted the fruit, he became a Christian. He was also martyred.

COMMEMORATIONS: Barsanuphius the Great and John the Prophet of Palestine; Bucolos, Bishop of Smyrna; Photios, Patriarch of Constantinople; Dorothea of Caesarea, and with her Christina, Callista, and Theophilus; James of Kyros; Julian of Emesa; Fausta, Evilasius, and Maximus at Cyzicus; Dorothea of Kashin; John of Thebes; Arsenios of Ikaltoi, Georgia; Amand, apostle of Maastricht; Vedast, Bishop of Arras; Mael, Bishop of Ardagh; Basil Nadezhnin of Moscow.

Friday   **Strict Fast**

February 7

Ephesians 4:17-25; Mark 6:45-53

Repentance is the gateway to mercy which is open for all who seek it. By way of this gate we enter into the divine mercy, and apart from this entrance one cannot find mercy.
                                                                    St. Isaac the Syrian

---

ST. RICHARD OF WESSEX. Not much is known about this English saint. More is known about his three children, Walburga, Winebald, and Willibald, and his brother Boniface, all of whom are also saints. Richard once obtained by his prayers the recovery of his son Willibald, when his life was despaired of by a grievous illness, by laying him at the foot of a great crucifix in England. Richard and two of his sons undertook a pilgrimage of penance and devotion to the west coast of France, visiting the holy places. Richard fell ill and died suddenly in Lucca, Italy and was buried in the church of San Frediano, where he remains today. Miracles were reported at his tomb. He is greatly venerated by the citizens there and in Germany where some of his relics were translated. In art, St. Richard is portrayed as a royal pilgrim with two sons, one a bishop and the other an abbot.

COMMEMORATIONS: Parthenios, Bishop of Lampsacus on the Hellespont; Aprionus, Bishop of Cyprus; Augulius, Bishop of Brittany; 1,003 Martyrs of Nicomedia; 6 martyrs of Phrygia; Mastridia of Jerusalem, woman ascetic of the desert; Luke of Mt. Steirion; Theopemptus and his brotherhood; Peter of Monovatia; Euthymius of Glinsk; George of Crete; Richard, King of Wessex; Roman, Bishop of Kilmaronen; Barlaam Ryashentsev, Archbishop of Perm.

Saturday   Fast-free

February 8
Ephesians 2:4-10; Matthew 10:16-22

*I*t is impossible for you to be completely removed from society. However, it is up to you as to how much time you spend in less desirable company. When you are in society, do not forget, to the extent you are able, to keep your attention on the true Lord, Who is close by and within, and do not forget the remembrance of death, which is ready to take you. Do not give your heart over to the pleasurable impressions of the eyes, ears or other senses. Life in that world is bad. Too many things, people and activities crowd into the soul; the mental impression on all this then disturbs it. It is also not conducive to proper prayer. There is one remedy for this: Guard your heart as much as possible from the pleasantness of impressions. Let everything go right past you without entering your heart.

St. Theophan the Recluse

HOLY PROPHET ZECHARIAH. Known as one of the Twelve Minor Prophets, Prophet Zechariah was descended from the priestly lineage of the Levite tribe. He foretold the coming of the Messiah and His earthly life five hundred years earlier. His prophecies included Christ's triumphant entry into Jerusalem on a young donkey, Judas' betrayal of Christ for thirty pieces of silver and the purchase of the potter's field, the scattering of the apostles from the Garden of Gethsemane, and the piercing of Christ's side at the Crucifixion.

COMMEMORATIONS: Theodore Stratelates the Commander, of Heraclea; Prophet Zechariah of the Twelve Minor Prophets; Sabbas II, Archbishop of Serbia; Conitus of Alexandria; Martha and Mary the sisters, and Lycarion the child Martyr of Egypt; Martyrs Nikephoros and Stephen; Martyrs Philadelphus and Polycarp; Martyr Pergetus; Macarios, Bishop of Paphos; John and Basil of the Kiev Caves; Lyubov of Ryazan, fool-for-Christ; Cuthman, hermit of Steyning; Kew, virgin of Cornwall; Agathangelus, Bishop of Damascus.

Sunday
February 9

Sunday of the Publican and Pharisee
Triodion Begins
Fast-free week
2 Timothy 3:10-15; Luke 18:10-14

The Kingdom of Christ is founded on the principle that whosoever would be first should be the servant of all (cf. Mark 9.3 5). The man who humbles himself shall be raised up, and vice versa: he who exalts himself shall be brought low. In our struggle for prayer we shall cleanse our minds and hearts from any urge to prevail over our brother. Lust for power is death to the soul.

+*Elder Sophrony of Essex*

ST. BRACCHIO OF TOURS. Bracchio was an avid hunter and nobleman in the court of Lord Sigiswald of Clermont. One day Bracchio pursued a wild boar that escaped into the hut of a Gallo-Roman hermit named St. Emilian. Bracchio's dogs were intimidated by St. Emilian, and they refused to attack the boar. Emilian offered Bracchio some wild fruit, and Bracchio, who was intrigued by the hermit and his evident power, discussed spiritual matters. Bracchio soon gave up his worldly life and became Emilian's spiritual student for three years. He learned how to read and soon knew the Psalter by heart. Others were also attracted to the hermitage. When St. Emilian died, he bequeathed the hermitage to Bracchio, and he turned it into a monastery. Later St. Bracchio became abbot of Menat in Auvergne and re-established strict monastic discipline there.

COMMEMORATIONS: Nicephorus of Antioch; Peter, Bishop of Damascus; Marcellus, Philagrius, and Pancratius, disciples of Apostle Peter; Aemilianus and Bracchio of Tours; Romanos the Wonderworker of Cilicia; Apollonia of Alexandria; Pancratius of the Kiev Caves; Gennadius and Nicephorus of Vazhe Lake (Vologda); Teilo, Bishop in Wales; Alexander and Ammon at Soli of Cyprus; Uncovering of the relics of St. Innocent of Irkutsk; Uncovering of the relics of St. Tikhon, Patriarch of Moscow and All Russia; (2nd Sunday of February: The 383 God-bearing Fathers of the Eighth Ecumenical Synod in 879-880).

Monday

February 10

St. Haralambos
Fast-free
2 Timothy 2:1-10
John 15:17-16:2

Offer ourselves alone to God, but each other also; for, according to the law of charity, we must seek the good of others as well as our own.
St. Nicholas Cavasilas

ST. ZENO THE LETTER CARRIER OF CAESAREA. Zeno became a civil servant in fourth-century Caesarea. He swiftly carried the letters of the emperor. Zeno revered the writings of St. Basil, and his admiration of Basil caused him to become a monk. He went to live in a sepulcher on the mountain of Antioch. Through ascetic contests he purified his soul that he might better be able to understand the vision of God. His tomb had neither bed, table, nor lamp. He rested on straw and leaves, and his shoes required straps to hold them together. A friend delivered bread every two days, and Zeno walked a considerable distance for water. A friendly stranger once insisted that he carry the water for Zeno, but the saint said he could never drink water carried by another. However, when the stranger persisted, Zeno permitted him to carry it but later poured it out and walked back for more. When he returned, he encountered pilgrims seeking him. Out of modesty, Zeno said that he knew of no monk by his name. Finally, they accompanied him to his dwelling. When it was time to leave, Zeno hesitated to give them his blessing, saying that he was a civilian and they were the soldiers. The group marveled at his poverty, asceticism, knowledge, and modesty. One day the Isaurians attacked and killed many of the monks and nuns, but Zeno prayed and miraculously they were not able to find the entrance to his sepulcher.

COMMEMORATIONS: Haralambos, Bishop of Magnesia, and Porphyrios and Baptos; Anastasius II, Archbishop of Jerusalem; Anatole, Metropolitan of Odessa; Zeno of Caesarea; Prochoros the Orach-eater; Ennatha, Valentina, and Paula of Palestine; John Chimchimeli of Bachkovo; Scholastica of Italy; Anna of Novgorod; Longinus of Vologda; Raphael and Ioannicius of Svatogorsk; Merwinna of Romsey; Synaxis of Novgorod Hierarchs; Commemoration of the Deliverance of Zakynthos from the Plague by St. Haralambos; "Areovindus" Icon of the Mother of God.

TUESDAY

February 11

St. Blaise of Sebaste
Fast-free
Hebrews 4:14-5:6
Matthew 10:1, 5-8

The first duty of a believer is to purify oneself from passions.
St. Theophan the Recluse

ST. BENEDICT OF ANIANE. Benedict was the son of a count and was educated in the eighth-century Frankish court of Pippin the Younger. He entered the royal service as a page and served at the court of Charlemagne. Benedict almost drowned one day while trying to save his brother, and this experience led him to act on a resolve to renounce the world and live the monastic life at the Abbey of Saint-Seine. Later he was made the abbot, but the monks would not conform to his strict practices, so he left. Around 780 he founded a monastery based on Eastern asceticism, but this effort also disappointed Benedict. His next monastery, based on Benedictine Rule, was a success and this gave him considerable influence and enabled him to establish and reform many other monasteries. Benedict became the effective abbot of all the monasteries of Charlemagne's empire. Later, Emperor Louis the Pious also entrusted all the monasteries within his domain to Benedict. Benedict had a vast knowledge of patristic literature, and churchmen sought his counsel. In 817 Benedict sought to restore the primitive strictness of the monastic observance. He was the head of a council of abbots, and they created a code of regulations which was binding on all their monasteries. After his death, these codes had a lasting effect on Western monasticism.

COMMEMORATIONS: Blaise, Bishop of Sebaste; Theodora the Empress, protectress of Orthodoxy; Lucius of Adrianople in Thrace; George of Kratovo, at Sofia; Demetrius of Priluki Monastery; Vsevolod (Gabriel), Prince of Pskov; Gobnait of Ireland; Caedmon of Whitby; Benedict of Aniane; Gregory of Sinai; Finding of the relics of Prophet Zacharias, father of St. John the Baptist; "Corfu" Icon of the Mother of God.

Wednesday

Fast-free

February 12

2 Peter 3:1-18; Mark 13:24-31

A person is never entirely bad. Each person has his good and bad points. When you remember his good points, you pray for him, you are moved, your soul feels for him, and you entreat God for him. And as for his bad side, he is not to blame, but our enemy the devil is.

+Elder Joseph the Hesychast

ST. PROCHORUS OF GEORGIA. Prochorus was born into a wealthy family and was raised in a monastery in the early eleventh-century country of Georgia. He was ordained as an adult and lived one year at the St. Savvas Lavra in Jerusalem. King Bagrat gave Prochorus a vast sum of money to restore the Holy Cross Monastery near Jerusalem. This monastery was built in the fifth century and was destroyed several times before Prochorus restored it. When he had accomplished the restoration, he assembled a group of eighty monks to labor there, and he established the monastic rule to reflect that of the Savvas Lavra. It is said that this monastery was built on the same ground where Abraham's nephew Lot planted three trees that grew into one: a cedar, a pine, and a cypress. When the Temple of Solomon was built in Jerusalem, the tree was cut down but not used for the temple. It is believed that the Cross of Jesus was made from this tree. At the end of his life, Prochorus and two disciples went to live in the wilderness where he died after some time.

COMMEMORATIONS: Meletios, Archbishop of Antioch; Anthony II, Patriarch of Constantinople; Alexis, Metropolitan of Moscow; Meletius, Archbishop of Kharkov; Mary, called Marinus, and her father Eugene, at Alexandria; Alexius, Bishop of Voronezh; Martyrs Plotinus and Saturninus; Bassian of Uglich; Nikoloz Dvali, Prochorus the Georgian, Luke of Jerusalem, and the Holy Fathers of the Georgian monasteries in Jerusalem; Chrestos at Constantinople; Meletios of Ypseni, Rhodes; Urbanus, Bishop of Rome; Ethilwald of Lindisfarne; Gertrude of Nijvel; Callia of Serbia; Appearance of the "Iveron" Icon of the Mother of God (Mt. Athos).

Thursday   **Fast-free**

February 13

1 John 1:8-2:6; Mark 13:31-14:2

Love humility and you will never fall into the devil's snare.
St. Theophan the Recluse

ST. SERAPHIM SOBOLEV OF BOGUCHARSK AND WONDER-WORKER OF SOFIA. The doctors decided to destroy Seraphim in the womb as they feared for his mother's well-being. However, she awoke and forbade this. He was an excellent student at the seminary, and his mother tried to find him a good wife so he could become a priest. But Seraphim had desired to become a monk. He decided to enter the Theological Academy, but the entrance exam questions were difficult. He ardently prayed that out of the hundreds of questions possible, he would only be given the ones he knew, and the Lord answered his prayer. After graduation, he taught the younger children and engaged them in soul-saving discussions, and they loved him. He was made rector of the seminary in Voronezh, where there were many undisciplined students. With affection, questions, and persuasion, he elicited sincere repentance. He was consecrated bishop and reassigned to Bulgaria, where he was appointed the director of all the Russian Orthodox monasteries. In poor health, Seraphim made the rounds of Russian parishes, caring for the poor and sick, getting them free hospital treatment, or placing them in homes for invalids. For some he obtained pensions, some he fed at his place, and some he put in a monastery. He also helped the destitute monks of Mt. Athos. Seraphim received the gift of clairvoyance. Since his death in 1950, St. Seraphim's tomb, in the Russian church of St. Nicholas in Sophia, has been a constant source of miracles.

COMMEMORATIONS: Eulogios I, Patriarch of Alexandria; Martinian of Caesarea; Aquila and Priscilla, Apostles of the Seventy; Symeon the Myrrh-gusher of Hilander; Zoe of Bethlehem and Virgin Photina; Joseph of Volokolamsk; a father and son, crucified; Timothy, Patriarch of Alexandria; George, Archbishop of Mogilev; Modomnoc of Ossory; Castor of Karden, Germany; Huna of Huneya; Ermenhilda of Ely; Seraphim (Sobolev) of Bogucharsk; Silvester (Olshevsky) of Omsk.

Friday   **Fast-free**

February 14

1 John 2:7-17; Mark 14:3-9

The time of repentance is short; the kingdom of heaven has no end.
St. Ephraim the Syrian

ST. HILARION THE GEORGIAN OF IMERETI. His uncle, a hermit Hierodeacon, raised Hilarion. Upon his uncle's death, his father took him to King Solomon II of Imereti, who recognized the youth's piety. He appointed Hilarion to be his spiritual adviser and arranged for him to marry the princess. He was soon ordained to the priesthood and appointed the confessor of the court church. Upon the death of the king and the princess, Hilarion put on beggar's clothes and departed for Mt. Athos and was tonsured a monk. A Greek archimandrite recognized him, and news spread that Hilarion had been the spiritual father of the king, so he withdrew to the wilderness. In 1822 a Turkish pasha and a vast army surrounded Mt. Athos and demanded all the abbots of the monasteries to submit to him. The pasha was delighted to see Hilarion because he was also of Georgian descent, but Hilarion condemned him. Hilarion was released, but the other monks were taken captive. With the blessing of the abbot, he went to the court of the pasha in Thessalonica. For four days he reasoned with the pasha, but in the end, he was sentenced to death, but some Georgian servants of the pasha convinced him to release the saint. Hilarion remained in Thessalonica for six months ministering to the sick prisoners, before returning to Athos. He compiled twelve volumes of the Lives of the Saints, entitled *The Flower Garden*. Three years after his death, his body was unearthed, and it was fragrant.

COMMEMORATIONS: Auxentios of Bithynia; Cyril, Equal-to-the-Apostles and teacher of the Slavs; Peter, Patriarch of Alexandria; Abraham, Bishop of Charres; Philemon, Bishop of Gaza; Theodore of Chernigov; Maron of Syria; George Paizan the Tailor of Mytilene; Nicholas of Corinth; Hilarion the Georgian; Isaac of the Kiev Caves; Damian the New of Philotheou and Kissavos, at Larissa; Onisimus, Bishop of Tula; 12 Greek Master-builders of the Dormition Cathedral in the Kiev Caves.

SATURDAY   Fast-free

February 15

Philemon 1:1-25; Luke 20:46-21:4

*W*hen tested by some trial, you should try to find out not why or through whom it came, but only how to endure it gratefully, without distress or rancor.

St. Mark the Ascetic

VENERABLE ANTHIMOS OF CHIOS. Anthimos was born into a poor but pious family in nineteenth-century Chios. At the age of nineteen, he visited the monastery founded by monk Pachomios, the spiritual counselor of St. Nektarios. He was so moved by the monks' spiritual life, that he built himself a small hut and lived in it when he returned home. He had an icon of the Mother of God, and this soon began to work miracles, which attracted many. Anthimos went to a monastery for a time, but when he fell ill, the abbot sent him home. He remained a monk, spending nights in prayer and living only on bread and water. Though the people wanted Anthimos ordained to the priesthood, the local bishop declined due to the saint's lack of education, but the Bishop of Smyrna ordained him instead. On Chios, Anthimos became chaplain to a leper hospital, which soon became a spiritual center. He worked many miracles of healing, and some of these patients became monks and nuns. During the Exchange of Populations of 1922-1924, refugees poured into Chios, and many were destitute nuns and young girls. In a vision, the Mother of God told Anthimos to build a monastery, which opened with thirty nuns and grew to house eighty. It was a model of monastic life, and Anthimos served as their priest. Each day he received sixty to seventy of the faithful for prayers and counseling. St. Anthimos continued this ministry for thirty years. He died peacefully at the age of ninety-one.

COMMEMORATIONS: Apostle Onesimos of the Seventy; Anthimos of Chios; Major of Gaza; Oswy of Northumbria; Eusebios of Syria; Paphnutius of the Kiev Caves; Dalmatus, in Siberia; Paul of St. Nilus Hermitage and Virgin-martyr Sophia; Theognius of Bethelia; Sigfrid of Sweden; Synaxis of St. John the Theologian at Diaconissa; "Vilensk" and "Dalmatian" Icons of the Mother of God.

Sunday

February 16

Sunday of the Prodigal Son
Fast-free
1 Corinthians 6:12-20
Luke 15:11-32

*W*hoever we are, whatever we are, wherever we have come to be, even at the very edge of the abyss, we must never let go of the moving image of the prodigal son's reception into the embrace of the father, who hugs him tightly and showers him with kisses. Let our final fall be into the arms of our Most-Compassionate Heavenly Father…

+Monk Moses of Mt. Athos

ST. MARUTHAS, BISHOP OF SOPHENE. Maruthas was a treasure of the fourth-century Church. Foremost among his endeavors were his peace-seeking missions. On two occasions he was sent by Emperor Theodosius the Younger to the Persian emperor to procure peace between the Byzantine Empire and Persia. He helped Christians in Persia gain their freedom, and he rebuilt churches that had been destroyed during the persecutions. He found the relics of the martyrs and had them transferred to Martyropolis, a city that he founded between Persia and the Byzantine empire. His works include "The 73 Canons of the First Ecumenical Council at Nicaea," which includes an account of the acts of the Council, the lives of the martyrs, and other works written in the Syrian language such as "Commentary on the Gospel." He was a member of the Second Ecumenical Council at Constantinople, convened against the heresy of Macedonius, and the Antioch Council against the Messalians. St. Maruthas died in Martyropolis, and later his relics were transferred to Egypt.

COMMEMORATIONS: Pamphilus, Paul, Valens, Seleucus, Porphyrius, Julian, Theodoulos, Elias, Jeremiah, Isaiah, Samuel, and Daniel, at Caesarea in Palestine; Flavian, Archbishop of Antioch; Maruthas, Bishop of Martyropolis, and others with him in Mesopotamia; Macarius (Nevsky), Metropolitan of Moscow; Flavian the Hermit; Romanus of Karpenesion; Basil Gryaznov of Pavlovo-Posadsky; Mary the New of Byzia; Persian martyrs under Shapur.

Monday

February 17

Great Martyr Theodore the Tyro
Fast-free
2 Timothy 2:1-10; Luke 20:46-21:4

*H*ow many mothers come crying to me begging, *'Pray for my child, Father.'* What agony! Very few men say, *'Pray for my child who has gone astray.'* Why even today, a mother— with what eagerness, the poor thing— forced her children, all eight of them, and put them all in line to take a blessing. For a father to do that would have been difficult. Russia survived because of mothers. A father's embrace, when without the Grace of God, is dry. While the mother's embrace, even when it is without God, has milk. The child loves its father and respects him; but due to the tender-hearted love and affection of a mother, the love for his father grows even stronger.

St. Paisios the Athonite

ST. AUXIBIOS, BISHOP OF SOLI ON CYPRUS. Auxibios was raised in a wealthy family in Rome during the first century. At an early age, he went to Jerusalem and learned about the new Christian faith. When his parents wanted to marry him off, he secretly sailed to Cyprus and there encountered the holy Apostle Mark. Auxibios later was appointed by the Apostle Mark to the bishop of the city of Soli, and Apostle Mark set off to Alexandria. Auxibios settled near the pagan temple of Zeus. He befriended and converted the pagan priest and gradually converted to Christianity, all the people. Before his death, many churches were built throughout the island. St. Auxibios was buried beneath the first church he had built, and for many years a spring of healing water flowed from his tomb.

COMMEMORATIONS: Theodore the Tyro; Mariamne, sister of Apostle Philip; Hermogenes, Patriarch of Moscow; Emperor Marcian and Pulcheria; Auxibios, Bishop of Soli; Theodosius the Bulgarian, and Romanus of Turnovo; Theodore the Silent; Righteous Theosterictus; Theodore of Byzantium; Barnabas of Gethsemane Skete; Theodore of Adjara; Finan of Lindisfarne; Uncovering of the relics of St. Menas the Melodius; Panagia Dakrirooussa of Prophet Elias Skete; Weeping "Tikhvin" Icon of the Mother of God.

TUESDAY   **Fast-free**

FEBRUARY 18

1 John 3:9-22; Mark 14:10-42

The perfect person does not only try to avoid evil. Nor does he do good for fear of punishment, still less in order to qualify for the hope of a promised reward. The perfect person does good through love. His actions are not motivated by desire for personal benefit, so he does not have personal advantage as his aim. But as soon as he has realized the beauty of doing good, he does it with all his energies and in all that he does. He is not interested in fame, or a good reputation, or a human or divine reward. The rule of life for a perfect person is to be the image and likeness of God.

St. Clement of Alexandria

VENERABLE COSMAS OF YAKHROMSK. Cosmas was the servant of a boyar-noble who had a severe sickness. He did his best to comfort his master by reading to him as they traveled from city to city. One day they stopped at the River Yakhroma, and there appeared to Cosmas in the forest an icon of the Dormition of the Most Holy Mother of God. He heard a voice telling him to become a monk and to build a monastery. His sick master was healed from the icon. Cosmas was tonsured a monk at the Pechersk monastery in Kiev and later returned to Yakhromsk to build a church in honor of the Mother of God. Other monks began to gather near Cosmas and a monastery soon formed, and he was chosen, abbot. His ascetic fame spread even to the great prince. St. Cosmas died peacefully in old age and was buried in the monastery he founded.

COMMEMORATIONS: Leo the Great, Pope of Rome; Leo and Parigorius of Patara; Nicholas the Catholicos of Georgia; Agapitus, Bishop of Synnada, and Martyrs Victor, Dorotheus, Theodulus, and Agrippa; Blaise of Mt. Athos; Martyr Piulius; Agapetus, Archbishop of Ekaterinoslav; Cosmas of Yakhromsk; Colman, Bishop of Lindisfarne; Commemoration of the New Martyrs who suffered during the "Holy Night" in St. Petersburg.

WEDNESDAY   **Strict Fast**

February 19   1 John 3:21-4:11; Mark 14:43-15:1

Ah, how effortless the road of humility is! Even without laboring ascetically or enduring illness, a person with humility and self-reproach, along with thanksgiving to God, is able to reach spiritual heights and feel the gift of sonship! While on the contrary, toiling ascetically without realizing one's own infirmity and weakness and wretchedness is a struggle without prizes, sweat without wages, a road without hope. What a misfortune to struggle without profit! To cultivate without reaping! Why does this happen? Because the struggle was not lawful. "If someone competes as an athlete, he is not crowned unless he competes according to the rules." (2 Tim. 2:5). Even in physical competitions an athlete is not crowned if he does not struggle lawfully.

Elder Ephraim of Arizona

APOSTLE PHILEMON OF THE SEVENTY. Philemon and his wife Apphia are numbered among the Seventy Apostles. Philemon was the bishop of Gaza. Together with Apostle Archippus of the Seventy, they ministered to the town of Colossae from its Christian center, Philemon's home. During a pagan feast, the Church was gathered at his home for prayer. When the pagans learned of this, they raided the home and took Philemon, Apphia, and Archippus to be killed. The three were whipped, buried up to their waists, and then stoned. Philemon and Apphia gave up their souls there. Apostle Onesimos of the Seventy was once St. Philemon's former slave, and he became a disciple of St. Paul.

COMMEMORATIONS: Apostles Philemon and Archippus of the Seventy and Martyr Apphia; Theodore of Sanaxar Monastery; Eugene and Macarius, priests and confessors at Antioch; Philothea the Athenian; Maximus, Theodotus, Hesychius, and Asclepiodote of Adrianople; Nicetas of Epirus and Mt. Athos, at Serres; Dositheus of Gaza; Rabulas of Samosata; Conon in Palestine; Mesrop the Translator of Armenia; Vladimir (Terentiev), abbot of Zosima Hermitage, Smolensk.

Thursday   **Fast-free**

February 20

1 John 4:20-5:21; Mark 15:1-15

The reason people sin is that they don't remember death as they should. The wise Isaac the Syrian says that the devil attempts in every way to remove the thought of death from man's mind. He fills man's mind with unprofitable and harmful recollections. He will give the whole world to man so long as he doesn't think or remember death and doesn't consider it in depth. We must reflect how we will die; well or badly? Ready or unprepared? All of us who fear death do so because we have not loved God as we should.
+*Elder Philotheos Zervakos*

THIRTY-FOUR HOLY MARTYRS OF VALAAM MONASTERY. In the year 1578, these venerable Fathers were beleaguered by converts to Lutheranism. This took place at the Monastery of the Transfiguration at Valaam on Lake Ladoga. The Lutherans tried to make them renounce Orthodoxy, and when they bravely refused, the 34 were massacred. An office of commemoration has been celebrated for them each year in the katholikon of the monastery. The Patriarchate of Moscow canonized them in the year 2000.

COMMEMORATIONS: Bessarion the Great, wonderworker of Egypt; Agatho, Pope of Rome; Sadoc, Bishop of Persia, and 128 Martyrs with him; Eleutherius, bishop in Byzantium; Leo, Bishop of Catania; Cindeus, Bishop of Pisidia; Cornelius of the Pskov Caves, and his disciple Bassian of Murom; Righteous Plotinus; Agatho of the Kiev Caves; Yaroslav the Wise, Great Prince of Kiev; Macarius and 34 monks and novices of Valaam Monastery; Eucherius, Bishop of Orleans; Eleutherius, Bishop of Tournai.

Friday   **Strict Fast**

February 21

2 John 1:1-13
Mark 15:20, 22, 25, 33-41

The devil does not have any power and authority over a believer who goes to church, confesses, takes communion. The devil only paws at such a person, the same as a toothless dog.
St. Paisios the Athonite

VENERABLE TIMOTHY OF SYMBOLA. Timothy was of Italian descent and became a monk at an early age in the eighth century. He struggled at the Monastery of Symbola on Mount Olympus. Timothy became known as a desert dweller. Through intense prayer and discipline, he mortified the impulses of his passions and became a pure vessel of the Holy Spirit. To remain chaste, he never wished to even gaze at a woman's face, lest he should suffer harm. Timothy received the gift of working miraculous cures of every disease, and to dispel demons. Despite his isolation, he showed his love for people by giving alms, protecting orphans and widows, showing kindness to strangers, and giving food and clothing to the needy. During the Iconoclast period, Timothy was a defender of the holy icons. He suffered scourging for confessing his veneration of the holy icons. He reposed in deep old age. St. Theophanes reports that St. Timothy's "honorable reliquary pours forth a torrent of healings" at the Monastery of Symbola.

COMMEMORATIONS: Timothy of Symbola on Mt. Olympus in Bithynia; John the Scholastic, Patriarch of Constantinople; Eustathius, Archbishop of Antioch; Zachariah, Patriarch of Jerusalem; George, Bishop of Amastris; Severian, Bishop of Scythopolis; Macarius of Glinsk Hermitage; "Cucuzelis" and "Kozelshchansk" Icons of the Mother of God.

SATURDAY

Commemoration of the Departed
Fast-free

FEBRUARY 22

1 Thessalonians 4:13-17
Luke 21:8-9, 25-27, 33-36

Indulging your ill temper at the expense of your wife may give some immediate relief to your emotions; but it brings no lasting joy or pleasure. Yet, if you treat your wife as a free woman, respecting her ideas and intuitions, and responding with warmth to her feelings and emotions, then your marriage shall be a limitless source of blessing to you.

St. John Chrysostom

ST. MAXIMIANUS, BISHOP OF RAVENNA. Maximianus was from the city of Pula, which is in modern-day Croatia. He was a 48-year-old deacon and friend of Emperor Justinian I. He was consecrated the bishop of Ravenna, the capital of the Roman-Byzantine Empire territories in Italy. His flock initially refused his leadership as he was not their initial candidate, and it was said that his elevation was politically arranged. However, he won the respect of the people by his discretion, generosity, and building of churches and their embellishment. Maximianus devoted himself to the revision of liturgical books and commissioned a large number of illuminated manuscripts. He died ten years after becoming a bishop, in the year 556.

COMMEMORATIONS: Thallasios, Limnaios, and Baradates of Syria; Telesphorus, Pope of Rome; Athanasius the Confessor of Constantinople; Titus, Bishop of Bostra in Arabia; Maurice and his son Photinos, and Martyrs Theodore, Philip, and 70 soldiers; Anthusa and 12 handmaidens; Holy Nine Children of Kola; Maximianus of Ravenna; Martyr Synetus; Theoktista of Voronezh; Peter the Stylite of Mt. Athos; Babylas and Comnita of Nicosa; Leontius of Lycia; Abilius, Patriarch of Alexandria; Papius of Hieropolis; Michael Lisitsyn of Ust-Labinskaya; Herman of Stolobny Monastery; Blaise, bishop; Uncovering of the relics of the Holy Martyrs at the gate of Eugenius at Constantinople.

SUNDAY

FEBRUARY 23

Meatfare Sunday
Fast-free
1 Corinthians 8:8-9:2
Matthew 25:31-46

For what purpose does the Lord add day after day, year after year, to our existence? In order that we may gradually put away, cast aside, evil from our souls, each one his own, and acquire blessed simplicity; in order that we may become truly gentle; in order that we may learn not to have the least attachment to earthly things, but as loving and simple children may cling with all our hearts, all our souls, and all our thoughts, to God alone, and so to love Him, and our neighbor as ourselves. Let us therefore hasten to pray to the Lord, fervently and with tears, to grant us simplicity of heart, and let us strive by every means to cast out the evil from our souls.
St. John of Kronstadt

ST. GORGONIA, SISTER OF ST. GREGORY THE THEOLOGIAN. Gorgonia was the daughter of Saints Gregory the Elder and Nonna, and her brothers were Saints Gregory the Theologian and Caesarius of Nazianzus. Gorgonia married and had children. She became known as the mother of orphans, eyes of the blind, and keeper of the poor. She became very ill when an epidemic struck her village. She prayed for God's will and recovered but continued to help others who were still sick. St. Gorgonia died peacefully at the age of thirty-nine.

COMMEMORATIONS: Polycarp, Bishop of Smyrna; Gorgonia, sister of Gregory the Theologian; John, Antioch, Antoninos, Zevinos, and Polychronios, Moses, and Damian of Syria; Alexander, founder of the Monastery of the Unsleeping Ones; John Theristes (the Harvester) of Stylos in Calabria; Damian of Esphigmenou, Mt. Athos; Polycarp of Briansk; Moses of White Lake; Michael Edlinsky of Kiev; Lazarus of the Peloponnese; Seraphim (Zenobius) of Tetritskaro; Milburga of Much Wenlock; Nazarius of Valaam Monastery; Martyr Clement; Martyr Thea; Sergius Bukashkin of Novo-Alexandrovka; Antipas Kyrillov of Tatarintsevo; Philaret Pryakhin of Trubino.

Monday

February 24

First & Second Finding of the Precious Head
of St. John the Baptist
Abstain from meat products.
2 Corinthians 4:6-15
Matthew 11:2-15

At least once in our life we must light a candle for those whom we insulted, whom we deceived, whom we stole something from, whom we owed, and whom we did not pay our debt.

St. Seraphim of Viritsa

FIRST AND SECOND FINDINGS OF THE PRECIOUS HEAD OF ST. JOHN THE BAPTIST. The head of St. John came to be known as the "Kara." His body was buried in Sebaste, Samaria. Herod's wife, Herodias, fearing that John would rise from the dead, ordered the head to be buried separately from the body, deep in the earth in an unworthy place. Herodias' lady in waiting, Joanna, the wife of Chuza, secretly removed the Kara and buried it reverently on the Mount of Olives. When Herod heard about the miracles of Jesus, he thought that it was John raised from the dead. However, while John was yet alive, he had never performed a miracle. Much later, a monk named Innocent accidentally dug up the Kara while building a church on the Mount of Olives. He later reburied it in the same place when its identity was revealed to him. In the fifth century, it came into the hands of an Arian monk named Eustachios, who buried it in a cave in Emesa. Bishop Uranios found it after Eustachios' death and had it placed in a church for all to venerate. In the ninth century, it was taken to Constantinople, and many miracles were performed there.

COMMEMORATIONS: First and Second findings of the Venerable Head of St. John the Baptist; Erasmus of the Kiev Caves; Montanus, Lucias, Julian, Victoricus, Flavian, and companions at Carthage; Cummain Ailbe, abbot of Iona; Uncovering of the relics of St. Romanus, Prince of Uglich.

TUESDAY   **Abstain from meat products.**

FEBRUARY 25
Jude 1:1-10
Luke 22:39-42, 45-71, 23:1

The knowledge of God does not reside in a body that loves comforts.

St. Isaac the Syrian

HIEROMARTYR REGINOS, BISHOP OF THE ISLE OF SKOPELOS. Reginos was from fourth-century Greece. He was an excellent student in both the secular and ecclesiastical, and he governed well his thoughts and desires. He fasted, kept vigil, and slept on the ground, all in an effort to master his body, make his soul more radiant, and to become a temple of the Holy Trinity. God rewarded Reginos with gifts of the Holy Spirit and the working of miracles by his prayers, and he became well known throughout Greece. When the bishop of the island of Skopelos died, the people elected Reginos. Multitudes of people rejoiced at his enthronement and beseeched him for the healing of their various diseases. The Arian heresy continued to rage within the Church. The Arians believed that Christ was not coessential with God the Father. A synod of 367 bishops was convened to debate this heresy. When Reginos spoke, he cited passages from the Gospel and Church writings proving the coessentiality of God the Father and the Son. The Church was disrupted again when Julian the Apostate took the throne, and he began persecuting Christians. Reginos was arrested and subjected to horrible torture. He was flattered and threatened to break his resolve and dishearten his flock, but this only further strengthened the faith of the Christians. Reginos remained steadfast, unshaken, and eager to the end. The ruler gave the order to behead St. Reginos. His holy relics were transferred to the Nativity of Christ Cathedral in Skopelos.

COMMEMORATIONS: Tarasios, Archbishop of Constantinople; Reginos, Bishop of Skopelos; Alexander at Drizipara of Thrace; Theodore, fool-for-Christ; Erasmus and Paphnutius of Kephala; Marcellus, Bishop of Apamea in Syria; Martyr Anthony; Martyrs Alexander and Hypatius at Marcianopolis; Walburga, abbess of Heidenheim; Ethelbert, King of Kent; Venerable Polycarp; Leo Korobczuk of Laskov.

WEDNESDAY   **Abstain from meat products.**

February 26

Joel 3:12-21; Joel 2:12-26

If you truly wish to put your thoughts to shame, to be serenely silent, and to live in the effortless enjoyment of a sober and quiet heart, let the Jesus Prayer cleave to your breathing, and in a few days, you will see all this realized.

St. Hesychios of Sinai

NEW MARTYR JOHN CALPHAS THE CABINETMAKER, AT CONSTANTINOPLE. John was a master cabinetmaker in the sixteenth-century suburb of Galata, in Constantinople. He was in charge of the work inside the sultan's palace. John was a Christian, and he was filled with good works. He provided for orphans and those in prison and helped any who came to him. An important official once asked him to take on his nephew as an apprentice, and John agreed. After his training, the young man was given an honorable position at court. Later, this young man, who was devoted to Islam, asked John what the Christian books had to say about Prophet Mohammed. John was reluctant to answer, but the young man persisted. Finally, John answered that Mohammed was an uneducated man who never performed a miracle. The young man told the other Muslims, and John was brought to trial, where they demanded him to renounce Christ. John bravely confessed his faith and was tortured and imprisoned for six months. Over the next three months, he was beaten and finally beheaded in the crowded town square.

COMMEMORATIONS: Porphyrios, Bishop of Gaza; Photina the Samaritan Woman, and her sisters Anatola, Phota, Photis, Parasceva, and Cyriaca; and her sons Victor (Photinus) and Joses, and Sebastian the Duke, Victor, and Christodulus, all martyred under Nero; John Calphas at Constantinople; Martyr Theoclitas, with St. Photina; Sebastian of Poshek-honye; John of Rylsk; "Mezhetsk" Icon of the Mother of God.

THURSDAY   **Abstain from meat products.**

FEBRUARY 27

1 Jude 1:11-25
Luke 23:1-31, 33, 44-56

*P*ray and then speak. That's what to do with your children. If you are constantly lecturing them, you'll become tiresome and when they grow up, they'll feel a kind of oppression. Prefer prayer and speak to them through prayer. Speak to God and God will speak to their hearts. That is, you shouldn't give guidance to your children with a voice that they hear with their ears. You may do this too, but above all you should speak to God about your children. Say, "Lord Jesus Christ, give Your light to my children. I entrust them to You. You gave them to me, but I am weak and unable to guide them, so, please, illuminate them." And God will speak to them and they will say to themselves, "Oh dear, I shouldn't have upset Mummy by doing that!" And with the grace of God this will come from their heart.

St. Porphyrios the Kapsokalyvite

NEW MARTYR ELIAS OF TREBIZOND. Elias was the son of a priest from the eighteenth-century village of Kryonero in Trebizond of Asia Minor. It is unknown why, but Elias was apprehended by Muslims and painfully tortured to force him to convert from his Christian faith. When he refused, he was sentenced to be hanged in 1749. Christians took up his sacred relics and buried them at the Monastery of Panagia Theoskepastos in Trebizond.

COMMEMORATIONS: Prokopios the Confessor of Decapolis; Julian, Chroniun and Besas at Alexandria; Asklepios and James of Syria; Gelasius the Actor of Heliopolis; Stephen of Constantinople; Thalaleos of Syria; Timothy of Caesarea; Pitirim of Tambov; Martyr Nesius; Titus of the Kiev Caves, the former soldier; Elias of Trebizond; Titus of the Kiev Caves, presbyter; Raphael, Bishop of Brooklyn; Macarius, Bishop of Jerusalem; Herefrith, Bishop of Lincolnshire; Leander of Seville.

FRIDAY **Abstain from meat products.**

FEBRUARY 28

Zechariah 8:7-17; Zechariah 8:19-23

Has a brother been the occasion of trial for you, and has your distress at this led you to hatred of him? Do not be overcome by hatred, but overcome hatred by love. This is how you will overcome hatred: by praying sincerely to God for him and accepting his apology, or by soothing him yourself through this apology—reckoning yourself responsible for the trial, enduring patiently until the cloud has passed. He is long-suffering who awaits the end of a trial with composure, and waits upon the glory of his perseverance.

St. Maximos the Confessor

APOSTLES NYMPHAS AND EUBULUS OF THE SEVENTY. Apostle Nymphas was a Christian from Laodicea, and the Apostle Paul mentions him in his Epistle to the Colossians. He was a person of outstanding worth and importance in Laodicea, for he had granted the use of his home for the ordinary weekly meetings of the Church. Moreover, a tiny house could not have accommodated all the Christian men and women. Apostle Eubulus is mentioned in the Second Epistle to Timothy. He was one of the members of the Church in Rome during St. Paul's second imprisonment in that city. At a time when the Roman Christians proved disloyal to St. Paul, Apostle Eubulus and a few others remained faithful to him.

COMMEMORATIONS: Proterius, Patriarch of Alexandria, and six companions; Apostles Nymphas and Eubulus; Nestor in Pamphylia; Barsus, Bishop of Damascus; Basil the Confessor; Marana, Kyra, and Domnica of Syria; Kyranna of Thessalonica; Sergius, priest; Martyr Avrikios; Romanus of Condat in Gaul; Arsenius of Rostov; Nicholas of Pskov.

SATURDAY

FEBRUARY 29

Commemoration of the Departed
Abstain from meat products.
Galatians 5:22-6:2; Matthew 6:1-13

*W*e are often indifferent to our brethren who are distressed or upset, on the grounds that they are in this state through no fault of ours. The Doctor of souls, however, wishing to root out the soul's excuses from the heart, tells us to leave our gift and to be reconciled not only if we happen to be upset by our brother, but also if he is upset by us, whether justly or unjustly; only when we have healed the breach through our apology should we offer our gift.

St. John Cassian

ST. OSWALD, ARCHBISHOP OF YORK. Oswald was raised by his uncle in England, who sent him to the abbey of Fleury in France to become a monk. When his uncle died, Oswald looked for a new patron and turned to another kinsman, the Archbishop of York. Oswald's work for him attracted the notice of Archbishop Dunstan, who had him consecrated as Bishop of Worcester. Oswald supported Dunstan's reforms of the Church, including monastic discipline and the effort to purify the church of secularism. He founded several monasteries and reformed another seven. Oswald regularly visited the monasteries he founded. It was Oswald's daily custom during Lent to wash the feet of the poor, and he died one day while doing this. Almost immediately after his death in the year 992, miracles were reported at his funeral and his tomb.

COMMEMORATIONS: John Cassian the Roman; John (Barsanuphius) of Nitria in Egypt; Cassian of the Kiev Caves; Martyr Theocteristos of Pelecete Monastery; Germanus of Dacia Pontica; Cassian of Mu-lake Hermitage; Leo, Cappadocian monastic; Oswald, Archbishop of York; Meletius, Archbishop of Kharkov; "Devpeteruv" Icon of the Mother of God.

Remember how none of the saints of old won their crowns of patient endurance by living luxuriously and being courted; but all were tested by being put through the fire of great afflictions. "For some had trial of cruel mockings and scourgings, and others were sawn asunder and were slain with the sword." These are the glories of the saints.

St. Basil the Great

Sunday
March 1

Forgiveness Sunday
Cheesefare Sunday
Abstain from meat products.
Romans 13:11-14:4; Matthew 6:14-21

*P*hysicians and Bishops say that frugal fasting is very beneficial to man. Once, a doctor told me: "Father, don't eat for five days, nor even drink a drop of water, because we will do a test to see what is going on with your body." Therefore I fasted for five days. It had done great things to me. How much more are we benefited when we fast for our soul! Because within our body inhabits an eternal soul. Therefore, let us take care for our soul, which is truly an immortal thing.

St. Iakovos Tsalikis of Evia

MARTYR ANTONINA OF NICAEA. In fourth-century Bithynia in Asia Minor, Antonina went before the Christian-hating Emperor Maximian and boldly confessed her belief in Jesus Christ. He tortured her and put her in prison. When he realized her firm resolve, he had her suspended, and her sides lacerated. Antonina belittled the Greek gods and Maximian for his beliefs. Again, he ordered her stripped and beaten. Angels protected her and beat the soldiers before they could remove her clothes. Later, she was placed on a red-hot bed, but she was protected. Finally, she was sewn into a sack and sunk it in a lake.

COMMEMORATIONS: Eudocia of Heliopolis; Antonina of Nicaea; Martyrs Charisius, Nikephoros, and Agapius; Agapios of Kolitsou Skete of Vatopedi, and his 4 companions; Domnina, ascetic of Syria; Martyrs Sylvester and Sophronius; Antonina of Kizliar; Anastasia Andreyevna, fool-for-Christ; Anthony (Korzh) of Kiziltash Monastery (Crimea); Martyrius, founder of Zelenets Monastery; David of Wales; Paraskevas of Trebizond; Leo-Luke of Corleone, Sicily; Albinus, Bishop of Angers; Swidbert (Suitbert), bishop in southern Westphalia and monastic founder on the Rhine River.

Monday

March 2

Clean Monday—Great Lent Begins
Strict Fast

Isaiah 1:1-20; Genesis 1:1-13
Proverbs 1:1-20

For I know, yes I know many, not merely fasting and making a display of it, but neglecting to fast, and yet wearing the masks of them that fast, and cloaking themselves with an excuse worse than their sin.

St. John Chrysostom

ST. NICHOLAS PLANAS OF ATHENS. Papa Nicholas was taught to read the Psalter by his grandfather, a priest, and he would try to liturgize with the few words he knew. He married at seventeen, had a son, and received ordination to the priesthood. Nicholas liturgized six hours every day for fifty years and commemorated many names of the living and the dead. His inner state was pure. Children would see him talking with saints or levitating during prayer. He would not keep the money that was given to him but gave it to the poor. Once when he lost his way to a little church, an angel of God appeared and guided him the rest of the way. Papa Nicholas knew how to correct and enlighten souls without sermons, but with his own life and presence. One time a rich woman got sick and her daughter requested a respectable priest from a big church, rather than the dusty Papa Nicholas. That night Nicholas appeared to her in gold vestments, and she immediately called for him the next morning. When he saw her, he asked if she was pleased with the way she had seen him? In this way, Papa Nicholas taught her about vanity. Another time, as he was communing a leper, a small part of the Holy Eucharist fell from the leper's mouth, and immediately Papa Nicholas knelt and consumed it. Papa Nicholas died at the age of eighty-four, in 1932, and the faithful rushed to embrace him for the last time.

COMMEMORATIONS: Hesychius the Senator; Quintus of Phrygia; Euthalia of Sicily; Theodotus of Cyrenia; Arsenius of Tver; Hesychius the Palatine; Troadios of Neo-Caesarea; Joachim of Vatopedi; Nestor, Tribimius, Marcellus, and Anthony of Perga; Martyrs Andronicus and Athanasia; Nicholas Planas of Athens; Sabbatius of Tver and Euphrosynus; 440 Martyrs in Italy; Chad of Lichfield.

Tuesday   **Strict Fast**

March 3

Isaiah 1:19-2:3; Genesis 1:14-23
Proverbs 1:20-33

If there is no spiritual person with whom one could talk, then do not grieve much. Sit at home, and the Lord, who loves everyone, will send you His consolation and admonition. God knows about your loneliness and will not leave you.

St. Nektarios of Aegina

ST. PIAMA OF EGYPT. Piama lived in her mother's home in a small village outside Alexandria, along the Nile River. She remained a virgin and lived as an ascetic. When she was not in prayer, she spun flax. God granted her the gift of insight. A more populated village nearby planned to destroy the saint's small village because they wanted to divert water from the overflowing Nile to their fields. Piama discerned what the other villagers intended to do, and she informed the elders of her village. She was asked to go and talk to them, but she eschewed contact with people and instead spent the night in prayer. Just as the enemy converged upon Piama's small village, they suddenly stopped, as if by an unseen hand, and were not able to proceed. When they learned about the saint's prayers, they repented of their evil intent. St. Piama died peacefully in year 337.

COMMEMORATIONS: Eutropius and Cleonicus of Amasea, and Basiliscus of Comana; Alexandra of Alexandria; Righteous Zeno and Zoilos; Hemetherius of Spain; Virgin Piama of Egypt; Theodoretus of Antioch; Caluppan of Auvergne (Gaul); John IV (Chrysostom), Catholicos of Georgia; Non, mother of David of Wales; Winwaloe, abbot of Landevennec, Brittany; "Volokolamsk" Icon of the Mother of God.

Wednesday   Strict Fast

March 4

Isaiah 2:3-11; Genesis 1:24-2:3
Proverbs 2:1-22

If we watch carefully, we shall often find a bitter joke played on us by the demons. For when we are full, they stir us up to compunction; and when we are fasting, they harden our heart so that, being deceived by spurious tears, we may give ourselves up to indulgence which is the mother of passions. We must not listen to them but rather do the opposite.

St. John Climacus

ST. GERASIMUS OF VOLOGDA. Gerasimus was tonsured a monk on March 4, the day commemorating St. Gerasimus of the Jordan. As was the custom, he was given the name of a saint celebrated that day. He labored at the Kiev Uspenie monastery. Wishing to imitate the fathers before him, he went to live in solitude in a dense forest near the Vologda River. He built a hut and settled into a life of unceasing prayer, work, and the contemplation of God. Then he built a church dedicated to the Holy Trinity, which became the first monastery in northern Russia. The monastery became a place of spiritual enlightenment to the people of the surrounding area. St. Gerasimus died peacefully on the same date that he was tonsured.

COMMEMORATIONS: Gregory, Bishop of Constantia; Gerasimus of the Jordan; Julian, Bishop of Alexandria; Gregory, Bishop of Assos; Paul, Juliana, Quadratus, Acacius, and Stratonicus, at Ptolemais in Syria; John of al-Sindiyana (Palestine); James the Faster of Phoenicia; Saints of Pskov martyred by the Latins: Ioasaph of Snetogorsk Monastery and Basil of Mirozh Monastery; Dimitry Ivanov of Kiev; Vyacheslav Leontiev of Nizhegorod; Daniel, Great Prince of Moscow; Gerasimus of Vologda; Basil, Prince of Rostov; Translation of the relics of St. Wenceslaus, Prince of the Czechs.

Thursday

Strict Fast

March 5

Isaiah 2:11-21; Genesis 2:4-19
Proverbs 3:1-18

In Holy Communion we receive the Living Lord Christ Himself, in the form of bread and wine; in almsgiving we give to the Living Lord Christ Himself, in the form of the poor and needy.
— *St. Nikolai Velimirovich*

ST. NIKOLAI VELIMIROVICH, BISHOP OF OCHRID. Nikolai was born in 1881 in western Serbia. His mother was the primary spiritual influence in his life, and he often walked three miles with her to church. He excelled academically and graduated from the seminary and King's College in Oxford. He spoke seven languages and taught at the seminary in Belgrade. He inspired people to repentance with his sermons that always focused on three main points and never lasted more than twenty minutes. During World War I, he went to England to seek help for the Serbs who were struggling with Austria. He was invited to America to speak and raised money for the orphanages he established. He became the leader of a spiritual revival that encouraged people to pray and read the Bible. Nikolai helped restore monasteries and revitalize monasticism, which helped reenergize the spiritual life of the Serbs. He criticized the Nazis during World War II, and for this was sent to the Dachau death camp, where he saw the horrors and was tortured. When the Americans liberated the prisoners, Nikolai went to America and taught at St. Sava's Seminary in Illinois. He later settled at St. Tikhon's Orthodox Monastery in Pennsylvania and also lectured at St. Vladimir's Orthodox Seminary in New York. His writings include the *Prologue from Ochrid*, *The Life of St. Sava*, and *A Treasury of Serbian Spirituality*. He died peacefully in 1956 in America.

COMMEMORATIONS: Mark the Faster; Mark of Athens; Conon of Isauria; Conon the Gardener; Onisius of Isauria; Eulampius of Palestine; Rhais of Antinoe, Archelaus and 152 Martyrs; Eulogius of Palestine; Theophilus, Bishop of Caesarea; Basil and Constantine of Yaroslavl; George of Rapsana; Hesychius the Faster; Nikolai Velimirovich of Ochrid; John the Bulgarian; Adrian of Poshekhonye, and Leonid; Theodore of Smolensk, with Yaroslav, David, and Constantine; Kieran of Munster; Virgil of Arles.

Friday

March 6

Salutations to the Virgin Mary
Strict Fast

Isaiah 3:1-14; Genesis 2:20-3:20
Proverbs 3:19-34

*W*hat does love look like? It has the hands to help others. It has the feet to hasten to the poor and needy. It has eyes to see misery and want. It has the ears to hear the sighs and sorrows of men. That is what love looks like.

St. Augustine of Hippo

ST. HESYCHIOS THE WONDERWORKER. Hesychios lived in Galatia, Asia Minor, in the eighth century. Thieves would attack those who ventured outside that city. After many years, Hesychios decided that with God's help, he would brave the badlands and climb to the peak of a nearby holy mountain to pray. His trip to the mountain of Maionos was surprisingly uneventful. He lived there in peace and prayer and built a church. Some Christians brought their daughter to him that had epilepsy. With his touch, he healed her, and he told the parents that after his death, that place would become a convent for virgins, and this prophecy was fulfilled. Hesychios mortified his body and grew in virtue. He became known in all of Asia Minor as a wonderworker. He was made worthy of talking with the holy angels. Before his death, he was visited by an angel who told him he was going to die in thirty days. He gave his final words to the brethren, and a heavenly light shined on him as his soul departed. The holy relics of St. Hesychios were transferred to Amasia later during the reign of St. Constantine and his mother St. Helen.

COMMEMORATIONS: The uncovering of the Precious Cross and the Precious Nails by Empress St. Helen; 42 Martyrs of Ammorium in Phrygia; Hesychios of Galatia; Conon and his son Conon of Iconium; Fridolin, enlightener of the Upper Rhine; Arcadius of Cyprus, with Julian and Bulius; Job (Joshua) of Anzersk Island; Martyrs Maximus and Euphrosynus; Martyrs Julian and Eubulus; Cyriacus and 12 companions, in Augsburg; Miraculous Icon of Jesus Christ at Agia Moni; "Chenstokhov" and "Blessed Heaven" Icons of the Mother of God.

SATURDAY

MARCH 7

Commemoration of the Departed
Abstain from meat and dairy products, and fish.
2 Timothy 2:1-10; Mark 2:23-3:5

He who lives in idleness, always sins.

St. Tikhon of Zadonsk

MARTYR AND CONFESSOR JOHANNES OF ILOMANTSI. From early childhood, Johannes espoused a deep Orthodox faith. At the age of twenty-two, he was asked by the archbishop of Vyborg and all Finland to open a religious school in his village. At this time the Evangelical Lutheran Church of Finland was trying to evangelize Orthodox Karelia. Together with the Karelian Brotherhood, the school was established. Johannes started working as a missionary across Karelia with the monks of Valaam Monastery. He was also active in the completion of the church of St. Anna the Prophetess. Because of this, the nationalists from Finland accused him of promoting the Russian faith and influence. He was called a collaborator of the Russian secret police, anti-Finnish in his politics, and the "dark force of North Karelia." However, Johannes did not defend himself. He just continued with his religious work, not politics. After the 1917 Russian Revolution, the schools and churches owned by the Karelian Brotherhood were closed. Johannes was harassed by the Finnish nationalists, calling him a Bolshevik, even though he supported the Tsarist regime. When the Finnish Civil War began, he was called to join the White Army but was arrested and placed in a prison camp for the Reds. Finally, he was executed by a firing squad and buried in a mass grave. St. Johannes' body was returned later to his wife, and a large crowd of Orthodox and Lutherans attended his funeral.

COMMEMORATIONS: Ephraim, Patriarch of Antioch; Hieromartyrs of Cherson: Basil, Ephraim, Eugene, Capiton, Elpidius, Agathorodus, and Aetherius; Emilian of Italy; Paul the Simple of Egypt; Laurence of Phaneromenh Monastery on Salamis; Nestor and Arcadius of Tremithus; Dandus and All Saints of Thrace; Nilus (Tyutyukin) of St. Joseph of Volokolamsk Monastery; Eosterwine of Wearmount; Johannes of Ilomantsi; Synaxis of All Saints of the Dodecanese; "Surety of Sinners" and "Of Czestochowa" Icons of the Mother of God.

Sunday

March 8

**Sunday of Orthodoxy
Abstain from meat and
dairy products, and fish.**
Hebrews 11:24-26, 32-40; John 1:43-51

*B*elieve me children, heresies and schisms have done nothing for the holy church except to make us love God and each other very much less than before.

St. Palladius of Antioch

APOSTLE HERMAS OF THE SEVENTY. According to tradition, the Apostle Hermas was the author of three spiritually beneficial books: *The Church, The Shepherd,* and *The Ten Parables.* As written in *The Shepherd,* Hermas was a wealthy man, but because of his sins and the sins of his sons, he fell into extreme poverty. Once while in prayer, an angel of repentance appeared to him and said that he would be with him until the end of his life. The angel gave him twelve mandates: 1) Believe in God; 2) Live in simplicity and innocence; do not speak evil and give alms to all who beg; 3) Love truth and avoid falsehood; 4) Preserve chastity in your thoughts; 5) Learn patience and generosity; 6) To know that in every man, there is a good and an evil spirit; 7) Fear God and not to fear the devil; 8) Do every good and refrain from every evil deed; 9) Pray to God from the depth of the soul with faith that our prayer will be fulfilled; 10) Guard against melancholy as the sister of doubt and anger; 11) Question true and false prophecies; 12) Guard against every evil desire. St. Hermas became Bishop of Philippopolis in Thrace and died in peace.

COMMEMORATIONS: Apostle Hermas of the Seventy; Theophylactos, Bishop of Nicomedia; Paul the Confessor, Bishop of Plousias in Bithynia; Martyr Dion; Venerable Dometius, monk; Quintilian and Capatolinus at Nicomedia; Athanasius and Lazarus of Murom Island; Felix of Burgundy, enlightener of East Anglia; Andronicus (Lukash), of Tbilisi, Georgia; Senan of Scattery Island (Inis Cathaigh); Julian of Toledo; "Kursk Root" Icon of the Sign of the Mother of God.

MONDAY

March 9

Holy 40 Martyrs of Sebaste
Abstain from meat and dairy products, and fish.
Hebrews 12:1-10; Matthew 20:1-16

*D*o you want to live a spiritual life—watch yourself. Every evening, look over what you have done good and bad, thank God for good, and repent of bad.

St. Alexy Mechev of Moscow

THE 42 NEW MARTYRS OF MOMISICI. Momisici is in Southeast Europe, bordered by the Adriatic Sea, Croatia, Bosnia, Serbia, and Albania. In the year 1688 at the St. George Church, two priests, serving as religious education teachers, and their 40 students, children from the parish, were burned alive by the Turkish military general. This was in retaliation for the defeat the Turks suffered in a battle against the Kuci tribe. The relics of the martyrs were gathered and buried beneath the holy altar table of the St. George Church and remained there until 1936. In 2006 the relics were taken out for the faithful to venerate on the feastday of the Holy 40 Martyrs of Sebaste. The relics were washed with wine and anointed with rose oil according to ancient Orthodox custom. They are located in a reliquary on the left side of the iconostasis in the Momisici church of St. George.

COMMEMORATIONS: Holy Forty Martyrs of Sebaste; Caesarius, brother of St. Gregory the Theologian; Philoromus, Confessor of Galatia; Urpasianus of Nicomedia; Tarasius the Wonderworker of Lycaonia; Jonah, Archbishop of Novgorod; Theodosius Levitsky of Balta (Odessa); Bosa, Bishop of York; Vitalius of Castronovo; Pacianus, Bishop of Barcelona; Mitrophan Buchnoff of Voronezh, and Ioasaph of Popovka; Dimitra, foundress of Vvedensk Convent in Kiev; 2 priests and 40 students of Momisici (Montenegro); "Albazin" (The Word was Made Flesh) Icon of the Mother of God.

Tuesday **Strict Fast**

March 10

Isaiah 5:7-16; Genesis 4:8-15
Proverbs 5:1-15

*W*herever you put a person suffering from an internal disease or oppressed with cruel sorrow, he will suffer, even if he is put in the most magnificent palace; that is because his disease and sorrow are always and everywhere with him and in him. It is the same in the case of a sinner who is impenitent and not cleansed of his sins—wherever you put him, he will suffer even in Paradise itself, because the cause of his suffering (i.e., sin) is in his heart. To a sinner everywhere is hell.

St. Innocent of Alaska

MARTYR KODRATOS OF CORINTH, WITH DIONYSIOS, ANEKTOS, PAUL, CYPRIAN, CRESCENS, AND OTHERS. During a third-century Christian persecution, a pious woman named Ruthyna fled from Corinth into the wilderness, and there gave birth to Kodratos. She died after giving birth, and God nourished the infant with sweet dew that dripped from a cloud that hovered over him. Kodratos spent his youth in the wilderness. When he was twelve years old, he met some Christians, who taught him the true faith. He studied grammar and later was educated as a doctor. He healed with medicine and prayer. He frequently went into the wilderness for solitude and prayer, and his friends followed him there for instruction. Later, during another persecution under Emperor Decius, Kodratos and his friends were arrested and thrown into prison. They were stoned and dragged through the streets to the place of execution. At the site of their beheading, a spring of water gushed from the ground. To this day, the spring is called Kodratos.

COMMEMORATIONS: Kodratos of Corinth, and those with him; Victorinus, Victor, Nicephoros, Claudius, Diodoros, Serapion, Papias, and others, at Corinth; Anastasia the Patrician of Alexandria; Martyr Marcian; Attalus, abbot of Bobbio; John of Khakhuli, Georgia, who was called Chrysostom; Michael Mavroeidis of Adrianople; Paul of Taganrog; Kessog, Bishop of Loch Lomond; Alexander (Badanin) of Vologda.

WEDNESDAY **Strict Fast**

March 11

Isaiah 5:16-25; Genesis 4:16-26
Proverbs 5:15-6:3

If your mind can pray without distraction, your heart will soon be softened.

St. Mark the Ascetic

ST. THEODORA, QUEEN OF ARTA. At a tender age, Theodora married Emperor Michael II Komnenos Doukas in the thirteenth century. She devoted herself to God and cultivated the virtues. Michael was weak with a lust for women and a noblewoman named Gangrene. Her sorcery beguiled his sanity, and he developed a hatred for Theodora. She was driven into exile for five years and lived in the open air, where she suffered from the cold and burning heat, and hunger and thirst. Still, she continued to pray and strove for virtue. One day a priest from the village found her picking greens while holding her baby. Theodora was pregnant when she went into exile. He took her home and concealed her. Finally, the leading officials seized the wicked Gangrene, and the whole affair came to light. Michael came to his senses and took Theodora back, and all things were filled with joy and rejoicing. Michael established two beautiful sacred monasteries and Theodora erected a women's monastery dedicated to Great Martyr George. When the emperor died, she immediately became a nun, and she conversed with God through psalms and hymns. Theodora served the nuns unceasingly, helping orphans and widows, the poor, the oppressed, and all with humility of heart. She foresaw her death but implored God through the help of St. George and the Mother of God to let her live six more months to finish a church, which came to pass. After her death, St. Theodora worked many great miracles for those both near and far.

COMMEMORATIONS: Trophimos and Thallus at Laodicea; George of Sinai; Sophronius of Jerusalem; Sophronius of Vratsa; Euthymius of Novgorod; George Arselaites; Pionios of Smyrna, with Asclepiades, Macedonia, Linus, and Sabina; John Moschos; Sophronius of the Kiev Caves; Theodora of Arta; George the New of Constantinople; Eulogius of Cordoba; Alexis of Goloseyevsky; Patrick of Valaam; Michael of Svyatogorsk; Angus of Clonenagh.

THURSDAY

MARCH 12

Strict Fast

Isaiah 6:1-12; Genesis 5:1-24
Proverbs 6:3-20

Once you learn to be patient, you will always pray in great joy.
+*Evagrios of Pontus*

RIGHTEOUS AARON THE HIGH PRIEST. Aaron was appointed the spokesman for Moses before Pharaoh and the people because Moses was "slow of speech." When Moses was young, Pharaoh's wise men and magicians perceived that he would one day raise an army against Pharaoh, so they put him to the test. They placed before the child a piece of gold and a lump of burning coal. If he reached for the gold, they would execute him, but if he took the coal, he would live. As he reached for the gold, suddenly the Archangel Gabriel appeared and moved his hand to the lump of coal. He picked it up and put it in his mouth, and from that day, Moses stuttered. The Lord told Moses that Pharaoh would ask for a miracle to release the Hebrews from slavery. Aaron threw down his rod before Pharaoh, and it turned into a snake. Also, he stretched forth his rod over the Nile River, and it turned to blood. On their journey to the Promised Land, the Hebrews fought Amalek in a battle. Moses stood on top of a hill, and when he raised his hand, the Hebrews prevailed. However, when he lowered it, Amalek prevailed. So Aaron and Hur held up the arms of Moses. Aaron received from God a monopoly over the priesthood for himself and his male descendants, and they were given instructions for performing their duties. A Levite led many in challenging Aaron's exclusive claim to the priesthood, but these rebels were swallowed up by the earth. Aaron died at the age of 123.

COMMEMORATIONS: Gregory the Dialogist, Pope of Rome; Symeon the New Theologian, and his elder Symeon the Reverent, of the Studion; Theophanes the Confessor of Sigriane; Aaron the High Priest, brother of Prophet Moses; Phineas, grandson of Aaron; Demetrius the Devoted, King of Georgia; Cyrus of Alexandria; 9 martyred by fire; Dragutin (Theoctistus) of Serbia; Paul, Bishop of Leon in Brittany; Nicodemus of Mammola in Calabria; Alphege, Bishop of Winchester, England; Vladimir of Islavskoe.

Friday

March 13

Salutations to the Virgin Mary
Strict Fast
Isaiah 7:1-14; Genesis 5:32-6:8
Proverbs 6:20-7:1

Every day you should try to plant in your soul something spiritual, which will eject something worldly and sinful. Gradually, the old self will be disclaimed, and you will be able to move freely in the spiritual realm. Replace the sinful images in your mind with holy ones. Replace songs with hymns, worldly magazines with spiritual books. If you do not break away from all that is worldly and sinful, if you do not commune with Christ, with Panagia, with the Saints, with the Church Triumphant, and if you do not place yourself completely in the hands of God, you will not be able to acquire spiritual health.

St. Paisios the Athonite

TRANSLATION OF THE RELICS OF NIKEPHOROS THE CONFESSOR, PATRIARCH OF CONSTANTINOPLE. The principle feast-day of St. Nikephoros is June 2. Today commemorates the finding and translation of his holy relics, after nineteen years in exile. As patriarch, Nikephoros confronted Leo the Armenian in defense of the icons. He spoke to Leo of the error of his ways and later condemned him for his iconoclast stance. Nikephoros was exiled for thirteen years and died in a monastery he had built on the island of Prochonis. In the year 846, his holy relics were found completely incorrupt and fragrant. They were transferred to Constantinople to the church of Hagia Sophia, and a vigil was held. The next morning, they were carried to the Church of the Holy Apostles.

COMMEMORATIONS: Publius, Bishop of Athens; Habib (Abibus) of Hermopolis; Alexander of Thessalonica; Africanus, Publius, and Terence at Carthage; Christina of Persia; Aninas of the Euphrates; Leander, Bishop of Seville; Stephen (Bekh), Bishop of Izhevsk; Ypomoni of Serbia; Translation of the relics of St. Nikephoros the Confessor, Patriarch of Constantinople; "Devpeteruv" Icon of the Mother of God.

SATURDAY

March 14

Abstain from meat and dairy products, and fish.
Hebrews 3:12-16; Mark 1:35-44

*E*ven if my body is defiled by force, my soul will never be defiled by renouncing Christ.

St. Irene of Thessalonica

ICON OF THE MOTHER OF GOD OF ST. THEODORE (FEODOROVSKAYA). St. Luke the Evangelist wrote this wonderworking icon, and it has many similarities to the Vladimir Icon of the Mother of God. According to tradition, St. Alexander Nevsky's uncle, St. Yuri, discovered it in a small wooden chapel. When he died in battle, Alexander's father, Prince Yaroslav-Theodore, inherited it, giving the icon his baptismal name, in honor of St. Theodore Stratelates, and it was located in the area of Kostroma. Alexander was blessed with this icon when he entered into marriage. Yaroslav is credited with rebuilding cities, churches, and monasteries after the Mongol invasions. He died by poisoning in the capital city of Mongolia. The icon was always with Alexander, and it was his prayer icon. When he died, it passed to his younger brother Vasili, and he remained under its protection during battles. He once went into battle to defend Russia against the Mongols, carrying with him the wonderworking icon. Bright rays shot out from the icon, striking the Mongols, and they were routed and expelled from Russia. The holy icon has remained in the Kostroma cathedral of St. Theodore Stratelates. Its veneration spread throughout all Russia. It was used in blessing the selection of Mikhail Romanov as the new tsar, and this event established the commemoration of the icon on this date. Copies of the icon have been enlarged to include scenes depicting events from the history of the icon.

COMMEMORATIONS: Euschymon, Bishop of Lampsacus; Benedict of Nursia; Eustathius and his company at Carrhae, Mesopotamia; Theognostus, Metropolitan of Kiev and Moscow; Alexander of Pidne; Andrew of Holy Trinity Monastery in Rafailovo, Siberia; Rostislav-Michael, Great Prince of Kiev; Talmach of Lough Erc; Kostroma "Feodorovskaya" Icon of the Mother of God.

SUNDAY

MARCH 15

Sunday of St. Gregory Palamas
Abstain from meat and
dairy products, and fish.
Hebrews 1:10-14, 2:1-3; Mark 2:1-12

The passion for popularity brings such injury upon those it masters that it shipwrecks faith itself. Our Lord confirms this when He says, "How can you have faith in Me when you receive honour from one another and do not seek for the honour that comes from the only God? (cf. Jn. 5:44).

St. Gregory Palamas

MARTYR LEOCRITIA OF CORDOBA. Leocritia was from a noble Muslim family in ninth-century southern Spain. She was converted to Christianity by a relative, which was a capital violation of Muslim law. She sought protection from her irate parents and waited for a chance to escape them. She went with them to the wedding of a friend and took the opportunity. She went to Father Eulogius who hid her for a time among Christian friends. Enormous pressure was put upon the Christian community to find her. Anyone suspected of helping her was arrested and interrogated. Eventually, Leocritia and Fr. Euologius were discovered, arrested, flogged, and condemned to death, but they were given time to reconsider and weigh their options. They could not embrace Islam, but neither would they renounce their Christian faith. Fr. Eulogius was beheaded for proselytization and Leocritia for apostasy. Her holy relics were thrown into the Guadalquivir River and were retrieved later by the faithful. They took their place beside those of St. Eulogius.

COMMEMORATIONS: Apostle Aristobulus of the Seventy, Bishop of Britain; Agapius, Pauplius, Timolaus, Romulus, two named Dionysius, and two named Alexander, at Caesarea in Palestine; Alexander of Side in Pamphylia; Zachariah, Pope of Rome; Nicander of Egypt; St. Habarestes; Nicander, founder of Gorodnoezersk Monastery (Novgorod); Manuel of Crete; Leocritia of Cordoba.

Monday　　　　　　　　　　　　　　　　　　　　　　　　**Strict Fast**

March 16

Isaiah 8:13-9:7; Genesis 6:9-22
Proverbs 8:1-21

The Lord seeks out the heart, not the appearance.
St. Paisius of Sihla

ST. AMBROSE THE CONFESSOR OF GEORGIA. In the mid-nineteenth century, Ambrose graduated from the Tbilisi Seminary and was ordained to the priesthood, where he served in northwestern Georgia for eight years. He also taught the Georgian language and directed the activity of several philanthropic societies. Ambrose followed the Georgian national independence movement with great interest. Several years after his wife's death, Ambrose received monastic tonsure and he fought for the autocephaly of the Georgian Orthodox, and for this, he was exiled. When Ambrose returned, he was appointed abbot of Chelishi Monastery. He spent much time restoring the old monastery manuscripts, and one day while walking, he heard a sound coming from the ground. He dug there and found an ancient copy of the Chelishi Gospel, a famous Georgian relic from a thousand years before. Four years later, in 1921, the Georgian Church achieved autocephaly, and Ambrose was elevated to the throne of Catholicos-Patriarch of All Georgia. Soon after, the Soviets plundered 1,200 churches, and throngs of the clergy were arrested and exiled or shot. Ambrose sent a letter to the conference at Genoa, where thirty-four nations met with a deep concern for Georgia, as well as for the human race. The Bolshevik regime arrested St. Ambrose; yet, he fearlessly criticized them and was imprisoned. He was granted amnesty two years later, but the experience had taken its toll, and he died within a few years.

COMMEMORATIONS: Alexander, Pope of Rome; Julian of Anazarbus; Ananias of Mesopotamia; Sabinas of Hermopolis, Egypt; John of Rufinianae; 10 Martyrs in Phoenicia; Serapion, Archbishop of Novgorod; Christodoulos of Patmos; Papas of Lycaonia; Pimen, fool-for-Christ of Dagestan, and Anthony of Meskhi, Georgia; Romanus at Parium on the Hellespont; Ambrose the Confessor of Georgia; Eutropia of Cherson; Abban of Kilabban; Malachi of Rhodes; Theodore of Tyre (1st Saturday of Great Lent).

TUESDAY **Strict Fast**

March 17

Isaiah 9:9-10:4; Genesis 7:1-5
Proverbs 8:32-9:11

We must thank the Lord for everything, the labor which he imposes on us to teach us patience, which ennobles the soul and is more beneficial for us than comfort. Evidently, this is pleasing to the Lord. Sorrows cannot befall us except through God's permission—for the sake of our sins. Moreover, these very sorrows protect us from other temptations.

St. Moses of Optina

ST. GURIAS, ARCHBISHOP OF TAURIA AND SIMFEROPOL. Gurias was the son of a priest from nineteenth-century Saratov, Russia. He graduated from the St. Petersburg Theological Academy and was later tonsured a monk and ordained to the priesthood. He became a member of the ecclesiastical mission to Beijing, China for the next 18 years, serving the last eight years as the mission head. He mastered the Chinese language, in speaking and writing, and translated the New Testament, Psalms, books on Church history, and Church services. He was made abbot of the Simonov Monastery in Moscow, then rector of the embassy church in Rome. He was consecrated bishop and did missionary work among the Tatars. In Crimea, he opened a seminary and two church schools for men and women. At the end of his life, St. Gurias was raised to the rank of archbishop.

COMMEMORATIONS: Alexis the Man of God, in Rome; Patrick, enlightener of Ireland; Theosterictus the Confessor of Pelecete; Marinus the Soldier, at Caesarea; Ambrose of Alexandria; Paul of Crete; Gertrude of Nivelles; Gabriel the Lesser of Gareji, Georgia; Gurias, Archbishop of Tauria and Simferopol; Beccan of Rhum; Withburga, solitary at Holkham; Macarius of Kalyazin Monastery; Commemoration of the Earthquake of 790 A.D.

WEDNESDAY

Strict Fast

March 18

Isaiah 10:12-20; Genesis 7:6-9
Proverbs 9:12-18

*D*o not lose your temper with those who sin. Do not have a passion for noticing every sin in your neighbor and judging it, as we usually do. Everyone will give an answer for himself before God. Especially, do not look with evil intention on the sins of those older than you, with whom you have no business. But correct your own sins, your own heart.

St. John of Kronstadt

HOLY 10,000 MARTYRS OF NICOMEDIA. Emperor Diocletian began his Christian persecutions in the year 303 A.D. in the city of Nicomedia. For nineteen years, these ten thousand martyrs were killed for their confession of Christ. In the nineteenth year of Diocletian's reign, the royal edict ordered the churches to be leveled to the ground, and the Scriptures burned. Also, those who held places of honor would be degraded. All the rulers of churches were thrown into prison and compelled to sacrifice. Entire families of the pious were put to death in masses, by sword or fire. However, with eagerness, some men and women rushed into the fire. Some were put on boats and cast into the depths of the sea. A raging Diocletian even forced his daughter and wife to be polluted by sacrifice. Once powerful eunuchs were slain. Presbyters and other officers of the Church with their families were executed. Prisons were crowded, and tortures invented. In the courts of justice, every litigant had to offer incense before being heard.

COMMEMORATIONS: Cyril, Archbishop of Jerusalem; Trophimos, Eukarpios, and those with them in Nicomedia; Tetricus, Bishop of Langres in Gaul; Daniel, monk of Egypt; Cyril of Astrakhan; 10,000 Martyrs of Nicomedia; Edward, King of England; Maria (Skobtsova), at Ravensbruck.

THURSDAY

Strict Fast

MARCH 19

Isaiah 11:10-12:2; Genesis 7:11-8:3
Proverbs 10:1-22

Go to God's temple more often, especially when you're in afflictions. It's good to stand in some dark corner and pray and weep from your heart.

St. Barsanuphius of Optina

MARTYR ALCMUND, PRINCE AND PASSION-BEARER OF NORTHUMBRIA. A passion-bearer is a saint who is not necessarily martyred for his religious beliefs, but who voluntarily gives his life for the truth. Prince Alcmund was the son of King Alchred of Northumbria in the eighth century. A revolution forced the king and prince to flee to Scotland. For many years Prince Alcmund preached Christianity to the Picts until the dynastic struggles were over in Northumbria, but they soon resumed. Some sources say that the prince participated in battles for freedom in Northumbria and Mercia. However, he was assassinated at the orders of the Northumbrian usurper Eardwulf. Alcmund was loved for his humility and acts of charity and support of the needy, widows, and orphaned. Six ancient churches were dedicated to him, and numerous miracles occurred at his relics. The wonderworking and sweet-smelling relics were translated to the city of Derby. When the saint's shrine was opened, an unearthly fragrance spread all through the church. The deaf, blind, and those suffering from diseases received miraculous help. Thousands flocked to his relics for healing and consolation. He is venerated as the heavenly patron of Derby.

COMMEMORATIONS: Chrysanthus, Daria, Claudius, Hilaria, Jason, Maurus, Diodorus, and Marianus, at Rome; Maria, wife of Vsevelod III; Innocent, founder of Komel (Vologda); Bassa, nun of Pskov Caves; Pancharios at Nicomedia; Sophia of Slutsk and Minsk; Nicholas Karamanos of Smyrna; Demetrios at Constantinople; Symeon (Popovic) of Dajbabe, Montenegro; Dimitri of Tornada; Alcmund, Prince of Northumbria; Commemoration of the Miracle of Kollyva wrought by St. Theodore the Tyro; Smolensk "Umileniye" (Tender Feeling) Icon of the Mother of God.

Friday

March 20

Salutations to the Virgin Mary
Strict Fast
Isaiah 13:2-13; Genesis 8:4-21
Proverbs 10:31-11:12

We should have spiritual nobility because when we have that, we become Christ's kin.

St. Paisios the Athonite

ST. MARTIN OF BRAGA IN IBERIA. Martin was from sixth-century Pannonia (modern-day Hungary). As a young man, he made a pilgrimage to Palestine and was tonsured a monk there. In the Holy Land, he met some pilgrims who encouraged him to go to Galicia in northwestern Spain to convert a Germanic tribe, some of whom were pagans. Also, to convert those who were following the Arian form of Christianity. Martin founded several monasteries and became the abbot of one. He was consecrated Bishop of Braga. St. Gregory of Tours called him "full of virtue and second to none among the learned men of his time." Martin wrote works of a moral, liturgical, and ascetical nature, translated into Latin the sayings of the Egyptian Fathers, and wrote a sermon to counter pagan superstitions. He converted the Arian Galicians to Orthodoxy and rooted out the remains of paganism. St. Martin is considered the Apostle to Galicia.

COMMEMORATIONS: Seven Virgin-martyrs of Amisus: Alexandra, Claudia, Euphrasia, Matrona, Juliana, Euphemia, and Theodosia; Nicetas the Confessor, Bishop of Apollonias in Bithynia; Holy Fathers martyred at the Monastery of St. Sabbas: John, Sergius, Patrick, and others; Martyrs Rodion, Aquila, Longinus, and Emanuel; Euphrosynus of Blue-Jay Lake (Novgorod); Tadros, Bishop of Edessa, at Jerusalem; Martin of Braga in Iberia; Austreigiselis, Bishop of Bourges; Wulfram, missionary; Cuthbert of Lindisfarne; Archil II, King of Georgia; Myron of Mega Castro on Crete; Herbert, hermit of Derwentwater; Michael the Sabbaite at Jerusalem; Nicholas Holz of Novosiolki.

SATURDAY

March 21

Abstain from meat and dairy products, and fish.
Hebrews 10:32-38; Mark 2:14-17

*T*his air which is spread out between heaven and earth is so thick with spirits, which do not fly about in it quietly and aimlessly, that divine providence has quite beneficially withdrawn them from human sight. For human beings, utterly unable to gaze upon these things with fleshly eyes, would be overwhelmed by an unbearable dread and faint away because of their frightening confluence and the horrible expressions that they can take upon themselves and assume at will… "our struggle is not against flesh and blood but against principalities, against powers, against the world rulers of this darkness, against spirits of evil in heavenly places" (Eph. 6:12).

St. John Cassian

MARTYRS PHILEMON AND DOMNINOS OF ROME. During the persecution of Christians in Italy, Philemon and Domninos fearlessly traveled from city to city preaching Christ. They converted and baptized many, and for this, they were arrested and taken to the ruler of Italy. Through bribes and threats, the idol-worshippers tried to dissuade Philemon and Domninos from their Christian belief, but instead, they called upon Jesus Christ in the face of these tormentors, and this angered the pagans. The martyrs were stripped and suspended to the ground, and mercilessly beaten. Then they were cast into prison, beaten again, and finally beheaded.

COMMEMORATIONS: Thomas, Patriarch of Constantinople; Philemon and Domninos of Rome; Cyril, Bishop of Catania; Beryllus, Bishop of Catania; Lupicinus, desert-dweller of the Jura Mountains (Gaul); James the Confessor, Bishop of the Studion; Michael of Agrapha; Seraphim of Vyritsa; Serapion the Sindonite of Egypt; Enda of Aran (Ireland); Pachomius of Nerekhta; Sophronius, abbot of St. Theodosius Monastery in Palestine; Serapion, Bishop of Thmuis, Egypt.

SUNDAY

MARCH 22

**Sunday of the Holy Cross
Abstain from meat and
dairy products, and fish.**
Hebrews 4:14-5:6; Mark 8:34-9:1

The demonic hosts tremble when they see the Cross, for by the Cross the kingdom of hell was destroyed. They do not dare to draw near to anyone who is guarded by the Cross. The whole human race, by the death of Christ on the Cross, received deliverance from the authority of the devil, and everyone who makes use of this saving weapon is inaccessible to the demons. When legions of demons appeared to St. Anthony the Great and other desert-dwellers, they guarded themselves with the Sign of the Cross, and the demons vanished. When they appeared to Saint Symeon the Stylite, who was standing on his pillar, what seemed to be a chariot to carry him to heaven, the Saint, before mounting it, crossed himself; it disappeared and the enemy, who had hoped to cast down the ascetic from the height of his pillar, was put to shame.

St. John Maximovitch

ST. LEA OF ROME. St. Jerome wrote an epistle about Lea who died in the year 384. She was a noblewoman of Rome, born into wealth. Lea married but was soon widowed and left financially sound. Instead of retiring, she left her social standing and joined a convent in Rome, where she later became the abbess. St. Jerome writes that Lea's virtues were worthy of heaven. She was a woman of austerity, obedience, and extraordinary penances. "She was careless of her dress, neglected her hair, and ate only the coarsest food. She avoided ostentation that she might not have her reward in this world." "She instructed her companions even more by example than by precept." St. Jerome also writes, "if we wish for immortality, we must realize that we are but mortal."

COMMEMORATIONS: Drosis of Antioch, and 5 Virgin-martyrs; Callinica and Basilissa of Rome; Lea of Rome; Basil of Ancyra; Schema-abbess Sophia (Grineva) of Kiev; Euthymius of Demitsana and Mt. Athos; Paul, Bishop of Narbonne, Brittany; Basil (Zelentsov), Bishop of Priluk; "The Izborsk" Icon of the Mother of God.

Monday	Strict Fast

March 23

Isaiah 14:24-32; Genesis 8:21-9:7
Proverbs 11:19-12:6

In case of a fall of some kind in deed, word, or thought, you should immediately repent and, acknowledging your infirmity, humble yourself and force yourself to see your sins, but not your corrections. From examining his sins, a person comes to humility and acquires a heart that is broken and humble, which God does not despise.

St. Hilarion of Optina

VENERABLE NICON, ABBOT OF THE KIEV CAVES. Nicon was an eleventh-century Russian monk and first disciple of St. Anthony, founder of the Kiev-Pechersk Monastery. His obedience was to tonsure all the new monks, including St. Theodosius of the Kiev Caves, who became Nicon's spiritual father. Though he proclaimed his unworthiness, Nicon was chosen abbot of the Kiev Caves monastery. He wanted to beautify his monastery, so he prayed for divine assistance. A few Greek iconographers from Constantinople had a vision of Sts. Theodosius and Anthony, requesting their help, and so they quickly traveled to Kiev to complete the work. St. Nicon died peacefully, and his relics lie incorrupt in the Nearer Caves of St. Anthony.

COMMEMORATIONS: Nicon and 199 disciples in Sicily; Bassian, Archbishop of Rostov; Dometius the Persian; Nicon, abbot of the Kiev Caves; Ephraim and Theodosios of Vologda; Pachomius of Nerekhta; Basil of Mangazea in Siberia; Luke of Adrianople and Mt. Athos; Helen of Florovsk Ascension Convent in Kiev; Gwinear of Cornwall; Sergius (Serebriansky) of Tver; Elijan (Vyatlin) of Vladimir; Macarius Kvitkin of Orenburg; Ethilwald of Farne.

Tuesday
March 24

Strict Fast
Forefeast of the Annunciation
Isaiah 25:1-9; Genesis 9:8-17
Proverbs 12:8-22

One cannot hide anywhere from temptations except in the depths of humility.

St. Macarius of Optina

HIEROMARTYR ARTEMON, PRESBYTER OF LAODICEA. During the third century, Emperor Diocletian sent an administrator named Patricius to Laodicea to persecute Christians. The bishop of Laodicea, St. Sisinios, along with Father Artemon and other Christians, smashed every pagan idol in the temple of Artemis. When Patricius heard this, he led a mob toward the church, intent on killing everyone within, but suddenly a high fever incapacitated him. When his pagan idols could not heal him, he beseeched the bishop to call upon his God, declaring that he believed in Christ, and the fever left him. However, he then rode towards Caesarea and happened upon Artemon, who was followed by two deer and six wild donkeys. When Artemon said that he controlled the animals with the word of Christ, he was chained and dragged to Caesarea, but he ordered the animals to go to St. Sisinios. Receiving the gift of speech from God, the deer told the bishop that Patricius was holding Artemon. Artemon was brought to trial, and he was tortured when he refused to offer sacrifice. The doe that had spoken to the bishop returned to Caesarea, and by God's command, it addressed Patricius, predicting that he would die in a cauldron of boiling pitch. Patricius gave orders to throw Artemon into a cauldron of pitch. Checking to see if the pitch was boiling, Patricius was suddenly thrown into the cauldron by two angels in the form of eagles. Artemon baptized the pagan priest and many of the pagans who came to believe in Christ. At the end of his life, St. Artemon was attacked by pagans and beheaded.

COMMEMORATIONS: Artemon of Seleucia; Artemon of Laodicea; Parthenios III, Patriarch of Constantinople; Zachariah the Recluse; Zachariah the Faster; Zachariah the Hospitable; James of Catania; Martin of Thebes; 8 Martyrs of Caesarea; Stephen and Peter of Kazan; Caimin of Holy Island on Lough Derg (Ireland); Thomas of St. Euthymius; Dunchad of Iona; Severus of Catania.

Wednesday

March 25

Annunciation of the Theotokos
Abstain from meat and dairy products.
Hebrews 2:11-18; Luke 1:24-38

If we do not forgive others, we find ourselves outside paradise.
St. Paisios the Athonite

ST. SENNUPHIOS THE WONDERWORKER OF LATOMOS. Sennuphios was a monk in the Egyptian desert. He often prayed that he might behold how the Lord would appear when He arrived to judge the earth. One day in a vision, he was told to travel to Thessalonica, to the Monastery of Latomos, where he would see this icon. Upon his arrival, Sennuphios inquired about the icon but was told that it was not there. He returned to his cell dejected, thinking the devil had deceived him, but again the voice told him to return to the monastery. As he was sitting in the monastery, a severe earthquake struck, and plaster and bricks fell from the ceiling, revealing the icon depicting Christ on Judgment Day. He is beardless with a fiery appearance, sitting on a cloud situated over the Four Rivers of Paradise, and surrounded by the four apocalyptic symbols of the Evangelists. In Christ's hand is a scroll that reads in part, "Behold our God, on whom we put our hope." Sennuphios was in awe of the icon's beauty, and he immediately gave up his soul. The origin of the icon is as follows. The bishop of Thessalonica baptized the daughter of the third-century emperor Maximian. She had a church built, disguising it as a bathhouse. On the ceiling, she had a mosaic created of the Mother of God. However, overnight it was miraculously transformed into the Judgment Day icon, to the amazement of the artist. For that reason, it is now called the Latomou mosaic, Not-Made-by-Hands. The princess covered the icon, first with ox hide, then with mortar and bricks.

COMMEMORATIONS: Annunciation of the Theotokos; Pelagia, Theodosia, and Dula of Nicomedia; Holy martyr that was formerly an executioner; Tikhon, Patriarch of Moscow and All Russia; Nicander, hermit of Pskov; Parthenius of the Kiev Caves; Justin Popovich of Chelije in Serbia; Sabbas the New of Kalymnos; Sennuphios the Wonderworker of Latomos.

THURSDAY
MARCH 26

Synaxis of the Archangel Gabriel
Abstain from meat and dairy products, and fish.
Isaiah 28:14-22; Genesis 10:32-11:9
Proverbs 13:19-14:6

The love of God is fiery by nature, and when it descends in an extraordinary degree onto a person, it throws that soul into ecstasy.
St. Isaac the Syrian

SYNAXIS OF THE ARCHANGEL GABRIEL. Archangel Gabriel is a faithful servant of Almighty God and the leader of the Heavenly Hosts. The name Gabriel means "might of God." Archangel Gabriel is the herald of the destinies of God about the salvation of man. He revealed to St. Anna that she would give birth to the Virgin Mary and appeared to Prophet Zachariah foretelling the conception of St. John the Baptist. He also announced to the Virgin Mary that she would conceive the Son of God. Archangel Gabriel appeared to Joseph and revealed the mystery of the Incarnation of Christ from the Theotokos and warned him of Herod's intentions, and to flee to Egypt. Archangel Gabriel also inspired Moses to write the Book of Genesis in the Old Testament.

COMMEMORATIONS: Synaxis of the Archangel Gabriel; Quadratus (Codratus), Theodosius, Manuel, and 40 other Martyrs; Stephen the Confessor and Wonderworker, abbot of Tryglia; 26 Martyrs of Gothia in Crimea, including presbyters Bathusius and Bercus; Basil the Younger; Eusebius, Bishop of Kival, and Pullius the Reader; Irenaeus, Bishop of Sirmium; Malchus of Chalcis in Syria; Montanus the priest, and his wife Maxima, at Sirmium; George of Sofia, at Adrianople; Eutychius of Alexandria; Braulio of Saragossa in Iberia; Ludger, Bishop of Munster.

FRIDAY

MARCH 27

Salutations to the Virgin Mary
Strict Fast
Isaiah 29:13-23; Genesis 12:1-7
Proverbs 14:15-26

Afflictions are a great teacher; afflictions show us our weaknesses, passions, and the need of repentance; afflictions cleanse the soul, they make it sober, as from drunkenness, they bring down grace into the soul, they soften the heart, they inspire us with a loathing for sin, and strengthen us in faith, hope, and virtue.

St. John of Kronstadt

ST. PAUL, BISHOP OF CORINTH. Paul was born in ninth-century Constantinople to pious parents. He had three brothers, named Dionysios, Plato, and Peter who became bishop of Argos. Paul was attracted to the monastic life. Hearing about a clairvoyant and wonderworking elder, he went with his brother Dionysios to become monastics. Paul rapidly acquired the virtues and became the spiritual father of his family. Inspired by their two sons, the entire family entered the monastic life. Later, Patriarch Nicholas I Mystikos appointed Paul bishop of Corinth. Peter lived in Corinth in silence and asceticism. Later he was made the Bishop of Argos. Paul proved to be a lover of peace and reconciliation, and together with his brother Peter, they produced many philanthropic works. St. Paul reposed in peace.

COMMEMORATIONS: Paul, Bishop of Corinth; Matrona of Thessalonica; John the Clairvoyant of Lycopolis, Egypt; Prophet Ananias; Cyricus of Thrace; Eutychius, monk; Ephraim, Archbishop of Rostov; Paphnutius, disciple of St. Anthony the Great; Philetos, Lydia, Macedonos, Theoprepios, Cronides, and Amphilochios in Illyria; Alexander of Voche; Anthony, Metropolitan of Tobolsk; Rupert, Bishop of Salzburg; Martyrs Baruch and John; "Sweet Kissing" (Glykophilousa) and "Of the Akathist" Icons of the Mother of God.

SATURDAY

March 28

Abstain from meat and dairy products, and fish.
Hebrews 6:9-12; Mark 7:31-37

*I*f the body does not tolerate fasting and labor, then pay attention to the soul, that is, to the heart and mind. Practice them in the Jesus prayer. And your acquisition will be more than those who labor physically. The main thing is to hold on to the Jesus prayer, sometimes with your mouth, and sometimes with your mind. This will eventually fall in love, but at the beginning, it is true, sometimes it is difficult.

St. Anatoly of Optina

ST. DIONYSIOS THE MERCIFUL, METROPOLITAN OF LARISSA. Dionysios is called "the Merciful" because he showed particular mercy towards people and was compassionate to people of low social status, and comforted those who suffered. Dionysios founded the monastery of St. Nicholas Anapausas at Meteora and was the metropolitan of Larissa in the late fifteenth century. He left this position to retire to the monastery of St. Nicholas. He reposed in peace in the year 1510.

COMMEMORATIONS: Apostle Herodion of the Seventy; Priscus, Malchus, and Alexander of Caesarea; Hesychius the Theologian of Jerusalem; Hilarion the New, abbot of Pelecete; Dionysius the Merciful, Bishop of Larissa; John, Bishop of Manglisi, Georgia; George, Bishop of Zagora, Parodus and Peter, priests, and Prince Enravota-Boyan, of Bulgaria; Eustratius of the Kiev Caves; Hilarion, founder of Pskovoezersk Monastery; Jonah, founder of Klimets Monastery (Olonets); Peter Ochryzko of Chartoviec; The miraculous occurrence of Taxiotis; "Of the Sign" Icon of the Mother of God.

SUNDAY

MARCH 29

Sunday of St. John Climacus
Abstain from meat and
dairy products, and fish.
Hebrews 6:13-20; Mark 9:17-31

All who enter upon the good fight, which is hard and close, but also easy, must realize that they must leap into the fire... A good foundation of three layers and three pillars is innocence, fasting and temperance. Let all babes in Christ begin with these virtues, taking as their model the natural babes. For you never find in them anything sly or deceitful. They have no insatiate appetite, no insatiable stomach, no body on fire, or raging like a beast.

St. John Climacus

EUSTATHIUS THE CONFESSOR, BISHOP OF KIOS IN BITHYNIA. Eustathius left the burdens and things of the world to become a monk. He was interested in taking care of his soul and following the commandments of God. He always gave thanks to God, in Whom he had an unshakable faith. He was humble, sympathetic, charitable, and filled with good works. He had a sincere love for everyone. Because of the entreaties of the people, he became a priest and later bishop, and he administered the post well for many years. When the iconoclast persecutions began, Eustathius armed himself with the study of the Holy Scriptures, which he used to fight the enemy. He was reported to the iconoclast king, who interrogated him. The saint was beaten, thrashed with a rod, and imprisoned. Again, he was beaten with heavy sticks and exiled. Finally, after many afflictions, troubles, poverty, hunger, thirst, and nakedness, St. Eustathius gave up his spirit.

COMMEMORATIONS: Mark the Confessor, with Cyril the Deacon of Heliopolis and others; Diadochus, Bishop of Photike; Jonah and Barachisius in Persia, with: Zanithas, Lazarus, Maruthas, Narses, Elias, Mares, Habib, Sivsithina, and Sabbas; Paul Voinarsky, and Paul and Alexis Kiryan, of Crimea; Eustathius the Confessor, Bishop of Kios; Jonah, Mark, and Vassa of the Pskov Caves; Eustasius of Luxeuil; Gundleus and Gwladys, parents of St. Cadoc.

Monday

Strict Fast

March 30

Isaiah 37:33-38:6; Genesis 13:12-18
Proverbs 14:27-15:4

*O*ne must not trust one's feelings, since because of his limitedness a man cannot know everything, and therefore his judgment is also relatively limited. Even if you see with your own eyes that someone sins, do not judge, for the eyes also may be deceived. One must in every way flee from judging, and pray in secret for those who have sinned. This form of love is pleasing to God. Judging is bound up with impudence and is incompatible with true repentance: "To judge is to impudently appropriate to oneself the rank of God."

St. John Climacus

ST. EUBOULA, MOTHER OF ST. PANTELEIMON. Euboula was from a family of Christians and the mother of St. Panteleimon, and she raised him to love God. However, Euboula was married to a Greek pagan named Eustorgios, and she lived during the reign and persecutions of Emperor Maximian between 286 and 305 A.D. Still, Euboula died in peace and her marble tomb is located east of Jerusalem in the Cave of the Magi, which is under the monastery of St. Theodosios the Cenobiarch. There are thirty-five other tombs of renowned saints there as well.

COMMEMORATIONS: John Climacus of Sinai, author of *The Ladder*; John the Hermit of Cilicia; Prophet Joel (Joad), who dwelled in Bethel; Zacharias, Bishop of Corinth; Euboula, mother of St. Panteleimon; John II, Patriarch of Jerusalem; Sophronius, Bishop of Irkutsk; Osburga of Coventry; Victor of Thessalonica and 11 Martyrs with him; Translation of the relics of Martyr-King St. Edmund of East Anglia.

Tuesday   **Strict Fast**

March 31

Isaiah 40:18-31; Genesis 15:1-15
Proverbs 15:7-19

The memory of insults is the residue of anger. It keeps sins alive, hates justice, ruins virtue, poisons the heart, rots the mind, defeats concentration, paralyzes prayer, puts love at a distance, and is a nail driven into the soul.

St. John Climacus

RIGHTEOUS JOSEPH THE FAIR, SON OF JACOB. Joseph was the son of Jacob and grandson of Abraham. His brothers were jealous of him, as their father loved him more than the others, and they feared him because of his dreams foretelling his future greatness. They intended to kill Joseph, until Rueben, the oldest brother, suggested that they throw Joseph into a pit. They later sold him to merchants in route to Egypt. They, in turn, sold Joseph to Potiphar, the head of the imperial bodyguards. Because Joseph was so handsome, Potiphar's wife tried to seduce him, but when Joseph refused, she accused him of trying to defile her. Joseph was imprisoned until he correctly interpreted Pharaoh's dream about an impending famine, and he appointed Joseph first counselor of Egypt. When famine struck, Joseph resettled his entire family in Egypt. He instructed that after his death, his bones were to be taken to the Promised Land, and this was done by the Prophet Moses about two hundred years later. Joseph's sons, Ephraim and Manasseh later became the leaders of two tribes of Israel.

COMMEMORATIONS: Blaise of Amorion and Mt. Athos; Akakios the Confessor, Bishop of Melitene; Hypatios the Wonderworker, Bishop of Gangra; Innocent, Metropolitan of Moscow and enlightener of Alaska and Siberia; Jonah, Metropolitan of Kiev, Moscow, and All Russia; Joseph the Fair, son of Jacob; Abdas, Bishop of Hormizd-Ardashir, the deacon Benjamin, of Persia, and Ormisdes the Confessor; Martyr Menander; Stephen the Wonderworker; Hypatius of Rufinus in Chalcedon; Philaret of Glinsk Hermitage; Hypatius the Healer of the Kiev Caves; Apollo, ascetic of the Thebaid; Appearance of the Iveron Icon of the Mother of God (Mt. Athos).

Our religion is founded on spiritual experience, seen and heard as sure as any physical fact in this world. Not theory, not philosophy, not human emotions, but experience.

St. Nikolai Velimerovich

WEDNESDAY   **Strict Fast**

April 1
Isaiah 41:4-14; Genesis 17:1-9
Proverbs 15:20-16:9

The best fast is to patiently endure everything that God sends.
St. Anatoly of Optina

ST. BARSANUPHIUS OF OPTINA. Barsanuphius was born in 1845 and was a descendant of the Orenburg Cossacks. After graduating from military and officers' school, he eventually rose to the rank of colonel. Once, when he was critically ill from pneumonia, he asked that the Holy Gospel be read to him and then he passed out. In a vision, his whole sinful life passed in front of him, and this caused him to repent. Then obeying a voice he heard, Barsanuphius visited the Optina Monastery. Two years later, the abbot of the monastery, St. Ambrose, gave him a blessing to enter the monastery in three months. During that time, he was offered the rank of general, and the people tried to arrange a marriage for him. He refused these offers and entered the monastery, and after one year, he was tonsured a monk. Over the next ten years, he was ordained to the diaconate and the priesthood. He served as a chaplain in the Russo-Japanese War, and when he returned, was made the abbot of the skete. He established order and discipline, repaired buildings, and paid off debts. Barsanuphius, like the other Optina elders, was granted the gifts of healing and clairvoyance. During a particular confession, he reminded the individual of events and people he had forgotten. Barsanuphius loved to read the Lives of the Saints as they helped to answer many of life's difficulties, and he commemorated many saints during his prayers. St. Barsanuphius died peacefully, and his relics were interred at Optina.

COMMEMORATIONS: Mary of Egypt; Macarius of Pelecete; Meliton of Sardis; Achaz, King of Judah; Abraham of Bulgaria; Martyrs Gerontius and Basilides; Gerontius of the Kiev Caves; Euthymius the Wonderworker of Suzdal; Barsanuphius of Optina; Macarius (Vasiliev), at the Pskov Caves Monastery; Pachomius of Roman and Galati (Moldavia); John of Shavta and Eulogius the Prophet, fool-for-Christ; Joachim of Nizhni-Novgorod; Tewdrig of Tintern; Simeon of Dajbabe; Cellach of Armagh.

Thursday

April 2

Strict Fast

Isaiah 42:5-16; Genesis 18:20-33
Proverbs 16:7-17:17

It is not right to speak of the former years and to bless them and to curse our own age. We must know that in every age and in every place, people who actually seek their salvation, find it.
St. Luke of Simferopol and Crimea

VENERABLE GREGORY OF NICOMEDIA. Gregory was born in twelfth-century Nicomedia. At a young age, he possessed excellent knowledge of the Lives of the Saints and the Gospel. He took monastic tonsure at a monastery in Bithynia. Out of jealousy, some of the monks falsely accused Gregory of stealing church property. He was proven innocent, and the monks were dismissed. Because of this, Gregory departed to another monastery where his brother lived and was ordained to the priesthood. His reputation attracted other monks, but desiring solitude, he moved into a mountain cave that was named after the Prophet Elias together with his brother. Gregory was endowed later with the gifts of healing and prophecy, and again his spirituality attracted many. Some evil men sought to discredit the saint and sent a prostitute to seduce him. When she stood before him, she became ill and weak, but Gregory healed her, and she became his ally. These same men then spread rumors, and the archbishop sent for Gregory for questioning. During the journey, witnesses saw Gregory on a horse riding on air above the waters of a river. Having heard about this miracle, the archbishop dismissed the rumors and left Gregory at peace. St. Gregory died peacefully.

COMMEMORATIONS: Gregory of Nicomedia; Titus the Wonderworker; Theodora (Theodosia) of Tyre; Polycarp of Alexandria; George of Matskveri; Amphianus and Aedesius of Patara, Lycia; Nicetius of Lyons; Sabbas, Archbishop of Sourozh.

Friday

April 3

Akathist to the Virgin Mary
Strict Fast
Isaiah 45:11-17; Genesis 22:1-18
Proverbs 17:17-18:5

It is impossible, someone says, impossible to spend the present day devoutly unless we regard it as the last of our whole life.
St. John Climacus

NEW MARTYR PAUL THE RUSSIAN, IN CONSTANTINOPLE. Paul was a Russian slave in seventeenth-century Constantinople during the Turkish domination. The Christian merchant later gave him his freedom. Paul attended church often, and there met and married a Russian Orthodox girl, and they became an integral part of the community. Paul had epilepsy, and one day during a particularly bad seizure, his friends carried him to the closest church seeking a cure for his condition. Paul was in a disoriented state and did not even recognize his friends, and asked not to go to the church, but they proceeded there anyhow. On the way, they encountered some Muslims, and Paul shouted, "I am a Hagarene." Thinking that Christians were taking Paul against his will, they offered him the protection of their mosque, and they informed the Grand Vizier. His friends spirited him away before the incident went further. A short time later, Paul was arrested and brought before the vizier, who asked him if he was a Muslim, and he responded that he was not. He was offered the choice to either become a Muslim or die, but Paul remained firm in his faith. He was flogged and thrown into prison. Three days later, he was beheaded.

COMMEMORATIONS: Joseph the Hymnographer of Sicily; Nicetas the Confessor, abbot of Medikion; Cassius, Philip, and Eutychius of Thessalonica; Paul the Russian at Constantinople; Evagrius, Benignus, Christos, Arestus, Kinnudius, Rufus, Patricius, and Zosima, at Tomis; Illyrios of Mt. Myrsinonos in the Peloponnese; Elpidephoros, Dius, Bithonios, and Galykos; Nectarius, founder of Bezhetsk Monastery (Tver); Ulphianus of Tyre; Fara of Faremoutiers; "The Unfading Flower" Icon of the Mother of God.

SATURDAY

April 4

Abstain from meat and dairy products, and fish.
Hebrews 9:1-7; Luke 1:39-49, 56

After denial of the faith, the greatest sin in the world is the murder of babies by abortion. These two sins quickly bring God's wrath and punishment upon men.

+Elder Paisius of Sihla

VENERABLE JOSEPH THE MUCH-AILING OF THE KIEV CAVES LAVRA. Joseph lived during the fourteenth century, and he suffered from various diseases. In this condition, he turned to God with prayer and vowed that if he was granted health, he would serve the brethren of the Kiev Caves Monastery until the end of his days. He returned to health, received monastic tonsure at that monastery, and began to work at prayer and fasting and to serve the brotherhood until the day he died. His incorrupt relics were buried in the Far Caves. Russian Orthodox literature cites Joseph as an example of the Christian attitude toward illness. He stayed in sickness not just because his infirmities saved him, atoning for some sins, but also St. Joseph received from God the grace to heal other people.

COMMEMORATIONS: Publius of Egypt; Theodulus and Agathopous of Thessalonica; Plato the Studite; Isidore, Bishop of Seville; Theonas, Archbishop of Thessalonica; Ferfoutha of Persia, with her sister and servants; George of Mt. Maleon; Zosimas of Palestine; Joseph the Much-ailing of the Kiev Caves; James of Old Torzhok in Galich, Kostroma; Basil of Mangazea; Zosimas, founder Annunciation Monastery at Lake Vorbozoma; Nicetas the Albanian of Mt. Athos; Theonas, Symeon, and Phorbinos of Egypt; Benjamin (Kononov) and Nichephorus (Kuchin) of Solovki; Elias of Makeyevka (Ukraine); Nicholas (Karaulov), Bishop of Velsk; Nun-martyr Maria (Lelyanova) of Gatchina.

Sunday
April 5

Sunday of St. Mary of Egypt
Abstain from meat and dairy products, and fish.
Hebrews 9:11-14; Mark 10:32-45

*W*hen one person's harmful behavior begins to affect a number of other people, that is not the time to show patience nor to look out for your own benefit; instead, you should look for what benefits the majority so that they may be saved. Virtue that benefits a multitude is better than virtue that benefits a single person.

St. Mark the Ascetic

NEW MARTYR PANAGIOTIS OF JERUSALEM. Panagiotis was born in Greece and raised in nineteenth-century Magnesia of Asia Minor. He was employed as a servant. One day after worshipping in the Tomb of Christ in the Holy Sepulcher, he was captured by some Turks who took him before the Pasha. He was offered the chance to convert to Islam to avoid death, but he remained steadfast in his Christian faith. He was stripped, one hand was broken, and his fingers on the other were severed. Finally, he was beheaded. The fathers of the Holy Sepulcher buried his body at the Cemetery of Holy Zion.

COMMEMORATIONS: Mark the Anchorite of Athens; Theodora and Didymus the Soldier of Alexandria; Philip I, first Metropolitan of Moscow; Theodora, nun of Thessalonica; Publius of Egypt; Martyrs Claudius, Diodorus, Victor, Victorinus, Pappia, Serapion, and Nicephorus; Martyrs Maximos and Terence; Theonas, Symeon, and Phorbinus of Egypt; Martyrs Thermus, Zenon, and Pompey; George of New Ephesus; Mark the Ascetic; 5 girls martyred at Neanidor; Panagiotis of Jerusalem; Constantine of Russia and those with him; Derfel of Lianderfel; Ethelburga, abbess of Kent; Translation of the relics of St. Job, Patriarch of Moscow.

Monday

Strict Fast

April 6

Isaiah 48:17-49:4; Genesis 27:1-41
Proverbs 19:16-25

Live in constant glorification of and thanksgiving towards God, for the greatest sin is ingratitude and the worst sinner is the ungrateful person.

St. Paisios the Athonite

ST. BRYCHAN OF BRECKNOCK. Brychan was born in fifth-century South Wales, the son of King Anlach and Queen Marchel. At the age of four, he was sent to be tutored for seven years by St. Drichan, who predicted a great future for Brychan. Later King Anlach lost a battle to King Banhadle of Powys. Brychan was sent as a hostage to the enemy's court. While there, he fell in love with Banhadle's daughter, but courtship was denied. Upon the death of his father, Brychan returned home with his pregnant wife and was elevated to king. He became known as a good king, a great patron of the Church, and an observer of its teachings. For this, the land was renamed in his honor. Throughout his reign, he married three times and had 24 children. Each child was enlightened, and some produced saints. However, Brychan was known to be ruthless to his enemies. Towards the end of his life, he abdicated the throne and went to live as a hermit. He reposed at an old age.

COMMEMORATIONS: Eutychius, Patriarch of Constantinople; Methodios, Equal-to-the-Apostles, and enlightener of the Slavs; Platonida of Nisibis; 120 Martyrs of Persia; Jeremiah and Archilias the presbyter, of Rome; Gregory the Sinaite; Gregory (Drimys) of the Great Lavra on Mt. Athos; Manuel, Theodore, George, Michael, and another George of Samothrace, at Makri in Thrace; Gennadios of Dionysiou, Mt. Athos; Martyrius of Glinsk Hermitage; 2 Martyrs from Ascalon; Sebastian (Fomin) of Optina and Karaganda; New Martyr Alexander Kosmich Fleginsky; Brychan of Brecknock.

Tuesday

Strict Fast

April 7

Isaiah 49:6-10; Genesis 31:3-16
Proverbs 21:3-21

Love for enemies gives the heart the fullness of love.
St. Ignatius Brianchaninov

VENERABLE GERASIMOS OF BYZANTIUM. Gerasimos was from a pious family in eighteenth-century Constantinople. He was well regarded as a wise and educated man. He became a disciple of St. Makarios Kalogeras at the seminary he founded on the island of Patmos. Makarios was known as the "Teacher of the Nation." Gerasimos became the rector of the seminary after the death of St. Makarios. He was tonsured a monk at the Patmos monastery of St. John the Theologian and was later ordained there to the priesthood. He was an excellent teacher to the students at the seminary. When Gerasimos fell ill, he traveled to Smyrna and then to Crete for treatment. He died in Crete and was buried in the Holy Trinity Monastery of Chania. Upon hearing about the death of Gerasimos, the monks of Patmos traveled there by boat. They asked for the relics to be returned, but the request was denied. During a vigil, the saint's right hand was miraculously cut off, and this holy relic was returned to Patmos, where it remains to this day as a source of many healings for those who venerate it with faith. St. Gerasimos' relic was kept under the altar in Chania until 1821 when the Ottoman Turks set fire to the monastery. However, the saint's holy skull is still there.

COMMEMORATIONS: George the Confessor, Bishop of Mytilene; Rufinus, Aquilina, and 200 soldiers at Sinope; Leucius of Volokolamsk; Daniel of Pereyaslavl; Gerasimus of Byzantium; George, Patriarch of Jerusalem; Hegesippus the Chronicler of Palestine; Gabriel, Archbishop of Ryazan and Zaraisk; Calliopios at Pompeiopolis; Sabbas the New of Kalymnos; George of Rabrichka, fool-for-Christ; Govan of Cornwall; Uncovering of the relics of St. Serapion, Archbishop of Novgorod.

Wednesday

Strict Fast

April 8

Isaiah 58:1-11; Genesis 43:26-31, 45:1-16
Proverbs 21:23-22:4

*D*o you have compassion for the poor? Don't pass judgment on them, my dear. If you can, help them. And even if you don't give them money, have pity on them. But if you have it, give it. Give alms by works or by word. Do both if you can. Don't give them too much, so that you end up regretting it. But don't ever judge them… And if you give, flee as much as you can from pride… There were saints who gave even the clothes off their backs. So we really never do anything great.

+Elder Paisius of Sihla

MARTYR PAUSILIPUS OF HERACLEA IN THRACE. During the second-century persecutions under the emperor Hadrian, Pausilipus was denounced by the pagans and brought to trial before the emperor, where he bravely made his confession of faith. Pausilipus was beaten with rods and taken to the governor Precius, who for a long time tried to persuade him to sacrifice to the idols. Pausilipus steadfastly refused, and finally, he was chained and led to the site of execution. Along the way, he prayed that Jesus would spare him from the hand of the executioner and grant him a quick death. Jesus heard his prayer. As battered and exhausted as he was, Pausilipus felt such a surge of strength that he shattered the chains that bound him and fled. Soon after, he gave up his soul after his captors tortured him. Christians reverently buried his relics.

COMMEMORATIONS: Apostles Hermes, Herodion, Agabus, Rufus, Asyncritus, and Phlegon, of the Seventy, and those with them; Celestine, Pope of Rome; Niphont, Bishop of Novgorod; Pausilipus of Thrace; Rufus the Obedient, recluse of the Kiev Caves; John Koulikas of Aegina; John Naukliros the Navigator, on Kos; Philaret of Seminara, Calabria; Josiah and Joseph of Mt. Kharasam, Persia; Spanish Icon of the Mother of God.

Thursday
April 9

Strict Fast

Isaiah 65:8-16; Genesis 46:1-7
Proverbs 23:15-24:5

If you feel that you cannot control your anger, remain silent, and for the time being say nothing, until, through continuous prayer and self-reproach, your heart has become calm.

St. Hilarion of Optina

MARTYRS HELIODOROS, DESAN, MARIABUS, ABDIESUS, AND 370 OTHERS IN PERSIA. During the fourth-century reign of Persian King Shapur II, Persian conquests and acquisitions included Mesopotamia and Armenia, and persecution of Christians began. The purpose was to persuade Christians to become Zoroastrians, who worship the sun and moon. When Shapur captured the fortress of Bet-Zabde, he imprisoned Bishop Heliodoros, the priests Dausas and Mariabus, and four hundred priests, monks, and nuns. Bishop Heliodors died on the way to prison but first ordained Dausas bishop. When Shapur heard that Dausus and the others blasphemed the Persian religion, he decreed that anyone who would not worship the sun would die. Five Christians denied their faith and were rewarded with land, but they soon suffered a premature death. The remaining prisoners were all massacred together, except Abdiesus who was wounded. Even though his neck was struck, it did not kill him, and he recovered to preach the Gospel. He was discovered by a fire-worshipper and was stabbed to death. The murderer, his family, and his entire village suffered a drought that lasted twenty years, and they left that area. When the persecution ended, the gravedigger's son built his house by the cave where the martyred were buried. The relics of the martyrs were miraculous, and a church was built there in their honor.

COMMEMORATIONS: Heliodoros, Desan, Mariabus, Abdiesus, and 370 others in Persia; Newly Revealed Martyrs Raphael, Nicholas, Irene, and Eleni of Lesvos; Eupsychios of Caesarea; Bademus (Vadim) of Persia; Acacius, Bishop of Amida in Mesopotamia; Woutruide, monastic foundress at Bergen (Netherlands); Martyr Patience; Fortunatus, Donatus, 12 virgins, and 6 laymen at Sirmium; Casilda of Toledo, Spain.

Friday   **Strict Fast**

April 10
Isaiah 66:10-24; Genesis 49:33-50:26
Proverbs 31:8-31

The angels are not absent when the saints perform their acts of courage, but keep them company.

St. Makarios of Egypt

NEW MARTYR DEMOS THE FISHERMAN AT SMYRNA. Demos was a fisherman in the eighteenth-century city of Adrianople. One year he worked at a breeding pool near Smyrna that was owned by an Ottoman. This work was unprofitable for Demos, and he was in debt to his employer. When the employer sold his business to another Turk, he asked Demos to remit the loan and to remain at the fishery. However, Demos decided to quit, and this upset the old employer, who slandered Demos, claiming that he had taken an oath to become a Muslim so he would not have to continue working in the fishery. Demos was abducted and taken to a judge, who ordered him to deny his Orthodox faith. Demos defended himself, saying that they were lying, that he did not take an oath, and confessed Jesus as true God. After severe tortures and beatings to the soles of his feet, he was imprisoned and placed in wooden stocks. He was brought out of prison on three occasions for interrogation. He was alternately promised gifts and threats. Finally, Demos was beheaded. Christians purchased his holy relics and buried them at the Church of Great Martyr George. Miracles began to occur at the saint's tomb. A tailor's wife, who was blind in both eyes for three years, venerated the holy relics of St. Demos and the next morning she could see. During the transfer of the saint's relics, they emitted a sweet fragrance.

COMMEMORATIONS: Gregory V, Patriarch of Constantinople; Terence, Africanos, Maximos, Pompeios, Zeno, Alexander, Theodore, and 33 others, at Carthage; Prophetess Huldah (Olda); Chrysanthos of Xenophontos; James, Azas, and Abdicius of Persia; Martyrs of Kvabtakhevi Monastery; George of Cyprus, at Acre (Palestine); Misael, Archbishop of Ryazan; Demos at Smyrna; Anastasia of Uglich and 34 nuns; Martyrs Beocca, Hethor, and companions, at Chertsey Abbey; Martyrs under the Danes.

SATURDAY

APRIL 11

Lazarus Saturday
Abstain from meat and
dairy products, and fish.
Hebrews 12:28-29, 13:1-8; John 11:1-45

Forgetting offences is a sign of sincere repentance. If you keep the memory of them, you may believe you have repented but you are like someone running in his sleep.

St. John Climacus

VENERABLE PHARMUTHIUS THE ANCHORITE. Pharmuthius was a fourth-century anchorite dwelling in the Egyptian desert. A young St. John of the Well once visited Pharmuthius in order to receive a blessing to go further into the desert to pray. Then as John continued on his journey, he happened upon a deep dry well filled with scorpions, snakes, and other reptiles. He entered into the well and prayed, staying there initially for forty days. An angel of the Lord would deliver food to Pharmuthius, who then delivered it to John. The food went to Pharmuthius to keep young John from falling into pride, and this continued for a few years until the devil deceived Pharmuthius to convince John to leave the well. John corrected this deception and told Pharmuthius to return to his cell, where he lived out the rest of his days until his peaceful repose.

COMMEMORATIONS: Antipas, Bishop of Pergamus; Processus and Martinian of Rome; Barsanuphius, Bishop of Tver; Pharmuthius, anchorite of Egypt; Euthymius and Chariton of Syandema; Callinicus of Cernica, Bishop of Rimnic; Tryphaina and Matrona of Cyzicus; Jakov (James), founder of Zheleznoborovsk Monastery, and his fellow-ascetic St. James; Guthlac of Crowland; Philip, Bishop of Gortyna; Domninus, Bishop of Salona, and 8 soldiers with him; Appearance of the Mother of God "The Footprint" at Pochaev.

Sunday

April 12

Palm Sunday
Abstain from meat and dairy products.
Philippians 4:4-9; John 12:1-18

*W*ho did not meet the Lord when He triumphantly entered Jerusalem as a king; and who did not cry out then, *Hosanna to the Son of David!* (Matt. 21:15)? But only four days passed, and the same crowd cried with the same tongues, *Crucify Him, crucify Him!* (John 19:6). An amazing change! But why should we be surprised? Do we not do the very same thing when, upon receiving the Holy Mysteries of the Body and Blood of the Lord, we barely leave the church before forgetting everything—both our reverence and God's mercy toward us? We give ourselves over as before to self-pleasing deeds—at first small and then also large. Perhaps even before four days have passed.

St. Theophan the Recluse

HIEROMARTYR ZENO, BISHOP OF VERONA. Zeno was from fourth-century Syria. While still a young man he became a monk, devoting himself to the study of the Holy Scriptures. He decided to settle in the city of Verona, and after some time he was made a bishop. This was during the time of the Arian heresy, which was condemned by the First Ecumenical Council of Nicaea in 325. However, due to the patronage of the emperors Constantius and Valens, the Arians began to persecute the Orthodox. Zeno defended true Orthodoxy in sermons and letters, and he wrote a total of 93 discourses against the Arians. For this, he bravely endured oppression and sufferings and died at the hands of the heretic Arians about the year 360. Two hundred years later, the Tiber River overflowed its banks, flooding the city of Verona. The waters surrounded the church dedicated to St. Zeno, rising up to the windows. When the church doors were opened, the water did not rush into the church but stopped at the front wall.

COMMEMORATIONS: Deposition of the Sash of the Most Holy Theotokos from Zela to Constantinople; Basil the Confessor; Hieromartyr Artemon; Anthusa of Constantinople; Isaac the Syrian; Zeno of Verona; Menas, David, and John of Palestine; Sergius II, Patriarch of Constantinople; Basil of Ryazan; Acacius the New; Martyrs Demes, Protion, and those with them.

Monday

April 13

Holy Monday
Strict Fast
Matthew 21:18-43; Matthew 24:3-35

Remembrance of Jesus' passion will heal your soul of resentment, by making it ashamed of itself when it remembers the patience of the Lord.

St. John Climacus

HIEROMARTYR BARNABAS, ARCHBISHOP OF ARCHANGELSK. Barnabas was from a peasant family in nineteenth-century Olonets, Russia. He became a gardener by profession. He was well-read in the works of the Holy Fathers, was zealous for Orthodoxy, and well-loved by the priests of that town. At the age of 36, he entered Klimenets monastery, and nine years later became the abbot. Over the next six years, he was appointed superior of three other monasteries and was consecrated bishop of Kargopol. In 1917 Barnabas undertook missionary work in Siberia and was a promoter of the canonization of St. John of Tobolsk, who was working many miracles and who had appeared to Barnabas, asking for his canonization. In 1918 Barnabas was arrested and imprisoned during the Russian Revolution, and he encouraged his fellow prisoners. In 1920 he was made the archbishop of Archangelsk, but he never arrived at his see. Barnabas died in Moscow in 1924 and was buried by Patriarch Tikhon.

COMMEMORATIONS: Martin the Confessor, Pope of Rome; Quintilian, Maximus, and Dada of Dorostolum; Eleutherius of Persia; Zoilus of Rome; Herman of Svyatogorsk; Martyrius, Patriarch of Jerusalem; Martius of Clermont; Stephen of Izhevsk; Anastasia, foundress of Protection Convent in Kiev; Martyr Theodosius; Guinoch of Buchan; Barnabas, Archbishop of Archangelsk.

TUESDAY

APRIL 14

Holy Tuesday
Strict Fast
Matthew 22:15-23:39; Matthew 24:36-26:2

Beware of measuring fasting by abstaining from food. Those who abstain from food but behave badly are likened to a devil who, although he does not eat anything, doesn't stop sinning.
St. Basil the Great

NEW MARTYR DEMETRIOS OF THE PELOPONNESUS. As a young Christian man in nineteenth-century Tripoli, Demetrios apprenticed with a Turkish contractor and became a Muslim at his employer's urging. His father reached him after several months had passed and brought him back to the faith. In the act of sincere repentance, Demetrios made his way to the island of Chios, where he spent time at a monastery and later took monastic tonsure. Though the abbot tried to convince him that even St. Peter the Apostle had denied Christ and was forgiven, Demetrios demanded of himself that he return to the Turks of Tripoli. When he confessed his faith in Jesus Christ, he was executed. The holy relics of St. Demetrios can be found today in the Holy Monastery of St. Nicholas Varson, and his skull in the Holy Church of St. Basil in Tripoli.

COMMEMORATIONS: Apostles Aristarchus, Pudens, and Trophimos of the Seventy; Thomais of Alexandria; Ardalion the Actor; Euthymius the Wonderworker; Azat the Eunuch and 1,000 Martyrs in Persia; Christopher of St. Sabbas Monastery; Anthony, John, and Eustathius of Vilnius (Lithuania); Demetrios of Peloponnesus, at Tripoli; Tassach, Bishop of Raholp (Ireland); Sergius Trofimov of Nizhni-Novgorod and companion; Pachomius of Gledin, Bishop of Roman; Commemoration of Sts. Raphael, Nicholas, Irene, and the other Newly-revealed Martyrs of Lesvos; "Vilna" Icon of the Mother of God.

Wednesday
April 15

Holy Wednesday
Strict Fast
John 12:17-50; Matthew 26:6-16

I think there is no greater labor than that of prayer to God. For every time a man wants to pray, his enemies, the demons, want to prevent him, for they know that it is only by turning him from prayer that they can hinder his journey. Whatever good work a man undertakes, if he perseveres in it, he will attain rest. But prayer is warfare to the last breath.

St. Agathon of Egypt

RIGHTEOUS DANIEL OF ACHINSK. Daniel was a poor Cossack from Ukraine, and he fought in the War of 1812. When he returned from Paris, he became an army officer. He also began reading spiritual books, and soon abandoned his military career to become a monk. Because he abruptly left the military, he was sentenced to hard labor in Siberia. However, when the governor saw Daniel's devout Christian character, he freed him. Daniel settled into a life of strict asceticism in Achinsk. He lived in solitude, wore chains, and fasted strictly. Over time he was granted the gift of clairvoyance and became a well-known elder.

COMMEMORATIONS: Leonidas, Bishop of Athens; Suchias of Iberia and 16 companions; Crescens of Myra; Anastasia and Vasilissa of Rome; Daniel of Achinsk, Siberia; Mstislav-Theodore, Prince of Kiev; Pausilipus of Thrace; Ruadhan, founder and abbot of Lothra, Ireland; Paternus (Padarn), Bishop of Llandbadam Fawr; Ananias Lampardes, Metropolitan of Lacedaemon.

Thursday

April 16

Holy Thursday
Strict Fast

1 Corinthians 11:23-32; Matthew 26:1-20
John 13:3-17; Matthew 26:21-39
Luke 22:43-44; Matthew 26:40-27:2

*L*et us now strive more, my children, and the benefits will be great. No one finds Grace without toil. If the farmer does not farm his field, he will not see the results. When our fasting coexists, is strengthened and is encompassed with prayer, with contemplation, with watchfulness, with church attendance, with Confession, with Holy Communion, with good works and charity giving, then is fulfilled the beauty of the soul's preparation for the reception of Holy Week. Then we feel the Holy and Honorable Passion of Christ more profoundly, because our hearts will soften, and they will alter and recognize how boundless the love of God is for man. Then the Holy Resurrection will be alive within us with great strength, we will feast in a divinely-fitting manner and celebrate together with the angels the Holy Pascha.

Elder Ephraim of Arizona

MARTYR IRENE OF CORINTH. During the third-century persecutions under the emperor Decius, St. Leonides was martyred, along with Saints Vasilissa, Nunekhia, Kallida, Galena, Nike, Charissa, and Theodora. Irene was celebrating Pascha with other Christians in a different church when she was reported to the magistrate and arrested. She was placed in prison, and later her tongue was cut out, and her teeth pulled. Finally, St. Irene was beheaded.

COMMEMORATIONS: Virgin-martyrs Agape, Irene, and Chionia in Illyria; Irene of Corinth; Leonidas, Charissa, Nike, Galina, Kallida, Nunekhia, Vasilissa, and Theodora; John, fool-for-Christ of Verkhoturye; Christopher of Dionysiou, Mt. Athos; Michael of Smyrna; Nicholas the Deacon of Mytilene; Fructuosis of Braga in Iberia; Theodora-Vassa, Princess of Novgorod; Felix, Januarius, Fortunatus, and Septimus of Lycaonia; "Ilyin Chernigov" Weeping Icon of the Mother of God.

Friday

April 17

Holy Friday
Strict Fast
1 Corinthians 5:6-8; Matthew 27:62-66

The entire purpose of our Lord's death was not to redeem us from sins, or for any other reason, but solely in order that the world might become aware of the love which God has for creation. Had all this astounding affair taken place solely for the purpose of the forgiveness of sin, it would have been sufficient to redeem us by some other means.

St. Isaac the Syrian

ST. EPHRAIM THE GREAT, BISHOP OF ATSQURI, GEORGIA. During his travels in the country of Georgia, the young Ephraim met St. Grigol of Khandzta. Grigol perceived that Ephraim would one day be a wonderworker and bishop of Atsquri, and Ephraim became his disciple. On their way back to Klarjeti, another youth named Arsenius accompanied them. When they arrived at the monastery, Grigol told the other monks that these two young men would one day be spiritual successors of St. Ephraim the Syrian and St. Arsenius the Great. Grigol entrusted the upbringing of the two youths to his two spiritual sons, Christopher and Theodore. Ephraim later became the bishop of Atsquri and strengthened the autocephaly of the Georgian Church. He was one of the most influential figures in the eighth- and ninth-century Georgian Church. He held this office for forty years and was granted the gifts of miracle-working, healing, and prophecy. St. Ephraim died peacefully in old age. Even to this day, those who approach his holy relics with faith are healed of their infirmities.

COMMEMORATIONS: Agapitus, Pope of Rome; Makarios Notaras, Metropolitan of Corinth; Symeon, Bishop in Persia, and with him: Abdechalas, Ananias, Usthazanes, Fusicus, Ascitrea, and Azat; Acacius II, Bishop of Melitene; Adrian of Corinthus in Persia; Ephraim the Great of Atsquri, Georgia; Paisius, fool-for-Christ of Kiev; Zosimas of Solovki; Elias of Makeevka, Ukraine; Donnan of Eigg and those with him (Scotland); Uncovering of the relics of St. Alexander of Svir.

Saturday

April 18

Holy Saturday
Strict Fast
Romans 6:3-11; Matthew 28:1-20

*A*lthough all of the New Testament saints are also blessed in heaven, they await an even more perfect bliss in the age to come, with a new heaven and new earth, when God will be all in all.

St. Theophan the Recluse

NEW MARTYR TOUNOM THE EMIR. In 1846 the Armenians had the Greeks locked out of the Holy Sepulcher and the Church of the Resurrection on Holy Saturday so that they might receive the Holy Light of the Resurrection themselves. Outside the Turkish army was standing around on guard, and the emir Tounom was one of these soldiers. On that day the sky was clear and blue, and suddenly there was a clap of thunder, and on the left side the middle marble column cracked and out of the fissure came forth a flame of fire. The Patriarch and all the Orthodox Christians lit their candles. The Orthodox Arabs began to run about all Jerusalem crying out, "Thou art our one God, Jesus Christ; one if our True Faith, that of the Orthodox Christians!" To this day, they do this every year in memory of this event. Seeing all of this, Tounom jumped down from his post, from a height of more than 35 feet, and landed on solid marble as though on soft wax, and to this day his footprints can be seen. He immediately believed in Christ and shouted, "One is the true God, Jesus Christ; one is the True Faith, that of the Orthodox Christians!" He thrust his weapon into the stone as though into soft wax and began to glorify Christ unceasingly. For this, the Turks beheaded him and burned his body. The Greeks gathered up his bones, put them in a case, and took them to the Convent of the Great Panagia, where they gush forth fragrance to this day.

COMMEMORATIONS: Sabbas the Goth; John, disciple of St. Gregory of Decapolis; Cosmas of Chalcedon, and Auxentius; Publius of Egypt; Euthymius of Karelia, and Anthony and Felix; Athanasia of Aegina; John the Tailor of Ioannina; Basil Ratishvili of Iveron; Tamara of Cheboksara; Alexis of Ekaterinburg; Nicholas and Basil Derzhavin, and the lay people of Gorodets; Tounom, the Arab emir; "Maximov" Icon of the Mother of God.

Sunday

April 19

Great & Holy Pascha
Fast-free Week
Acts 1:1-8; John 1:1-17

It is love that shows who is the true shepherd, for by reason of love the Great Shepherd was crucified.

St. John Climacus

VENERABLE SYMEON THE BAREFOOT. Symeon was the son of a priest and the spiritual child of Bishop Pachomios. He was tonsured a monk and went to a monastery near Mt. Olympos, and from there to Mt. Athos, to the Great Lavra of St. Athanasius the Athonite. He proved to be a model of humility and obedience and was ordained a hieromonk. He later transferred to Philotheou Monastery, where he was unanimously chosen abbot. Later, some monks unjustly slandered Symeon, so he left there and went to Mount Flamourion in Zagora. He lived there in total isolation without roof or fire, yet always in prayer, either standing or kneeling. After living three years in these conditions, others happened upon Symeon, and inspired by his example, they became his disciples. Over seven years, a monastery and church were founded, and the Divine Liturgy was celebrated every day. Once the life of the monastery was properly established, Symeon went to teach Orthodoxy in the cities of Athens, Thessalonica, and Epirus. He ordered the spiritual footsteps of the uncertain and strengthened those firm in the faith. Once again, envious enemies slandered Symeon. This time he was accused of converting Turks to Christianity, and he was sentenced to be burned to death. However, as he stood before the governor barefoot and chained, he answered so wisely that he was released. Symeon continued to teach, and by his prayers, he wrought miracles. St. Symeon died peacefully, and after two years his relics were unearthed and found fragrant and miraculous.

COMMEMORATIONS: Tryphon, Patriarch of Constantinople; George the Confessor; Theodore of Perga, his mother Philippa, and Dioscorus, Socrates, and Dionysius; Symeon the Barefoot; Agathangelos of Esphigmenou; Victor of Vyatka; Nicephorus of Katabad; Paphnutius of Jerusalem; Ioasaph (Bolotov), enlightener of Alaska; Alphege of Canterbury; Uncovering of the relics of St. Joachim of Opochka Monastery, Pskov.

Monday

April 20

Bright Monday
Fast-free
Acts 1:12-17, 21-26; John 1:18-28

*E*very day you provide your bodies with good to keep them from failing. In the same way your good works should be the daily nourishment of your hearts. Your bodies are fed with food and your spirits with good works. You aren't to deny your soul, which is going to live forever, what you grant to your body, which is going to die.

St. Gregory the Great

HOLY APOSTLE ZACCHAEUS, BISHOP OF CAESAREA. Zacchaeus was a chief tax collector at Jericho. Tax collectors were despised as corrupt traitors and working for the Roman Empire, not for their Jewish community. When Jesus was passing through Jericho on his way to Jerusalem, Zacchaeus ran ahead and climbed a sycamore tree because he was short of stature and would be unable to see Jesus through the crowd. When Jesus reached the sycamore tree, he looked up and called Zacchaeus by name, telling him to come down, for he was to visit his house. Consequently, Zacchaeus gave half his possessions to feed the poor. He also became a faithful disciple, and after the Resurrection, a companion of the Apostle Peter. Zacchaeus became the Bishop of Caesarea in Palestine and served faithfully until his peaceful repose.

COMMEMORATIONS: Apostle Zacchaeus, Bishop of Caesarea; Theodore Trichinas of Constantinople; Gregory, Anastasius I, and Anastasius II, Patriarchs of Antioch; Victor, Zoticus, Zeno, Acindynus, Christopher, Theonas, Caesarius, Antoninus, and Severian of Nicomedia; John the Ancient of Old Lavra; Ioasaph and Athanasius of Meteora; Alexander of Oshevensk; Gabriel of Zabludov, Poland; Theodosius of Kolomna; Betran and Theotimos I, Bishops in Scythia Minor; Caedwalla, King of the West Saxons; Translation of the relics of St. Nikolai Velimirovich; "Cyprus" and "Keepiazh" Icons of the Mother of God.

Tuesday

April 21

Bright Tuesday
Fast-free
Acts 2:14-21; Luke 24:12-35

It is useless to subdue the flesh by abstinence, unless one gives up his irregular life, and abandons vices which defile his soul.
— St. Benedict of Nursia

ST. MAELRUBA OF APPLECROSS, IRELAND. Maelruba has been venerated as one of the seventh-century apostles of the Picts in Scotland. He was descended from King Nial of Ireland. He became a monk, and his role model was St. Columba of Iona, who had lived 100 years earlier, so Maelruba decided to evangelize the pagan Picts in Scotland. At first, he lived on the Isle of Iona. He was noted for his piety, learnedness, and the many miracles he wrought. He traveled extensively and founded many churches. He also founded the Monastery of Applecross (Apur Crossan), where the revival of monastic traditions in Scotland began. It flourished until the ninth-century Viking raids. There is a holy well associated with St. Maelruba on Isle Maree that has curative powers for those who bathe in it, especially those with mental illness. St. Maelruba is one of the principal saints of northwestern Scotland after St. Columba.

COMMEMORATIONS: Januarius, Bishop of Benevento, with Proclus, Sosius, Festus, Desiderius, Gantiol, Eutychius, and Acutius, at Pozzuoli; Maximianos, Archbishop of Constantinople; Anastasius of St. Catherine's on Mt. Sinai; James of Stromynsk; Alexandra the Empress, wife of Diocletian and her servants Isaakios, Apollo, and Kodratos of Nicomedia; Niphon, Bishop of Novgorod; Maelruba of Apur Crossan, Ireland; Beuno, abbot of Clynnog Fawr, Wales; Basil Martysz of Teratyn (Poland); Alexis of Bortsumany, Nizhni-Novgorod; Uncovering of the relics of St. Theodore of Sanaxar Monastery; "Mozdok" Icon of the Mother of God.

Wednesday

April 22

Bright Wednesday
Fast-free
Acts 2:22-38; John 1:35-51

*A*bide in the bond of mutual love, for love is the beginning and the end—the foundation. It is on love towards God and your brothers that "all the law and the prophets hang." (Mt.22:40). Without love we are a clanging symbol—a big zero. According to the Apostle Paul, even if we give our body to be burned for Christ and distribute our belongings to the poor and mortify our life with harsh ascesis for Christ, yet lack love, we have accomplished nothing. (1 Cor.13:3). Therefore, with all our strength we must see to it that we keep a strong hold on mutual love, so that our trivial works may be approved by Him Who examines the secret thoughts of our hearts.

Elder Ephraim of Arizona

MARTYR LEONIDAS OF ALEXANDRIA. Leonidas lived in the late second century and was the father of the Christian writer Origen. Leonidas was persecuted for Christianity by imperial decree. First, all his property was confiscated, then he was imprisoned and condemned to death. Origen wrote his father a letter of encouragement, saying, "Father, do not worry about us, and do not flee from martyrdom on our account."

COMMEMORATIONS: Apostle Nathaniel of the Twelve; Apostles Apelles, Luke, and Clement, of the Seventy; Theodore the Sykeote, Bishop of Anastasiopolis; Leonidas of Alexandria; Platon, Bishop of Banja Luka; Vitalis of the monastery of Abba Seridus at Gaza; Epipodius of Lyons; Martyr Nearchus; Ananias of Malles (Crete); Sabbas, Bishop of Gornji Karlovac; New Martyrs of Jasenovac Concentration Camp; Translation of the relics of St. Vsevolod (Gabriel), Prince and Wonderworker of Rostov.

Thursday
April 23

Bright Thursday
St. George the Great Martyr
Fast-free
Acts 12:1-11; John 15:17-16:2

When children learn to read books, they first learn the letters, then spelling, and later on they learn to read. Christians should proceed in the same way in Christian doctrine. First of all they should learn to return good for good, which is gratitude; then not to return evil for evil, insult for insult, offense for offense, and not to take revenge either in word or in deed on the offender; and then after this, even to love their enemies and to do good to those that hate them, and to return good for evil.

St. Tikhon of Zadonsk

MARTYR GLYKERIOS THE FARMER OF NICOMEDIA. When Great Martyr St. George was in prison, the fame of his miracles spread across the city and surrounding area, and many people visited the prison every night. They gave large gifts to the guards to see the saint, and they received strength, joy, faith, and love. Glykerios was very poor, and he had only one ox to plow his field, and it died. He fell on his knees before St. George and begged for help. Seeing his sincere confession and belief, St. George said to Glykerios that his ox was alive. When Glykerios went and confirmed this, he returned to St. George crying out, "Great is the God of George!" For this, Glykerios was arrested and killed by the sword.

COMMEMORATIONS: George the Great Martyr; Anatolios and Protoleon, soldiers converted by the martyrdom of St. George; Glykerios the Farmer, Athanasius the Magician, Valerius, and Donatus, at Nicomedia; Gerontios and Polychronia, parents of St. George; George of Cyprus, at Ptolemais; George of Shenkursk, fool-for-Christ; Egor (George) of Russia; George Kosov of Spas Chekriak village, Orel; Sergius Zacharczuk of Nabroz (Poland); John, priest (1940); Lazarus the Shepherd of Bulgaria, at Pergamus; Iberius (Ibar) of Beggerin; Therinus of Bothrotus in Epirus; Adalbert Voitech, Bishop of Prague.

Friday

April 24

Bright Friday
Life-Giving Spring of the Theotokos
Fast-free
Acts 3:1-8; John 2:12-22

Honor the Most Holy Theotokos as… true mother, not as a mere supplicant and intercessor, but as the nourisher of all.
St. Theophan the Recluse

ST. ELIZABETH THE WONDERWORKER OF CONSTANTINOPLE. At an early age, Elizabeth entered the Monastery of Saint Kosmas and Damian in sixth-century Constantinople. She wore only one coarse garment her entire life, and it remained like new even though she lived in the extreme desert conditions of hot days and cold nights. Once while praying in her cell, Elizabeth opened her eyes and saw a poisonous snake before her. She closed her eyes and continued to pray, and when she opened them again, it was dead. Other times during prayer, she was seen resplendent with a heavenly light. She healed the sick and blessed those who visited her. After her death, her relics continued to heal the sick and suffering.

COMMEMORATIONS: Savvas Stratelates of Rome, and 70 soldiers with him; Sabbas the Commander, the Goth, at Buzau in Wallachia; Elizabeth the Wonderworker of Constantinople; Thomas, fool-for-Christ of Syria; Pasicrates, Valentine, and Julius, at Dorostolum; Eusebius, Neon, Leontius, Longinus, and others at Nicomedia; Xenophon, founder of Xenophontos Monastery, Mt. Athos; Alexander of Lyons; Innocent, on the Mount of Olives; Sabbas and Alexis the Hermit of the Kiev Caves; Nicholas of Magnesia; George in Anatolia; Joseph the Confessor, Bishop of Maramures; Symeon, Elias, and Sava, Metropolitans of Ardeal; Doukas of Mytilene; Branko of Veljusa, Serbia; Wilfrid, Bishop of York; Egbert, Bishop of Iona; Mellitus, Archbishop of Canterbury; Stephan, Metropolitan of Transylvania; Uncovering of the relics of St. Yvo, bishop; "Molchensk" Icon of the Mother of God.

SATURDAY

APRIL 25

Bright Saturday
St. Mark the Evangelist
Fast-free
1 Peter 5:6-14; Luke 10:16-21

A Christian is not the religious man, the man who stays at a ritualistic worship or a habitual worship. A Christian is the citizen of a kingdom. A Christian is the person who keeps calling upon the Lord. He is the disciple. He is the saint, the holy one. So, we have tribulation, patience and then, the kingdom. Along the way, we do have companionship or koinonia. This companionship not only exists between the faithful in the form of fellowship, but also between the faithful and Christ, because Christ is the one who suffered. Saint Paul captures this very beautifully. The saying is sure: If we have died with him, we shall also live with him; if we endure, we shall also reign with him (2 Tim. 2:11).
+*Elder Athanasios Mitilianos*

ST. MELLA, ABBESS OF DOIRE-MELLE IN IRELAND. Mella had two sons in eighth-century western Ireland. Through her holy example, they both became saints of the Church, St. Cannech, a priest, and St. Tigernach, an abbot. When her husband died, she became a nun and went to live at the monastery founded by her son Tigernach. After some time, he left Mella to oversee the monastery, and he retired to another named "the church of the field." St. Mella lovingly governed the nuns at her community, which came to be known as Doire-Melle, meaning "oak grove of Mella."

COMMEMORATIONS: Holy Apostle and Evangelist Mark; Stephen, Patriarch of Antioch; Macedonias II, Patriarch of Constantinople; Aninanus, second Bishop of Alexandria; Sylvester, abbot of Obnora Monastery; Martyr Nike, who believed in Christ through St. George; 8 martyred anchorites; Basil of Poiana Marului, Romania; Mella of Doire-Melle in Ireland; Commemoration of the Consecration of the Church of the Apostle Peter next to Hagia Sophia in Constantinople; "Constantinople" Icon of the Mother of God.

Sunday

April 26

Thomas Sunday
Fast-free
Acts 5:12-20; John 20:19-31

The soul perishes, if you do not defend your faith, and if you perish, defending your faith, the gates of the Kingdom of Heaven open before you.

St. Gabriel Urgebadze

ST. LEO, BISHOP OF SAMOS. Leo was born a pagan in the sixth century. He was humble, pious, and philanthropic. He converted to Christianity and later served as the Bishop of Samos. He was a wonderworker during his life and after his death, for those who approached his grave with faith. Five hundred years later, a ship from Venice was docked at Samos on St. Leo's feastday. On two occasions severe thunderstorms prevented the ship from leaving. The crowds took this as a sign from heaven. After the crowds left, a sailor suggested that the Venetians should take St. Leo's relics with them. By night they went to the church that housed the saint's relics and the doors miraculously unlocked, which confirmed for them that this was God's will. Many miracles happened along the way. Once in Venice, St. Leo's relics were placed in several churches over time, ending up in the Church of Santa Maria dell'Umilta, but from there it somehow disappeared and was never seen again.

COMMEMORATIONS: Stephen, Bishop of Perm; Glaphyra of Nicomedia; Basil, Bishop of Amasea; Andrew and Anatole, disciples of St. Euthymius the Great; George of Cyprus; Ioannicius of Devich (Serbia); Nestor the Silent; Cyril, Cindeus, and Tasie of Axiopolis; Righteous Justa; Richarius, abbot in Picardy; Calantius of Tamassos on Cyprus; Leo, Bishop of Samos; Kalandion of Cyprus; New Martyrs of Novo Selo, Bulgaria.

MONDAY   Fast-free

APRIL 27   Acts 3:19-26; John 2:1-11

*W*hen in pain, muster your spiritual strength, and try to comprehend the purpose of pain, through which God opens the Heavens for you. Do you for a moment think that He who measures the number of hairs on your head isn't aware of the extent of your pain? He is. So, rest trustingly in our heavenly Father. Don't not give up. With Christ, you'll get through everything. Because you'll become His heir and you'll inherit the infinite riches of our common Father and God. Amen.
Elder Ephraim of Arizona

VENERABLE STEPHEN, ABBOT OF THE KIEV CAVES AND BISHOP OF VLADIMIR IN VOLHYNIA. At a young age, Stephen pursued asceticism at the eleventh-century Kiev-Pechersk monastery under the guidance of St. Theodosius. Before his death, Theodosius appointed Stephen abbot of the monastery. Stephen completed the building of a church started by St. Theodosius, in honor of the Repose of the Holy Mother of God, as well as new cells for the brethren. He later left that monastery and founded a new one in honor of the Mother of God. Stephen was chosen to be the bishop at Vladimir-Volynsk, and he converted many inhabitants to Christianity. St. Stephen led the Church well into old age and died peacefully.

COMMEMORATIONS: Eulogius the Hospitable of Constantinople; Symeon the Kinsman of the Lord, Bishop of Jerusalem; Floribert, Bishop of Luik; John the Confessor of Cathares Monastery at Constantinople; Elias (Ardunis) of Mt. Athos; Seraphim, Bishop of Phanar; Stephen, abbot of the Kiev Caves; Lollion the Younger; Pollion the Reader of Cibalis in Pannonia; Nicon, abbot of the monastery of St. Gerasimus; Machalus of the Isle of Man; Burning of the relics of St. Sava I of Serbia by the Turks; Glorification of New Hieromartyr Hilarion (Troitsky), Archbishop of Verey; "Panagia Chrysafitissa" of Monemvasia (Monday of St. Thomas).

Tuesday

April 28

Fast-free

Acts 4:1-10; John 3:16-21

The silence of your heart is the voice of God, and the bustle of your heart is the voice of the world.

Monk Simeon of Mt. Athos

COMMEMORATION OF THE MIRACLE IN CARTHAGE. Near Carthage, in the town of Tunisia, in the seventh century, an epidemic ravaged the people. A young soldier, named Tounezi, and his new bride fled the area. They went to a small village where they had a country home. Tounezi committed adultery, and very soon after fell ill and died. Three hours after being buried, his shouts for help were heard, his grave was opened, and he was found alive. Unable to speak, he sat quietly until the Patriarch of Alexandria arrived. After three days, he began to speak and tell his story. He said that a terrible dark presence appeared when his soul left his body, presumably to take his soul into hell for his sin. He suddenly saw two beautiful angels dressed in white, and his soul rejoiced as they took him to heaven, but then the demons appeared, taking him through the tollhouses in the air, examining his every sin. As the demons examined each sin, the angels responded with his good deeds. However, when the sin of adultery was revealed, the demons immediately took him into hell. He cried out to the angels for pity and to help him repent. They told him it was not possible for him to repent unless he was in his body, so the angels sent his soul back to his body, and he began to yell. For forty days, he did not eat or drink, and with tears repented for his sins. A short time later, he died.

COMMEMORATIONS: Memnon the Wonderworker; Nine Martyrs at Cyzicus—Theognes, Rufus, Antipater, Theostichus, Artemas, Magnus, Theodotus, Thaumasius, and Philemon; Dada, Maximus, and Quintilian at Dorostolum; Auxibius II, Bishop of Soli on Cyprus; Cyril, Bishop of Turov; Basil Kishkin of Glinsk; Cyril, founder of Syrinsk Monastery (Karelia); Cronan, abbot of Roscrea Monastery, Ireland; Cyriacus, abbot of Kargopol; Tibald of Pannonia; Commemoration of the Miracle at Carthage of Africa.

Wednesday

April 29

Abstain from meat and dairy products, and fish.
Acts 4:13-22; John 5:17-24

He who prays in his mind with faith beholds the Lord before himself. For in Him do we live, move and exist.

St. Isaac the Syrian

ST. JOHN THE NEW MERCIFUL ONE, METROPOLITAN OF THEBES. During his life, John was known for his charitable works, and was named "the New Merciful." He was born in twelfth-century Constantinople to a well-to-do family. He was an excellent student, especially in theology. He became a monk in Constantinople and later was made the bishop of Thebes. This was a difficult and declining time for that city. It was once a flourishing center of the Byzantine silk industry, until the Norman sack of 1147, when the silk weavers were carried off to southern Italy. All five bishoprics remained vacant, which led to a decline of the religious sentiments of the local population. John appointed new bishops without informing the patriarchal synod, which angered Emperor Manuel I Komnenos. However, John stood firm, and the synod confirmed his appointments. Most importantly, John led a simple and austere life, performed works of charity for the poor and weak, and established new churches and monasteries. John also built a hospital, hospices for the poor and elderly, and a school for the education of girls. Economically, John financed the diversion of the Isminos river to the Boeotian plain, to ensure the functionality of the twenty water mills that supplied local irrigation. Coupled with this was the construction of an aqueduct system, which survived until the twentieth century. The river was named Agiannis, meaning "St. John."

COMMEMORATIONS: Jason and Sosipater of the Seventy, and companions; Zeno, Eusebius, Neon, and Vitalis; John Kaloktenes, Metropolitan of Thebes; Basil of Ostrog; Martyrs Quintian and Atticus; Secundellus in Gaul; Diodorus and Rhodopianus in Anatolia; John Tolaius of Alexandria; Arsenius of Suzdal; Nicetas of Synnada; John of Romania; Nectarius of Optina; Nicephorus of Sebaze; Stanko of Montenegro; Endellion of Cornwall; Holy Martyrs of Lazeti (Georgia).

Thursday

April 30

Holy Apostle James
Fast-free

Acts 12:1-11; Luke 9:1-6

Only those religious books that are written by the Holy Fathers of the universal Orthodox Church are acceptable to read.
St. Ignatius Brianchaninov

ST. IGNATIUS BRIANCHANINOV. Ignatius was born in nineteenth-century Vologda, the son of an aristocratic landowner. He was intellectually gifted, reflective, and peaceful. He was drawn to a life of stillness and prayer, but at the age of fifteen, his father enrolled him in a military academy. His excellence there caught the attention of the future Tsar Nicholas I. Ignatius graduated first in his class but fell gravely ill and attempted to resign the military, but Nicholas refused it. A year later, he fell ill again, but this time imperial authorities accepted it. Over the next four years, Ignatius lived in various monasteries searching for a spiritual father. Finally, at the age of 24, he became a deacon then a priest. Two years later, Tsar Nicholas inquired into the whereabouts of Ignatius. He was ordered to the capital, and Nicholas raised Ignatius to the rank of archimandrite and abbot of St. Sergius Monastery, one of the most influential in St. Petersburg. The tsar asked him to transform the monastery into a model community, where all could see monasticism as it should be. Ignatius remained there for 24 years. He was a prolific writer, completing much of the five volumes of his collected works. Later he was made a Bishop of the Caucasus, and the Black Sea area, a greatly disorganized diocese, until his health again forced him to resign. St. Ignatius spent the last six years of his in seclusion at the Nicolo-Gabaevsky Monastery.

COMMEMORATIONS: Apostle James, the brother of St. John the Theologian; Maximus of Ephesus; Clement the Hymnographer; Ignatius, Bishop of the Caucasus; Maximus of Ephesus; Argyra of Prusa; James, his wife, and son Alexis of Plotava; Donatus of Euroea; Eutropius and Estelle of Saintes; Erconwald of London; Endelienta of Cornwall; Translation of the relics of St. Argyre of Proussa, St. Theodore of Byzantium, and St. Sabbas of Zvenigorod Monastery; Uncovering of the relics of St. Basil of Amasea and St. Nicetas of Novgorod.

Friday

May 1

Abstain from meat and dairy products, and fish.
Acts 5:1-11; John 5:30-6:2

Life without Christ is tasteless, sad, and forlorn.
+*Elder Sophrony of Essex*

NEW MARTYR EUTHYMIOS OF PELOPONNESOS. Euthymios went to the Patriarchal Academy in Constantinople and later worked in Romania with his father and brothers. He decided to become a monk on Mt. Athos, but because of a war between Russia and Turkey, he could only travel as far as Bucharest. He pursued a life of pleasure and put aside thoughts of monasticism. After the war, he made his way back to Constantinople, but along the way, he embraced Islam. Soon his conscience began to bother him. One day he was seen wearing a cross, so the Moslems kept a close watch on him. Still, Euthymios escaped to Mt. Athos and was chrismated back into the Orthodox Church and became a monk. He read the New Martyrology of St. Nicodemos and was consumed with a desire to erase his apostasy with the blood of martyrdom. He returned to Constantinople dressed as a Muslim, went to the palace of the Grand Vizier, and said that he would never deny Christ again. The Vizier thought that Euthymios was either drunk or crazy, so he put him in prison to reconsider. Even after being beaten, his resolve remained unchanged. He walked to the place of execution joyfully, unbound, and unafraid. The executioner struck a fierce blow several times, attempting to behead him, but failed. Finally, he cut the martyr's throat. The head of St. Euthymios is in the Monastery of St. Panteleimon on Mt. Athos.

SAINTS OF THE DAY: Prophet Jeremiah; Panaretus, Bishop of Paphos; Philosophos of Alexandria; Maria of Merambelos; Isidora of Tabenna; Tamara, Empress of Georgia; Nicephorus of Chios; Ultan of Fosse; Macarius, Metropolitan of Kiev; Batas of Nisibis; Zosimas of Kumurdo; Michael of Chalcedon; Euthymius, Ignatius, and Acacius of Serres; Paphnutius of Borovsk; Gerasimus of Boldino; Luke Shvets of Glinsk; Brieuc, in Brittany; Romanus of Raqqa; Asaph, Bishop of Llanelwy, Wales; Walpurga of Germany; Commemoration of the Dreadful Earthquake at Sinai; "Unexpected Joy" Icon of the Mother of God.

SATURDAY   Fast-free

May 2
Hebrews 13:7-16; Matthew 5:14-19

There is no end to the love of the Lord Christ for man!
St. Justin Popovich of Celije

ST. ATHANASIOS III PATELLARIOS. Athanasios joined a monastery in Thessalonica in the sixteenth century. He received monastic tonsure and was ordained to the priesthood, spreading the Gospel of Christ among the Vlachs and Moldavians, for whom he translated the psalter. He drew the attention of Patriarch Cyril of Constantinople and was appointed a preacher of the Patriarchal throne. Soon he was consecrated bishop and Metropolitan of Thessalonica. When Cyril was slandered and imprisoned, Athanasios took the throne for a series of short tenures. After the death of Patriarch Cyril, Athanasios took the throne a third time but was deposed after only fifteen days, as he was not acceptable to the other faiths there. He traveled to Moscow and set forth the procedure for the Divine Liturgy celebrated by a bishop, which is still in use today. Athanasios died and was buried in a solid silver coffin. In the Greek tradition, he was buried in a sitting position in full vestments, thus the name "the Sitter." Eight years later, his relics were uncovered and found incorrupt. He was reburied in new robes, and the saint began to appear in many people's dreams, healing the sick, blessing, and teaching. When the Bolsheviks wanted to remove the silver coffin in 1922, tens of thousands of people traveled there and formed a ring around the church. The military brought in machine guns and artillery fire and 3,000 soldiers to disperse the crowds, but they would not leave. Finally, monks placed the holy relics of St. Athanasios into a wooden coffin, and the silver one was given to the Bolsheviks.

SAINTS OF THE DAY: Hesperus, Zoe, and their sons Cyriacus and Theodulus, at Attalia; Athanasius III Patellarios, Patriarch of Constantinople; Boris-Michael, Prince of Bulgaria; Athanasius of Syandem and Valaam; Jordan the Wonderworker; Basil of Kadom; Matrona the Blind; Translation of the Relics of St. Athanasius the Great and Sts. Boris and Gleb of Russia; "Putivilsk" Icon of the Mother of God; (1st Saturday of May: George of Gomati; Gervasios of Gomati the Athonite).

Sunday

May 3

Sunday of the Myrrhbearing Women
Fast-free

Acts 6:1-7; Mark 15:43-16:8

The tireless women! They would not give sleep to their eyes nor slumber to their eyelids until they found their Beloved!
                                                St. Theophan the Recluse

---

MARTYRS TIMOTHY AND MAURA. The third-century Christian persecutions by the emperor Diocletian had reached even to Egypt. Timothy was from a village called Penapeon, and he was a Reader in the church. After twenty days of marriage to Maura, he was captured by the governor Arianos and ordered to relinquish his sacred books. Refusing to give over his "children," hot burning rods were placed into his ears. He was fastened to a wheel with a bridle over his mouth. Then he was hung upside down until his flesh was torn. Timothy's wife received this news and prayed that God would relieve her husband's pain. Her prayers were answered, and Timothy was healed. Many who saw this confessed the faith, but the governor thought it was sorcery. Maura confessed her faith before the governor, and this angered him. He had her hair shaved off her head, fingers cut off, then submerged in a cauldron of boiling water, but she remained unharmed. Finally, Timothy and Maura were crucified and left hanging for nine days. She had a vision of their reward in heaven before she died. The governor later became a Christian and martyr. The demon-possessed have been miraculously healed before the icon of St. Maura, in the church dedicated to her on the island of Zakynthos.

SAINTS OF THE DAY: Timothy the Reader and his wife Maura of Antinoe in Egypt; Peter, Bishop of Argos; Ecumenius, Bishop of Tricca; Diodoros and Rodopianos the Deacon of Aphrodisia; Ansfried of Utrecht; Mamai, Catholicos of Georgia; Xenia of Peloponnesus; Paul of Vilnius, Lithuania; Holy 27 Martyrs; Eupraxia and Juliana of Conception Monastery in Moscow; Gregory, Bishop of Rostov; Irodion of Romania; Theophanes of Vatopedi; Theodosius of the Kiev Caves Monastery; Ahmet the Calligrapher of Constantinople; Michael and Arsenius the Georgians; Glywys of Cornwall; Sergius of Buzuluk.

Monday

Fast-free

May 4

Acts 6:8-7:5, 47-60; John 4:46-54

Begin on every action that is for God's sake joyfully.
St. Isaac the Syrian

ST. NIKEPHOROS THE HESYCHAST. Nikephoros was from thirteenth-century Italy. He converted from Catholicism to Orthodoxy during a time when the papacy wanted union with the Orthodox as well as submission in return for soldiers that the Orthodox needed to fight Turkish armies. Also, the Latin Church was unwilling to acknowledge Orthodox practices. After this time, Nikephoros went to Mt. Athos where he lived in stillness and quiet in a remote part of the mountain. St. Gregory Palamas was instructed by Nikephoros at the Great Lavra Monastery on Mt. Athos. Concerning the art of prayer of the heart, the Jesus Prayer, Nikephoros said that we must first enter into ourselves to practice this art of arts and science of sciences, called attentiveness, the guarding of the intellect. Attentiveness is the sign of repentance, the soul's restoration, a rejection of sin where God reveals Himself to the intellect, and faith is needed to endure outward afflictions, to bear them gladly and to make the Most High a refuge. It is the basis of faith, hope, and love. Nikephoros was the first to write down this technique of restraining the intellect from wandering, and bringing it into the heart with each inhaled breath in prayer. He recommended finding a spiritual guide to attain this spiritual gift. He said that the Jesus Prayer with attentiveness will help to attain the virtues of love, joy, peace, long-suffering, kindness, goodness, faith, meekness, and self-control and that with these virtues every prayer to God would be fulfilled. St. Nikephoros died peacefully.

SAINTS OF THE DAY: Silvanus of Gaza and 40 martyrs; Nikephoros the Hesychast; Pelagia of Tarsus; Hilary the Wonderworker; Erasmus of Formia; Aphrodisius, Leontius, Anthony, Valerian, Macrobius, and others, at Scythopolis; Athanasius of Corinth; Nicephorus of the Medicium; Dimitry Lyubimov of Gdov; Alphanov Brothers: Nicetas, Cyril, Nicephorus, Clement, and Isaac of Novgorod; Monica of Tagaste; Florian and 40 companions at Lorsch; Ethelred of Mercia; New Martyr Vasily Martysz; Synaxis of the Venerable Fathers of Mount Sinai.

TUESDAY

MAY 5

Fast-free

Acts 8:5-17; John 6:27-33

Let the person who seeks forgiveness for his sins love humility.
St. Mark the Ascetic

GREAT MARTYR IRENE OF THESSALONICA. In the fourth century, Irene converted over 100,000 pagans. At the age of six, her father, King Licinius, confined her to live in a tower. It was revealed to her that she would be baptized a Christian and many souls would be saved. Later, when she destroyed her father's idols, he ordered that horses trample her in the arena. However, he was there, but Irene's prayers raised him. He believed in Christ and was baptized, together with his wife and three thousand others. After the death of Licinius, the new king, Sedecian, demanded that she deny Christ. When she would not, he threw her into a pit of poisonous snakes, and after fourteen days she emerged unharmed. Then her legs were sawn off, but an angel of God restored her. When the water that powered a torture wheel miraculously ceased to flow, eight thousand more souls believed in Christ. When the king's son, Shapur, succeeded him, it is said that Irene blinded his entire army, then restored their sight. When they still tortured her, the earth split and swallowed up ten thousand soldiers. Then thirty thousand people converted. The next king attempted to burn her in a red-hot bronze bull, but Irene emerged unharmed. She worked many miracles, and thousands more believed in Christ. King Shapur II of Persia had her beheaded, but an angel of God resurrected her from her tomb. When she went to the king, he believed and received Baptism. At the end of her life, she had her teacher Apellian seal her in a stone tomb. When he went back after two days, he found the stone overturned and St. Irene missing.

SAINTS OF THE DAY: Great Martyr Irene of Thessalonica; Martyrs Neophytos, Gaius, and Gaianus; Barlaam of Serpukhov; Martin and Heraclius of Illyria; Eulogius the Confessor of Edessa; Adrian of Monza Monastery; Ephraim of Nea Makri; Efthymios, Bishop of Madytos in Thrace; Hydrock of Cornwall; Translation of the relics of St. Aldhelm, Bishop of Sherborne; Uncovering of the relics of St. James of Zhelezny Borok Monastery; "Inexhaustible Cup" Icon of the Mother of God.

WEDNESDAY

MAY 6

Abstain from meat and dairy products, and fish.
Acts 8:18-25; John 6:35-39

*T*he present generation has a laziness that gets brought into the monastic life too. We want to become holy without effort.
St. Paisios the Athonite

RIGHTEOUS PROPHET JOB THE LONG-SUFFERING. The story of Job is told in the Old Testament. He lived in a land called Uz, near Arabia. He led a peaceful life and was close to God, and God rewarded his piety with great wealth. In a classic confrontation of good and evil, God allowed Satan to visit Job with catastrophes to test his soul and to see if poverty would diminish his faith. At the age of seventy-nine, Job lost his wealth and all eight of his children in one day. Job did not complain against God, and this put the devil to shame, so he was not satisfied. The disease of leprosy struck Job, and he was reduced to lying on a pile of rubbish, scraping his boils with bits of broken pottery. Even Job's wife encouraged him to blaspheme God, but he remained firm. Though the Book of Job records much of his and others' dialogue, including that from God, Job best summed up his story when he said, "The Lord gives, and the Lord takes away. Blessed be the name of the Lord." God restored his health, gained back his wealth to an even greater extent, and gave him another seven sons and three daughters. St. Job lived another one hundred and forty years.

SAINTS OF THE DAY: Barbarus the Soldier, Bacchus, Callimachus, and Dionysius, in Morea; Barbarus the former robber, in Epirus; Mamas, Pachomius, and Hilarion, monks; Martyrs Danax, Mesiurs, Therin, and Donatus; Job the Long-Suffering; Job of Pochaev; Micah of Radonezh; Demetrios of Peloponnesus; Seraphim of Mt. Domvu; Sophia of Pontus and Kastoria; Edbert of Lindisfarne; Sinaites of Serbia: Romilus of Ravanica, Romanus of Djjunisa, Sisoes of Sinai, Martyrius of Rukumije, Gregory of Gornjak, Zosimas of Tuman, and Gregory of Sinai; Translation of the relics of St. Sava I of Serbia and St. Pachomius of Nerekhta.

Thursday

Fast-free

May 7

Acts 26:1, 12-20; John 6:40-44

*G*od appointed the salvation of the world to His Son and not to us... We must first look at our soul and if we can, let's help five or six people around us.

+*Elder Epiphanios of Athens*

MARTYR MAXIMOS. Maximos was a Christian and merchant in third-century Asia when Emperor Decius published edicts to enforce idolatry. He was arrested and brought before the proconsul. Under interrogation, Maximos said he was born free and was a slave of Jesus Christ and said he would sacrifice to none but God. As the torments began the proconsul continually offered to stop them if Maximos would sacrifice to the idols, but he said that if he abandoned the precepts in the Gospel, then real and eternal torments would be his portion. He continued that neither clubs nor iron hooks nor fire gave him any pain because the grace of Jesus Christ dwelled in him, and by the prayers of the saints, he obtained courage and strength. He was condemned to death by stoning, as an example of terror to all Christians.

SAINTS OF THE DAY: Commemoration of the Appearance of the Sign of the Precious Cross over Jerusalem; Domitianus, Bishop of Maastricht; Quadratus (Codratus), Rufinus, and Saturninus of Nicomedia; Acacius the Centurion at Byzantium; Nilus, founder of Sora Skete; John of Zedazeni in Georgia and 12 disciples; Thaddeus of Urbnisi; Pachomius the Russian of Usaki; John Psychaites the Confessor; John of Beverley, Bishop of York; Martyr Maximos, in Asia; Repose of St. Alexis Toth in America; Translation of the relics of St. Euthymius the Great; Finding of the relics of St. Nilus the Myrrh-gusher of Mt. Athos; "Zhirovits" and "Lubech" Icons of the Mother of God.

Friday

May 8

Synaxis of St. John the Theologian
Abstain from meat and dairy products, and fish.
1 John 1:1-7; John 19:25-28, 21:24-25

Our work is not in persuasion, for Christianity is most powerful when it is hated by the world.

St. Ignatius of Antioch

VENERABLE ARSENIOS VARNAKOVITES, FOUNDER OF VARNAKOVA MONASTERY. Arsenios was from the eleventh-century village of Karyes, Phokida. At first, he lived as an ascetic in a cave within a vast forest, but after attracting many disciples, it soon grew into a monastery. The Komneni emperors Alexios, John, and Emmanuel gave considerable financial assistance and are considered benefactors and founders of the monastery as well. After Arsenios died, his disciples made the cave into a chapel, and the altar is deep within where one must descend fifteen steps to get to it. In 2017 a fire broke out and spread throughout the entire monastery, even though eleven fire trucks quickly arrived. The miraculous icon of the Panagia there was saved. Before World War II, nine-year-old George Theocharopoulos became very sick and died in his mother's arms. She turned towards the Chapel of St. Arsenios and prayed. As soon as she finished, George stood up and walked. John Andreopoulos, who was blind, washed his eyes with holy water from the cave and immediately was cured. A miracle takes place every year in the cave on the feast of the saint. At the edge of the altar, holy water drips from a rock during the Divine Liturgy. As soon as the Liturgy ends, the water stops dripping.

SAINTS OF THE DAY: Synaxis of St. John the Theologian; Arsenios the Great of Scetis; Pimen the Faster of the Far Caves; Macarius of Ghent; Milles the Hymnographer; Arsenius the Lover of Labor of the Kiev Caves; Arsenios Varnakovites of Varnakova Monastery; Iduberga of Nivelles; Zosima and Adrian of Volokolamsk; Hierax of Egypt; Wiro of Utrecht; Plechelm and Otger of Odilienberg; Soldier martyrs slain by the sword; Translation of the relics of St. Arsenius of Novgorod, fool-for-Christ; Miracle wrought by the icon of the Mother of God of Cassiope.

Saturday

May 9

Fast-free

Acts 9:19-31; John 15:17-16:2

What is death? The age with which our true life begins.
St. Ignatius Brianchaninov

VENERABLE MARTYR NICHOLAS THE NEW OF VOUNENIA. Nicholas joined the Imperial Army and advanced through the ranks because of his virtues and bravery. The emperor made him a commander, and Nicholas trained his soldiers to be brave and fearless and to have faith in God. When the barbaric Avars arrived in Thessaly, they compelled the Christians to worship idols, torturing and killing those who refused. Nicholas and twelve soldiers decided to join a group of ascetics in the wilderness. One night an angel of the Lord appeared to Nicholas and the ascetics, telling them to prepare for martyrdom. Nicholas encouraged the group, saying that they should not fear mundane death nor cower before it, but to demonstrate their courage to inherit the heavenly kingdom. The Avars tortured these monastics on wheels and racks that wrenched their limbs, and then they were beheaded. They tried to persuade Nicholas to renounce his faith, but he said that he would not deny the true God who fashioned him. The saint was beaten and tortured with his spear and then was beheaded and his body abandoned. Many years later, St. Achilles appeared to a nobleman with leprosy, telling him to find the relics of St. Nicholas and he would be healed. When he found the relics in Vounenia, they were whole, unravaged, and fragrant, and immediately he was healed. He later built a church on that spot and dedicated it to St. Nicholas. To this day, the holy relics are fragrant and have worked many miracles for the faithful.

SAINTS OF THE DAY: Isaiah the Prophet; Christopher of Lycia, and with him Callinica, Aquilina, and 200 soldiers; Epimachus of Pelusium; Gordion at Rome; Maximus III, Bishop of Jerusalem; Nicholas of Vuneni, of Larissa in Thessaly; Joseph of Optina Monastery; Shio of Mgvime, Georgia; Translation of the relics of St. Nicholas the Wonderworker from Myra to Bari; Translation of the relics of Child-martyr St. Gabriel of Slutsk; "Zarazsk" Icon of St. Nicholas the Wonderworker.

SUNDAY

MAY 10

Sunday of the Paralytic
Fast-free
Acts 9:32-42; John 5:1-15

No matter where [difficulties] come from, the main task is to try to deal with the situation wisely and use it to advance spiritually, by converting the hardship into a blessing and the deep darkness into the true light. No one is exempt from hardship, neither sinners nor holy men, nor rich or poor; everybody is bound to taste the bitterness of tribulation at some point.
Metropolitan Athanasios of Limassol (Cyprus)

HOLY APOSTLE SIMON THE ZEALOT. Simon was the groom at the wedding in Cana where Jesus performed his first miracle, turning water into wine. When Simon witnessed this miracle, he forsook his bride and followed the Lord with zeal, thus the name "the Zealot." Simon was numbered among the twelve apostles. When Simon received the Holy Spirit, he went and preached Christ in faraway places like Africa and Great Britain. Simon was tortured and finally crucified in pagan Britain.

SAINTS OF THE DAY: Apostle Simon the Zealot; Alphaeus, Philadelphus, Cyprian, Onesimus, Erasmus, and 14 others, in Sicily; Simon, Bishop of Vladimir; Hesychius the Palantine of Antioch; Simon of Yurievets and Zharki, fool-for-Christ; Lawrence, of Mt. Pilion in Volos; Eustathius the Youth at Theodosia (Crimea); Conleth of Kildare; Synesius of Irkutsk; Lawrence, monk of Egypt; Comgall, founder of Bangor; Translation of relics of St. Basil of Mangazea, Siberia; "Kiev-Bratsk" Icon of the Mother of God.

Monday   Fast-free

May 11

Acts 10:1-16; John 6:56-69

What we say remains to eternity.

+Gerontissa Gavrielia of Greece

SAINTS OLYMPIA AND EUPHROSYNE OF KARYES. On the thirteenth-century island of Mytilene, near the village of Thermi, there was a monastery on a hill called Karyes, and the abbess was Olympia. Hundreds of years later, in 1961 and 1962, she appeared in a series of dreams to various people relating her story. She became a nun at the age of nineteen, and at twenty-five was made the abbess of a community of thirty nuns. In 1235 pirates attacked the convent, and at first, tried to defile the nuns. Some nuns fled into the mountains, but many were raped and slaughtered. Mother Euphrosyne was old and infirm and could not hide, and she was tortured much and burned alive. Olympia decided not to flee. Her flesh was burned with torches. She was nailed to a board with twenty nails, and three large nails were hammered into her head. After she died, they burned down the monastery and its beautiful church. In 1962 a man named Kostas Kanellos had a dream of Mother Olympia, and she told him where to dig. Thinking that he was digging for an icon, he instead discovered an ancient tomb. The bones inside were half powder mingled with large nails. After a few days, a woman named Anthoula Alaterou had a dream where she was helping nuns wash the bones and nails that had been found. St. Raphael, who was martyred two hundred years after Olympia, appeared and confirmed that the bones and nails found were those of St. Olympia. The relics of St. Olympia can still be venerated at Thermi in Mytilene at the Monastery of Saints Raphael, Nicholas, and Irene.

SAINTS OF THE DAY: Cyril and Methodius, Equal-to-the-Apostles; Mocius of Amphipolis; Nicodemus of Pech; Dioscorus the New and Argyros of Thessalonica; Sophronius of the Kiev Caves; Rostislav of Greater Moravia; Cathan of Bute; Joseph of Astrakhan; Olympia and Euphrosyne of Karyes; Mayeul of Cluny; Asaph of Llanelwy; Acacius of Lower Moesia; Theophylactus of Stavropol; Christesia of Gareji; Bassus of Persia.

Tuesday   **Fast-free**

May 12

Acts 10:21-33; John 7:1-13

*G*od never abandons a soul that puts its trust in Him, even though it is overpowered by temptations, for He is aware of all weaknesses. A man knows the weight that can be placed on the back of an ass, a mule or a camel, and burdens each beast with as much as it can carry; the potter knows how long he must keep his clay in the fire, for if he exposes it too long to the flames, the pot will crack, and if he does not bake it long enough, it will not be fit for use. Now if a man has judgment as precise as this, how infinitely greater is the wisdom of God in judging the degree of temptation which a soul is able to bear?

St. Nilus of Sora

ST. GERMANOS, PATRIARCH OF CONSTANTINOPLE. Germanos was the son of Justinian the Patrician who was killed by Constantinos Pogonatos in seventh-century Constantinople. Germanos was sent to a monastery where he studied the Holy Scriptures. He led a holy life and was later ordained Bishop of Cyzicus. During this time the Church needed a sensible and knowledgeable man to lead it, so he was elevated to the patriarchal throne in Constantinople, where he remained for over fourteen years. From this position, he rebuked the heretic emperor Leo the Isaurian and the iconoclasts. Isaurian forced Germanos to resign over their conflict, and he had soldiers beat the aged patriarch and physically remove him from the Patriarchate. St. Germanos lived out his days at a monastery and died peacefully at the age of ninety-five. His writings were numerous. Three of his letters were read after his death at the Seventh Ecumenical Council.

SAINTS OF THE DAY: Germanus, Patriarch of Constantinople; Sabinos of Cyprus; Pancratius of Rome; Epiphanios of Cyprus; Polybius of Cyprus; Athanasia of Smolensk Hodigitria Convent; Philip of Sicily; Theodore of Cythera; John of Serres; John of Wallachia; Dionysius and Anthony, Archimandrite of St. Sergius Lavra; Glorification of St. Hermogenes, Patriarch of Moscow and All Russia.

Wednesday

May 13

Mid-Pentecost
Abstain from meat and dairy products.
Acts 14:6-18; John 7:14-30

We try to stand before God with the whole of our being. Invocation of the Name of God the Savior, uttered in the fear of God, together with a constant effort to live in accordance with the commandments, little by little leads to a blessed fusion of all our powers. We must never seek to hurry in our ascetic striving. It is essential to discard any idea of achieving the maximum in the shortest possible time. God does not force us, but neither can we compel Him to anything whatsoever. Results obtained by artificial means do not last long and, more importantly, do not unite our spirit with the Spirit of the Living God.

+*Elder Sophrony of Essex*

MARTYR LAODICIUS, KEEPER OF THE PRISON. In the city of Heraclea in Thrace, Saint Glykeria was tortured during the second-century persecutions of Emperor Antoninus. When she was imprisoned, they threw her onto sharp stones, but she prayed without ceasing, and at midnight, an angel of God appeared and completely healed her. When Laodicius walked into her cell in the morning, he did not recognize her. He was about to kill himself, thinking that he would be punished, but Glykeria stopped him. Amazed at this miracle, he came to believe in Christ. He asked Glykeria to pray that he might suffer and die for Christ with her. At St. Glykeria's trial, Laodicius told everyone about the miracle, confessed that he also was a Christian, and for this, he was beheaded. Christians buried his relics.

SAINTS OF THE DAY: Glyceria and Laodicius, at Heraclea; Sergios the Confessor; George the Confessor of Constantinople, his wife Irene, and children; Pausicacius of Synnada; Alexander of Rome; Nicephorus of Ephapsios Monastery; John, Euthymius, George, and Gabriel of Iveron; Servatius of Maastricht; Alexander of Tiverias; Leander of Seville; Macarius, Amphilochius, and Tarasius of Glushitsa; Glyceria of Novgorod; Basil, Christopher, Alexander, Macarius, and Sergius of Moscow; Translation of the relics of St. Macarius of Kanev.

THURSDAY   **Fast-free**

May 14

Acts 10:34-43; John 8:12-20

Never judge priests, because when a priest is destroyed in the consciousness of the world, many Christians are ruined together with him.

+Elder Bessarion the Agathonite

HIEROMARTYR THERAPON, BISHOP OF CYPRUS. It is believed that St. Therapon lived sometime between the sixth and eighth centuries. According to tradition, he traveled to Jerusalem on a pilgrimage, where he became a monk. From there he arrived in Cyprus and became Bishop of Kition, where he was known as a wonderworker. He was killed by Arab pirates while celebrating the Divine Liturgy. A church was built dedicated to him, where his relics became a source of miracles. In the year 806, Therapon appeared in a vision to the sexton of that church, warning him that infidels would attack the island. Therapon instructed him to take his relics to Constantinople. During the transfer, fragrant myrrh streamed from the saint's relics. A great storm arose, and the ship miraculously was saved. At first, the holy relics were kept in the Church of the Theotokos at Blachernae, but later they were moved to a church dedicated to him. The myrrh continued to flow, and the sick with the gravest of illnesses were cured.

SAINTS OF THE DAY: Isidore of Chios; Serapion the Sindonite; Leontios, Patriarch of Jerusalem; Aprunculus of Clermont; Maximus, under Decius; Nicetas, Bishop of Novgorod; Alexander, Barbarus, and Acolythus in Constantinople; Alexander of Kentoukellai; Isidore, fool-for-Christ of Rostov; Mark of Crete; Nicetas, recluse of the Kiev Caves; John-Raiko of Bulgaria; Anthony, abbot in Russia, with 40 monks, 1,000 laymen, and Daniel, with 30 monks and 200 laymen; Andrew, abbot in Tyumen; Matthew of Yaransk; Therapon, Bishop of Cyprus; Uncovering of the relics of St. Tikhon, Bishop of Zadonsk; "Yaroslavl" (Pechersk) Icon of the Mother of God.

FRIDAY

MAY 15

Abstain from meat and dairy products, and fish.
Acts 10:44-11:10; John 8:21-30

"If you help a poor person in the name of the Lord, you are making a gift and at the same time granting a loan. You are making a gift because you have no expectation of being reimbursed by that poor person. You are granting a loan because the Lord will settle the account. It is not much that the Lord receives by means of the poor, but He will pay a great deal on their behalf. 'They who are kind to the poor lend to the Lord' (Prov. 19:17)."

St. Basil the Great

VENERABLE PANEGYRIOS THE WONDERWORKER. What we know of Panegyrios is information gathered from his Divine Service and depiction on his icon. He is portrayed as both a monk and priest in a liturgical vestment. From his Divine Service, it seems that he lived during a period of Arab raids in Cyprus. He taught the Christian way, and living as an ascetic, Panegyrios always had in mind the glory of the next life. St. Panegyrios was made worthy of performing miracles. He once expelled devastating locusts and cured the sick of various diseases.

SAINTS OF THE DAY: Pachomios the Great; Euphrosynus of Pskov and Serapion; Barbarus the Myrrh-gusher of Greece; Isaiah, Bishop of Rostov; Isaiah of the Kiev Caves; Andrew the Hermit of Epirus; Silvanus and Pachomius of Nerekhta; Dymphna of Geel; Hallvard of Husaby, Norway; Arethas of Valaam; Pachomius of Chernigov, Abercius, Priest Nicholas, and Vladimir Zagarsky; Achilles of Larissa; Jacob of Putna; Panegyrios of Cyprus; Kali of Crete; Martyrdom of Crown Prince Demetrius of Moscow; Translation of the Sacred Head of Apostle Titus; "Acheiropoieton" Icon of Christ in Kamouliana.

SATURDAY   Fast-free

May 16   Acts 12:1-11; John 8:31-42

God can fix everything in an instant. Correct all distortions. People make their plans, but God has His own plans. You would know how many times the devil wrapped the earth with his tail in order to destroy it. But God does not let him, He destroys his plans. And even the evil that is allowed to the good one, God uses for His own purposes, sends good. Do not worry!
St. Paisios the Athonite

ST. BRENDAN THE ANCHORITE, KNOWN AS "THE VOYAGER." Brendan was born in the late fifth century, near the present-day city of Tralee, Ireland. He was baptized by St. Erc and began his education in the priesthood at a very young age. He studied under St. Ita, as well as St. Erc, who ordained him. Over the next twenty years, he sailed all around the islands surrounding Ireland, spreading the word of God and founding monasteries. The most notable is Clonfert in Galway, founded in 557 A.D., which endured for over one thousand years. Brendan is most celebrated for his voyage to the "Land of Promise," a land far to the west. He and a small group of monks fasted forty days and set sail to investigate and convert the inhabitants. Altogether the journey took seven years, and this is why Brendan was made famous as a voyager. Many now believe that this land was Iceland. They explored a part of the area then returned to Ireland. Only a few survived the journey. St. Brendan died while visiting his sister, who was a nun. His grave can be found today at Clonfert Cathedral.

SAINTS OF THE DAY: Theodore the Sanctified; Nicholas I Mystikos, Patriarch of Constantinople; Abdas and Abdiesus, with 38 martyrs, in Persia; Peter of Blachernae; George II of Mytilene; Nicholas of Metsovo; Isaacius, Symeon and Bachthisoes of Persia; Martyr Papylinos; Alexander of Jerusalem; Euphemia near Neaorion; Cassian and Laurence of Komel; Ephraim of Novgorod; Musa of Rome; Bardas of Petra; Brendan the Voyager; Carantoc of Carhampton; Theodore of Vrsac; Vukasin of Klepci; Matthew of Yaransk; Silas, Paisios, and Nathan of Putna; Monk-martyrs of the community of St. Sava the Sanctified.

SUNDAY

MAY 17

Sunday of the Samaritan Woman
Fast-free
Acts 11:19-30; John 4:5-42

Let us honor one only, and everyone will honor us, for if we despise one, that is God, everyone will despise us, and we will be lost.
St. John the Dwarf

ST. ATHANASIOS THE NEW, ARCHBISHOP OF CHRISTIANOPOLIS. Athanasios was from Karytaina in southern Greece around 1604. When he was of age to marry, despite his desire to become a monk, his father insisted on marriage and betrothed his son to the daughter of a wealthy ruler in Patras. Then he sent his son to buy the wedding items. Athanasios obeyed and set off for Nafplion. On the way, he passed the church of the Panagia in Vidoni and asked for divine enlightenment. Then he bought what was needed for the wedding, but before his return trip, the Panagia appeared to him in a dream with St. John the Baptist. She told Athanasios to send his servants back with the wedding garments, so his betrothed could marry another, and that he should go to Constantinople to become a monk. He became a deacon and then a priest, and later Metropolitan of Christianopolis, within the city of Kyparissia. However, he inherited a province that was religiously, morally, and economically a disaster. He founded schools for the training of priesthood candidates and waived financial payments. He arranged for repair and maintenance of churches, which were the meeting place of Greeks. He worked to alleviate the suffering of his people, for orphans, widows, the needy, the elderly, and the persecuted. God made Athanasios worthy within his life and after to perform miracles. A few years after his death, St. Athanasios was exhumed, and his relic was found incorrupt and fragrant.

SAINTS OF THE DAY: Apostle Andronicus of the Seventy, and Junia; Solochon, Pamphamer, and Pamphalon at Chalcedon; Nectarios and Theophanes, builders of Varlaam Monastery; Athanasios the New of Christianopolis; Nicholas of Sofia; Andronicus the Gravedigger of Zverinets Monastery; Euphrosyne (Princess Eudocia) of Moscow; Melangell of Wales; Jonah Atamansky of Odessa; New Martyrs of Batak.

Monday

Fast-free

May 18

Acts 12:12-17; John 8:42-51

*W*hen we want mercy from God, we must first show ourselves worthy of this mercy.

St. John Chrysostom

MARTYRS PETER OF LAMPSAKOS, DIONYSIOS, ANDREW, PAUL, CHRISTINA, HERACLIOS, PAULINOS, AND VENEDIMOS, AT EURIDINOS. Peter was of noble lineage, but because he was a Christian, he was ridiculed and scorned. When he sought to reverse this scorn into reverence for Jesus Christ, he was arrested. When he denounced his idol-worshipping accusers as an affront to Christ and his convictions could not be altered, he was beaten to death. Andrew and Paul were military guards, who accompanied the Christian-hating Emperor Decius. They were sent to Athens to arrest the Christians Dionysios and sixteen-year-old Christina. The governor sent Andrew and Paul to the prison to violate Christina, but instead, she converted them to believe in Christ. When the soldiers openly confessed their faith, they were stoned to death, together with Dionysios. Christina was beheaded. Heraclios, Paulinos, and Venedimos were from Athens, and they converted many pagans. They were arrested, tortured, and thrown into a fiery furnace, in which they emerged unharmed by the power of God. Finally, they were beheaded.

SAINTS OF THE DAY: Peter of Lampsakos with Dionysia, Andrew, Paul, Christina, Heraclios, Paulinos, and Venedimos, at Euridinos; Tecusa with Alexandra, Claudia, Phaine, Euphrasia, Matrona, Julia, and Theodotus of Ancyra; Stephen the New, Patriarch of Constantinople; Theodore, Pope of Rome; Christina of Athens; Euphrasia of Nicaea; Symeon, Isaac, and Bachtisius of Persia; Potamon, Bishop of Heraclea; Anastaso of Lukada; Martinian of Areovinthus; Martyr Julian; Theodore in Orenburg; Davit and Tarichan of Georgia; Elgiva, Queen of England; Macarius, apostle to the Altai; Damian Strbac of Serbia; John Gashkevich of Korma; Commemoration of all Orthodox Martyrs slain under the Emperor Valens.

Tuesday   **Fast-free**

May 19

Acts 12:25-13:12; John 8:51-59

*K*now, my child, that the spirit of pride is difficult to overcome; the spirit of vainglory is many-headed and thorny. No matter how you change your thoughts or your way of life, you will find it in front of you like a thorn. And if this is how things are, what can we do? We should employ every means, whether mental or material, that leads us towards humility. Above all we have to coerce our mind to think humbly, and leave it to Divine Providence to arrange the deliverance from or reduction of this passion. On our part, we should persevere with a fighting spirit, and God, in proportion to our struggle, will intervene as a succor and helper.

St. Pambo of Nitria

VENERABLE JOHN, BISHOP OF THE GOTHIA IN CRIMEA. John showed his closeness to God by his gift of discernment and foretelling the day of his death. John was born to a Gothic family in Crimea during the eighth century. From an early age, he pursued asceticism. John made a pilgrimage to Jerusalem, visiting all the holy places. He returned to his country of Georgia, where he later became a bishop. He returned to the Goths who compelled him to become their bishop. John managed to escape to Amastris when the Khazars overtook the city of Gothia. He returned to guide his flock after the Khazar leader died and said that he would stand before God with him to be judged. Forty days later, St. John died. Many miracles took place at his grave.

SAINTS OF THE DAY: Patrick, Bishop of Prusa, and Acacius, Menander, and Polyenus; John, Conon, Jeremias, Cyril, Theoctistus, Barnabas, Maximus, Theognostus, Joseph, Gennadius, Gerasimus, Mark, and Herman of Cyprus; John, Bishop of the Goths; Kyriake and Theotima of Nicomedia; Demetrius Donskoy of Moscow; Acoluthus of the Thebaid; Memnon, wonderworker; Cornelius of Komel; Onuphrius of Kursk; Cornelius of Paleostrov; John (Ignatius) of Uglich; Ivan of Vologda; Sergius of Shukhtom; Dunstan of Canterbury; Valentin of Moscow; Synaxis of the Hieromartyrs of Kharkov.

WEDNESDAY

May 20

Abstain from meat and dairy products, and fish.
Acts 13:13-24; John 6:5-14

*D*o not believe your thoughts, neither when they tell you that you are terrible, nor when they tell you that you are a Saint.
St. Paisios the Athonite

STS. ZABULON AND SUSANNA, PARENTS OF ST. NINA OF GEORGIA. During a time of widespread pagan religions and Christian persecutions, Zabulon and Susanna converted many to Christianity. According to tradition, Nina and Great Martyr George were relatives on her father's side. At the time of St. George's martyrdom, Zabulon arrived in Rome, where he entered the emperor's army, and soon became famous as a courageous soldier. During a battle, he captured the Frankish king and his entourage and presented them to the Roman emperor who sentenced them to death. However, before this occurred, they asked to be baptized into the Christian faith. Zabulon himself became their godfather, then he implored the emperor to spare the life of his godchildren, and they were set free. Because of this, most of the Franks converted to Christianity. Zabulon later went on a pilgrimage to Jerusalem and entered into the service of Patriarch Juvenal. He gave away all his possessions to the poor, and shortly after married Susanna, the Patriarch's sister. The couple moved to Cappadocia and had their daughter Nina, whom they raised together to the age of twelve. With the Patriarch's blessing, Zabulon departed into the wilderness to live as an ascetic and Susanna continued to help the poor in Jerusalem, as she had in Cappadocia. A Georgian hymn relates that Zabulon converted the Gauls with his sword and Nina converted the country of Georgia with the cross.

SAINTS OF THE DAY: Thalaleos with Alexander and Asterios, at Aegae in Cilicia; Lydia of Philippi; Thalassios the Myrrh-gusher of Libya; Zabulon and Susanna, parents of St. Nina; Stephen of Piper; Asclas of Egypt; Dovmont-Timothy, Prince of Pskov; Nicetas, John, and Joseph, monks on Chios; Ethelbert, King of East Anglia; Austregiselus, Bishop of Bourges; Dodo of St. Davit-Garesja Monastery, Georgia.

THURSDAY

MAY 21

Sts. Constantine & Helen,
Equal-to-the Apostles
Fast-free
Acts 26:1, 12-20; John 10:1-9

In reality man's vocation in life is one. It is love: an exodus, a departure from the narrow prison of self-love for the promised land, the land of the Other, of my brother, my God.
Archimandrite Vasileios of Iveron, Mt. Athos

STS. CONSTANTINE, MICHAEL, AND THEODORE OF MUROM. The Christian Prince Constantine and his two sons, Michael and Theodore, had charge over a pagan people in Murom during the eleventh and twelfth centuries. Constantine sent Michael as an emissary to the Murom people, but they murdered him. When Constantine arrived with his entourage, the anger subsided, but the people would not give up paganism. Once, they went to the prince's house, intending to kill him, but he came out carrying the Murom-Ryazan Icon of the Mother of God, which placated the crowd, and they agreed to accept holy baptism at the Oka River. Constantine passionately helped Theodore spread Christianity, and he also built a church in honor of the Annunciation at the place where Michael was murdered. Constantine and his sons are buried next to each other in the church of the Annunciation in Murom.

SAINTS OF THE DAY: Equal-to-the-Apostles Emperor Constantine and Helen, his mother; Basil, Bishop of Ryazan; Constantine, Michael, and Theodore, wonderworkers of Murom; Cassian the Greek, monk of Uglich; Secundus and those with him, in Alexandria; Cyril, Bishop of Rostov; Pachomios of Patmos (Mt. Athos); Hospicius of Trier; Helen of Dechani, Serbia; Agapitus of Markushev; Synaxis of the Saints of Simbirsk and Karelia; Synaxis of the Hieromartyrs of Ufa; Meeting of the Vladimir Icon of the Mother of God; Pskov-Pechersk "Virgin of Tenderness," "Zaonikievsky," "Oransk," and "Krasnogorsk" Icons of the Mother of God.

Friday

May 22

Abstain from meat and dairy products, and fish.
Acts 15:5-12; John 10:17-28

As far as the truth of Orthodoxy is concerned, there is no room for the slightest doubt. The Holy Spirit presided over the Ecumenical Councils. Whatever the saints of God said, they said with the Spirit of God, and as proof of this, we have the sanctity of their holy relic.

Elder Ephraim of Arizona

MARTYRS CASTUS AND AIMILIUS OF CARTHAGE. Castus and Aimilius were imprisoned in Carthage in the year 250 A.D. during the persecutions of the emperor Decius, and under torture and the threat of fire they denied that they were Christians and were released. However, the second time they were arrested, they endured the tortures for martyrdom. Their bodies were lacerated, and blood flowed, then they were burned to death. St. Augustine writes that perhaps at the first trial, they relied presumptuously on their own powers, and that is why they fell away. The Lord squashed them in their self-assurance. The second time he called them in their faith and came to their aid as they fought. St. Augustine writes, "Let us remember that we shouldn't have too much confidence in ourselves. Let us entrust to God whatever good qualities we have; what we have rather less of, let us implore from Him."

SAINTS OF THE DAY: Commemoration of the Second Ecumenical Council; Melchisedec, King of Salem; John-Vladimir, King of Serbia; Basiliskos, Bishop of Comana; Donatus, Bishop of Thmuis, with Macarius and Theodore; James of Borovichi (Novgorod); Markella and Codratus; Sophia the Healer; Zachariah of Prusa; Paul and Demetrius of Tripoli, near Kalavryta; Maxim, Bishop of Serpukhov; Castus and Aimilius of Carthage.

SATURDAY   Fast-free

May 23
Acts 15:35-41; John 10:27-38

The Lord prolongs or shortens our days, judging by whether we can expect some good from us or not.
St. Theophan the Recluse

MARTYRS DONATIAN AND ROGATIAN OF NANTES. Donatian and Rogatian were brothers during the third- and fourth-century reign of Roman Emperor Maximian. Donatian, the youngest, was a nobleman and he was baptized. Then Donatian evangelized Rogatian, and he became a catechumen. They were denounced as Christians and arrested. When they appeared before the provincial governor, they were asked to sacrifice to idols. They refused, were tortured, and spent their last night together praying while bound in chains. Rogatian lamented that he was not baptized, but Donatian assured him that the blood of his martyrdom would take its place. Their joints were dislocated on the rack; they were whipped, speared in the throat, and beheaded. They were buried by St. Similien, Bishop of Nantes, and a church was built over the graves. Twenty-one years later, their relics were placed in a sarcophagus which attracted many pilgrims and required a monastic guard of honor. The saints' relics were displaced during the Norman invasions and were scattered during the French Revolution. Today a small portion of their relics survive.

SAINTS OF THE DAY: Michael the Confessor, Bishop of Synnada; Mary Cleopa the Myrrh-bearer; Michael the Black-robed of St. Sabbas Monastery; Salonas the Roman; Paisius, abbot of Galich; Martyr Seleucus; Damian of Georgia; Euphrosyne, Princess of Polotsk; Ioannicius I, Archbishop of Serbia; Desiderius, Bishop of Vienne; Donatian and Rogatian of Nantes; Theodore of Murom; Translation of the relics of St. Joachim of Ithaca; Uncovering of the relics of St. Leontios, Bishop of Rostov; Uncovering of the relics of St. Abramius of Rostov; Synaxis of All Saints of Rostov and Yaroslavl; "Thou Art the Vineyard" Icon of the Mother of God.

SUNDAY

May 24

Sunday of the Blind Man
Fast-free

Acts 16:16-34; John 9:1-38

Almsgiving must be done in secret.

+*Elder Paisius of Sihla*

MARTYR MARTHA OF MONEMVASIA, ABBESS OF MOST HOLY THEOTOKOS MONASTERY. This monastery was located below the Church of the Hodegetria in Monemvasia. Bishop Paul of Monemvasia wrote the life story of St. Martha in the tenth century. Martha suffered from a hemorrhage. One day an elder monk went to visit her, and he asked her for one of her garments. She said that due to her hemorrhage, she only had two garments; one she would wear while the other was being laundered. However, Martha gave him the laundered garment. As soon as he left, Martha noticed that the hemorrhage had ceased, and she realized the miracle. The monk was nowhere to be found. On that very day, at that same hour, the monk appeared to Martha's relatives in Thessalonica. He gave them her garment and instructed them to tell Martha, "Many things await you." Then he disappeared. They went to Monemvasia and told Martha all that had happened, including the day and hour, and they all surmised that the old monk was St. John the Theologian and Evangelist. Another time, Martha had a vision of the Mother of God, sitting in the sanctuary while the nuns were chanting Matins for her Dormition. When the Doxology began at the end of Matins, the sisters began to sing too loudly, and the Theotokos disappeared. St. Martha revealed the vision to the nuns, and from that time on, they chanted the Doxology more quietly and with a contrite heart.

SAINTS OF THE DAY: Meletios Stratelates with Stephen, John and 1,218 soldiers with women and children, including Serapion of Egypt, Callinicus the Magician, Theodore, Faustus, Marciana, Susanna, Palladia, Cyriacus and Christian, and 12 tribunes, all suffering in Galatia; Gregory, Archbishop of Novgorod; Symeon Stylites (the Younger) of Wonderful Mountain; Vincent of Lerins; Nicetas the Stylite, wonderworker of Pereyaslavl-Zalesski; Martha, abbess of Monemvasia; Sava Brancovic.

MONDAY

MAY 25

Third Finding of the Precious Head of St. John the Baptist
Fast-free
2 Corinthians 4:6-15; Luke 7:17-30

*C*hrist in His justice rewards the living, the dead, and every single action.

St. Thalassios the Libyan

ST. ZENOBIUS, BISHOP OF FLORENCE. Zenobius was from a noble pagan family in Florence, Italy, in the fourth and fifth centuries. Bishop Theodore baptized Zenobius, and he brought his parents to Christianity. Zenobius rose rapidly to the position of an archdeacon. Because of his virtues and notable powers as a preacher, he became known to St. Ambrose and then to Pope Damasus I, who called him to Rome. He was given important missions, including delivering to Constantinople the papal message against the Arian heresy. When the pope died, Zenobius returned home to Florence, and when the bishop died, Zenobius was elevated to the see, to the great joy of the people. He evangelized Florence and the surrounding areas and fought against Arianism. He died at the age of ninety, and his relic is now at the church of Santa Maria del Fiore. Many miracles are attributed to him. It is said that St. Zenobius resurrected five dead people. One story relates that a child was run over and killed by a cart while playing. His crying mother brought the body to St. Zenobius' deacon, and by prayer to St. Zenobius, the saint revived and restored the child to his mother. Also, during the transfer of the saint's relics to the Florence Cathedral, his body touched a dead elm, and it burst into life.

SAINTS OF THE DAY: Third Finding of the Precious Head of St. John the Baptist; Martyr Celestine; Olbian, monk; Mary of Ustiug; Therapontus, Bishop of Cyprus; Innocent of Cherson; Aldhelm, Bishop of Sherborne; Thaddeus of Svyatogorsk; Zenobius, Bishop of Florence; Dionysius, Bishop of Milan; Synaxis of Saints of Volhynia: Yaropolk, Stephen, Macarius, Igor, and Juliana; Commemoration of the reunion of 3,000,000 Uniates with the Orthodox Church at Vilna in 1831; Commemoration of the Finding of the Sacred Icon of Great Martyr Demetrios the Myrrhgusher; "The Helper of the Sinners" Koretsk Icon of the Mother of God.

Tuesday   Fast-free

May 26
1 Corinthians 4:9-16; John 12:19-36

Many complain against technology. Many accuse modern technology for all the woes in the world. Is technology really to blame, or those who create technology and use it? Is a wooden cross to blame if somebody crucifies someone on it? Is a hammer to blame if a neighbor breaks his neighbor's skull? Technology does not feel good or evil. The same pipes can be used for drinking water or the sewer. Evil does not come from unfeeling, dead technology, but from the dead hearts of people.
St. Nikolai Velimirovich

ST. SYNESIOS, BISHOP OF KARPASIA. Synesios was the second bishop of the city of Karpasia on Cyprus. By the gentleness and sweetness of his words and convincing arguments reinforced by his many miracles, he confronted the numerous heresies of his time to protect his flock. He taught the enemies of the Church the true Gospel message and the correct path of the Christian faith. Even after his death, he continued to grant healings and miracles to those who ran to him with faith; most notably those who suffer from dysuria, which is pain during urination. In the village of Rizokarpaso, there is a church dedicated to Synesios. It is next to a cave where the saint had lived, in the central square. It is one of only three Orthodox churches in the occupied areas of Cyprus that is still functioning, and that has not been converted into a museum or mosque because of the few hundred Greek Cypriots that still live there.

SAINTS OF THE DAY: Apostles Carpus and Alphaeus, of the Seventy; Abercius and Helen, children of Apostle Alphaeus; Alexander of Thessalonica; Synesios, Bishop of Karpasia on Cyprus; Augustine of Canterbury, evangelizer of England; Milan Banjac and Milan Golubovic of Drvar, Serbia; Translation of the relics of St. George of Kratovo and Sofia, Bulgaria; Uncovering of the relics of St. Macarius, abbot of Kolyazin; "Tabynsk" Icon of the Mother of God.

Wednesday

May 27

Leave-taking of Pascha
Abstain from meat and dairy products.
Acts 18:22-28; John 12:36-47

Anybody who would attain a certain virtue cannot succeed unless he first hates the vice which is the antithesis of that virtue. If you wish to attain sorrow, then you must hate laughter. Do you long for humility? Then hate haughtiness. Do you wish to be temperate? Then hate gluttony. If you want to be pure, then hate lewdness. If it is poverty you long for, then hate material possessions. If you wish to be an almsgiver, then hate the greed for money.

+Abba John of Cyzicus

VENERABLE BEDE THE CONFESSOR. Bede was from seventh-century Jarrow, on the border of England and Scotland. At the age of seven, he was placed under the care of St. Benedict Biscop at the Monastery of St. Peter at Wearmouth to be educated. He became a monk and maintained his monastic disciplines while he continued to study the sciences. However, his chief preoccupation was the study of the Holy Scriptures. He also studied Greek and Hebrew. He was ordained deacon at the age of nineteen, and a priest at thirty. He hated sloth and used his time to read and pray, often bathed in tears. He wrote many books for the faithful and gained such a reputation that he was alternately known as the "Light of the Church," "Teacher of the English," and "Doctor of the Church." His teachings were powerful because he lived a holy life. At the age of 62, he suffered a terrible illness, but he never stopped praying and translating into English the Gospel of John. Just before his death, he completed the last sentence of his project. St. Bede's final words were, "Glory to the Father, and to the Son, and to the Holy Spirit."

SAINTS OF THE DAY: Helladius, bishop in the East; John the Russian; Therapontus of Sardis; Venerable Bede; Therapontes of White Lake; Martyrs Alypius and Eusebiotus; Michael of Parekhi, Georgia; Basil Khakhuli of Georgia; Julius the Veteran at Dorostolum; Therapontus of Monza; Lazarus the Clairvoyant; Translation of the relics of St. Nilus of Stolben Island and Sts. Cyprian, Photius, and Jonah, Metropolitans of Kiev.

Thursday

May 28

The Ascension of our Lord
Fast-free

Acts 1:1-12; Luke 24:36-53

*W*ho can describe the bond of God's love? Who is able to explain the majesty of its beauty? The height to which love leads is indescribable… In love the master received us, Jesus Christ our Lord, in accordance with God's will gave his blood for us, and his flesh for our flesh, and his life for our lives.

St. Clement of Rome

ST. NIKETAS, ARCHBISHOP OF CHALCEDON. Niketas was an eighth-century monk who helped widows, orphans, and the poor. He took care of strangers in his home and fought for those who had been wronged. He was made Metropolitan of Chalcedon and was a Confessor of the Orthodox faith. When Leo the Armenian began his attack on the icons and those who venerated them, Niketas took a stand and denounced these iconoclasts, encouraging his people to continue venerating the icons. Niketas was tortured and exiled, where he reposed in peace. His relics caused many miraculous healings.

SAINTS OF THE DAY: Niketas the Confessor, Bishop of Chalcedon; Eutychius, Bishop of Melitene; Crescens, Paul, and Dioscorides of Rome; Germanus, Bishop of Paris; Ignatius, Bishop of Rostov; Heliconis and Dapni of Thessalonica; Gerontius, Metropolitan of Moscow; Demetrios (Mitros) of Tripoli; Helen of Diveyevo; Macarius, Dionysius, Nicholas, Ignatius, and Peter; Zacharias of Prusa; Heraclius of Turkistan; Rodion (Fyodorov) of St. Sergius Lavra; Domnica of Cherson; Andrew, fool-for-Christ of Constantinople; Sophronius of Bulgaria; William of Languedoc (Gaul); "The Consoler of Angry Hearts" and "Unbreakable Wall" Icons of the Mother of God.

FRIDAY

May 29

Abstain from meat and dairy products, and fish.
Acts 19:1-8; John 14:1-11

*N*othing is more precious to man than intelligence. Its power is such as to enable us to adore God through intelligent speech and thanksgiving. By contrast, when we use futile or slanderous speech we condemn our soul. Now it is characteristic of an obtuse man to lay the blame for his sin on the conditions of his birth or on something else, while in fact his words and actions are evil through his own free choice.

St. Anthony the Great

HIEROMARTYR OLBIAN, BISHOP OF ANAEA, WITH HIS DISCIPLES. Olbian was a third-century bishop from Asia Minor. Emperor Maximian issued a decree to the governors demanding that all Christians offer sacrifice to the pagan god Rhea. When Olbian spoke before his persecutors, he denigrated their idols and gave sound evidence of the validity of his Christian faith. Since Olbian was a miracle-working leader and example for the Christians, the pagans began torturing him. They burned his body and organs with hot iron rods. When this failed to persuade him, he was stripped and beaten with clubs. After this, a great fire was lit, in which they threw Olbian and his three disciples, Symphoros, Callistos, and Macedonios. Wonderworking miracles were worked by St. Olbian during his life and after his repose.

SAINTS OF THE DAY: Commemoration of the First Ecumenical Council; Alexander, Patriarch of Alexandria; Theodosia of Constantinople; Theodosia of Tyre; John of Thessalonica, at Smyrna; Euthymios of Zela; Luke, hierarch-surgeon of Simferopol; Constantine XI, last Byzantine emperor; Olbian, Bishop of Aneus, and his disciples: Symphoros, Callistos, and Macedonios; Andrew Argentes of Chios; John of Ustiug, fool-for-Christ; Cyril, Carellus, Primolus, Phinodus, Venustus, Gissinus, Alexander, Tredentius, and Jocunda, at Caesarea; Commemoration of the Fall of Constantinople; "Surety of Sinners" Icon of the Mother of God in Moscow.

Saturday

Fast-free

May 30

Acts 20:7-12; John 14:10-21

The salvation of the soul is the only meaning of labor of man on earth.

St. Nikolai Velimerovich

VENERABLE BARLAAM OF CAESAREA. During the time of Constantine the Great, there lived in India a pagan king named Abenner. When his son Joasaph was born, he called together his astrologers and wise men to prophesy the child's future. Only one dared to tell the king that Joasaph would become a Christian and give up his throne. Abenner became furious and gave orders to kill all the Christians in his kingdom and to ban them from entering. He put Joasaph in a private, guarded castle in order to shield him, and he remained there for twenty years. During this time, he learned the skills of warfare and wisdom. He grew up into a fine and strong man, and finally, his father allowed him to see the kingdom. Joasaph saw that even though the world was a beautiful place, there were sorrows, sins, and death, so he sought to find what filled the soul. At this time, there was a desert-dwelling ascetic named Barlaam, and by a revelation from God, he changed his monastic clothing for a lay dress and sought out Joasaph. Barlaam under the guise of a merchant got into the castle and explained the Orthodox Christian faith to Joasaph, who then demanded to be baptized. In the following months, the entire household was converted, including King Abenner, who later became a hermit. Joasaph did become king, but he gave the kingdom to relatives. Wearing the hair shirt given to him by Barlaam, he searched for two years and finally found Barlaam at his cave. The two began to struggle together and Barlaam, who had struggled there for seventy years, died at the age of one hundred. Joasaph labored there for thirty-five years and died at the age of sixty.

SAINTS OF THE DAY: Isaac the Confessor; Emilia, mother of St. Basil the Great; James of Starotorzhok; Martyr Natalius; Barlaam of Caesarea; Martyrs Romanus, Meletius, and Euplius; Macrina, grandmother of St. Basil the Great; Hubert of Liege; Venantius of Gaul; Walstan of Bawburgh; Felix I, Pope of Rome.

SUNDAY

May 31

Fathers of the First Ecumenical Council
Fast-free
Acts 20:16-18, 28-36; John 17:1-13

Only he who leaves everything to the will of God can feel truly joyous, light and peaceful.

+*Elder Thaddeus of Vitovnica*

ST. PHILOTHEUS, METROPOLITAN OF TOBOLSK. Philotheus was from a seventeenth-century noble Ukrainian family. After completing his education, he married and was ordained to the priesthood. He served as a parish priest for several years, but when his wife died, he entered the Kiev Caves Lavra, eventually becoming the abbot. Tsar Peter I had Philotheus consecrated to the episcopate of the vast territory of Tobolsk and Siberia. He exerted great efforts to evangelize there. During his tenure, the number of churches in Siberia grew from 160 to 448. Thirty-six monasteries were created, and more than 40,000 pagans were converted to Orthodoxy. Because of illness, he interrupted his administration of the diocese. When he recovered, he concentrated on missionary work, making numerous trips to teach and convert the natives. He resumed his duties as metropolitan for a short time and died peacefully at the age of seventy-seven.

SAINTS OF THE DAY: Hermeias at Comana; Marus the Magician, who converted witnessing the martyrdom of St. Hermias; Hierotheus, Bishop of Nikolsk, and Seraphim Nikolsky; 5 Martyrs of Ascalon; Eustathius, Patriarch of Constantinople; Martyrs Eusebius and Charalampus; Philosophos of Alexandria; Philotheus, Metropolitan of Tobolsk; Philosophus Ornatsky, with Nicholas and Boris, in St. Petersburg; Winnow, Mancus, and Myrbad of Cornwall; First translation of the relics of St. Philip, Metropolitan of Moscow and All Russia; Finding of the relics of St. Nicholas the Deacon of Mytilene; (Last Sunday of May: Neomartyrs of Eurytania; the Co-Workers of the Apostle Paul; Finding of the Icon of Holy Great Martyr Demetrios the Myrrhgusher).

Just as a man sees another face to face, try thus to stand before the Lord, so that your soul is face to face with Him. This is something so natural that there should have no need to mention it specially, for by its very nature the soul should strive always towards God. And the Lord is always near. There is no need to arrange an introduction between them for they are old acquaintances.

St. Theophan the Recluse

MONDAY   Fast-free

JUNE 1
Acts 21:8-14; John 14:27-15:7

*L*ove has rightly been called the capital city of all virtues, the fulfillment of the Law and the Prophets. So let us make every effort to attain this holy love. By means of love we will be liberated from the tyranny of evil obsessions and be raised up high to heaven on the wings of goodness, and we will even see the face of God, so far as this is possible for human nature.
St. Theodoros the Ascetic

ST. DAVID OF GAREJI, GEORGIA. David was one of thirteen missionaries sent to the country of Georgia from Antioch by the command of the Theotokos, who was seen in a vision. Their assignment was to strengthen Orthodoxy, which they did by founding monasteries and performing miracles. In old age, David left the desert of Gareji to venerate the holy places in Jerusalem. When he saw the city from a distance, his humility would not allow him to walk in the footsteps of Jesus. Instead, he sent his disciples, and he carried back home three stones. An angel of God appeared to the patriarch of Jerusalem, telling him that one stone was a sufficient blessing for David. Some messengers overtook David and conveyed the angel's message. The one stone now lies on the saint's grave.

COMMEMORATIONS: Justin the Philosopher, and those with him at Rome: Justin, Chariton, Charita, Euelepistus, Hierax, Paeon, Liberianus, and Justus; Thespesius of Cappadocia; Metrios the Farmer of Myra; Dionysius of Glushitsa; Onuphrius of Kharkov; Firmus of Magus; Shio the New, David, Gabriel, and Paul of Gareji, Georgia; Justin Popovich of Chelije in Serbia; Martyr Neon; Ronan of Locronan; Agapitus of the Kiev Caves; Martyr Neon; Pyrros the Virgin; Wistan of Mercia; Caprais of Lerins; Deliverance of the Island of Lefkada from the Plague of 1743.

Tuesday

Fast-free

June 2

Acts 21:26-32; John 16:2-13

Anyone who is sick should seek the prayer of others, that they may be restored to health.

St. Ambrose of Milan

GREAT MARTYR JOHN THE NEW OF SUCEAVA. John was an Orthodox Christian trading merchant from fourteenth-century Trebizond. Once while traveling by ship, John discussed the Christian faith with a Venetian merchant, and this man developed a grudge against John because he had always won his arguments. When they docked in Cetatea Alba, the Venetian spread a rumor that John wanted to become a Muslim. When this reached the ears of the Tartar ruler, he called for John, who remembered Christ's words, "When they shall lead you, and deliver you up, take no thought beforehand what you shall speak…but whatsoever will be given you in that hour, speak that, for it is not you that speaks, but the Holy Spirit" (Mark 13:11). Indeed, the Holy Spirit helped John to repudiate the claims of the ruler and to confess his faith in Christ. He was beaten with canes so harshly that pieces of flesh fell away, but he was thankful to be found worthy. Then he was chained and imprisoned. The next morning, John cheerfully called the governor a tool of Satan. They beat him again, then tied him to a horse and dragged him through the streets. Finally, he was beheaded and left in the street. At night a pillar of light illuminated his body, and three angels sang Psalms and censed the relics. A Jew, thinking that Christians were taking the martyr away, took a bow and tried to shoot an arrow, but a force from heaven restrained him, and he was motionless all night. Many miracles are associated with St. John's relics.

COMMEMORATIONS: Nikephoros the Confessor; John the New of Suceava; Pothinus of Lyons; Sanctus, Maturas, Attalus, Blanding, Biblis, Ponticus, Alexanders, and others, at Lyon; Marinus of Constantinople; Constantine the Hagarene; Nicholas the Pilgrim; Marcellinus and Peter of Rome; Nicephorus of Milet; Demetrius of Philadelphia; Andrew of Nizhegorod; Martyr Asprocastron; Erasmus of Formia, and 20,000 Martyrs; Odo of Canterbury; Marino, known as Baanes.

WEDNESDAY

JUNE 3

Abstain from meat and dairy products, and fish.
Acts 23:1-11; John 16:15-23

*B*lessed is he who is enriched with good hopes and illuminated with good thoughts: his glory is great and everlasting.
St. Ephraim the Syrian

HIEROMARTYR LUCIAN THE BISHOP, IN GAUL. The miracles of God can be extremely difficult for the finite mind to conceptualize. Lucian was a pagan living in Rome. He was converted to Christ by the Apostle Peter and accepted holy baptism. Lucian preached the Gospel in Italy. St. Clement, Pope of Rome, sent Lucian to Gaul and Belgium to preach, along with St. Dionysios the Areopagite. Lucian was successful in converting large numbers of pagans until almost all of Belgium converted to faith in Christ. During this time, the Roman Emperor Dometian began a second persecution of Christians. Soldiers were sent to Belgium to kill the missionaries and anyone else who would not offer sacrifice to the pagan gods. Lucian gathered his flock and urged them not to be afraid of threats, torture, or death. Lucian and the others were led away to trial, and the judge accused them of sorcery. After fierce beatings, Lucian was beheaded. A bright light shone on his body, and a Voice from heaven was heard. By the power of God, the saint stood up, and taking his severed head, he crossed the river, laid down upon the ground, and reposed. About 500 pagans who witnessed this miracle were converted to Christ. A church was built over the relics of St. Lucian.

COMMEMORATIONS: Lucillian and those with him at Byzantium: Hypatios, Paul, Claudius, Dionysios, and Virgin Paula; Athanasius the Wonderworker of Cilicia; Lucian the bishop, and Maxianus, Julian, Marcellinus, and Saturninus, at Beauvais (Gaul); Achilles, Bishop of Alexandria; Barsabus of Ishtar, and 10 companions in Persia; Hieria of Mesopotamia; Chlotilda, Queen of France; Joseph, Metropolitan of Thessalonica; Cyprian Nelidov of Moscow; Kevin of Glendalough; Pappos, Bishop of Chytri in Cyprus; Isaac of Cordoba; Dorotheos Proios, Metropolitan of Adrianople; Gregory, Bishop of Derkoi.

Thursday

June 4

**St. Metrophanes,
Archbishop of Constantinople
Fast-free**
Hebrews 7:26-8:2; John 10:1-9

We must not approach Christ out of fear of how we will die and of what will become of us. Rather, we must open out hearts to Him, as when we tug at a window curtain and the sun immediately shines in. In this way Christ will come to us, that we might truly love Him. This is the best way.

St. Porphyrios the Kapsokalyvite

MARTYR CONCORDIOS OF SPOLETO, ITALY. Concordios, by the example of his father, the presbyter Gordian, fasted, prayed, and gave alms to the poor. Because of his piety, Bishop Pius of Rome made him a sub-deacon. With his father's permission, he moved in with a relative not far from Rome and spent his days in prayer and good works. When Torquatus, the head of the Tussa region, heard of the saint's piety, he sent for him and offered to make him a priest of his pagan gods. Concordios tried to persuade the ruler to become a believer in Jesus Christ. For this, he was beaten and imprisoned, but Bishop Anthymus secured his release from prison. He took him into his home and sometime later ordained him a priest. Concordios was summoned again to Torquatus and was asked what he thought about his life. When he answered that life for him was Christ, he was imprisoned and chained to a wall by his neck for three days. When they demanded that he worship Zeus, Concordios declared glory to Jesus Christ and spat on the idol. St. Concordios willingly bent his neck and was beheaded, about the year 175.

COMMEMORATIONS: Metrophanes, first patriarch of Constantinople; Andronicus, Archbishop of Perm; Basil, Archbishop of Chernigov; Mary and Martha, sisters of St. Lazarus; Concordios of Spoleto; Alonius of Scete in Egypt; Frontasius, Severinus, Severian, and Silanus of Gaul; Astius of Dyrrachium; Zosimas of Cilicia, Bishop of New Babylon; Sophia of Thrace; Optatus, Bishop of Milevum; Methodius of Peshnosha; Eleazar and Nazarius of Olonets; Titus, Bishop of Byzantium; John of Monagria; Ioannicus of Montenegro; Petroc of Cornwall; Martyrs of Niculitsel.

Friday

June 5

Leave-taking of the Holy Ascension
Abstain from meat and dairy products, and fish.
Acts 27:1-28:1; John 17:18-26

Suffering reminds the wise man of God, but crushes those who forget Him.

St. Mark the Ascetic

ST. PETER OF KORISHA. Peter was a meek child from thirteenth-century Russia, near the city of Pech. From an early age, he and his sister Helena fasted and prayed. When Peter was ten, he told his parents that he wanted to become a monk. Within two years of each other, both parents died, and Peter, then sixteen years old, received monastic tonsure. Peter built separate cells for himself and Helena and lived in asceticism. Before long, pilgrims began to seek them out for healing and counseling, so they moved to a more remote area on a mountaintop named Korisha. Peter soon decided to leave his sister to live alone in a cave for greater solitude, enduring winters, summers, and the incessant attacks of demons. He would sing Psalms and hymns all night to ward off these attacks. Archangel Michael once appeared to Peter and drove off the demons. The Archangel told him to call upon the name of the Lord whenever he was attacked. Many monks came to live near him, and he accepted and guided them. Foreseeing his death, Peter instructed the monks to dig him a grave inside his cave. On the night of the saint's death, the monks saw a heavenly light shining in the cave, and they heard angelic singing. St. Peter's face was radiant, and the cave was filled with a beautiful fragrance. Many Orthodox believers receive spiritual and bodily healing through his miracle-working relics.

COMMEMORATIONS: Dorotheos, Bishop of Tyre; Dorotheos of Gaza; 10 Martyrs of Egypt; Christopher of Rome; Conon of Rome; Constantine, Metropolitan of Kiev; Illidius of Clermont; Dorotheus of Chiliokama; Agapius and Nicodemus of Vatopedi; Dorotheus of Thebes; Theodore of the Jordan; Theodore Yaroslavich, brother of St. Alexander Nevsky; Peter of Korisha; Boniface of Mainz (Germany); Mark of Smyrna; Nicholas of Vladimirskoye; Uncovering of the relics of Sts. Jonah and Bassian of Solovki; Translation of the relics of St. Igor-George of Kiev; "Igor" Icon of the Mother of God.

Saturday
June 6

Commemoration of the Departed
Fast-free
1 Thessalonians 4:13-17; John 21:14-25

The Church breathes prayer. Just as it is in nature, when during pregnancy a mother breathes and the strength she receives from this breath passes on to her child, so also in a grace-filled way the Church breathes a prayer which is shared by all, and the power of the prayer passes on to the reposed, who are held in the bosom of the Church, which is made up of the living and the dead, the militant and the triumphant. Do not be slothful about zealously commemorating all of our departed fathers and brothers whenever you pray. It will be your alms for them.

St. Theophan the Recluse

MARTYR GELASIOS. During a time of Christian persecution, Gelasios was filled with holy zeal, so he distributed all his possessions to the poor. He dressed in white garments and went to the place where the martyrs were being tormented. Gelasios showed them affection, asked for their prayers, and urged them to stand firm in the faith. When the pagans saw this, they arrested him and took him to the governor for interrogation. Gelasios answered the charges by ridiculing the pagan idols as senseless and deaf and confessed Jesus Christ as the true God. The ruler, however, did not perceive the saint as a threat and thought him worthless. After a light flogging, St. Gelasios was beheaded.

COMMEMORATIONS: Bessarion the Great of Egypt; 5 Virgin-martyrs of Caesarea in Palestine: Martha, Mary, Cyria, Valeria, and Marcia; Virgin-martyrs Archelais, Thecla, and Susanna, at Salerno; Attalus the Wonderworker; Hilarion the New; Justus, Patriarch of Alexandria; Anoub of Egypt, the Worker of Signs; Martyr Gelasius; Amandus, Amantius, Alexander, Lucius, Alexander, Alexandria, Donatus, and Peregrius in Scythia Minor; Claudius of Besancon, Gaul; Raphael of Optina Monastery; Jonah of Klimetsk; Paisius of Uglich; Jonah, Bishop of Perm; Jarlath of Cluainfois (Ireland); "Pimen" Icon of the Mother of God.

Sunday

June 7

Holy Pentecost
Fast-free Week
Acts 2:1-11; John 7:37-8:12

The whole praise and blessedness of the saints consists of these two elements—their orthodox faith and praiseworthy life, and the gift of the Holy Spirit and His spiritual gifts.
                                St. Symeon the New Theologian

---

VENERABLE PANAGIS BASIAS OF CEPHALONIA. Panagis was born in 1801 in Lixouri, Cephalonia to a pious and wealthy couple, and they gave him an excellent education. He spoke four languages, and he became a teacher. Inspired by the great ascetics of Cephalonia, he went to live at a monastery for a short time but returned home for his mother and sisters. At the age of 35, he was ordained to the priesthood and served at the Monastery of St. Spyridon near Lixouri. He distributed all his wealth to the needy. He liturgized and preached every day and would visit the faithful. He was an excellent confessor, and God granted him the gift of clairvoyance and prophecy. He could read the hearts of the faithful and lead them to repentance. His widespread fame as a miracle worker forced him to claim to be a fool-for-Christ's sake, to avoid egotism. Panagis did suffer a nervous breakdown. For the rest of his life, he lived with his family and liturgized at the church of St. Spyridon. During his last five years, he remained bedridden, and many would visit day and night for counsel and confession. St. Panagis died peacefully at the age of eighty-eight. There was a massively attended funeral service held over three days. A portion of his relics is displayed for veneration at Holy Cross Theological School in Brookline, Massachusetts.

COMMEMORATIONS: Marcellinus, Bishop of Rome, and those with him; Cyria, Valeria, and Marcia, of Caesarea; Theodotus of Ancyra; Lycarion of Hermopolis; Daniel of Scetis; Sebastiane the Wonderworker; Potamiane of Alexandria; Aesia and Susanna of Taormina; Panagis Basias of Cephalonia; Anthony of Kozha Lake; Zenaidos of Caesarea; Stephen and Anthimos of Constantinople; Martyrs Tarasius and John; Colman of Dromore, Ireland; Andronicus of Perm; Synaxis of All Saints of Ivanovo.

Monday

June 8

Feast of the Holy Spirit
Fast-free

Ephesians 5:8-19; Matthew 18:10-20

Revere every work, every thought of the Word of God, of the writings of the Holy Fathers, and amongst them, the various prayers and hymns which we hear in church or which we read at home, because they are all the breathing and words of the Holy Spirit.

St. John of Kronstadt

VENERABLE ZOSIMAS OF PHOENICIA. Zosimas was from the village of Synada in Syria. He was zealous in fasting, prayer, and the other virtues, and for this was granted the gift of clairvoyance. While in Caesarea, he foresaw the earthquake that destroyed Antioch in the year 526. Another time, when a patrician was visiting Zosimas, a messenger arrived informing the patrician that his wife was suffering terribly from a needle puncture to her eye. Zosimas assured the man that his wife was in the care of St. John Khozevites. The saint reached such spiritual heights that even animals obeyed him. Once, while on his way to Caesarea by donkey, a lion attacked the donkey and began eating it. Zosimas told the lion to carry his load the rest of the way, then to return to the wilderness. The lion did as he was told, and St. Zosimas set him free.

COMMEMORATIONS: Ephraim, Patriarch of Antioch; Nicander and Marcian at Dorostolum; Athre of Nitria; Naucratios of the Studion; Naukratios of Caesarea; brother of St. Basil the Great; Kalliope, at Rome; Theophanes at Constantinople; Medardus, Bishop of Noyon; Theodore, Bishop of Rostov; Zosimas of Phoenicia; Theophilus of Luga; Melania the Elder; Barlaam and Herman of Russia; Theodore of Kvelta, Georgia; Paul the Confessor of Kaiuma in Constantinople; Martyrs Mark and Nikandros; Chlodulf, Bishop of Metz; Uncovering of the relics of Sts. Basil and Constantine of Yaroslavl; Translation of the relics of St. Theodore Stratelates; Synaxis of the Mother of God and Archangel Michael at the Sosthenion; Synaxis of the Church of the Cross at Mtskheta, Georgia; Commemoration of the Blood-flowing Icon of St. Theodore in Karsatas.

TUESDAY   **Fast-free**

JUNE 9
Romans 1:1-7, 13-17; Matthew 4:23-5:13

We must always remember that the Lord sees us wrestling with the Enemy, and so we must never be afraid. Even should all hell fall upon us, we must be brave.

St. Silouan the Athonite

MARTYRS PRIMUS AND FELICIAN OF ROME. Primus and Felician were brothers in late third-century Rome. They spent their years in the practice of all good works. They gave whatever they had to the poor, spent nights and days with the confessors of Christ in the dungeons, or their places of torment and execution. Others who had fallen, they encouraged and raised up. The brothers escaped the dangers of many bloody persecutions, and they grew old in these heroic endeavors. However, the pagans raised such an outcry against them, that by joint order of both emperors Diocletian and Maximian, they were arrested and put in chains. Primus was eighty years old when this happened. They were inhumanly scourged in several towns as enemies of the pagan gods. They were tortured together, and later separately, telling each brother that the other had offered sacrifice. Both were beheaded and their bodies cast into a field, where Christians took them up and buried them. The relics were translated in the seventh century to the Church of Santo Stefano Rotondo in Rome, under an altar dedicated to them, where they now remain.

COMMEMORATIONS: Cyril, Archbishop of Alexandria; Holy 5 Virgins: Thecla, Mariamne, Martha, Mary, and Ennatha in Persia; Alexander, Bishop of Prusa; 3 Virgin-martyrs of Chios; Righteous Cyrus; Martyr Ananias; Cyril, founder of White Lake (Belozersk); Primus and Felician of Rome; Alexander, founder of Kushta (Vologda); Cyril of Velsk (Vologda); John of Shavta; Raphael of Moldavia; Columba of Iona; Baithene of Tiree; Alexius Mechev of Moscow.

WEDNESDAY

JUNE 10

Fast-free

Romans 1:18-27; Matthew 5:20-26

*W*hy did the Lord give me life? So that I would turn with my whole heart to God, for my purification and correction. Remember this and correct yourself.

St. John of Kronstadt

HIEROMARTYR TIMOTHY, BISHOP OF PRUSA. Timothy was a priest in fourth-century Bithynia. He governed his flock well, leading them to salvation. Because of his purity, God granted him the gift to work various miracles, and he converted many pagans to the faith. There was a great dragon that lived in a cave not far from Prusa, that with its very breath would kill the people who passed by the place. One day, as Timothy was passing by on his way to a neighboring village, the dragon rose up against him. The saint tightly rolled up his holy vestment and threw it at the dragon, and it withdrew from him, and he was able to pass. On his return, Timothy found the dragon dead, and he picked up his vestment and returned to his home. This miracle became known everywhere. When the emperor Julian the Apostate heard this and the many other miracles, he had Timothy put in prison. When St. Timothy would not deny his faith, he was beheaded. His relics were later transferred to Constantinople.

COMMEMORATIONS: Theophanes and Pansemne of Antioch; Timothy, Bishop of Prusa; John Maximovitch, Metropolitan of Tobolsk; Asterius, Bishop of Petra; Alexander and Antonina at Constantinople; Bassian, Bishop of Lodi in Lombardy; Canides of Cappadocia; Neaniscus the Wise of Alexandria; Mitrophan, the first Chinese priest, and the Chinese New Martyrs of the Boxer Uprising, at Peking and other places in 1900; Alexios of Bithynia; Silouan of the Far Caves in Kiev; Apollo, bishop; Landry, Bishop of Paris; Savvas the Stageiritis; Tamar, abbess of St. Seraphim-Znamensky Skete (Moscow); Translation of the relics of St. Basil, Bishop of Ryazan; Synaxis of the Saints of Siberia and Saints of Ryazan.

Thursday

June 11

Holy Apostle Bartholomew
Fast-free
1 Corinthians 4:9-16; Matthew 5:14-19

Let us therefore, both poor and rich, cease from taking the property of others. For my present discourse is not only to the rich, but to the poor also. For they too rob those who are poorer than themselves. And artisans who are better off, and more powerful, outsell the poorer and more distressed, tradesmen outsell tradesmen, and so all who are engaged in the market-place. So that I wish from every side to take away injustice.
St. John Chrysostom

VENERABLE BARNABAS THE WONDERWORKER OF VASA. As a young man, Vasa was admired for his modesty, and it is said that he was full of piety and goodness. When he decided to dedicate himself to the Lord, he went to live in a cave west of the village of Vasa in Cyprus. The cave was eighteen feet wide by twenty-eight feet long, and eight feet in height, and it exists to this day. Through continuous prayer, fasting, study, and repentance, he became an ascetic illumined with the Holy Spirit, and he received the grace to work miracles. The locals came to him for advice and prayers. When he died, his face was illuminated by divine grace, as bright as the sun. Some of the relics of St. Barnabas are preserved in Vasa, in the church dedicated to Panagia Evangelistria. On one of the saint's icons in the church is the inscription, "The memory of Jesus illumines the nous and dispels the demons."

COMMEMORATIONS: Holy Apostles Bartholomew and Barnabas; Niphon, Patriarch of Constantinople (Romania); Barnabas of Vetluga; Barnabas of Vasa in Cyprus; Martyr Theopemptus and 4 with him; Arcadius of Vyazma; Zafeirios of Halkidiki; Uncovering of the relics of St. Ephraim of New Torzhok; Commemoration of the appearance of Archangel Gabriel to a monk on Mt. Athos and the revelation of the hymn "It is Truly Meet" (Axion Esti); "It is Truly Meet" Icon of the Mother of God.

Friday

Fast-free

June 12

Romans 2:14-28; Matthew 5:33-41

The main goal of the monastic life is to unite monks very strongly with God, Who is the ultimate. When a person is united with God and God dwells within his heart, he lacks nothing. There is no void within his soul. Furthermore, he does not even lack any material thing necessary for living in this present life. This is but one more proof of how much God loves those who obey Him.

Elder Ephraim of Arizona

VENERABLE ONOUPHRIOS THE GREAT OF EGYPT. Abba Paphnutios desired to visit all the holy monks living in the desert to learn about their lives in serving God. An angel took him to an old ascetic in the desert that was about to die. The ascetic had lived there in solitude for seventy years, and his name was Onouphrios. He was born to a royal couple that prayed fervently for a son. An angel of God foretold his birth and name and that he must be dedicated to Jesus Christ. When they reposed, he was given over to the care of desert monks. He moved into a cave near Mt. Sinai, where he struggled, and his only sustenance was dirt until an angel finally brought him bread. A palm tree grew, providing him with dates, and a new spring gave him water. On Saturdays, an angel of God brought him Holy Communion. His beard and hair had reached his ankles, and white hair covered his whole body. The day after Abba Paphnutios arrived, Onouphrios told him that God had sent him, for he was about to die. Then kneeling in prayer, St. Onouphrios gave up his spirit. Paphnutios buried the saint under the palm tree.

COMMEMORATIONS: Onuphrius the Great; Onuphrius of Malsk; Onuphrius and Auxentius of Vologda; Antonina of Nicaea; Amphianos in Cilicia; Olympius in Thrace; Julian of Dagouta Church; John the Soldier; John of Trebizond; Peter of Mt. Athos; John Tornike of Mt. Athos; Stephen of Komel; Timothy of Egypt; Arsenius of Konevits; Bassian and Jonah of Solovki; Cunera of Rhenen; Synesios, Benedict, Timothy, and Paul of Thessalonica; Miracle-working icons of the Theotokos and St. Onuphrius at St. Onuphrius Monastery.

SATURDAY

JUNE 13

Leave-taking of Pentecost
Fast-free
Romans 1:7-12; Matthew 5:42-48

*H*ave you ever observed the life of the heart? Try it even for a short time and see what you find. Something unpleasant happens, and you get irritated; some misfortune occurs, and you pity yourself; you see someone whom you dislike, and animosity wells up within you; you meet one of your equals who has now outdistanced you on the social scale, and you begin to envy him; you think of your talents and capabilities, and you begin to grow proud... All this is rottenness: vainglory, carnal desire, gluttony, laziness, malice—one on top of the other, they destroy the heart. And all of this can pass through the heart in a matter of minutes. For this reason, one ascetic, who was extremely attentive to himself, was quite right in saying that "man's heart is filled with poisonous serpents. Only the hearts of saints are free from these serpents, the passions."

St. John Maximovitch

VENERABLE PHILOTHEOS OF SKLATAINA. St. Stephen Monastery at Meteora was initially built in the twelfth century. In the fifteenth century, Philotheos rebuilt the elegant Katholicon from its foundations. He also rebuilt the cells and other buildings of the monastery, so he became known as the second founder. Philotheos and another monk, Gerasimos, funded all the work. In 2004 a church was consecrated in Rizoma of Thessaly, the hometown of St. Philotheos, and dedicated to his memory.

COMMEMORATIONS: Aquilina of Byblos in Lebanon; Eulogius, Patriarch of Antioch; Anna and her son John of Constantinople; Antonina of Nicaea; Diodoros of Emesus; Antipater, Bishop of Bostra in Arabia; Triphyllios of Leukosia; Sabbas and Andronicus, abbots of Moscow; Anthimus the Georgian, Metropolitan of Wallachia; Alexandra, foundress of Diveyevo Convent; Philotheos of Sklataina; Synaxis of New Martyrs and Confessors of Zaporozhie (Ukraine); Finding of the relics of St. Nicholas of Karyes of Lesvos; "Lugansk" Icon of the Mother of God.

Sunday

June 14

All Saints Sunday
Fast-free
Hebrews 11:33-12:2
Matthew 10:32-33, 37-38, 19:27-30

The spirit of the saints burned with a bright flame, which the wind of temptation failed to extinguish but set burning stronger still.
St. Silouan the Athonite

VENERABLE JULITTA OF TABENNISI. Julitta and her mentor and closest friend Euphrasia lived in a fifth-century convent of 130 nuns in Tabennisi, Egypt. One day the abbess had a vision that Euphrasia would be leaving them in ten days. Upon hearing about the vision, one of the nuns told Euphrasia. Julitta speculated that perhaps Euphrasia's former fiancé had persuaded the emperor to remove her from the monastery, but she firmly replied that she would never abandon her Lord Christ. Julitta went to the abbess' cell and overheard her, saying that she saw in the vision two men in monastic habits coming to take Euphrasia, and the monks took her to Heaven. The abbess saw 10,000 angels and a numberless multitude of saints looking on, and the Mother of God escorted Euphrasia. Julitta told Euphrasia what she had heard, and that tomorrow she would die. The two nuns spent the night in the church alone, in silent vigil. Julitta told her friend to remember how close they had been on the earth and that she did not want to be separated from her. She asked Euphrasia to pray that the Lord will find her worthy to be together with her in the next life. The next day Euphrasia died. For three days, Julitta wept at her grave. On the fourth day, Julitta told the abbess that through Euphrasia's intercession, Christ was calling her, and the next day she died. St. Julitta was buried in the same tomb with St. Euphrasia. Thirty days after this, by the prayers of St. Euphrasia, Christ also called the abbess.

COMMEMORATIONS: Elisha the Prophet; Methodius, Patriarch of Constantinople; Niphon of Kapsokalyvia; Julitta of Tabennisi; John of Euchaita; Cyril of Gortyna; Methodius of Peshnosha; Sabbas, fool-for-Christ of Vatopedi; Elisha of Solovki; Joseph of Thessalonica; Mstislav-George, Prince of Novgorod; 11 Estonians Martyred during the Soviet occupation of Estonia; Synaxis of the Saints of Diveyevo.

Monday

JUNE 15

Fast of the Holy Apostles Begins
Abstain from meat and dairy products.
Romans 2:28-3:18; Matthew 6:31-7:9-11

*B*ecause we cannot see the Sun of righteousness Himself, let us see the mountains bathed in His brightness, I mean the holy apostles. They shine with virtues and gleam with miracles. The brightness of the risen Sun has poured over them. Since He is invisible Himself, He has made Himself visible to us through them, as if through mountains bathed in light.

St. Gregory the Great

HOLY PROPHET AMOS. "O Jerusalem, Jerusalem, the one who kills the prophets and stones those who are sent to her!" (Matthew 23:37). Amos was a prophet 800 years before Jesus Christ. He was born near Bethlehem and was a shepherd around Jerusalem. He became a powerful prophet who chastised King Uzziah and his idol-worshipping priests, who worshipped golden calves like the Hebrews that Moses had led through the desert. He prophesied that Israel would be defeated by the Assyrians, killing the king and sons of Amaziah. Amaziah had also led his people into idol-worship, for this Amos was persecuted. The son of an idol-worshipping priest struck down Amos, and he died from the blow.

COMMEMORATIONS: Prophet Amos; Apostles Stephanas, Achaicus, and Fortunatus, of the Seventy; Augustine, Bishop of Hippo, and his mother Monica; Dulas of Cilicia; Cedronus, Patriarch of Alexandria; Ephraim II, Patriarch of Serbia; Jonah, Metropolitan of Moscow; Modestus, Vitus, and Crescentia at Lucania; Doulas the Passion-bearer of Egypt; Hesychius the Soldier of Dorostolum; Lazar, Tsar of Serbia; Gregory and Cassian of Avnezh; Orsiesius of Tabennisi; Michael, first Metropolitan of Kiev; Martyr Grace; Symeon, Archbishop of Novgorod; Spyridon, Patriarch of Serbia; Abraham of Auvergne; Sergius and Barbara of Oyatsk; Jerome of Stridonium; Theophan of Roslavl Forests and Optina; Job of Ugolka; Synaxis of New Martyrs of Serbia; "Marianica" Icon of the Mother of God.

Tuesday

June 16

Abstain from meat and dairy products.

Romans 4:4-12; Matthew 7:15-21

How do we count the fruits of earthly blessings? If we … add to our account those who have fared well in combat through inflicting defeats in battle and other recorded deeds, these examples do not suit our objective. A Christian is ashamed at anything contrary to the faith and rejoices at praise coming from persons who love Christ much like those in the shadow of a notable person exult in his victories. Let us be silent about this world's glories despite their numerous accounts.

St. Gregory of Nyssa

HIEROMARTYR MARK, BISHOP OF APOLLONIA. According to Hippolytus in his work "On the Seventy Apostles," there were three named Mark that belonged to the Seventy Apostles: Mark the cousin of Barnabas, John Mark the Bishop of Byblos, and Mark the Evangelist. Hippolytus said that Mark, the cousin of Barnabas, was a leader of the apostolic Church and Bishop of Apollonia, and St. Paul calls him a "fellow worker." According to the Synaxarion of Constantinople, Bishop Mark of Apollonia was martyred when he was hanged upside down with boulders tied to his hands.

COMMEMORATIONS: Tychon the Wonderworker, Bishop of Amathus in Cyprus; Tigrius and Eutropius of Constantinople; Mnemonios, Bishop of Amathus; Mark the Just of Apollonia; 5 Martyrs of Nicomedia; 40 Martyrs of Rome; Kaikhosro the Georgian; Tikhon of Krestogorsk; Hermogenes, Bishop of Tobolsk, and Euphremius, Michael, Peter, and Constantine; Tikhon of Lukh; Tikhon of Kaluga and Medin; Moses of Optina, founder of Optina Skete; Translation of the relics of St. Theophan the Recluse; Synaxis of the Theotokos at Maranakios.

WEDNESDAY

Strict Fast

JUNE 17

Romans 4:13-25; Matthew 7:21-23

It is well to raise the hands in prayer and beg God that the soul after its departure might safely pass all those who strive to impede its way to Heaven.

St. Theodora of Alexandria

MARTYRS ISAUROS, BASIL, INNOCENT, FELIX, HERMIAS, PERIGRINOS, RUFUS, AND RUFINUS. In third-century Athens, the priest Isauros, together with Basil and Innocent, went to live the ascetical life in a cave in Apollonia, Albania because a divine angel instructed them to do so. There they found the Christians Felix, Peregrinos and Hermias. Isauros instructed them in the faith in exchange for food that the youths provided. Through these lessons, the three young men gradually began to change their ways, and they shunned their pagan families. However, the families of the three youths became incensed and reported the group to the prefect who had them arrested. Since the youths would not deny their faith in Christ, they were beheaded. Isauros, Basil, and Innocent were tortured by fire, water, the sword, and they endured terrible pain coupled with imprisonment. Through all of this, these confessors of the faith remained unharmed by divine providence. Because of this, many Greek pagans were converted to faith in Christ, including two brothers, Rufus and Rufinus, who were senators in the city of Apollonia. Finally, they were all beheaded.

COMMEMORATIONS: Joseph and Pior, disciples of St. Anthony the Great; Manuel, Sabel, and Ishmael of Persia; Philoneides, Bishop of Kurion in Cyprus; Aetius the Eunuch, enlightener of Ethiopia; Isauros, Basil, Innocent, Felix, Hermias, Perigrinos, Rufus, and Rufinus, of Apollonia; Ananias the Iconographer of Novgorod; Ismael of Russia; Shalva of Akhaltsikhe, Georgia; Nectan of Hartland; Botolph of Boston (England) and Adolph the Confessor; Nicander of Yaroslavl; Hypatius of Rufinianos; Martyrs of Atchara, Georgia; Uncovering of the relics of the Alfanov Brothers of Novgorod: Nicetas, Cyril, Nicephorus, Clement, and Isaac.

Thursday

June 18

Abstain from meat and dairy products.

Romans 5:10-16; Matthew 8:23-27

*T*he bodies of fellow human beings must be treated with greater care than our own. Christian love teaches us to give our brethren not only spiritual gifts, but material gifts as well. Even our last shirt, our last piece of bread must be given to them. Personal almsgiving and the most wide-ranging social work are equally justifiable and necessary. The way to God lies through love of other people and there is no other way. At the Last Judgment I shall not be asked if I was successful in my ascetic exercises or how many prostrations I made in the course of my prayers. I shall be asked, did I feed the hungry, clothe the naked, visit the sick and the prisoners: that is all I shall be asked.

St. Maria Skobtsova of Paris

VENERABLE LEONTIOS THE ATHONITE AND MYRRH-GUSHER. "From here to eternity" are the words of encouragement to a monk when he receives his new cell. It is there that he is to battle and defeat his passions. Leontios was born in sixteenth-century Argos of the Peloponnese. At the age of seventeen, he went to live in a monastery near his home. He fasted, prayed, studied Holy Scripture, kept vigil, and did good works. After the fall of Nafplio, he went to live on Mt. Athos at the monastery of Dionysiou. He lived in a small cell there for sixty years, without ever leaving the monastery grounds. He was granted the gift of prophecy and discernment, and for this reason, he was named the "Seer." With these gifts, he was able to guide his spiritual children. Having foreseen his death, he soon reposed peacefully. The relics of St. Leontios gushed fragrant myrrh.

COMMEMORATIONS: Marina the Virgin of Bithynia; Leontius, Hypatius, and Theodulus at Tripoli in Syria; Aetherus of Nicomedia; Leontius the Myrrh-flowing of Dionysiou Monastery, Mt. Athos; 2 Martyrs of Cyprus; Leontius, canonarch of the Kiev Caves; Nicanor (Morozkin) of Spas-Ruzsky; Leontius of Phoenicia; Erasmus, monk; Amand of Bordeaux; Alena of Belgium.

FRIDAY

JUNE 19

Holy Apostle Jude
Strict Fast
1 Jude 1:1-25; John 14:21-24

What has happened has happened—it is in the past. Just keep on going, all the while asking for help from God.
+Elder Thaddeus of Vitovnica

VENERABLE ZENO THE WONDERWORKER OF EGYPT. Zeno was a fifth-century monk in Egypt. He traveled in Egypt, Syria, and Palestine with the thought that he would never settle near a monk with a great name, never live in a famous place, and never build himself a permanent place to live. Zeno never wanted to be given anything but found that people were disappointed when he refused their gifts. He also noted that visitors hoped to be given some token but were always disappointed. Finally, he decided to take what was offered and gave from that. Zeno once wandered from his cell for three days and nights and became so exhausted that he fell to the ground. Suddenly, a child carrying bread and water stood before him, telling him to nourish himself. The child, who was a divine angel, told him to follow him, and immediately they were at the monk's cell. Zeno observed that Egyptian ascetics hid their virtues, accusing themselves of faults they did not have whereas the Syrian and Greek ascetics pretended to have virtues and hid their faults. Once during his travels, Zeno thought to take a cucumber from a plant that was not his, but after five days of prayer and self-examination, he realized he could not bear the penalty if caught. St. Zeno said, "If a man wants God to hear his prayer quickly, then before he prays for anything else, even his own soul, when he stands and stretches out his hands towards God, he must pray with all his heart for his enemies. Through this action, God will hear everything that he asks."

COMMEMORATIONS: Apostle Jude, the Brother of the Lord; Paisios the Great of Egypt; Paisius the Bulgarian of Hilander; Holy Myrrh-bearer Mary, mother of Apostle James; Zosimas the Soldier; Macarius of Petra; John the Solitary of Jerusalem; Romuald of Ravenna; Job, Patriarch of Moscow; Zeno of Egypt; Barlaam of Shenkursk; Parthenius of Russia; Asyncretus, martyred at the Church of Holy Peace by the Sea in Constantinople.

SATURDAY   **Abstain from meat and dairy products.**

JUNE 20

Romans 3:19-24; Matthew 7:1-8

Forgiveness is better than revenge.

St. Tikhon of Zadonsk

ST. LUCIUS THE CONFESSOR, BISHOP OF BRINDISI. Lucius was born in mid-fourth-century Alexandria to pious parents. At the age of eleven, his mother died. His father, desiring to become a monk, took the child with him to the Monastery of St. Hermias. Lucius was raised under the spiritual guidance of the abbot, and he diligently studied Holy Scripture. He became quiet, meek, and obedient. At the age of eighteen, the abbot died, and the monks chose Lucius as abbot, even though he was not yet tonsured a monk. He refused, and for seven years, the monastery was without an abbot. During this time, Lucius reached a high degree of virtue and spirituality. His father had a vision that his end was near and that his son would become the bishop of Brindisi. The bishop also heard a voice from heaven blessing Lucius for archpastoral service. When the monks of St. Hermias asked the bishop to install Lucius as abbot, Lucius was ordained to the priesthood and was made abbot. Because of his ascetic efforts, he was granted the gift of working miracles and casting out demons. Soon after, the bishop of Alexandria died, and Lucius replaced him. He converted many pagans to Christianity, so the eparch decided to kill Lucius. Lucius departed there by ship to the city of Brindisi. The head of the city, Antiochus, said to Lucius that if he wanted them to believe in the God he preached, to send down rain on the land to end a two-year drought. Then the rain poured, and 27,000 people accepted holy Baptism. After a short illness, St. Lucius died. Many miracles occurred at his grave.

COMMEMORATIONS: Callistus I, Patriarch of Constantinople; Studius of the Studion; Methodius of Patara; Lucius the Confessor; Paul, Cyriacus, Paula, Felicilana, Thomas, Felix, Martyrius, Vitaly, Crispinus, and Emilius in Tomi; Nicholas Cabasilas of Thessalonica; Nahum of Ochrid; Gleb of Vladimir; Minas of Polotsk; Florentina of Spain; Govan of Pembrokeshire; Finding of the relics of St. Raphael of Lesvos; "Directress" Icon of the Mother of God of Xenophontos.

Sunday

June 21

Second Sunday of Matthew
Abstain from meat and dairy products.
Romans 2:10-16; Matthew 4:18-23

Anger is implanted in us as a sort of sting, to make us gnash with our teeth against the devil, to make us vehement against him, not to set us in array against each other. We have arms, not to make us at war among ourselves, but that we may employ our whole armor against the enemy. Are you prone to anger? Be so against your own sins: chastise your soul, scourge your conscience, be a severe judge, and merciless in your sentence against your own sins. This is the way to turn anger to account. It was for this that God implanted it within us.

St. John Chrysostom

HIEROMARTYR TERENCE, BISHOP OF ICONIUM. Terence, also known as Tertius, was a wonderworker, martyr, and one of the Seventy Apostles. He was the second Bishop of Iconium, after St. Sosipater. Terence converted many pagans through his words and deeds done in the power of the Holy Spirit. He baptized those converted by St. Sosipater. He was also the scribe of the Apostle Paul's letter to the Romans. "I Tertius, the one writing this letter, greet you in the Lord (Romans 16:22)." Terence died after being pricked with thorns, perhaps by being dragged over them.

COMMEMORATIONS: Terence, Bishop of Iconium and Apostle of the Seventy; Julian of Tarsus in Cilicia; Theodore of Starodub; Julian of Egypt (Libya), and with him: Anthony, Anastasius, Celsius, Basilissa, Marcianilla, 20 prison guards, and 7 brothers; Aphrodisios in Cilicia; Demetria of Rome; Julius and Julian of Novara; Archil II and Laursab II, kings of Georgia; Nicetas of Nisyros, near Rhodes; Cormac of the Sea; Raoul, Archbishop of Bourges (Gaul); George (Lavrov) of Kaluga; Finding of the "Panagia Eleusa" Icon of the Mother of God in Xyniada; (2nd Sunday after Pentecost: Olga of Kwethluk; Finding of the relics of St. Basil of Ryazan; Synaxis of the Saints of Ryazan and Siberia; Synaxis of the Saints of North America); (9th Sunday after Pascha: "Tabynsk" Icon of the Mother of God).

Monday

Abstain from meat and dairy products.

June 22

Romans 7:1-14; Matthew 9:36-10:8

If you think little about yourself, you will have rest wherever you reside.

St. Poemen the Great

ST. GREGORY THE TEACHER OF VATOPEDI. Gregory was from eighteenth-century Bucharest. He studied at the most prestigious schools of the time, acquiring a serious theological grounding. Afterward, Gregory and two fellow students went to the Monastery of Neamt, and he was tonsured a monk. Because he knew Latin and Greek, his obedience was to translate the writings of the Holy Fathers. Gregory lived for a time on Mt. Athos at a dependency of Vatopedi Monastery. He returned to the Neamt monastery and for eight years continued to translate sacred books. He lived humbly in a small cell with the bare necessities. When the Prince of Wallachia heard of Gregory's wisdom and humility, he appointed him to the metropolitan's throne. Gregory refused to travel in a carriage and chose to walk to Bucharest. Along the way, he asked to stay at the home of a priest, but when the priest saw only an ordinary monk, dusty from the road, he sent him to the stable to sleep with the pigs. After his enthronement, Gregory appointed bishops and built churches, and founded schools in villages and towns. He also founded four seminaries, cared for the poor, the widows, and children. He also began repairs on the metropolitan cathedral church in Bucharest. Gregory published the Lives of the Saints in twelve volumes. The Russians exiled him for four years towards the end of his life. St. Gregory died shortly after his return to Bucharest.

COMMEMORATIONS: Paulinus, Bishop of Nola; Eusebius, Bishop of Samosata; Zenas and Zenon of Philadelphia in Arabia; Pompianos, Galacteon, Juliana, and Saturninos of Constantinople; Basil of Patalaria Monastery; Athanasius, Bishop of Chytri on Cyprus; Anastasia of Serbia, mother of St. Sava; Alban, Protomartyr of Britain; Gregory, Metropolitan of Wallachia; 1,480 Martyrs of Samaria in Palestine; Aaron of Britain.

Tuesday   **Abstain from meat and dairy products.**

June 23

Romans 7:14-8:2; Matthew 10:9-15

*B*efore holy baptism, grace encourages the soul toward good from the outside, while Satan lurks in its depths, trying to block all the intellect's ways of approach to the Divine. But from the moment that we are reborn through baptism, the demon is outside, grace is within. Thus, whereas before Baptism error ruled the soul, after baptism truth rules it.

St. Diadochos of Potiki

ST. ARTEMIOS OF VERKOULA. Artemios was the son of pious parents in the sixteenth-century village of Verkola. From his youth, he was known for his mild manner, fortitude, and diligence in doing good deeds. While out in a field with his father, a thunderstorm erupted and lightning killed twelve-year-old Artemios. The superstitious people believed that this was a sign of judgment by God, so they left the boy in the woods unburied, with no funeral. Thirty-two years later, a deacon out picking berries, saw a light emanating from the place where Artemios had been laid. He found the body of Artemios totally incorrupt as if he were sleeping. The local priest and villagers brought the relics of St. Artemios to the local church dedicated to St. Nicholas. Many miraculous healings have occurred.

COMMEMORATIONS: Eustochius, Gaius, Probus, Lollius, and Urban of Ancyra; Agrippina of Rome; Joseph, Anthony, and Ioannicius of Vologda; Dionysius of Polotsk; Leonty, Maximus, and Mitrophan of Russia; Artemius of Verkola; Aristocles, Demetrianos, and Athanasios of Cyprus; Nicetas of Thebes, with Theodore, Gregory, and Daniel; Etheldreda of Ely; Fomar (Tamara) of Moscow; Barbaros the Pentapolitis; Translation of the relics of St. Michael of Klops; Translation of the relics of St. Herman of Kazan; Synaxis of All Saints of Vladimir; Synaxis of the New Martyrs of Crete; The Meeting of the "Vladimir" Icon; Pskov "Umileniye" and "Zaonikiev" Icons of the Mother of God.

Wednesday
June 24

Nativity of St. John the Baptist
Abstain from meat and dairy products.
Romans 13:11-14:4; Luke 1:1-25, 57-68, 76-80

Your soul's coat must shine with the whiteness of simplicity.
St. Ignatius Brianchaninov

ST. ATHANASIOS OF PAROS, THE KOLLYVAS. Athanasios helped to spearhead the Kollyvades Movement, which began on Mt. Athos in the eighteenth century. Other members of the movement were St. Makarios Notaras, St. Neophytos Kavsokalyvitis, and St. Nicodemos the Hagiorite. The movement's name came from the Greek word for boiled wheat, *kollyva*. The members of the movement strictly followed the holy traditions of the Orthodox Church, to the exclusion of the progressive philosophies of the Age of Enlightenment that prevailed at that time. They were adherents of frequent Holy Communion and the Jesus Prayer, known as the "prayer of the heart." They were against having memorial services on Sunday, the day of the Lord's Resurrection, and said that Saturday was the usual day for the memorial service. Athanasios was ordained to the priesthood on Mt. Athos by St. Makarios. Twenty-five years later, Athanasios was labeled a heretic, stripped of his priesthood, and driven from Mt. Athos because he upheld the strict traditions of Orthodoxy. Five years later, the charges against him were proved unfounded, and he was restored to his former rank. Athanasios was a writer of the Lives of the Saints and the liturgical services held in their honor. He wrote other useful books, including his most important work, *Epitome*, on Orthodox dogma. St. Athanasios spent the last twenty-five years of his life on the island of Chios.

COMMEMORATIONS: Nativity of St. John the Baptist; Athanasios of Paros, the Kollyvas; John the New of Romania; Michael, Great Prince of Tver; John of Solovki; John and James of Novgorod; John the Hermit of Bohemia; Anthony, founder of Dymsk; Panagiotes of Caesarea; Nicetas, Bishop of Remesiana; Gerasimus, Bishop of Astrakhan and Enotaeva; Synaxis of the Righteous Zacharias and Elizabeth, parents of St. John the Baptist; Translation of the relics of St. John the New to Suceava, Romania.

Thursday

June 25

Abstain from meat and dairy products.

Romans 8:22-27; Matthew 10:23-31

Like an enormous ocean, like great rivers and valleys, may the Lord grant us so much patience. The grace of patience is the strongest grace, because patience is at the foundation of all virtues. We cannot perform a single virtue without patience.
+*Blessed Makrina of Portaria*

STS. PETER AND FEBRONIA, WONDERWORKERS OF MUROM. Peter was the second son of Prince Yuri Vladimirovich from twelfth-century Murom. As a young man, Peter contracted leprosy, which was incurable at the time. He had a vision that the daughter of a beekeeper in the village of Laskova could heal him. He sent for Febronia, and she healed him. Because of her piety, wisdom, and virtue, he fell in love with her and they married. They remained in love throughout their trials. The nobles of Murom railed at the fact that Febronia was of common birth and the royal couple was banished from the city. The wrath of God fell upon the city of Murom, and the people begged for their return. Peter and Febronia became famous for their charity and piety. Eventually, they entered different monasteries and received monastic tonsure. They died on the same day and same hour, and they were buried in the same grave. Saints Peter and Febronia are patron saints of newlyweds.

COMMEMORATIONS: Febronia of Nisibis; Gallicianus the Patrician; Symeon of Sinai; 7 Martyred Brothers: Orentius, Pharnacius, Eros, Firmus, Firminus, Cyriacus, and Longinus, near Lazica; Nikon of Optina; Dometius and Dionysios of the Monastery of the Forerunner, Mt. Athos; Theoleptus, Metropolitan of Philadelphia; Cyprian of Svyatogorsk Monastery; Methodius of Nivritos; George of Attalia; Peter and Febronia of Murom; Procopios of Varna & Mt. Athos, in Smyrna; Orosia of Spain; Adelbert, archdeacon; Virgin-martyrs Leonida, Liby, and Eutropia of Syria; Moluac of Lismore (Scotland).

Friday   **Strict Fast**

June 26

Romans 9:6-19; Matthew 10:32-36, 11:1

As a moth gnaws a garment, so doth envy consume a man.
St. John Chrysostom

WONDERWORKING ICON OF THE MOTHER OF GOD OF LYDDA, "THE ROMAN." According to tradition, the Apostles Peter and John were preaching in Lydda near Jerusalem. They built a church there dedicated to the Most Holy Theotokos and asked her to visit and sanctify the church. She said to them, "Go in peace, and I shall be there with you." When they arrived back in Lydda, they saw an icon of the Mother of God imprinted in color on the church wall. The icon was not made by hand, but by divine power. Then she appeared, happy about the number of people who had gathered there, and she blessed the icon and gave it the power to work miracles. When Julian the Apostate heard about the icon in the fourth century, he sent masons to chip away the image, but the paint and lines just penetrated further into the stone, and they were unable to destroy it. As word of this miracle spread, millions of people came to venerate it. In the eighth century, St. Germanos, the future Patriarch of Constantinople, had a copy made of the icon. He later sent it to Pope Gregory in Rome for protection during the iconoclast period. It is said that the icon miraculously arrived by itself. It was placed in the Church of St. Peter and became a source of many miracles. Over 100 years later, the icon was returned to Constantinople and was known as the Roman Icon. The transfer took place as follows: The icon would move and stand upright on its own during Matins and Vespers, and occasionally during the Divine Liturgy. It hovered over the heads of the faithful, and slowly left the church, arriving the next day in Constantinople.

COMMEMORATIONS: David of Thessalonica; John, Bishop of the Goths; Dionysius of Suzdal; David of St. Anne's Skete; Anthion, monk; Perseveranda of Spain; Brannock of England; Translation of the relics of Sts. Nilus of Stolobny and Tikhon of Lukhov; "Tikhvin," "Of the Seven Lakes," "Neamts," and "Lydda" Icons of the Mother of God.

SATURDAY

Abstain from meat and dairy products.

June 27

Romans 3:28-4:3; Matthew 7:24-8:4

Let us, therefore, forsake the vanity of the crowd and their false teachings, and turn back to the word delivered to us from the beginning.

St. Polycarp of Smyrna

HIEROMARTYR KIRION II, CATHOLICOS-PATRIARCH OF ALL GEORGIA. Kirion was from the nineteenth-century country of Georgia. He graduated from the Kiev Theological Academy, was appointed assistant dean of the Odessa Theological Seminary, and was active in the educational life of several cities. He was appointed a supervisor of the Georgian monasteries and dean of schools for the renewal of Christianity. He directed parochial schools, established libraries, and wrote articles on the history of the Georgian Church, folklore, and literature. At the age of thirty-one, he was tonsured a monk and was also selected abbot of the monastery. Twelve years later, he was made Bishop of Alaverdi, and immediately began to rebuild the Church using his own resources. When the Monophysites confiscated the Georgian churches, he sent a letter to the Russian exarch demanding their return. When Kirion was appointed Bishop of Gori, he led a movement of priests to regain the autocephaly of the Georgian Church, but the Russian government frustrated his efforts. Then the Russian regime became even more restrictive with him, and he was imprisoned. When he was finally released, he was elevated to archbishop of the areas in western Russia. When the Georgian Church declared its autocephaly in 1917, Kirion returned and was enthroned as Patriarch of All Georgia. One month after this, Georgia declared independence in the face of the communist revolution, and St. Kirion was found murdered in the Patriarchal residence.

COMMEMORATIONS: Joanna the Myrrh-bearer; Sampson the Hospitable; Kirion II of Georgia; Crescens, Maximus, and Theonest of Mainz; Martin of Turov; Anectus of Caesarea; Severus of Interocrea; Martin of Turov; Pierios of Antioch; Gregory Nikolsky of Kuban; Serapion of Kozha Lake; George of Mt. Athos; Martyrs Marcia and Mark; Luke (Mukhaidze), in Jerusalem; Uncovering of the relics of the Optina Elders.

Sunday
June 28

Third Sunday of Matthew
Abstain from meat and dairy products.
Romans 5:1-10; Matthew 6:22-33

Anger is a natural attribute of the intellect, and without anger man will never reach cleanliness or purity if he does not first become wrathful against all wicked and cunning thoughts.
— *St. Anthony the Great*

ST. PAUL THE PHYSICIAN. Paul was born to pious Christian parents in seventh-century Corinth. In his youth, he went to a monastery where he labored under an experienced ascetic. Paul had a difficult struggle with fornication. The demon would appear to him with temptations, but with the name of Christ and the power of the Cross, Paul drove out the evil spirit. One day, an evil woman went to the monastery and maliciously accused Paul of being the father of her child. She thrust the infant child into Paul's arms, but he accepted the slander as a trial for his benefit. Some men took Paul from the monastery and made him walk through the city so the people could ridicule and spit on the false monk. Paul fervently prayed to God and said, "Behold, let the child himself say who is his father." The infant child pointed to a blacksmith, and said, "That man is my father and not Paul the monk!" The people asked Paul for forgiveness. God granted Paul the gift of healing, and for this reason, he received the name "the Physician." St. Paul died peacefully at the age of seventy.

COMMEMORATIONS: Paul the Physician of Corinth; Sennuphius the Standard-bearer of Egypt; Sergius and Herman of Valaam; Serenus, Plutarchus, Heraclides, Heron, Raiso and others in Alexandria; Venerable Magnus; Sergios the Magistrate of Paphlagonia; Xenophon of Novgorod; Donatus of Libya; Austell of Cornwall; 3 Martyrs of Galatia; 70 Martyrs of Scythopolis; Moses the Anchorite; Martyr Pappias; Heliodorus of Glinsk Hermitage; Martyr Macedonius; Finding of the relics of Sts. Cyrus and John the Unmercenaries; "Of the Three Hands" Icon of the Mother of God.

Monday
June 29

Holy Apostles Peter and Paul
Fast-free
2 Corinthians 11:21-12:9; Matthew 16:13-19

It is not necessary to seek the truth among others which it is easy to obtain from the Church; since the apostles, like a rich man [depositing his money] in a bank, lodged in her hands most copiously all things pertaining to the truth.
— St. Ireneaus of Lyons

ST. COCHA OF ROS-BENNCHUIR IN IRELAND. Although not much is written, the following has been passed down to us about St. Cocha. She was at first the nurse and guardian of St. Kieran of Saigir, around the beginning of the fifth century. He is also associated with St. Patrick in southern Ireland. Cocha then embraced the religious life and became the abbess of the monastery of Ros-Bennchuir, situated on the seacoast. She was of great assistance to St. Kieran in propagating the Christian faith. It is written in the life of St. Kieran that every year, he would send oxen to Cocha's convent to plow her fields. They would go the considerable distance, without even being conducted by a driver, and when the plowing was done, they would return to Kieran. Each year on the feast of the Lord's Nativity, St. Kieran would go to Ros-Bennchuir to offer up the Holy Sacrifice to the nuns.

COMMEMORATIONS: Holy and All-Praised Apostles Peter and Paul; Peter, Prince of the Tatar Horde, wonderworker of Rostov; Mary, mother of John-Mark, nephew of Apostle Barnabas, at Jerusalem; Cassius of Narni; Cocha of Ros-Bennchuir in Ireland; Uncovering of the relics of St. Nicander of Pskov; "Kasperov" Icon of the Mother of God.

Tuesday

June 30

Synaxis of the Twelve Holy Apostles
Fast-free
1 Corinthians 4:9-16; Matthew 9:36, 10:1-8

*B*lessed are those who rejoice when unjustly accused, rather than when they are justly praised for their virtuous life. Here are the signs of holiness, not in the dry exertion of bodily asceticism and the great number of struggles, which, when not carried out with humility and the aim to put off the old man, create only illusions.
St. Paisios the Athonite

SYNAXIS OF THE HOLY, GLORIOUS, AND ALL-PRAISED TWELVE APOSTLES. The Twelve Apostles and Apostle Paul are commemorated collectively on this day. In addition, they are commemorated on their individual feastdays throughout the year. (1) St. Andrew was crucified on an X-shaped cross. (2) St. Bartholomew was crucified, saved, and later beheaded. (3) St. James, the son of Zebedee, was beheaded. (4) St. James, the son of Alphaeus, was crucified. (5) St. Matthew the Evangelist was burned alive. (6) St. Matthias was stoned and then beheaded after death. (7) St. Paul was beheaded. (8) St. Peter was crucified upside down. (9) St. Philip was crucified. (10) St. Simon the Zealot was crucified. (11) St. Thaddeus (Jude), the brother of James, was crucified. (12) St. Thomas was pierced with five spears. (13) St. John the Theologian asked to be buried alive and was not found when others rushed out to unearth him.

COMMEMORATIONS: Synaxis of the Holy Twelve Apostles: Peter, Andrew, James and John the sons of Zebedee, Philip, Bartholomew, Thomas, Matthew, James the son of Alphaeus, Jude the brother of James, Simon the Zealot, and Matthias; Basilides the Soldier at Alexandria; Stephen of Omsk; Gelasius of Rimet; Peter of Sinope; Erentrude of Salzburg; Andrew, Prince of Bogoliubsk; Michael Paknanas the Gardener of Athens; Martial of Limoges; Dinar, Queen of Khereti (Georgia); Nicander of Yaroslavl; Theogenes of Kazakhstan; Milan Popovic of Rmanj; Alexander of Munich; Peter the Prince of Ordinsk, Rostov; Martyr Meleton; Glorification of St. Sophronius, Bishop of Irkutsk and All Siberia; "Balikin" Icon of the Mother of God.

Wednesday
July 1

**Sts. Cosmas & Damian
the Holy Unmercenaries**
Abstain from meat and dairy products, and fish
1 Corinthians 12:27-13:8; Matthew 10:1, 5-8

You should ask God to forgive you of your sins. And because you have asked him humbly, and with pain of heart, God will forgive you all your sins, and heal your body too.
St. Porphyrios the Kapsokalyvite

VENERABLE PETER THE PATRICIAN. Peter was a Byzantine general and nobleman in ninth-century Constantinople under Emperor Nikephoros the Patrician. The emperor took him to Bulgaria, where there was a war between the Bulgarians and Romans. Peter was captured and taken prisoner along with fifty commanders, and the emperor was mortally wounded. Peter prayed and St. John the Theologian appeared to him in prison, released him from his chains, and fled back to his own land. After this experience, Peter left the world and became a monk on Mt. Olympus in Asia Minor. His spiritual guide was St. Ioannikios the Great, and in time, Peter received the angelic schema. After thirty-four years later, Peter returned to Constantinople. He built a church and a hut where he continued his ascetic labors for another eight years. He endured many hardships, fasted, held vigil, wore a hair shirt, and never wore shoes. St. Peter died peacefully at the age of seventy-seven.

COMMEMORATIONS: Cosmas and Damian the Unmercenary Physicians, at Rome; Potitus at Naples; Peter the Patrician; Gallus, Bishop of Clermont; Eparchius the Recluse of Gaul; Basil, founder of the Monastery of the Deep Stream in Cappadocia; 25 Martyrs at Nicomedia; Leo the Hermit; Nicodemus of Svyatogorsk; Leontius, Bishop of Radauti in Moldavia; Servanus (Serf), apostle of Western Fife, East Scotland; Julius and Aaron, first martyrs of Wales; Constantine of Cyprus, and those with him; Juthwara of England; Second translation of the relics of St. John of Rila from Turnovo to Rila.

Thursday
July 2

Deposition of the Precious Robe of the Theotokos in Blachernae
Fast-free
Hebrews 9:1-7; Luke 1:39-49, 56

He who flees the vain glory of this world, feels the glory of the future life in his soul.

+*Elder Justin Parvu of Romania*

ST. PHOTIUS, METROPOLITAN OF KIEV AND ALL RUSSIA. Photius was born a Greek in the city of Monemvasia, Peloponnesus. While still a youth, in the late fourteenth century, he became a monk. Later, Photius accompanied the patriarch to Constantinople for church business. St. Cyprian, the Russian metropolitan, had died and Photius was named to replace him since he was known for his holiness of life. Photius moved the metropolitan's headquarters from Kiev to Moscow. He led the Church there for twenty-two years, while the country endured war and pillaging by the Tatars. Under the leadership of Photius the Church prospered spiritually and financially. From this position of strength, he also helped the Patriarch of Constantinople and the international status of the Russian Orthodox Church. However, he was not without attacks from heretics and enemies. Russia was under siege by the Tatar Khan Edigei, and he intended to capture Photius, who hid in a settlement surrounded by swamps, and the enemy was unable to catch him. Photius wrote many important church documents, including, "Order of Selection and Installation of Bishops," "Discourse on the Seriousness of the Priestly Office and the Obligations of Church Servers," and "Spiritual Testament," which tells his life story. St. Photius was foretold his death by an angel, and he died peacefully.

COMMEMORATIONS: Placing of the Honorable Robe of the Most Holy Theotokos at Blachernae; John Maximovitch, Archbishop of Shanghai and San Francisco; Juvenal, Patriarch of Jerusalem; Juvenal, Protomartyr of America and Alaska; Photius, Metropolitan of Kiev and All Russia; Quintus of Phrygia; Basil, Patriarch of Jerusalem; Stephen the Great of Moldavia; Lampros of Makri; Monegunde of Gaul; Paul, Bilonus, Theonas, and Heron, at Thessalonica; Swithun of Winchester; Oudoceus of Llandaff; Uncovering of the relics of St. Sergius Florinsky, of Estonia.

Friday   **Strict Fast**

July 3

Romans 11:25-36; Matthew 12:1-8

We should receive everything as a command of God. When someone shames you, say that God commanded him to do it. When someone takes something of yours, God commanded him to take it, in order to make you a monk. When you are removed from a higher place, God changed your place so that you would change from your passions and bad habits. This is true humility.

+*Elder Paisius of Sihla*

ST. JOHN THE FOOL-FOR-CHRIST OF MOSCOW. John was from sixteenth-century Vologda in Russia. As a young man, he worked as a water carrier at a saltworks. Even with this heavy work, he added fasting and prayer to his life. After some time, he moved to Rostov and met the monk Irinarh the Recluse, after which John decided to become a fool-for-Christ's sake. As an ascetic burden, he wore heavy iron crosses and chains, and on his head a heavy iron cap, for which he was called "John Big Cap." He went about Moscow nearly naked and barefoot, even in the most terrible of winters. He foretold the great adversities and invasions that Russia would suffer, saying that in Moscow there will be many devils, visible and invisible. He spoke the truth to everyone, including the Tsar. Towards the end of his life, John removed his chains and healed the sick with his prayers. He indicated where he wanted to be buried, at the Pokrov church on Rva, which later was called the Cathedral of Basil the Great. St. John is venerated as a wonderworker.

COMMEMORATIONS: Hyacinth of Caesarea, and Theodotus and Theodota; Diomedes, Eulampius, Asclepiodotos, and Golinduc of Caesarea; Anatolios, Patriarch of Constantinople; Anatolios of Laodicea, and Eusebius; Symeon the Stylite; Anatolius of the Near Caves; Anatolius of the Far Caves; Isaiah the Solitary; Martyrs Mark and Mocius; Alexander of the Monastery of the Unsleeping Ones; John and Longinus of Yarenga; Basil and Constantine of Yaroslavl; Gerasimos of Carpenision; Nicodemus of Kozha Lake; John "Iron Cap" of Moscow; Germanus of the Isle of Man; George of the Black Mountain; Joachim of Notena; Jacob of Hamatoura.

SATURDAY   Fast-free

JULY 4
Romans 6:11-17; Matthew 8:14-23

How pathetic the complacency of our outlook on this present life is! The insubstantial little island of our "normal" existence will be washed away in the worlds beyond the tomb.
+Fr. Alexander Elchaninov of Russia

ST. MICHAEL CHIONIATES, METROPOLITAN OF ATHENS. Michael was from the twelfth- and thirteenth-century ancient city of Colossae in Asia Minor. His younger brother Niketas was a bishop and scholar. Michael was appointed Metropolitan of Athens, and for decades worked for the education and spiritual development of his clergy and to reverse the moral and material deterioration of tax-laden Athens. Niketas defended Michael from his enemies and the impunity of state officials. Michael was also a writer, and he described those times and their dismal conditions. He composed homilies, speeches, and poems. In 1203 a brutal landowner of the Peloponnese attacked Athens until Michael defended the city with the aid of some members of the Fourth Crusade in 1205. Michael was exiled to Kea for about twelve years for not submitting to the papacy. Finally, he retired to a monastery for the remaining five years of his life.

COMMEMORATIONS: Theodore, Bishop of Cyrene, with Cyprilla, Aroa, and Lucia; Donatus, Bishop of Libya; Hieromartyrs Theophilus and Theodotus; Righteous Menignos; Andrew, Archbishop of Crete; Asclepias the Wonderworker; Martha, mother of St. Symeon Stylites the Younger; Innocent and Sabbatios and 30 others in Sirmium; Andrew the Russian of Cairo; Euthymius of Suzdal; Nilus of Poltava; Andrew of Bogoliubsk; Michael Choniates of Athens; Ulrich of Augsburg; Andrew (Rublev), iconographer of Moscow; Translation of the relics of St. Martin the Merciful, Bishop of Tours; "Galatea" Icon of the Mother of God.

Sunday

July 5

Fourth Sunday of Matthew
Fast-free
Galatians 5:22-6:2; Matthew 8:5-13

*A*re you a sinner? Do not become discouraged, and come to Church to put forward repentance. Have you sinned? Then tell God, 'I have sinned.' What manner of toil is this, what prescribed course of life, what affliction? What manner of difficulty is it to make one statement, 'I have sinned'?

St. John Chrysostom

NEW MARTYR ELIZABETH ROMANOV, GRAND DUCHESS OF RUSSIA, AND VENERABLE BARBARA. Elizabeth was the sister of Empress Alexandra of Russia and granddaughter of Queen Victoria of England. She was one of the most illustrious women of her day, known for her modesty, beauty, and goodness of heart. She married Grand Duke Sergei Alexandrovich and converted to Orthodoxy, though she was not required. After her husband's assassination in 1905, she founded the Saints Mary and Martha Convent, where she lived in prayer, fasting, and the caring of the poor and the sick. During the Bolshevik Revolution, she was exiled to the Urals and martyred in 1918, the same year as her sister. She and those with her, including Nun Barbara from Elizabeth's convent, were thrown into an abandoned mineshaft and left to die. Their relics were later taken to Jerusalem to the Church of St. Mary Magdalene. In 2004, portions of the relics of St. Elizabeth and St. Barbara were taken to Russia and were housed at the Saints Mary and Martha Convent.

COMMEMORATIONS: Athanasios of Mt. Athos and his 6 disciples; Cyprian of Koutloumousiou, Mt. Athos; Stephen, Bishop of Rhegium, and Bishop Suerus, Agnes, Felicitas, and Perpetua; Anna at Rome; Athanasius, disciple of Sergius of Radonezh; Basil and 70 Martyrs of Scythopolis; Theodosius of Cherepovets; Athanasius of Jerusalem; Lampados of Hirenopolis; Elizabeth Romanova and Nun Barbara, and with them John, Igor, Constantine, Sergius, Vladimir, and Theodore; Agapitus of Optina Monastery; Morwenna of Morwenstow; Synaxis of 23 Saints of Lesvos; "Economissa" Icon of the Mother of God.

Monday

Fast-free

July 6

Romans 12:4-5, 15-21; Matthew 12:9-13

*D*o you wish to lead a proper life? Exercise humility, for without it, it is impossible to lead a proper life.

St. Theophan the Recluse

VENERABLE SISOES THE GREAT OF EGYPT. Sisoes pursued asceticism in the cave once inhabited by St. Anthony the Great in the Egyptian desert. He labored there for sixty years and was granted the gift of wonderworking. He healed the sick, drove out demonic spirits, and raised the dead. Many came to him from a great distance for his counsel. He always taught humility as the most necessary virtue. He said, "It is a great thing to regard yourself as inferior to everyone else. This leads to the acquisition of humility." As he lay dying in great old age, the disciples that surrounded him saw his face radiant. His eyes became intent, and he said, "See the Prophets are coming." Then he became even more radiant, saying, "See, the Apostles are coming." Once again, "See, the angels are coming to take my soul." Finally, his countenance was so bright that the brethren were no able to look at him. St. Sisoes said, "See, the Lord is coming. He is saying, 'Bring Me the chosen vessel from out of the wilderness.'" Then he gave up his soul, and the whole room became fragrant.

COMMEMORATIONS: Synaxis of the Apostles Archippos, Philemon, and Onesimus; Sisoes the Great of Egypt; Marinus and Martha at Rome, and their children Audifax and Abbacum, and those with them at Rome: Cyrinus, Valentine, and Asterios; Astius, Bishop of Dyrrachium; Lucy at Rome, and 24 companion martyrs; Cyril of Hilander, Mt. Athos; Simon of Ufa; Sisoes of the Kiev Caves; Isaurus, Innocent, Felix, Hermias, Basil, Peregrinus, Rufus, and Rufinus of Apollonia in Macedonia; Martyrs Alexander, Epimachos, and Apollonius; Theodore (Bogoyavlensky) of Moscow; Euthymius of Optina Monastery; Barnabas of Gethsemane Skete; Monenna of Ireland; Goar, hieromonk and missionary along the Rhine; Synaxis of the Saints of Radonezh; Uncovering of the relics of St. Juliana Olshansky.

TUESDAY   Fast-free

JULY 7
Galatians 3:23-4:5 Mark 5:24-34

How easy it is to say, "My Lord Jesus, have mercy on me! I bless Thee, my Lord Jesus; help me!
St. Makarios the Great

NEWLY-REVEALED HIEROMARTYR VLASIOS OF AKARNANIA. Vlasios was a retired bishop or an abbot of a monastery in the town of Palairos Sklavaina. He was martyred by pirates in 1006 A.D., along with five fellow monastics and a multitude of men, women, and children of his flock. During the uncovering of the saint's relics, it was found that the pirates had driven five nails into Vlasios, then beheaded him. Beginning in 1915, the residents of that town would see a priest in their sleep, telling them to dig to uncover his relics, and indicating the place. Fearing ridicule, they kept it to themselves. The dreams continued, and finally, in 1923, Vlasios appeared to Euphrosyne Katsara. She was praying next to her daughter's death bed when the doors and windows opened automatically, and Vlasios appeared in an indescribable light. He made the Sign of the Cross over her daughter, and after a few days, she was healed. Vlasios led Euphrosyne to his gravesite, where sheep were trampling, which he could not bear. On the third day of digging, most of the saint's relics were found, and a beautiful fragrance filled the air. At the insistence of Vlasios, his skull was also uncovered. Vlasios continued to appear to the people with wonderworking power. In 1980 an iconographer asked St. Paisios to pray that St. Vlasios would appear to him, to get an accurate description for the saint's icon. St. Vlasios appeared to the Elder Paisios, and when the icon was completed, he was relieved to see that the image was captured correctly.

COMMEMORATIONS: Kyriake of Nicomedia; Acacius of Sinai; Hieromartyr Eustathius; Epictetos and Astion in Scythia; Peregrinus, Lucian, Pompeius, Hesychius, Pappias, Saturninus, and Germanus, in Macedonia; Pantaenus of Alexandria; Thomas of Mt. Maleon; Evangelus, Bishop of Tomi; Euphrosyne (Eudocia) of Moscow; New Martyr Polycarp; Vlasios of Akarnania; Willibald of Eichstatt; Hedda of the West Saxons; Maelruin of Tallaght; Translation of the "Blachernae" Icon of the Mother of God.

WEDNESDAY

JULY 8

St. Procopius the Great Martyr
Abstain from meat and dairy products, and fish.
1 Timothy 4:9-15
Luke 6:17-19, 9:1-2, 10:16-21

In the Church we become one with every sorrowful, aching and sinful person. Nobody should want to be saved alone, without the salvation of others.

St. Porphyrios the Kapsokalyvite

"THE SITKA" ICON OF THE MOTHER OF GOD. The famous iconographer, Vladimir Lukich Borovikovsky wrote the Sitka Icon of the Mother of God on canvas. He also wrote many icons for the Cathedral of the Kazan Icon in St. Petersburg. The icon is located in the Cathedral of St. Michael the Archangel in Sitka, Alaska. It was a gift to the cathedral in 1850 and was paid for by the meager wages of a group of laborers of the Russian American Company. The Sitka icon depicts the Theotokos and the Christ child, and the image of God the Father blessing from above. A detailed riza of silver covers the icon. The icon is described as a "pearl of Russian ecclesiastical art of ineffable gentleness, purity, and harmony." Because of the peaceful gaze of the Theotokos, the more one looks at the icon, the more difficult it is to look away. It is said that the gaze of the Theotokos has restored to health the faithful who have prayed before it.

COMMEMORATIONS: Procopius of Caesarea in Palestine, and with him: Theodosia, his mother, tribunes Antiochus and Nicostratus, and 12 women of senatorial rank; Anastasios at Constantinople; Theophilus the Myrrh-gusher of Pantocrator Monastery; Mirdat, King of Kartli, Georgia; Procopius, fool-for-Christ of Ustiug (Vologda); Procopius, fool-for-Christ of Usya; Martyr Abdas; Edgar the Peaceable of England; Sunniva and companions on Selje Island, Norway; Hieritha (Urith) of Chittlehampton; Translation of the relics of St. Demetrius of Basarabov, Bulgaria; Appearance of the "Kazan" Icon of the Mother of God; "Our Lady of Sitka," "Of Tender Feeling," Ustiug "Annunciation," and "Peschanskaya" Icons of the Mother of God.

Thursday   **Fast-free**

July 9

Romans 15:17-29; Matthew 12:46-13:3

In those in whom mercy and truth prevail, everything is godlike; for truth judges no one without mercy, while mercy never manifests compassion apart from truth.

St. Ilias the Presbyter

VENERABLES DIONYSIOS AND METROPHANES OF MT. ATHOS. Dionysios acquired much wisdom from secular and sacred studies. He became a monk and priest at the Monastery of Stoudios in Constantinople. The Proverbs of Solomon was a fountain of life for him and his disciple Metrophanes. Dionysios was a skilled orator and had a great ability to simplify the words of the Holy Fathers. His writings are in monastery libraries throughout Mt. Athos. He deemed the pleasures and riches of this world deceitful. He bemoaned anything that did not lead to the knowledge of Christ. Dionysios and Metrophanes moved to Mt. Athos for quiet and solitude, but many came to Dionysios for counsel, confession, and correction. Seeking greater solitude, they settled into a cave that became the future site of Little Anne's Skete. Through unceasing prayer, they purified the passions of body and soul. Many Orthodox Christians asked the Fathers of Mt. Athos for a spiritual father, and Metrophanes was chosen. He left Mt. Athos for a short time and visited the villages and countryside, preaching the word of God and confessing the local people. St. Dionysios died peacefully around the year 1606. St. Metrophanes died shortly after that.

COMMEMORATIONS: Pancratius, Bishop of Taormina; Cyril, Bishop of Gortyna in Crete; Dionysius the Rhetorician and Metrophanes of Mt. Athos; Patermuthios, Copres, and Alexander the soldier, in Egypt; Photios, founder of Akapniou Monastery in Thessalonica; Methodius, Bishop of Lampes in Crete; Peter of Vologda; Martyrs Andrew and Probus; Theodosius, Stylite of Edessa; Euthymius of Karelia; Everilda of Northumbria; Killian, Colman, and Totman, at Wurzburg; Uncovering of the relics of St. Gabriel, of St. Elias Skete, Mt. Athos.

Friday   **Strict Fast**

July 10

Romans 16:1-16; Matthew 13:3-9

To believe one does not need counsel is great pride.
St. Basil the Great

VENERABLES PARTHENIOS AND EVMENIOS OF CRETE. Parthenios and Evmenios were brothers from the island of Crete. They wanted to become monks, but their mother refused to give her blessing until a miracle occurred that convinced her. One day she wanted to bake bread and asked her sons to bring wood to light the oven. They encouraged her to put the loaves in the oven without fire and allow them to bake in this way. The miracle happened, and she gave them her blessing to go. They became monks at the Odigitria Monastery on Mt. Athos, and later became hermits in the sacred caves of Martsalo, where many came seeking their guidance. The brothers moved to St. John's Cave and St. Anthony's Cave in the Koudoumas area. But the Panagia appeared to Parthenios and asked him to build her a monastery at Koudoumas. This seemed impossible since they were destitute, but because of their sanctity and miracles, the local people helped the monks. They built there on the ruins of an older fourteenth-century monastery. They got advice on how to organize their monastery from a monk from Vatopedi Monastery. He also donated many books and vestments. Parthenios was given the power to work miracles. He drove away crop-devouring locusts, made seawater sweet, and filled the beach with the stone that was needed to build the monastery. Before his death, St. Parthenios sat up, and extended his hand, saying, "Welcome my Panagia!" The relics of the two saints are housed at the Koudoumas Monastery.

COMMEMORATIONS: Deposition of the Precious Robe of the Lord at Moscow; 45 Martyrs at Nicopolis; 10,000 Fathers of Scetis; Anthony of the Kiev Caves; Bianor and Silvanus of Pisidia; Apollonios of Sardis; Silouan of the Far Caves; Evmenios and Parthenios of Crete; Joseph of Damascus, and companions; Athanasios of Pentaschoinon; Synaxis of All Saints of Vatopedi; Synaxis of St. John the Theologian in Beatus.

Saturday
July 11

St. Euphemia the Great Martyr
Fast-free
2 Corinthians 6:1-10; Luke 7:36-50

Do not expect to find in your heart any remarkable gift of prayer. Consider yourself unworthy of it. Then you will find peace.
St. Macarius of Optina

VENERABLE CYRIL THE NEW OF PAROS. Cyril was from eighteenth-century Paros. He went to Mt. Athos as a young man and was educated at the School of Vatopedi. His teacher was St. Athanasios Parios, whom Cyril imitated and applied fiery zeal and tireless action. He stayed on the holy mountain for a considerable time, teaching sacred letters and secular wisdom, and was associated with the renewal movement of the Kollyvades fathers. Cyril's virtues and learning were greater than any other Athonite ascetic. Later the Patriarch of Constantinople appointed him preacher general of the Aegean. He became a zealous preacher, setting up a cross wherever he went and delivering fiery sermons. They were both constructive and discreetly corrective, and as a confessor, he was compassionate, consoling, and supportive. He also did not hesitate to reprimand politicians and men of the Church for misconduct. For this, he was threatened and survived many attempts on his life. He spent time on Paros, where he had an impact on the pious people and the revival of monasticism. He renovated several monasteries, including a nun's convent, providing for all their needs as a spiritual father. Cyril had the gift of foresight and the ability to work miracles. He could travel on his monastic cassock when he spread it out upon the sea. When he struck a rock at an arid monastery, a spring gushed forth, which is still flowing to this day. St. Cyril's relics are at the Monastery of St. George.

COMMEMORATIONS: Euphemia the All-praised of Chalcedon; Olga, Princess of Russia; Cindeos of Pamphylia; Januarius and Pelagia of Nicopolis; Nicodemus of Elbasan and Mt. Athos; Nicodemos of Hilander; Arcadius of Vyazemsk; Nectarios of St. Anne's Skete; Cyril of Paros; Leo of Mandra; Drostan of Old Deer; New Hieromartyrs of Serbia (1941–1945); Translation of the relics of St. Barbara from Constantinople to Kiev; "Rudensk" Icon of the Mother of God.

Sunday

Fifth Sunday of Matthew
Fast-free

July 12

Romans 10:1-10; Matthew 8:28-9:1

If I did not trust in God, I do not know what would have happened to me. People can make things happen up to a point. After that, it is up to God. We have got to have complete trust in Him.

St. Paisios the Athonite

WONDROUS "PRODROMITISSA" ICON OF THE MOTHER OF GOD. In 1863 the founders of the Romanian Skete of the Honorable Forerunner, Fathers Niphon and Nektarios, wanted to acquire a beautiful icon of the Panagia. They found a pious iconographer, Iordakin Nicholas, and asked him to write it with prayer and fasting. Every day he read the Supplication Service to the Panagia. He began by painting the vestments of the Panagia and the Lord, but when he tried to paint the face, he failed. This pained Iordakin, so he covered the icon with a cloth and retired to his room to pray harder. The next day, he removed the cloth and saw the sacred faces miraculously and perfectly made without hands. The holy fathers received and transferred the wondrous icon to Mt. Athos. During the journey, it accomplished numerous miracles and continues to do so to this day.

COMMEMORATIONS: Proclus and Hilary of Ancyra; Andrew the Commander, Heraclius, Taustus, Menas, and others; Mamas, near Sigmata; Serapion, Bishop of Vladimir; Serapion the New, at Alexandria; Veronica, who was healed by the Lord; Michael of Maleinus; Arsenius of Novgorod; Simon of Volomsk Monastery; Theodore and John of Kiev; John and Gabriel of Mt. Athos; Paisios the New of Mt. Athos; Translation of the relics of Momcilo Grgurevic of Serbia; Translation of the relics of St. Anthony of Leokhnovo Monastery; "Of the Three Hands" Icon of the Mother of God of Hilander, Mt. Athos; Wondrous "Prodromitissa" of the Mother of God.

Monday

Fast-free

July 13

Hebrews 2:2-10; Matthew 13:10-23, 43

If someone prays correctly, God listens to him.
St. Paisios the Athonite

ST. ONESIPHOROS THE WONDERWORKER OF ANARITA IN PAPHOS. Onesiphoros was from a pious and wealthy family in Constantinople. He was brought up in the emperor's palace and was educated in the knowledge of the law, specializing in military seamanship. The emperor made him head of the imperial fleet. He built new naval units, repaired old warships, took care of military exercises, and increased the navy's militancy. At one point, enemies attacked the Roman Empire, and Onesiphoros engaged them. However, all of the Roman ships, except the one Onesiphoros was on, went down during the conflict. The pitch which glued together the wood of the vessels had failed. Saddened, Onesiphoros decided to leave the world, along with ten of his friends, to seek the silence of asceticism. They went to Paphos in Cyprus, and each departed to where God led them. Onesiphoros settled in a cave where he fasted, prayed to God, and made vigils. He also built a small church there. At that time, a horrible drought caused the crops and trees to dry up, and the animals were dying of thirst. For three days, Onesiphoros neither ate, drank, nor slept. With unending tears, he prayed to God, and the rains came. Crowds of people came to thank him, but he told them to praise God and always to lead clean lives. Even after his death, his miracles would cleanse lepers, heal the blind, the mute, the lame, and cure cancer patients. Parts of the saint's relics are at the Monastery of Kykkos and Monastery of Chrysorrogiatissa.

COMMEMORATIONS: Synaxis of the Holy Archangel Gabriel; Stephen of St. Sava's Monastery; Sarah of Seeds; Mary (Golinduc) of Persia; Julian, Bishop of Cenomanis; Martyr Serapion, under Severus; Marcian of Iconium; Alamannia in Cyprus; Heliophotus, Epaphrodites, Ammon, Auxouthenius, and Euthenius, of Cyprus; Onesiphoros of Anarita; Mildred of Minster; Juthwara of Cornwall; Just of Cornwall; Commemoration of the first recorded miracle of St. Spyridon in Corfu; Synaxis of Hilander Saints, Mt. Athos.

Tuesday   **Fast-free**

July 14

Romans 16:1-16; Matthew 13:24-30

Those who want to be saved scrutinize not the shortcomings of their neighbor but always their own and they set about eliminating them.

St. Dorotheos of Gaza

VENERABLE NIKODEMOS OF MT. ATHOS. In his thirty-three years as a monk, Nikodemos authored many of the important and classical books of Orthodoxy. He committed to writing eleven hundred years of Orthodox monastic wisdom in the four books of the *Philokalia*. He compiled the rules of the Church from the fourth century in the *Rudder* and wrote a two-volume collection of the Lives of the Saints covering seventeen centuries. To bolster the faithful in the face of four centuries of Turkish domination and Orthodox conversions to Islam, he wrote *Neon Martyrologion*. These were his accounts of ordinary people from the sixteenth to eighteenth centuries who refused to deny Jesus Christ and died for Him. St. Nikodemos became a monk on Mt. Athos at the age of twenty-seven and died at the relatively young age of sixty, in the early nineteenth century.

COMMEMORATIONS: Apostle Aquila of the Seventy, and St. Priscilla; Justus at Rome; Joseph, Archbishop of Thessalonica; Heraclius, Patriarch of Alexandria; Onesimos of Magnesia; Hellius of Egypt; John of Merv; Marcellinus of Utrecht; Nicodemos of Mt. Athos; Stephen of Makhrishche Monastery; Martyr Aquila; Longinus of Svyatogorsk Monastery; Constantine Oprisan of Jilava, Romania; Procopius of Sazava in Bohemia; Uncovering of the relics of St. Theophilos of Kiev.

WEDNESDAY

July 15

Sts. Cyricus and Julitta his Mother
Strict Fast
1 Corinthians 13:11-14:5; Matthew 17:24-18:4

*W*hen we lack abstinence and do not practice self-control with our mouth and stomach, then we anger God. As I mentioned before, watchfulness is superior to prayer. When one achieves watchfulness, he will find prayer and will be able to feel and understand with Whom he is speaking. When we are able to comprehend the prayer within our heart, we will perceive the grace of God guiding us, taking us by the hand like a small child, and telling us, "This is how you will walk; this is how you will speak."

+Gerondissa Makrina of Volos

MIRACLE OF ST. BARBARA IN POLYDENDRI IN ATTICA. In 1917 an epidemic struck the village of Polydendri. Eight people died, and others were on the verge of death. Everyone panicked and many took to the mountains. Homes and surrounding areas were quarantined, and the wells and fountains guarded. Lime was spread over the graves to prevent the spread of the epidemic. A villager named Panagiotis Spyridon Sotirchos had a vision of St. Barbara in her church, and she said, "Come and get me so that I can chase away the sickness." The priest and others took the wonderworking icon of St. Barbara to the intersection of the village. The Christians received her with reverence and tears. Then the saint's icon was processed around the town, and not only did the epidemic cease, but all the sick became well. Out of gratitude, a feast was established to commemorate this miracle.

COMMEMORATIONS: Julitta and Kyrikos of Tarsus; Equal-to-the-Apostles Great Prince Vladimir, enlightener of Russia; Abudimus of the isle of Tenedos; Donald of Ogilvy, and his 9 virgin daughters, nuns of Abernathy (Scotland); Asiya of Tanis in Syria; Zosima of Alexandrov (Vladimir); Job of Malaya Ugolka; Martyr Lollianus; Commemoration of the Miracle of St. Barbara in Polydendri in Attica; Finding of the head of St. Matrona of Chios; Translation of the relics of St. Swithun, Bishop of Winchester.

THURSDAY   **Fast-free**

JULY 16

1 Corinthians 3:18-23; Matthew 13:36-43

((The Gospel is) …a workshop of souls and a storehouse of spiritual herbs by which any disease can be cured.

St. Basil the Great

MARTYR HELIER OF JERSEY. Helier was from what is now modern-day Belgium. His pagan father was the governor of that area. Because they had difficulty conceiving, St. Cunibert advised them to pray to God and raise the child in the Christian faith. Helier's father eventually got angry with Cunibert because of his influence over Helier, who was already causing youthful miracles. The governor had Cunibert killed, and Helier fled. He found refuge in the monastic community of St. Marculf of Nantus, but it did not provide him with the quiet needed for contemplation. So Marculf sent him and a companion, St. Romard, to the island of Jersey, where the few inhabitants asked for someone to bring them the gospel. Helier settled on a tidal islet, known as Hermitage Rock, and Romard settled in a small community of fishermen. Romard would travel between the village and Helier's rock, which had a vantage point to see approaching attackers. Helier would signal the villagers, and they would hide in the marshes. His prayers and the Sign of the Cross once raised a storm, driving off a raiding party. The story is that St. Helier was beheaded by pirates, and he picked up his head and walked to shore where St. Romard found him still holding his head in his hands.

COMMEMORATIONS: Athenogenes, Bishop of Heracleopolis, and his 10 disciples; Antiochus, physician of Sebaste; 15,000 Martyrs of Pisidia; Julia of Carthage; Ardalion (Ponamarev) of Kasli; John of Turnovo; Theodotus of Glinsk Hermitage; Seraphim, Theognostus, and others of Alma-Ata; Helier of Jersey; James, Archbishop of Barnaul, and with him: Peter, John, Theodore, and John; Matrona Belyakova of Anemnyasevo; Anastasios and Euxitheos, Bishop of Thessalonica; Basil Kalika of Novgorod; Magdalena of New Tikhvin Convent; Martyr Athenogenes; Martyr Faustus, under Decius; Commemoration of the Fourth Ecumenical Council.

FRIDAY

JULY 17

St. Marina the Great Martyr
Abstain from meat and
dairy products, and fish.
Galatians 3:23-4:5; Mark 5:24-34

Put the lover of legality to shame by your compassion.
St. Isaac the Syrian

GREAT MARTYR MARINA OF ANTIOCH. Marina's father was a pagan priest in the third century, and her mother died giving birth. Her foster mother taught her about Jesus Christ. The Christian faith took root in Marina, and she vowed to remain a virgin and one day become a martyr. Her father despised her for her faith. The pagan eparch of the land admired Marina's purity and wanted her for his wife, but she refused. When he demanded that she sacrifice to idols, she responded that nothing would separate her from Christ. She was beaten, imprisoned, suspended, and her sides raked with iron nails. She prayed, and it was as if another person was receiving the torture. Again imprisoned, the devil tried to frighten her three times. He appeared as a dragon, attempting to devour her, holding half of her body in its mouth. She made the Sign of the Cross, and the dragon was torn apart and vanished. Again, he appeared as a man, black as night. She seized his hair and beat him with a hammer until he left her sight. Still, he grabbed her and threatened to kill her if she would not stop praying, but she whipped him. The Archangel Michael appeared to her and healed her of all her wounds. The next day she was burned with torches and thrown into a cauldron of boiling water. She prayed, and an earthquake struck the land, and a voice was heard by all, saying, "You are blessed, Marina. You were baptized, and became worthy of the crown of virginity." Many declared their faith and received Baptism. The governor then ordered the saint's beheading, at the age of fifteen.

COMMEMORATIONS: Marina of Antioch; Timothy, fool-for-Christ of Svyatogorsk; Euphrasius of Ionopolis; Holy Royal Martyrs: Tsar Nicholas II, Empress Alexandra, Alexis, Olga, Tatiana, Maria, and Anastasia, and others; Eugene Botkin, the Passion-bearer; Sabbas of Gornji Karlovac and George Bogich of Nasice; Irenarchus of Solovki; Leonid of Ustnedumsk; Scillitan Martyrs; St. Marcellina; Translation of the relics of St. Lazarus of Mt. Galesion and St. Gabriel of Seven Lakes; "Svyatogorsk" Icon of the Mother of God.

SATURDAY   Fast-free

July 18

Romans 9:1-5; Matthew 9:18-26

The worldly man is not known by his hairstyle and clothing, but by his evil manner of life and his greed for worldly and material luxuries; for it is these that make the soul sinful.

St. Ephraim the Syrian

ST. JOHN IX THE HIEROMNEMON, PATRIARCH OF CONSTANTINOPLE. John was a cleric from within the scholarly, philosophical branch of the Church hierarchy, and rose through the ranks to become Patriarch of Constantinople. Between the years 1111 and 1134, he worked to reverse the secularizing trend within the clergy by banning them from being advocates in civil courts. He also sought to reclaim the great but scattered collection of books within Constantinople. To that end, he acquired the book collections of powerful men who had died, then had them recopied, and this greatly expanded the number of titles in the Great Church. John also worked to make the patriarchal clergy, rather than the monastic community, the authoritative voice of Orthodoxy. He also condemned the heretical Nestorian doctrine of Eustratios of Nicaea. During John's time as Patriarch, efforts were made by Emperor Alexios I Komnenos to bridge the schism between the Orthodox and the Papal church. However, these efforts failed since Pope Pascal II in 1112 demanded that the Patriarch of Constantinople recognize the Pope's primacy over "all the churches of God throughout the world." The opposition came from the majority of the secular clergy, the monastic world, and the laity.

COMMEMORATIONS: Hyacinth of Amastris; Martyrs Dasius and Maron; Paul, Chionia (Thea), and Valentina in Caesarea of Palestine; Emilian of Silistra in Bulgaria; Athanasius of Klysma, Egypt; Stephen II, Archbishop of Constantinople; Pambo, hermit of Egypt; Cozmas of Georgia; John the Confessor, Metropolitan of Chalcedon; Pambo, recluse of the Kiev Caves; Apollinarius of Verkhoturye; Leontius, abbot of Karikhov; Barlaam of Bald Mountain; Frederick, Bishop of Utrecht; John the Long-suffering of the Kiev Caves; Martyr Marcellus; "Tolga" Icon of the Mother of God.

Sunday

July 19

Sunday of the Holy Fathers of the Fourth Ecumenical Council
Fast-free
Titus 3:8-15; Matthew 5:14-19

*B*ringing one soul close to God by repentance is much better, in the eyes of God, than all other offerings, for there is nothing in the world better for God than the human soul, for everything in the world will perish except the soul because it is eternal.
St. John Climacus

BLESSED ROMANUS, PRINCE OF RYAZAN. Romanus was descended from a line of princes who gave their lives for their country. Both his grandfathers were killed in wars. Romanus was devout in his faith, prayed with tears, and loved his country. At this time, the people of Ryazan were under the oppression of the Tatars and Khan Mengu-Timur. Romanus defended his people against the intimidation and theft of the khan's tax collectors. The Tatar tax collectors hated Romanus for this and slandered him before the Tatar khan, who threatened him to either join the Tatar faith or die a martyr's death. Romanus responded that a follower of Christ could not change from the true faith to a false one. The saint was subjected to hideous torments. His tongue was cut out, eyes were gouged, and his ears, lips, hands, and feet were cut off. The skin from his head was torn off. Finally, Romanus was beheaded and impaled with a spear, in the year 1270. In the nineteenth century, a church was built and dedicated to St. Romanus at Ryazan.

COMMEMORATIONS: Macrina, sister of Sts. Basil the Great and Gregory of Nyssa; Theodore the Sabbaite, Bishop of Edessa; Abba Diocles of *The Paradise*; Dius, abbot of Antioch; Paisius of the Kiev Caves; Victor, Bishop of Glazov; Militsa (Eugenia in schema), Princess of Serbia; Stephen Lazarevic, King of Serbia; Romanus Olegovich, Prince of Ryazan; Sophronius of Svyatogorsk Monastery; Synaxis of All Saints of Kursk; Commemoration of the Miracle of St. Haralambos in Filiatria of Messenia; Translation of the relics of St. Seraphim of Sarov; The Seraphim-Diveevsk "Tenderness" Icon of the Mother, before which St. Seraphim reposed.

Monday

July 20

Glorious Prophet St. Elias
Fast-free
James 5:10-20; Luke 4:22-30

The Lord is quick to forgive the sins of the merciful!
St. Silouan the Athonite

UNCOVERING OF THE RELICS OF VENERABLE ATHANASIOS OF BREST. Athanasios was the abbot of the Brest Monastery. He singlemindedly devoted his life to the defense of Orthodox Christians, in word and deed, in inspiring speeches and writings, and against the Uniates who oppressed them. The Uniates were Eastern Christians who were in communion with the Roman Catholic Church but retained their own languages, rites, and codes of canon law. This took place seven centuries after the schism between the two Churches. Athanasios saw himself as a servant and a tool for God whose purpose was to speak the truth in defense of Orthodoxy. He always vowed and predicted that the Uniates would die out. Athanasios lived to see the complete undoing of the Uniates and the reaffirmation of Orthodoxy in Russia. However, he had developed enemies because of the conflict, and they finally killed him and hid his body in the ground. Eight months later, a boy showed the monks of Simonov Monastery where the incorrupt relics were hidden on the Jesuit lands. They secretly removed them and performed a church funeral. Then they were placed in a copper reliquary in the main church of the monastery. Many believers venerated the wonderworking relics.

COMMEMORATIONS: Elias (Elijah) the Prophet; Elias and Flavius II, Patriarchs of Jerusalem and Antioch; Lydia, Alexis, and Cyril of Russia; Elias Chavachavadze of Georgia; Philosoph Omalsky, and those with him; Salome of Jerusalem and Kartli; Abramius of Galich; Deacon Juvenal; Alexis Medvedkov of Ugine, France; Elias Fondaminsky, Priest Demetrius Klepinine, George Skobtsov, and Nun Maria Skobtsova of Paris; Tikhon, George, Cosmas, John, Sergius, Theodore, Alexander, George, Euthymius, and Peter, at Voronezh; Ethelwida, widow of King Alfred the Great; Uncovering of the relics of St. Athanasius of Brest.

Tuesday

Fast-free

July 21

1 Corinthians 6:20-7:12; Matthew 14:1-13

*L*et us make our body an altar of sacrifice. Let us place all our desires on it and beseech the Lord that he would send down from heaven that invisible and mighty fire to consume the altar and everything that is on it.

St. Makarios the Great

MARTYR VICTOR OF MARSEILLES. Victor was a Roman military officer. He was known for his bravery, intelligence, and noble background. However, he would not sacrifice to the Roman gods, calling them dead idols. His opponents seized this opportunity to denounce him. Victor was brought before two prefects, but they recognized his nobility and decided that he should appear before Emperor Maximian. Maximian told Victor to repent for his verbal sin against the empire, but when he refused to become an idolater, he was severely beaten. He was put on the rack and tortured slowly, hoping he would lose his resolve. They dragged him through the streets in the hope that humiliation would shake his conviction. He was then imprisoned under the guard of three soldiers, but he converted them, and the soldiers were beheaded that day. Maximian became enraged and confused, so he stood Victor before a statue of their god Jupiter, telling him to burn incense. The saint kicked the figure, and it fell to the ground. Then Maximian gave orders to cut off Victor's offending foot. St. Victor was then beaten and finally crushed to death by a millstone.

COMMEMORATIONS: Symeon of Emesa and his fellow faster John; Parthenius, Bishop of Radobysdios; Acacius of Constantinople; Eleutherius of "Dry Hill"; Justus, Matthew, and Eugene of the 13 who suffered at Rome with Trophimos and Theophilos; Victor of Marseilles; Bargabdesian at Arbela; Paul and John, near Edessa; Raphael and Parthenios of Old Agapia Monastery; Onuphrius the Silent of the Kiev Caves; Zoticus of Comana; Onesimus of the Kiev Caves; 3 Martyrs of Melitene; Simo Banjac, Milan Stojisavljevic, and his son Milan of Glamoc, Serbia; Praxedes at Rome; Arsenia of Ust-Medveditsky; "Armatia" Icon of the Mother of God.

WEDNESDAY

JULY 22

Holy Myrrhbearer St. Mary Magdalene
Abstain from meat and dairy products, and fish.
1 Corinthians 9:2-12; Luke 8:1-3

We are created for God and only in Him do we find the paramount bliss for which our heart is constantly yearning.
+Archimandrite Seraphim Aleksiev

VENERABLE MENELAOS THE WONDERWORKER. Menelaos was from an eminent aristocratic family in early eighth-century France. When he reached manhood, his father pushed him to attain the social position of a prince and to marry a blueblood. But Menelaos said that he did not want to marry, so a continuous conflict ensued. Together with his two trusted friends, they left their parental home and settled in the ancient and famous Monastery of St. Menas, which had been abandoned. Eventually, a monk visited and suggested that they should all go and submit themselves to the spiritual elder St. Eudos, which they did. After some time, the three hermits obtained great fame. One day, Menelaos' mother, sister, and former fiancé arrived at the monastery, wanting to become nuns. The years passed peacefully, and many novice monks came to Menelaos. He was granted the gift to work miracles, and he healed the blind, those with paralysis, raised a dead child, and drove out the devil with just a slap. St. Menelaos died peacefully.

COMMEMORATIONS: Myrrh-bearer and Equal-to-the-Apostles Mary Magdalene; Cyril I, Patriarch of Antioch; Marcella of Chios; Cyprian, fool-for-Christ of Suzdal; Cornelius of Pereyaslavl; Wandregislus of Caux (Gaul).

Thursday
Fast-free

July 23
1 Corinthians 7:24-35; Matthew 15:12-21

*S*orrows are that very threat of fire, or trial, but we must not fear them; rather we must be like the godly children and sing unto God in our sorrows, believing that they are sent to us by God for our salvation.

St. Barsanuphius of Optina

"JOY OF ALL WHO SORROW" ICON OF THE MOTHER OF GOD. A bishop traveling through Volhynia in Ukraine gave a pious woman an icon of the Mother of God. It soon began to work miracles, including healing her blind brother. The Mother of God is depicted standing and surrounded by the sick and suffering who are receiving Her aid, and angels are giving gifts of consolation. In some copies of the image, the Panagia is holding Jesus in her arms. In 1597 the icon was given to the monks in Pochaev. When Turks attacked the monastery in 1675, the Mother of God miraculously saved her image. At the end of the seventeenth century, one copy of this icon healed the sister of Patriarch Joachim, from which the feast was established. Another copy was found in St. Petersburg during the nineteenth century. During a thunderstorm, lightning struck a chapel housing the icon, and it remained unharmed by the flames. But it had fallen to the floor, broke open, and twelve copper coins were found stuck to the icon in different places. After this, many miracles were worked by the grace of the Joy of All Who Sorrow Icon. Wonderworking copies have been found throughout Russia.

COMMEMORATIONS: Ezekiel the Prophet; Trophimos, Theophilos, and 13 others, in Lycia; Anna (Hannah), mother of Prophet Samuel; 8 Martyrs of Carthage; Nectarius of Yaransk; Anna of Leucadia; Apollonius at Rome; 250 Martyrs killed by the Bulgarians; John (Jacob) of Neamts; Apollinarius of Ravenna; Theodore Ushakov; Pelagia of Tinos; Repose of St. John Cassian the Roman; Translation of the relics of St. Phocas, Bishop of Sinope; Icon of the Mother of God of Pochaev and Her Miraculous Intercession; "Pochaev" and "The Joy of All Who Sorrow" Icons of the Mother of God.

Friday   **Strict Fast**

July 24

1 Corinthians 7:35-8:7; Matthew 15:29-31

A tempest on the high seas is a great hardship; a tempest in one's soul is an even greater one. But neither the high seas are calm and clear, nor the soul is at peace and purified until the storm is over.
St. Nikolai Velimirovich

GREAT MARTYR CHRISTINA OF TYRE. In third-century Tyre, Christina's pagan father put her in a tower he had built to hide her beauty. He placed idols there to which she could sacrifice. As she reflected on the beauty of the sun and stars, her natural wisdom led her to believe in the true God. She smashed the idols, so she was beaten and thrown into prison to starve to death. A divine angel appeared and fed and healed her wounds. She was cast into the sea with a stone around her neck, and by this means she received holy Baptism. An angel rescued her, but again she was put into prison. When her father saw her, he ordered her beheading, but he died that evening. A few days later, the new governor named Dion interrogated her, then had her beaten. She worked many miraculous signs, and three thousand Greeks converted to the faith. Dion died from distress, and the next governor, Julian, had her burned in a furnace for six days, but she emerged unharmed. She was thrown to deadly snakes, her tongue was cut out, and her breasts removed, and again she remained unharmed. Two soldiers were ordered to stab her, and she gave up her spirit. Julian went home and died with great suffering. The incorrupt relics of St. Christina are preserved in the Church of San Francesco della Vigna in Venice, Italy.

COMMEMORATIONS: Christina of Tyre; Boris and Gleb of Russia; Pachomius, abbot; Hilarion of Tvali; Bernulphus, Bishop of Utrecht; Theophilos of Zakynthos; Athanasius of Nicaea; Polycarp of the Kiev Caves; John Kalinin of Olenevka; Bogolep, child schemamonk of Cherny Yar; Declan of Ardmore (Ireland); 17 New Martyrs of Mgarsk Monastery (Poltava); Alexander of Bolshaya Rechka; Martyrs Capito and Hymenaeus; Martyr Hermogenes; Serbian New Martyrs of Prebilovci (Herzegovina).

SATURDAY

JULY 25

**Dormition of St. Anna,
Mother of the Theotokos
Fast-free**
Galatians 4:22-27; Luke 8:16-21

We should never lose hope. No matter what we do, no matter how far we fall, no matter how often we are injured and hurt—we should never ever despair or lose hope!

Elder Ephraim of Arizona

MARTYRS SANCTUS, MATURUS, ATTALUS, BLANDINA, VETTIUS EPAGATHUS, BIBLIS, AND MARTYR POTHINUS, BISHOP OF LYONS. In second-century Gaul, a persecution of Christians arose under Marcus Aurelius. Christians were shut out from their houses and the markets, forbidden to be seen, subjected to shame, harmed by stoning, dragging, blows, and imprisoned. An honorable Christian named Epagathus testified in defense of the Christians but was also taken to prison. Some prisoners suffocated to death. Pothinus, the bishop of Lyons, was over ninety years old. Hardly able to breathe, he was dragged to the judgment seat, where he gave an excellent witness of his faith. He was beaten with hands and feet and stoned by those from a distance. He died in prison. Those who remained steadfast in their confession were only accused as Christians. However, those who denied the faith were punished twice as severely as the others. The confessors Muturos, Sanctus, Blandina, and Attalos were subjected repeatedly to the gauntlet, wild beasts, and roasted on an iron chair. The pretext against all these Christians was incest and cannibalism, to enrage the mob that watched. The relics of all of these martyrs were left unburied for six days, then burned to ashes and swept into the River Rhone.

COMMEMORATIONS: Dormition of St. Anna; Sanctus, Maturus, Attalus, Blandina, Vivlia, Vetius, Egapathus, Ponticus, Alexander, and others, at Lyons; Olympiada the Deaconess of Constantinople; Eupraxia of Tabenna; Vukosav Milanovic and Rodoljub Samardzic of Serbia; Theodore Tonkovid of Lovets (Pskov); Gregory Kallides of Thessalonica and Heraclea; Christopher of Solvychegodsk; Macarius of Zheltovod and Unzha; Synaxis of the Holy 165 Fathers of the Fifth Ecumenical Council.

Sunday
July 26

Seventh Sunday of Matthew
Fast-free
Galatians 3:23-29, 4:1-5; Matthew 9:27-35

If God is with us invisibly on earth, this is a sign that He will be with us in heaven. If we do not see God on earth with the heart, we will not see Him in heaven.

+*Elder Parthenius of Kiev Pechersk*

VENERABLE IOANNIKIOS THE NEW OF ROMANIA. Ioannikios was from sixteenth- and seventeenth-century Muscel in Romania. From a young age, he rejected worldly things. He went to the Cetatuia Monastery and lived in asceticism in a cave on Mount Negru Voda for fifty years. He fasted and prayed with tears for the whole world. Once a week a monk would bring him bread and water, and the abbot would go very often with Holy Communion. Ioannikios was the spiritual guide of the great prince Micheal the Brave and the ruler Matei Basarab. The saint foresaw the year of his repose, which was 1638, and inscribed it on a wall in his cave. Over three hundred years later, the abbot of the monastery was lowered through a hole into the cave, down fourteen meters, and found lying on a stone the relics of St. Ioannikios. On a rock, he found engraved in Cyrillic letters, "Ioannikios monk, 1638." Today the relics are in a chapel of the Cetatuia Monastery.

COMMEMORATIONS: Paraskeve of Rome; Jerusalem of Byzantium; Hermolaus, Hermippos, and Hermocrates at Nicomedia; Oriozela of Reuma in Byzantium; Ignatius of Mt. Stirion; Sava III, Archbishop of Serbia; Gerontios, founder of St. Anne Skete; Ioannikios the New of Muscel (Romania); Theodosius of the Caucasus; Isaac of Svyatogorsk; Moses the Hungarian of the Kiev Caves; Jacob, Enlightener of the peoples of Alaska; "Emvolon" Icon of the Mother of God, in Constantinople.

Monday

July 27

St. Panteleimon the Great Martyr
Fast-free
2 Timothy 2:1-10; John 15:17-16:2

Seek refuge in prayer.

St. John the Short

GREAT MARTYR AND HEALER PANTELEIMON. Panteleimon was a renowned physician of the people and the court of Emperor Maximian. The saint's father was a pagan, and his mother, Euboula, was from a family of Christians. Panteleimon learned about the Christian faith from the priest St. Hermolaos, who baptized him. A blind man went to Panteleimon, asking to be healed, and through the saint's prayer, the man received his sight. When the emperor asked the man who healed him of his blindness, he said Panteleimon, and he also said he was a Christian. Immediately, the emperor ordered the man to be beheaded. Panteleimon was found and brought to the emperor. When he would not abandon Christ for the idols, he was stretched on a rack and burned with candles. He was thrown into a pit of fire and to wild beasts, was cast into the sea and tied to a wheel nailed with sharp knives. Jesus appeared to him many times and kept him whole and unharmed. The idol-worshipers believed it was sorcery. Finally, Panteleimon was sentenced to beheading. As he knelt in prayer, the executioner swung the sword, but it suddenly melted like wax. When the soldiers saw this miracle, they believed in Christ. Then St. Panteleimon knelt and was beheaded in the year 304, at the age of twenty-nine.

COMMEMORATIONS: Great Martyr and Healer Panteleimon; The blind man who confessed Christ and was healed by St. Panteleimon; Clement of Ochrid, and Angelarius, Gorazd, Nahum, and Sabbas, disciples of Sts. Cyril and Methodios; Anthousa, abbess of Mantinea in Asia Minor, and 90 sisters; 853 Martyrs of Thrace who were drowned; Christodoulos of Kassandra, at Thessalonica; Ambrose (Gudko), Bishop of Sarapul; Joasaph, Metropolitan of Moscow; Nicholas Kochanov of Novgorod; Righteous Manuel; Aurelius, Sabigotha (Natalia), Felix, Liliosa, and George the Sabbaite, at Cordoba; Glorification of St. Herman of Alaska.

TUESDAY   Fast-free

JULY 28   Acts 6:1-7; Matthew 16:6-12

We receive salvation by grace and as a divine gift of the Spirit. But to attain the full measure of virtue we need also to possess faith and love, and to struggle to exercise our free will with integrity.

St. Symeon Metaphrastis

MARTYR EFSTATHIOS THE SOLDIER OF ANCYRA. Efstathios was a Christian soldier. He was taken before the pagan governor Cornelius of Ancyra, where he confessed his faith. He was beaten, holes were drilled in his ankles, and a rope pulled through so that they could drag the saint to the river. Cornelius went with them to observe the tortures. Finally, Efstathios was put into a wooden chest and thrown into the river, but a divine angel brought the chest back to shore. When Efstathios saw that God had healed every injury, he began to chant Psalm 91: "He that dwelleth in the secret place of the most High shall abide under the shadow of the Almight." When Cornelius heard that Efstathios survived, he was so humiliated and disgraced that he killed himself with a knife. Having received Holy Communion from the hand of an angel, St. Efstathios gave up his spirit. His relics were buried in the city of Ancyra.

COMMEMORATIONS: Apostles Prochorus, Nicanor, Timon, and Parmenas; Paul of Xeropotamou; Julian of Dalmatia; Eustathius of Ancyra; Acacius of Apamea; Irene Chrysovolantou of Cappadocia; Ursus and Leobatius of Gaul; Anastasius of Ancyra; Anthony of Rostov; George the Builder of Iveron; Pitirim of Tambov; Samson of Dol; Basil of Sarov; Ignatius of Jablechna; Moses of the Kiev Caves; Translation of the relics of St. John the New Chozebite; Synaxis of All Saints of Tambov; Smolensk "Hodigitria," "Of the Lavra in Suprasl" (Poland), "Grebensk," and "Yugsk" Icons of the Mother of God.

Wednesday
July 29
Strict Fast

1 Corinthians 10:12-22; Matthew 16:20-24

Slandering someone who is deaf means backbiting one who is absent and cannot hear you. Just as the deaf man cannot hear or understand what is said, so it is with the absent person someone slanders. That person who is absent cannot reply or rectify the errors of which he is the object.

St. Gregory of Nyssa

VIRGIN-MARTYR SERAPHIMA OF ANTIOCH. Seraphima was a young Christian woman living in the home of an illustrious Roman named Sabina, in second-century Antioch. When Seraphima converted Sabina to Christianity, she was taken to the governor Birillus, who tortured Christians. He imprisoned her and sent two youths to violate her. When they arrived at her cell, an angel of God appeared holding a sword, rendering them unconscious. The next day Berillus asked her to revive the youths, and with prayer, they stood up. The young men told Berillus about the miracle and how an angel shielded Seraphima. Dismissing this as sorcery, the governor gave orders to have her burned with torches and beaten with canes. Chips from the cane flew through the air, striking the eyes of the governor, and blinding him. St. Seraphim was beheaded, and Sabina buried her. Healing myrrh flowed from her relics.

COMMEMORATIONS: Kallinikos of Gangra; Theodota and her 3 sons, in Bithynia; Theodota of Asia Minor; Benjamin and Berius of Constantinople; Constantine III Leichoudes, Patriarch of Constantinople; Seraphima of Antioch; Bessarion of Bulgaria; John the Soldier at Constantinople; Constantine and Cosmas of Kosinsk; Mamas in Darii; Romanus of Kirzhach; Eustathius of Mtskheta; Lupus of Troyes; Theodosius the Younger, emperor; Basiliscus the Elder; Bogolep of Black Ravine; Olaf of Norway; Anatole of the Caucasus Mountains; Seraphim and Theognostus at Kazakhstan; Pachomius of Kazakhstan; Daniel Kushnir of Mlievich (Ukraine).

Thursday

Fast-free

July 30

Acts 15:35-41; Matthew 16:24-28

*E*very adversity and affliction, if not accompanied by patience, produces double torment; for a man's patience casts off distress, while faintness of heart is the mother of anguish. Patience is the mother of consolation and is a certain strength which is usually born of largeness of heart. It is hard for a man to find this strength in his tribulations without a gift from God received through the ardent pursuit of prayer and the outpouring of his tears."

St. Isaac the Syrian

HIEROMARTYR VALENTINE, BISHOP OF INTERAMNA IN ITALY. Valentine was a third-century bishop in Umbria, Italy, in the city of Interamna. He had the gift from God to heal various illnesses through prayer, and he healed the brother of a Roman tribune. Because of this, the tribune sent the eminent pagan philosopher Craton to Bishop Valentine to ask him to heal Craton's son, Cheriton, whose spine was so cramped that his head was stuck between his knees. Valentine spent a whole night in prayer with the youth, and in the morning, he was found healed. Because of this, Craton and his entire household received Baptism, and Cherimon became Valentine's disciple. Later, Valentine baptized the son of a Roman eparch. Infuriated, the eparch tortured and beheaded St. Valentine along with some of Craton's pupils.

COMMEMORATIONS: Apostles Silas, Silvanos, Crescens, Epenetos, and Andronikos, of the Seventy; Julitta at Caesarea; Valentine, Bishop of Interamna, and Proculus, Ephebus, Apollonius, and Abundius; Polychronius of Babylon, and Parmenius, Helimenas, Chrysotelus, Luke, Mocius, Abdon, Sennen, Maximus, and Olympius; Stephen (Vladislav) of Serbia; Anatole II of Optina; Alexander the Chanter; Angelina Brancovich of Serbia; Tsotne Dadiani the Confessor of Mingrelia; Uncovering of the relics of St. Herman of Solovki; Synaxis of the Saints of Samara; "Okonsk" Icon of the Mother of God.

FRIDAY

JULY 31

Forefeast of the Precious Cross
Strict Fast
1 Corinthians 11:8-23; Matthew 17:10-18

Cast aside cares, strip yourself from thoughts, and abandon your body; for prayer is nothing other than detachment from the visible and invisible world.

St. John Climacus

ST. GERMANUS, BISHOP OF AUXERRE. Germanus was born in Auxerre in the fourth century. He was educated in Rome, where he studied law and rhetoric and became a lawyer. The emperor sent him to Gaul to serve as a provincial governor. He was later chosen as bishop of Auxerre. Germanus prayed more, and his faith grew stronger. He wore a simple monk's robe, fasted for many days, ate only barley bread in the evening, and gave away all his earthly goods to the poor. Pope Celestine I sent him to Britain to fight the Pelagian heresy. This heresy was the brainchild of Pelagius, who professed that original sin never existed and the concept of Christian grace was an error. Germanus succeeded in defeating this doctrine. During one of his trips to Britain, he took over the command of the army and defeated the Picts and Saxons. The city of Armorica, now Brittany, was being threatened by barbarians. Germanus met with their leader, grabbed his horse by the bridle, and turned him around, thus diffusing their attack. Then the saint went to Ravenna to meet with the emperor to ask for a pardon for the same rebels. St. Germanus died there, and his body was taken back to Auxerre for burial. Hundreds of years later, his relics were seized by the Huguenots and scattered.

COMMEMORATIONS: Joseph of Arimathea; Julitta, at Caesarea in Cappadocia; Eudokimos of Cappadocia; John the Exarch of Bulgaria; Germanus of Auxerre; 12 Martyrs of Rome; Dionysius of Vatopedi; Benjamin, Sergius, George, and John of Petrograd; Basil of Kineshma; Neot, in Cornwall; Arsenius of Ninotsminda; Anonymous New Martyr from Crete; Consecration of the Church of the Most Holy Theotokos of Blachernae; Translation of the relics of Apostle Philip to Cyprus.

Let us humble ourselves, and the Lord will grant us to know the power of the Jesus Prayer...Learn how to have Christ-like humility, and the Lord will grant you to taste the sweetness of prayer. And if you want to achieve pure prayer, become humble, exercise temperance, confess sincerely, and the prayer will love to swell in you. Become obedient, submit yourself with a sincere conscience to all authorities, and be content with all things; then your mind will be cleansed from vain thoughts. Remember that the Lord sees you, and be careful lest you sadden your brother with something— do not condemn him, and do not sadden him even with a single glance. Then, the Holy Spirit will love you, and He will help you in all things.

St. Silouan the Athonite

SATURDAY

AUGUST 1

Procession of the Precious Cross
Dormition Fast Begins
Abstain from meat and dairy products, and fish.

Hebrews 11:33-12:2; Matthew 10:16-22

The apostle Peter leads the righteous to heaven, and the Queen of Heaven Herself leads sinners.

St. Ambrose of Optina

FEAST TO THE ALL-MERCIFUL SAVIOR AND THE MOST HOLY MOTHER OF GOD. This Russian feast was established on events from icons of the Savior, the Most Holy Mother of God, and the Venerable Cross marking the victory of the Russian armies over the Volga Bulgars in 1164. There are three feastdays in August celebrating the All-Merciful Savior, and these connect with the Dormition Fast, which is is the first of the three feasts. The second feast is the Transfiguration of our Lord on August 6, and the third is the Transfer of the Icon Not-Made-With-Hands of the Lord Jesus Christ from Edessa to Constantinople on August 16. The August 1 feast is also called the "Honey Savior/Spas" because in the Ukraine beekeepers harvest honey and hold honey markets during this time. A famous market is held at the Kiev Caves Lavra to this day, which marks the day in 988 that St. Vladimir the Great baptized his people into Orthodox Christianity. This is also the day water is blessed.

COMMEMORATIONS: Procession of the Life-Giving Cross; Feast to the All-Merciful Savior and the Most Holy Mother of God; Holy Seven Maccabees: Abimus, Antonius, Gurias, Eleazar, Eusebonus, Alimus, and Marcellus, and their mother Solomonia, and their teacher Eleazar; 9 Martyrs of Perga: Leontius, Attius, Alexander, Cindeus, Minsitheus, Cyriacus, Menaeus, Catanus, and Eucleus; Timothy, Archbishop of Priconissus; Nicholas, enlightener of Japan; Eusebius, Bishop of Verceil (Italy); Basil, Archbishop of Chernigov; Elessa of Cythera; Papas the New; Martyr Eleazar; Martyrs Theodore and Polyeuctus; Anthony the New of Beroia; Menas, Menais, and others of England; Sidwell of Exeter; Ethelwold, Bishop of Winchester; Cennydd of Llangenydd (Wales); Almedha of Wales; Alexander (Urodov) of Sanaxar and Seven Lakes; "Tripolitsa" and "Tavriotissa" Icons of the Mother of God.

SUNDAY

AUGUST 2

Eighth Sunday of Matthew
Abstain from meat and
dairy products, and fish.
1 Corinthians 1:10-17
Matthew 14:14-22

During the great fast of the first fifteen days of August, some persons wore black clothes, in order to honor the Theotokos. But if this is not accompanied by fasting and by prayer it is in vain.

St. Raphael of Lesvos

VENERABLE PHOTINI (FOTOU) OF CYPRUS. St. Photini the Cypriot, known in Cyprus as Fotou, lived as an ascetic in a cave that she carved out herself. The cave is in the village of Agios Andronikos of Yialousa. The fifteenth-century historian Leontios Macheras writes in his "Chronikon" that in the cave was a Holy Altar and a place of worship, which has holy water deep in depth. At every new moon, the top of the water turns into ice and people lift it off, which then starts melting into small particles as thin as dust. The blind take this dust and rub it on their eyes, and they can see. This holy water is said to have dried up since the Turkish settlement of Northern Cyprus in 1974. Every year on the eve of Fotou's feast, thousands of faithful from around Cyprus filled the village and made temporary huts. This began one of the island's biggest festivals, with food drink, song, and dance. Until 1964 the village was mixed, and Turkish Cypriots celebrated with the Greeks. Fotou is one of the most beloved saints of the region. According to tradition, she was granted the power to perform miracles. She died peacefully and was buried by devout Christians. Later her tomb was discovered by divine revelation. In it were written the following words: "Photini, Virgin Bride of Christ."

COMMEMORATIONS: Theodore of the Dardanelles; Friardus of Gaul; Basil the Fool-for-Christ of Moscow; Marco of Belavinsk; Justinian of Byzantium and Theodora; Stephen, Pope of Rome; Martyr Phocas; Basil of Kuben Lake; Platon of Chasovo (Komi); Friardus of Vindumitta and Secundellus (Gaul); Etheldritha (Alfreda) of England; Alexis Medvedkov of Uzine; Fotou (Photini) the Cypriot; Consecration of the Church of St. John the Theologian; Translation of the relics of Protomartyr and Archdeacon Stephen.

Monday

Strict Fast

August 3

1 Corinthians 11:31-12:6
Matthew 18:1-11

*T*he devil extremely despises the person who prays, and when someone is about to pray, he employs every means to spoil man's goal. He does not cease stirring thoughts of different things in our memory and arousing all the passions through the flesh, in order to obstruct this excellent work of prayer and prevent the mind's ascent to God.

St. Neilos the Ascetic

ST. SALOME THE MYRRHBEARER. Salome the Myrrhbearer was the first cousin of the Panagia. Her husband was Zebedee, and her sons were James and John the Apostles. She was distinguished for her zealous faith and philanthropy. Salome was among the women who followed and ministered to Jesus and His disciples. She is also the one who asked Jesus to have in His kingdom her two sons to sit one on His left and the other on His right. Later, after the Crucifixion, when all the Apostles fled except for John, Salome stood with the other women mourning and beating their chests out of grief. Three days after the Crucifixion, Salome was made worthy of being among the Myrrhbearers to witness the Resurrection of the Lord. She helped and served the Church of Jerusalem after Pentecost. St. Salome died in peace after Herod's soldiers beheaded her son James.

COMMEMORATIONS: Isaac, Dalmatius, and Faustus of the Dalmatian Monastery; Salome the Myrrh-bearer; Stephen, Pope of Rome; John, abbot of Patalaria Monastery; Theodora of Thessalonica and her daughter Theopisti of Aegina; Cosmas, hermit of Palestine; Olympios the Prefect; Anthony the Roman of Novgorod; Theocleto the Wonderworker of Optimaton; Rajden of Tsromi, Georgia; Nine Kherkheulidze brothers, with their sister and mother and 9,000 martyrs of Marabda, Georgia; Trea of Ardtrea.

Tuesday

Strict Fast

August 4

1 Corinthians 12:12-26
Matthew 18:18-22, 19:1-2, 13-15

You must conquer anger through silence. The angry man is a murderer of his soul. It is not possible to not get angry, if you are not humble.

+Elder Efstratios of Glinsk

HOLY SEVEN YOUTHS OF EPHESUS: MAXIMILIAN, JAMBLICUS, MARTINIAN, JOHN, DIONYSIUS, EXACUSTODIAN (CONSTANTINE), AND ANTONINUS. During the third-century Christian persecution under Emperor Decius, an edict demanded that everyone submit to idol-worship. These seven youths, as well as many other Christians, went into hiding. The seven young men hid in a cave, but when they were found, the cave was sealed, and the men left to die within. This was the same cave in which Mary Magdalene had been buried. Almost two hundred years later, a new property owner curiously unearthed the cave opening, only to have the seven men walk out. They had fallen asleep the night the cave was sealed, and now they assumed they had been uncovered the next day. God had preserved them. When they tried to use money that was two hundred years old, the story began to unfold. The Christian Emperor Theodosios, who caused this story to be recorded, received them. Multitudes of people came to visit and see the living miracles. It was said that after forty days, the seven youths reposed. In a dream, the seven saints appeared to the emperor asking that their relics be left in the cave.

COMMEMORATIONS: Holy Seven Youths of Ephesus—the "Seven Sleepers": Maximilian, Jamblicus, Martinian, John, Dionysius, Exacustodian (Constantine), and Antoninus; Eleutherius of Constantinople; Michael (Zhuk) of Staroye Zubarevo (Mordovia); Martyr Thathuil; Molua of Killaloe (Ireland); Eudocia of Persia; Consecration of the Church of Jesus Christ the Pantocrator in Constantinople; Translation of the Relics of Martyr Ia of Persia.

WEDNESDAY

AUGUST 5

Forefeast of the Transfiguration
Strict Fast
1 Peter 1:1-2:10; Matthew 20:1-16

The Lord clothes his chosen souls in the garments of the ineffable light of his kingdom, the garments of faith, hope, love, joy, and peace, the garments of goodness and kindness and all comparable things. They are divine garments pulsating with light and life, and they bring us peace that passes all description.

St. Makarios the Great

VENERABLE JOB THE GORGE-DWELLER. Job was a seventeenth-century monk of the Solovki Monastery in Russia. He was ordained a hieromonk and was sent to the Mezensk frontier on the Mezen River, where he built a chapel in honor of the Nativity of Christ. Monks began to gather there, but they had to live close by with family because the monastery was so poor. When the tsar granted the monastery lands with fishing rights, they built a church and monastic cells. One day on August 5, 1628, while all the monks were working in the fields, robbers attacked the monastery. Job was tortured, then beheaded when they demanded he open the monastery treasury. Finally, when they found nothing, they fled. Pilgrims soon began to venerate Job as a saint because of numerous miracles that took place at his tomb. Thirty years later, an icon of St. Job was written, and a chapel was built over his relics, which was later rebuilt and dedicated to Righteous Job the Much-Suffering. In the icon St. Job is depicted holding a scroll with the words, "Fear not those who kill the body, but are not able to kill the soul."

COMMEMORATIONS: Eusignius of Antioch; Pontius at Cimella in Gaul; Nonna, mother of St. Gregory the Theologian; Fabian and Antherus, Popes of Rome; John Jacob of Neamt, the Chozebite; Cantidius, Cantidian, and Sibelius of Egypt; Eugenius the Aitolos; Job the Gorge-dweller; Eudocia Shikova of Puzo, with Daria, Daria, and Maria of Diveyevo; Euthymius, Patriarch of Constantinople; Simon (Shleyev), Bishop of Ufa; Chrestos of Preveza; Oswald of Northumbria; Soleb of Egypt; Afra of Augsburg; Uncovering of the relics of St. Arsenios the New of Paros.

Thursday

August 6

Holy Transfiguration
Abstain from meat and dairy products.
2 Peter 1:10-19; Matthew 17:1-9

*H*asten as early as possible, before anything interferes, to lift yourself up to the Lord in mind and heart in solitude, to confess your needs and intentions to Him, and to beg for His help. Having attuned yourself by prayer and thoughts of God from the first moments of the day, you will then spend the whole day in reverence and fear of God, with collected thoughts.

St. Theophan the Recluse

NEW MARTYR DIMITRI, ARCHBISHOP OF GDOV, AND THOSE WITH HIM. Dimitri Lyubimov was born into the family of a protopriest from the St. Petersburg province, who was a benefactor, church builder, and friend of St John of Kronstadt. Dimitri graduated from the Theological Academy in 1882 and was a reader and then a teacher at the local theological school. He married and was ordained to the priesthood. His charitable works included running an orphanage, old age homes, and schools. He had a great love for the poor. During the time of the Russian Revolution, Dimitri was arrested and exiled many times. Metropolitan Sergius had fallen away from the true Orthodox faith and represented the interests of the State instead. Dimitri pleaded and reasoned with him to stop these activities but to no avail. The true Orthodox were labeled counter-revolutionaries. Dimitri was appointed archbishop and became the leader of the Catacomb Church in the Petrograd area, and accepted many other parishes. But Sergius was relentless in his pursuit and banishment of Dimitri. One mass arrest included Dimitri and forty-six others, including protopriests, monastics, and laypeople. Dimitri spent years in solitary confinement and was savagely tortured. He died in prison.

COMMEMORATIONS: Transfiguration of our Lord, God and Savior Jesus Christ; Theoctistus, Bishop of Chernigov; Abbacum of Thessalonica; New Martyrs Dimitri (Lyubimov), Archbishop of Gdov, and Nicholas Prozorov, Andrew Zimin, Sergius Tikhomirov, Domnik, Lidia, and Mary Zimin, of Russia; New Virgin Martyr Eudocia, near Sarov.

Friday   Strict Fast

August 7

1 Corinthians 14:26-40; Mark 9:2-9

Many Christians, unaware of the great value of fasting, either keep the fast with difficulty or reject it altogether. We should not be afraid to fast but embrace it with joy.

St. John Chrysostom

MARTYR DOMETIOS OF PERSIA AND TWO DISCIPLES. Dometios was born in fourth-century Persia. He was taught the faith of Christ and abandoned his relatives. He entered a monastery, was baptized, and began to take great strides towards perfection. When he sought greater solitude, he placed himself under obedience to Archimandrite Urbil, who for sixty years did not eat any cooked food, nor lie down or sit. When Urbil attempted to elevate Dometios to the priesthood, he left there and went into a mountain cave. He endured the heat of summer and cold of winter for many years. Through prayer, fasting, and vigils, Dometios was granted the gift of healing the sick. He converted Greek pagans to the faith in Christ. When Julian the Apostate heard about this, he gave orders to kill Dometios. When the soldiers arrived at the cave, they found Dometios and two disciples chanting. St. Dometios and his two disciples were stoned to death.

COMMEMORATIONS: 10,000 Ascetics of Thebes; Narcissus, Patriarch of Jerusalem; Marinus and Asterius the Senator at Caesarea; Sozon of Nicomedia; Horus of the Thebaid; Nicanor of Mt. Callistratus; Hyperechius of *The Paradise*; Potamia of Alexandria; Dometius of Persia and 2 disciples; Mercurius of Smolensk; Dometios of Philotheou; Theodora of Sihla (Romania); Anthony of Optina; Pimen the Much-ailing of the Kiev Caves; Theodosius the New of Argos; Nikanor the Wonderworker; Mikallos of Akanthou; Pimen, faster of the Kiev Caves; Joseph of Kapsa; Victricius of Rouen; Irene and Pulcheria of Constantinople; Alexander Hotovitzky, Peter Tokarev, Michael Plishevsky, John Voronets, Demetrius Milovidov, Alexei Vorobiev, Elisha Sholder, and Athanasius Egorov, of Moscow; Paphnutius the Mute of Romania.

SATURDAY

AUGUST 8

Abstain from meat and dairy products, and fish.
Romans 14:6-9; Matthew 15:32-39

How many hours of each day have I spent in sleep, how often have I enjoyed voluptuous thoughts in bed and defiled my flesh! How many hours have I spent in empty and futile pastimes and pleasures, in frivolous talk and speech, jokes and laughter, games and fun, and how much time have I wasted conclusively in chatter, and gossip, in criticizing others and reproaching them; how many hours have I spent in time-wasting and emptiness! What shall I answer to the Lord God for every hour and every minute of lost time? In truth, I have wasted my entire life in laziness.

St. Basil the Great

ST. MYRON, BISHOP OF CRETE. Myron was an extremely charitable farmer from the third-century island of Crete. From his youth, he was known for his faith in God and wonderworking. He assisted everyone who asked for help. One evening he came upon thieves stealing his grain. Myron helped them lift the sacks of grain onto their shoulders, and said to them, "God forgive you. This is my advice: go, but do not steal again." When Myron's wife died, the people of Crete asked him to be ordained to the priesthood. He was later appointed bishop and held the office for seventy years. One time during a flood, Myron stopped the flow of a river and commanded it to resume after he had crossed over. St. Myron lived to one hundred years of age.

COMMEMORATIONS: Gregory of Sinai; Myron, Bishop of Crete; Eleutherius and Leonides of Constantinople, and many infants; Emilian the Confessor, Bishop of Cyzicus; Gormizdas of Persia; Gregory of Sinai; Gregory, iconographer of the Kiev Caves; Gregory, wonderworker of the Kiev Caves; Anastasius of Radovishte in Strumica; Philaret of Ivanovo; 12 Ascetics of Egypt; Euthymius of Georgia; Triandaphillos of Zagora; 2 Martyrs of Tyre; Zosimas the Sinaite of Tumana Monastery, Serbia; Martyr Styracius; Joseph of Tolga; Nicholas of Pokrovskoye; Nicodemus of Kostroma; Theodosios of Orov.

SUNDAY

AUGUST 9

Ninth Sunday of Matthew
Abstain from meat and dairy products, and fish.
1 Corinthians 3:9-17
Matthew 14:22-34

If you avoid having children, you avoid salvation.
+*Elder Paisius of Sihla*

NEW MARTYR IGNATIUS BAZYLUK OF POLAND. Ignatius was from mid-nineteenth-century Poland. Between the time of the First and Second World Wars, he was a monk at the St. Onuphrios Monastery in Jableczna. When he first entered there, there were about twelve monks, and it was their task to spread true Orthodoxy and offset the propaganda of other religions in that area. Ignatius' obedience was the ringing of the bells for church services. At one point, around 1915, the school that was created at the monastery had four hundred pupils and eighty monks. But in that same year, the Germans occupied the monastery, and the monks fled to Moscow. Only four monks returned to the monastery, and it was found in ruins. In 1939 German soldiers occupied the monastery again, confiscating the food supply and livestock. Then in 1942, they set fire to the monastery. The monks fled into the courtyard, and Ignatius began ringing the bell to warn the residents in the area of danger. He was attacked and beaten to death. Some residents arrived at the monastery to help, but the soldiers detained them. Then everyone in the courtyard was shot.

COMMEMORATIONS: Apostle Matthias; Herman of Alaska; 10 Martyrs at the Chalke Gate: Julian, Marcian, John, James, Alexius, Demetrius, Photius, Peter, Leontius, and Maria the Patrician; Psoes of Egypt; Anthony of Alexandria; Macarius of Oredezh Monastery; Philaret Humilevsky of Chernigov; Felim of Kilmore; Nathy of Achonry; Ignatius Bazyluk of Poland; Euthymios, Metropolitan of Rhodes; Synaxis of the Saints of Solovki; Glorification of St. Herman of Alaska; Finding of the Acheiropoeton Icon of Christ in Kamouliana.

Monday

August 10

Strict Fast

1 Corinthians 15:12-19
Matthew 21:18-22

We mustn't despair when we struggle and continuously see nothing but the slightest progress. We all do nearly nothing, some a little more, some a little less. When Christ sees our little effort, He gives us an analogous token, and so our nearly nothing becomes valuable and we can see a little progress. For this reason, we mustn't despair, but hope in God.

St. Paisios the Athonite

HOLY MARTYR LAWRENCE THE ARCHDEACON. Lawrence was one of seven archdeacons under Pope Sixtus II of Rome during the third century. His charge was to oversee efforts to help the poor. He was effective and respected by those he helped, as well as those who donated. During this time, the emperor Valerian instituted another Christian persecution and began by martyring the St. Sixtus. When Lawrence was ordered to bring the treasures of the Church of Rome to the emperor, he brought all the sick and poor Christians he could find. Enraged, the emperor sent the crowd away and promised unheard-of tortures for Lawrence. He was grilled alive over a fire, and he did not make a sound. He asked his torturers to turn him over since his one side was cooked enough. God kept the saint unharmed. Lawrence's last words to the emperor and his entourage were that he was done enough, and it was time to eat. He prayed for Rome to turn from idol-worship and gave up his spirit. His martyrdom brought many to the faith in the Western Church. St. Lawrence is depicted in icons with St. Stephen the First Martyr.

COMMEMORATIONS: Archdeacon Lawrence and Pope Sixtus, Felicissimus, and Agapitus, deacons, and others with them; Hippolytus of Rome and 18 martyrs with him, including Concordia, Irenaeus, and Abundius; Romanus, soldier of Rome; 6 Martyrs of Bizin; Bertram, King of Merica; Lawrence, fool-for-Christ at Kaluga; Blaine of the Isle of Bute; Heron the Philosopher; Synaxis of New Martyrs and Confessors of Solovki.

Tuesday **Strict Fast**

August 11

1 Corinthians 15:29-38
Matthew 21:23-27

Just as you would seek the best possible doctor, you should do the same for a spiritual father.

St. Porphyrios the Kapsokalyvite

NEW MARTYRS ANASTASIOS AND DEMETRIOS THE BASKETWEAVERS. Anastasios and Demetrios were from different villages on the island of Lesvos. Anastasios took on the family trade of basket weaving and later moved to Asia Minor to make a better living. Demetrios was from a poor family and orphaned at a young age. His new stepfather was hard on him and his brother, depriving them of food and clothing, so they would not go home to sleep. A kind Turkish man saw this and felt sorry for Demetrios. He took the child under his wing, supporting him until he came of age. At that time, he sought to have Demetrios marry his daughter and change his faith. To avoid any further pressure, Demetrios decided to go to Asia Minor, and there he met Anastasios and joined him in basket weaving. The Christians admired the work of these two men, and in turn, they encouraged them in their Orthodox faith. But some from the Turkish community approached Anastasios and Demetrios and suggested that they convert to Islam and told them of the advantages. When the two saints declined, the Turks were offended. They were taken to a judge who tried to convince them, and when they refused to leave their Orthodox faith, they were tortured and hanged. With great honor, their bodies were buried by Christians, and their relics became a source of healing. Magnificent churches were erected in their honor.

COMMEMORATIONS: Euplus of Catania; Niphon II, Patriarch of Constantinople; Theodore and Basil of the Kiev Caves; Taurinus of Evreux; Susanna, with Gaius and Gabinus; Maximus, Claudius, Praepedigna, Alexander, and Cuthias; Anastasios Paneras of Asomaton, and Demetrios Begiazis of Lesvos; Theodore, Prince of Ostrog; John of Svyatogorsk; Passarion of Palestine; Martyrs Neophytus, Zeno, Gaius, Mark, Macarius, and Gaianus; Blaan of Bute; Commemoration of the Miracle of St. Spyridon against the Hagarenes on Corfu.

WEDNESDAY   Strict Fast

August 12
1 Corinthians 16:4-12
Matthew 21:28-32

Be extremely careful with your imagination. Do not accept any image, because it will become an idol that you will worship.
Elder Ephraim of Arizona

ST. PALAMON THE ANCHORITE OF EGYPT. A young St. Pachomios the Great went to Abba Palamon in the fourth century, asking to become his disciple. Together they made hair sacks, which they gave to the poor who came to them. Palamon admonished his disciple to keep vigilant so the adversary could not steal all his toils. Once, when Pachomios offered his elder vegetables with oil for their Pascha meal, Palamon refused. He said that Jesus was just crucified a few days before, how could he partake of oil today? Another time, a monk filled with demonic pride visited the ascetics and challenged them to walk on hot coals to test their faith. With discernment, Palamon told him to ignore those soul-injuring antics. However, the visitor proudly walked on the hot coals, but the devil later possessed him for a different prideful act. This reminded them of the need for humble-mindedness to avoid this type of punishment. Palamon fell sick from his rigorous regimen. He would not drink water with his bread. The doctor advised him to eat properly to prolong his life, but Palamon said that if the martyrs persevered while being cut up and tormented, then he would be a coward to back away from his severe fasting. One month later, St. Palamon died. His disciple, St. Pachomios buried him.

COMMEMORATIONS: Alexander, Bishop of Comana; Palamon of Egypt; Martyrs Pamphilus and Capito; 12 Soldiers Martyrs of Crete; Sergius and Stephen, monks; Anicetus and Photius of Nicomedia; Gerontius, Serapion, Germanus, Bessarion, Michael, Simeon, and Otar of Garesja; Molaise of Devenish; Jambert of Canterbury; Seigine of Iona; Muredach (Murtagh) of Killala; Barlaam, Anthony, Sergius, Elijah, Vyacheslav, Ioasaph, John, Micah, Bessarion, Euthymius, Matthew, Euthymius, Barnabas, Demetrius, Sabbas, Hermogenes, Arcadius, Marcellus, John, James, Peter, James, Alexander, Theodore, Peter, Sergius, and Alexis – of the Belogorsk St. Nicholas Monastery (Perm).

Thursday

Strict Fast

August 13

1 Corinthians 1:1-7
Matthew 21:43-46

An arrow of evil cannot reach you when you are fasting. Never!
  +Gerontissa Gavrielia of Greece

ST. TIKHON OF ZADONSK, BISHOP OF VORONEZH. Tikhon was from a poor family in eighteenth-century Novgorod. At the age of thirteen, he went to a clergy school, then to the Novgorod seminary, where he later taught Greek, Rhetoric, and Philosophy. He was tonsured a monk, and that same year was ordained a deacon, then a priest. Shortly afterward he was named rector of the seminary and was elevated to Bishop of Voronezh. However, because of the size of the diocese, its transient population, and the number of schismatics, Tikhon's health began to suffer. He resigned and went to the Tolshevsk Monastery for rest. Two years later, he transferred to the Monastery of the Theotokos in Zadonsk. He prayed and wrote books there until he died at the age of fifty-nine. He has become known as the "Russian Chrysostom." He wrote in a simple style, mostly about the duties of Christians, with quotes from Holy Scripture. Sixty years after his death, it was necessary to move his body during the construction of a new cathedral in Zadonsk. St. Tikhon's relics were uncovered and found incorrupt, and many miracles occurred. Three hundred thousand people attended the canonization of this beloved Russian saint in 1863. People often pray to St. Tikhon for the protection and upbringing of their children.

COMMEMORATIONS: Tikhon of Zadonsk; Dorotheos of Gaza; Maximos the Confessor; Xenia-Irene of Hungary; Dositheos of Thawaitha; Eudocia the Empress, wife of Theodosius the Younger; Empress Irene (Xene) of Constantinople; Serid (Seridus), abbot of Gaza; Radegunde of Poitiers; Wigbert, abbot of Hersfeld; Seraphim (Zvezdinsky), Bishop of Dmitrov; Translation of the Relic of St. Maximos the Confessor; Uncovering of the relics of St. Maximus of Moscow, fool-for-Christ; "Of the Passion," "Minsk," "Of the Seven Arrows," and "The Softening of Evil Hearts" Icons of the Mother of God.

Friday

August 14

Forefeast of the Dormition
Strict Fast
2 Corinthians 1:12-20
Matthew 22:23-33

The Panagia is the only mother of all Christians. And who does not call upon her? Because the sufferings of mankind are many in this vain world, nowhere else can we all find relief, except in the Panagia. When you are sitting there quietly, a thought suddenly comes to you and brings darkness. Where will you go to be loosed from this darkness? To the Panagia.

St. Anthimos of Chios

HIEROMARTYR MARCELLUS, BISHOP OF APAMEA. In the fifth century, Marcellus was a wealthy, well-educated boy living on the island of Cyprus. Emperor Theodosios later appointed him governor of the island for his leadership ability. Gradually, he felt an increasingly strong calling to work with the Church. Therefore, he resigned, studied for the priesthood, and was ordained. Soon he was consecrated bishop of Apamea in Syria. When he arrived, he found only a seed of Christianity against a backdrop of idol-worship, but he caused Christianity to flourish. However, the Christian converts, as was their practice, would destroy their former places of worship, and this was perceived as an outright attack on idol-worshippers. Bishop Marcellus received permission from the emperor Theodosius the Great to destroy the strong temple of Zeus in Apamea. By divine intervention, the temple collapsed. The pagans seized St. Marcellus and threw him into a fire.

COMMEMORATIONS: Forefeast of the Dormition; Prophet Micah; Ursicius at Nicomedia; Nazarius, Herman, Hierotheus, Simon, and Bessarion, of Georgia; Marcellus, Bishop of Apamea; Symeon of Trebizond; Luke the Soldier; Basil, Archbishop of Chernigov, and with him, Matthew and Alexis; Fachanan, abbot of Ross Carbery, Ireland; Matthew and Eleutherius of Holy Trinity Monastery (Smolensk); Eve (Pavlova), abbess of Holy Trinity Convent in Penza; Synaxis of the New Martyrs of Georgia who suffered under the Atheist Yoke; Commemoration of the Honorable and Life-Giving Cross to the Palace; "Narva" and "Converser" Icons of the Mother of God.

SATURDAY

Dormition of the Mother of God
Fast-free

AUGUST 15

Philippians 2:5-11
Luke 10:38-42, 11:27-28

She does not complain, is not stressed, has no fear and is not in a hurry. She has abandoned herself to the divine will and has identified her will with the divine will. She lives in Paradise — freely, as Eve did before the Fall. She has no worries, no misfortunes, no superficialities, no reservations and no ulterior motives. She has completely, honorably and joyfully given herself to God. This is why Mary, the all-virtuous Panagia, is significant, exceptional, amazing and extraordinarily unique.
+*Blessed Moses of Mt. Athos*

ST. TARCISIUS THE ACOLYTE. One day Tarcisius was entrusted with the task of taking the Eucharist to condemned prisoners in third-century Rome. On the way, he was attacked by a mob who wanted to take the Divine Mysteries. Tarcisius preferred death than to lose them. The fourth-century Pope Damasus composed a poem in his honor, comparing Tarcisius, who was beaten to death, to First Martyr Stephen, who was stoned to death. Cardinal Wiseman made this story well known in his novel "Fabiola." The story of the young Tarcisius is dramatized by a very moving account of his martyrdom. St. Tarcisius is known as one of the patron saints of altar boys. It is said that he was an acolyte of the pope.

COMMEMORATIONS: Dormition of the Theotokos; Chrestos of Ioannina; Alexis, archpriest of Petrograd; Stephen, elder of Vyatka; Priest Paul Szwajko and Presbytera Joanna of Graboviec (Poland); Macarius the Roman and his disciple Chariton of Novgorod; Tarcisius the Acolyte; Remembrance of the Love of God for Mankind; Synaxis of the Panagia Fidousa in Kefallonia; "Diasozousa" and "Chajnicke" Icons of the Mother of God.

SUNDAY

Tenth Sunday of Matthew
Fast-free

AUGUST 16

1 Corinthians 4:9-16
Matthew 14:22-34

We invoke the Mother of God as "truly more honored than the Seraphim," for she is a powerful intercessor above all others.
St. Symeon of Thessalonica

MARTYR DIOMEDES THE PHYSICIAN OF TARSUS. Diomedes was a doctor and Christian in the city of Tarsus in the third century. He was from a wealthy family, and as he healed the sick, he taught them the Christian faith and converted many during his travels. When he arrived in the city of Nicaea, a persecution of Christians was underway by the emperor Diocletian, who sent soldiers to arrest him. On the way from Nicaea to Nicomedia, Diomedes gave up his soul as he was praying. As proof that they carried out the emperor's orders, the soldiers beheaded the saint, but they became blind. Diocletian ordered the soldiers to return the saint's head to his body, and when they did, their sight was restored, and they believed in Christ.

COMMEMORATIONS: Translation of the Image "Not-Made-by-Hands" of Our Lord Jesus Christ from Edessa to Constantinople; Diomedes the Physician of Tarsus; Anthony the Stylite of Georgia; Cherimon of Egypt; Akakios, Bishop of Liti and Rendini; Romanus the Sinaite of Serbia; Nicodemus of Meteora; 33 Martyrs of Palestine; Timothy of Euripos, founder of Penteli; Apostolos of St. Lawrence; Gerasimos of Kephalonia; Eustathius II of Serbia; Stamatios of Volos; Martyr Alcibiades; Raphael of Banat; Nilus, brother of Emperor Laskaris; Christopher of Guria; Joachim of Osogovo; Constantine Brancoveanu of Wallachia and his sons Constantine, Stephen, Radu, and Matthew, and counselor Ioannicius; Joseph of Varatec Monastery (Romania); Finding of the relics of Sts. Seraphim, Dorotheus, James, Demetrius, Basil, and Sarantis of Megara; "Feodorovskaya" of Kostroma and "Triumph of Holy Theotokos" of Port Arthur Icons of the Mother of God.

Monday Fast-free

August 17

2 Corinthians 2:3-15
Matthew 23:13-22

Have you asked yourself why is it so stifling in the world? Why is it hard to live? Why can we not put up with each other? The answer is because sin has poisoned the atmosphere of life. We are all sick with sin. And if untreated body wounds emit intolerable stench, how much more terrible is the stench of sin!
+*Archimandrite Seraphim Aleksiev*

BLESSED THEODORETUS, ENLIGHTENER OF THE LAPPS. Theodoretus became a monk at the age of thirteen at the Solovki Monastery in Russia. He remained there sixteen years in obedience and attained virtue and wisdom. He received permission to travel to other monasteries, and each place profited from the experience of other ascetics and hermits who lived in the forest. Theodoretus then undertook missionary labors among the Lapps who were idol-worshippers. He learned their language so he could translate prayers and teach them about Christ. He lived with them for over twenty years. Theodoretus established a monastery and served as abbot at several other monasteries, and was a help to Tsar Ivan the Terrible. St. Theodoretus died peacefully at the Solovki Monastery.

COMMEMORATIONS: Straton, Philip, Eutychian, and Cyprian of Nicomedia; Paul and Juliana of Syria; Patroclus of Troyes; Myron of Cyzicus; Thyrsus, Leucius, and Coronatus, with others at Caesarea; Alypius the Iconographer of the Kiev Caves; James the Deacon; Agapius at Thermes; Elias the Younger of Calabria; Demetrius of Samarina in Epirus; Macarius of Mt. St. Auxentius; Theodoretus, enlightener of the Laps; Tbeli Abuseridze of Georgia; Archilleus of Stavropol; Pimen of Ugresh; Philip of Vologda; Jeroen at Noordwijk; George of Romania; "Armatia" and "Svensk" Icons of the Mother of God.

TUESDAY   Fast-free

AUGUST 18
2 Corinthians 2:14-3:3
Matthew 23:23-28

My rule of life: to change our residence only when circumstances become pressing.

+Fr. Alexander Elchaninov of Russia

STS. BARNABAS, SOPHRONIOS, AND CHRISTOPHER, FOUNDERS OF SOUMELA MONASTERY. According to tradition, Barnabas was the uncle of Sophronios. They were born and raised in fourth-century Athens. While celebrating the Divine Liturgy, Barnabas in a vision received a command from the Theotokos to build a monastery in Trebizond. Under the protection of the icon of Panagia Atheniotissa, which was believed to have been one of about seventy icons written by St. Luke the Evangelist, they survived many dangers. The famous monastery of the Panagia of Soumela was built in 386 A.D. The icon was placed in the monastery, and the two saints lived there for twenty-six years. Many pilgrims came to the monastery, and it enjoyed fame, imperial favor, and prosperity. Barnabas and Sophronios died on the same day in the year 412. Later, the monastery was attacked and eventually deserted, but the invaders failed to destroy the icon, which was hidden in a cave church. Once again, the monks returned, and the monastery flourished until a seventh-century enemy killed all the monks. Sometime later, the Panagia to a farmer named Christopher and sent him to the ruined monastery to revive it. He found the cave church and the icon safe. Other men soon joined him. Pilgrims returned, and Roman emperors became patrons of the monastery. One even traveled there to give thanks for deliverance from death. The icon worked great wonders.

COMMEMORATIONS: John of Rila; Christodoulos of Georgia; Florus and Laurus of Illyria, with Maximos and Patroklos, and many paupers; Sophronius of St. Anne's Skete; Juliana, near Strobilus; Leo, near Myra; Hermes, Serapion, and Polyaenus of Rome; Emilian of Trebia, with Hilarion, Dionysius, Hermippus, and 1,000 others; Barnabas and Sophronius of Mt. Mela; Christopher of Mt. Mela; Demetrius the Vlach; John and George, Patriarchs; Arsenios the New of Paros; Matthew of Crete; Agapios of Galatista; Agapios and Porphyrios of Santorini; Augustine of Orans; Constantine of Kappua.

WEDNESDAY

Strict Fast

AUGUST 19

2 Corinthians 3:4-11
Matthew 23:29-39

Always entreat the Creator to forgive you. He knows all the hidden deeds and thoughts which people do not confess, perhaps from shame, from lack of strength to tell the truth.

St. Raphael of Lesvos

ST. PITIRIM, BISHOP OF PERM. Pitirim was the abbot of the Chudov Monastery in fifteenth-century Moscow. He wrote the life story of St. Alexis, Metropolitan of Russia, and composed a Canon to him. When Pitirim became a bishop, he sought to create peace between two warring factions, the Christian Zyryani, and the pagan Voguli people, who pillaged and killed defenseless people. The angry landowners marched against the Voguli, defeated them, and took their leader Asyka prisoner. When Asyka vowed to attack the Christians no longer, he was set free. However, he waited for an opportunity to kill Pitirim, whom he credited for his army's defeat. Then Asyka began robbing and killing both the Zyryani and Voguli people, who had accepted the teachings of Pitirim and became Christians. Finally, Asyka murdered Bishop Pitirim when he was out blessing the waters. His body remained forty days buried in the hot climate where he had been killed, and his relics were found undecayed. St. Pitirim was buried in the Ust'-Vym cathedral church of the Annunciation.

COMMEMORATIONS: Andrew Stratelates and 2,593 soldiers with him in Cilicia; Timothy, Agapius, and Thecla of Palestine; Pitirim, Bishop of Perm; Theophanes, wonderworker of Macedonia (Mt. Athos); Credan, abbot of Evesham; Mochta of Britain; Namadia of France; Uncovering of the relics of St. Gennadius, abbot of Kostroma; "Of the Don" Icon of the Mother of God.

Thursday   **Fast-free**

August 20

2 Corinthians 4:1-12
Matthew 24:13-28

The theatre lulls the Christian life to sleep, destroys it, communicating to the life of Christians the character of the life of heathens.

St. John of Kronstadt

NEW MARTYR THEOCHARIS OF NEAPOLIS. Theocharis was orphaned at a young age. Because of the Ottoman State war in the year 1740, Theocharis was taken with other Christian boys to a concentration camp for training as soldiers. A judge liked Theocharis and brought him to his estate to work. Later he offered Theocharis his daughter in marriage, under the condition that he convert to their religion. When he refused, he was threatened and imprisoned without food. While there, he passed his time in prayer. Again, he was given a chance to change his mind, and when he refused, he was taken to a place where there was a white poplar tree. He was hanged and stoned to death, then buried under that tree. The sky became dark, and a big storm with thunder and lightning broke out, even though it was sunny. To this day, a blood-like substance flows from the broken branches of the tree. It is a place of pilgrimage for Christians and Ottomans. The relics of St. Theocharis were taken to the Church of St. Katherine in Thessalonica and can be seen there today.

COMMEMORATIONS: Samuel the Prophet; Philip, Bishop of Heraclea, with Severus, Memnon, and 37 soldiers, in Thrace; Lucius the Senator of Cyprus; Heliodorus and Dosa in Persia; Photina, at the Church of Blachernae; Hierotheus, first bishop and enlightener of Hungary; Stephen I, King of Hungary; Theocharis of Neapolis in Asia Minor; Reginos and Orestes of Cyprus; Oswin, King of Deira; Philibert of Jumieges (Gaul); New Martyrs of Estonia.

FRIDAY

AUGUST 21

Holy Apostle Thaddaeus
Strict Fast
2 Corinthians 4:13-18
Mark 3:13-21

It is in vain that some unenlightened people seek the greatest evil for man somewhere else, rather than in sin. Some consider disease to be the greatest evil, others—poverty, and others—death. But neither disease, nor poverty, nor death, nor any other earthly disaster can be such a great evil for us as is sin. These earthly misfortunes do not separate us from God if we are seeking Him sincerely, but, on the contrary, they bring us closer to Him.
+Archimandrite Seraphim Aleksiev

NEW HIEROMARTYR SYMEON, BISHOP OF SAMOKOV. Symeon was the beloved bishop of the Samokov diocese in eighteenth-century Bulgaria. During this time, Turkey was at war with the Moscovites, and the Germans captured the area of Nish and its surrounding towns. The Turkish soldiers invaded and pillaged Bishop Symeon's house, while he was away in the village of Doupnitsa. He was captured, bound him in chains, and put in a dungeon for twenty-three days. Then he was taken to a pasha, who ordered tortures for the saint until he renounced Christ. When St. Symeon showed his resolve through all the pains, he was hanged.

COMMEMORATIONS: Holy Forefathers Abraham, Isaac, and Jacob; Thaddeus, of the Seventy; Vassa of Edessa, with Theognios, Agapios, and Pistos; Avitus of Clermont; Theocleta of Asia Minor; Sarmean, Catholicos of Georgia; Symeon of Samokovo; Isaiah of Mt. Athos; Donatus, Romulus, Silvanus, and Venustus of Romania; Abramius of Smolensk, and Ephraim; Abramius of the Kiev Caves; Cornelius of Paleostrov, and Abramius; Raphael of Serbia; Ignatius of Optina; Martha of Diveyevo; Hardulph of Breedon; Jacob of Serbia; Commemoration of the Appearance of the Theotokos at Panteleimon Monastery.

SATURDAY   Fast-free

August 22

1 Corinthians 1:3-9
Matthew 19:3-12

You must always exercise discretion in your ascetic struggles.
+Elder Efstratios of Glinsk

VENERABLE ISAAC I OF OPTINA. Isaac came from a family of wealthy merchants who sold livestock at fairs, but this life did not satisfy him. One day, at the age of thirty-six, while on his way to a fair, he turned the horses around and ended up at the Optina Monastery. He worked as a cook, sang in the choir, and was a bookbinder. Seven years later, he was tonsured a deacon, then to the priesthood. There are many stories about Isaac's extraordinary silence. Once when everyone was having a spirited conversation with the abbot, Isaac was silent. The abbot asked him if he had anything to say. Isaac replied, "If everyone speaks, then who will listen?" Later, Isaac forsook his beloved solitude to spend thirty years as an abbot. He restored the economic stability of the monastery and undertook many building projects. Isaac acquired forest plots for firewood, a candle factory opened, and monastic gardens were cultivated. Thus, Optina Monastery flourished in Russia in the second half of the nineteenth century. Even though he was an abbot, Isaac was always obedient to the Elder Ambrose, and he said that he had known no sorrow for the thirty-two years of obedience. He also said, "You have to go to the elder to cleanse your conscience." Isaac would humbly wait in line with the other monks to see Elder Ambrose. St. Isaac gave up his soul at the age of eight-five, having been stricken with paralysis and dysentery.

COMMEMORATIONS: Agathonicus of Nicomedia, with Zotikos, Theoprepios, Akyndinos, Severian, Zeno, and others; Eulalia and Felix of Barcelona; Athanasius of Tarsus; Anthousa of Syria and Charesimos and Neophytos; Bogolep of Uglich Monastery; Isaac I of Optina; Macarius, Bishop of Orel, with Andrew, Alexis, Theodore, John, Hierotheus, John, Hilarion, and Gorazd; Martyrs Irenaeus, Or, and Oropsis; Ephraim of Selenginsk and John Vostorgov; Symphorian of Autun; Sigfrid of Wearmouth; "Prusa" and "Georgian" Icons of the Mother of God.

Sunday

August 23

Eleventh Sunday of Matthew
Fast-free
1 Corinthians 9:2-12
Matthew 18:23-35

*C*onfess, and receive Holy Communion so long as you practice love towards your fellow men and do for them all the good that lies within your power. This is therapeutic for both the soul and the body.

St. Raphael of Lesvos

HIEROMARTYR IRENAEUS, BISHOP OF LYONS. Irenaeus became known as one of the foremost Fathers of the Church in the third century, both articulating and defending Orthodoxy. He was born in the city of Smyrna of Asia Minor, and was a student of St. Polycarp, who was a disciple of St. John the Theologian. Polycarp ordained Irenaeus to the priesthood and sent him to preach in Gaul. He became Bishop of Lyons and converted many pagans to Christianity. His major battles were with the heretics in the Church. A deluded priest named Montanos declared himself a prophet, replete with visions and two assistants that would verify anything he said. Montanos claimed that Jesus Christ would return within a few days to prove his statements. The next heretical battle came from the Gnostics, who claimed that angels, not God, created the world. Then there was the dispute over what day Pascha should be celebrated. One faction argued for the old Asia Minor tradition of celebrating on the fourteenth of the month of Nisan, regardless of the day of the week it fell on. Bishop Victor of Rome summoned Irenaeus to help clarify this, and the best solution was to narrow it down to two alternatives. According to St. Gregory of Tours, St. Irenaeus was beheaded for confessing his faith during the reign of Severus.

COMMEMORATIONS: Irenaeus, Bishop of Lyons; Irenaeus, Bishop of Sirmium; Callinicus, Patriarch of Constantinople; Pothinos of Lyons; Victor of Marseilles; Eutychius and Florentius of Nursia; Nicholas the Sicilian; 38 Martyrs of Thrace; Lupus, slave of Demetrios of Thessalonica; Haralambos of Crete; Anthony of Sardis; Ebba the Younger of Coldingham, and companions; Ephraim (Kuznetsov) of Selenginsk, John Vostorgov of Moscow, and Nicholas Varzhansky; Tydfil of Merthyr Tydfil.

Monday   **Fast-free**

August 24

2 Corinthians 5:10-15
Mark 1:9-15

Unless a man can bring himself to say to his heart that he alone and God are present in this place, he will never find peace and rest of soul.

St. Alonios of Egypt

VENERABLE ARSENIUS OF KOMEL. Arsenius was from a noble family in sixteenth-century Moscow. In his youth, he was tonsured a monk, and he copied books at the monastery, including the Gospel. He later became the abbot, though he often spent time in solitude. Great Prince Basil once visited this prosperous monastery and was surprised to find Arsenius dressed in old clothes covered with patches. One day, Arsenius left his monastery carrying a large wooden cross he had made on his shoulders, intent on finding a location for a new monastery. Arriving at a marshy place through a swamp, he stumbled and fell. A heavenly light flashed on him, and this convinced him to build on that site. Monks soon gathered at his new monastery, and when many settled around there, he founded another monastery on land that the prince deeded to him. Through prayer, he tamed the wild beasts, and again monks gathered around him, and he built a church. He instructed the peasants to observe Sundays and feast days. After a lifetime of work, prayer, and fasting, St. Arsenius died peacefully.

COMMEMORATIONS: Cosmas of Aitolia, Equal-to-the-Apostles; George Limniotes the Confessor of Mt. Olympus; Eutychios, disciple of St. John the Theologian; Serapion of St. John the Baptist Monastery at Garesja, Georgia; Dionysius of Zakynthos, Archbishop of Aegina; Cyra of Persia; Arsenius of Komel; Tation at Claudiopolis; Maxim Sandovich of the Lemkos, Poland; Ouen, Archbishop of Rouen (Gaul); Athanasius II, Patriarch of Jerusalem; Seraphim of Grodno; Aristokles of Moscow and Mt. Athos; Martyrius, Archbishop of Novgorod; Holy Martyrs of Utica; Commemoration of the Appearance of the Most Holy Theotokos to St. Sergius of Radonezh; Translation of the relics of St. Dionysios of Zakynthos; Translation of the relics of St. Peter, Metropolitan of Kiev.

Tuesday

August 25

Translation of the Relics of Holy Apostle Bartholomew
Fast-free

Titus 1:1-5, 2:15, 3:1-2, 12-15
Matthew 5:14-19

I think there is no labor greater than that of prayer to God. For every time a man wants to pray, his enemies, the demons, want to prevent him, for they know that it is only by turning him from prayer that they can hinder his journey. Whatever good work a man undertakes, if he perseveres in it, he will attain rest. But prayer is warfare to the last breath.

St. Agathon of Scetis

ST. CONSTANTIA OF PAPHOS. Constantia was a holy woman from the city of Paphos in Cyprus. She was a disciple of St. Hilarion the Great, who lived as an ascetic in the village of Episkopi in Paphos. Hilarion had once anointed Constantia's daughter and son-in-law with oil and saved them from death. When St. Hilarion died, he was buried in his beloved garden. Constantia would spend whole nights in a vigil at his tomb, talking with him as if he were present. However, Hesychius, a disciple of St. Hilarion, stole the saint's body and took it to Palestine. When a message was brought to Constantia that Hilarion's body was taken to Palestine, she immediately died of unbearable grief. Great miracles are wrought every day in the garden of St. Hilarion, as well as in Palestine. St. Constantia is considered the patron saint of the city of Paphos.

COMMEMORATIONS: Apostle Titus of the Seventy; Menas, Patriarch of Constantinople; John the Cappadocian and Epiphanius, Patriarchs of Constantinople; Gennadios, Patriarch of Constantinople; Barses and Eulogius of Edessa; Protogenes of Carrhae; Gregory of Utrecht; John of Karpathos; Aredius of Limousin; Genesius of Arles; Constantia of Paphos; Ebba the Elder; Moses (Kozhin) of Solovki Monastery; Lucilla and Nemesius, at Rome; Synaxis of the Hierarchs of Crete: Andrew the Wonderworker, Eumenius of Rome, and Cyril of Gortyna; Translation of the relics of Apostle Bartholomew from Anastasiopolis to Lipari; Translation of the relics of St. Hilda of Whitby; Translation of the relics of St. Luke of Adrianople.

WEDNESDAY

Strict Fast

AUGUST 26

Hebrews 6:9-12; Mark 1:23-28

If you see your neighbor committing sin, take care not to dwell exclusively on his faults, but try to think of the many good things he has done and continues to do.

St. Basil the Great

COMMEMORATION OF THE VLADIMIR ICON OF THE MOTHER OF GOD. It is believed that the Vladimir Icon was written in Constantinople, and later in the twelfth century, it was sent to Prince Yuri in Kiev. The icon was kept in a monastery and was later taken to Vladimir. It is one of the most venerated icons in all of Russia. It is carried in military campaigns by princes, prayed before by rulers for the welfare of their people, and flocked to by the faithful. Whenever patriarchs or metropolitans are elected, their names are placed before the icon. In the year 1395, the Tatar King Tamerlane surrounded Moscow with a vast army. The holy Vladimir Icon of the Mother of God was brought from Vladimir to Moscow. With tears, all the people began to pray to the Mother of God to save them. Suddenly, the Tatar army retreated hurriedly. King Tamerlane had a vision in a dream of the Mother of God surrounded by an army of angels waving their staffs at him, and she threatened and ordered him to leave Russia. He awoke terrified, and at dawn, he ordered his troops to retreat.

COMMEMORATIONS: Adrian, Natalia, and 23 companions of Nicomedia; Tithoes of the Thebaid; Ibestion the Confessor; Adrian of Ondrusovsk; Cyprian of Storozhev; Zer-Jacob, missionary of Ethiopia; Maria of Diveyevo, fool-for-Christ; Nectarius (Trezvinsky) of Yaransk; Roman Medved of Moscow; Ioasaph, Prince of India; Adrian of Poshekhonye; Bassian of Alatyr Monastery; Abenner the King, father of St. Ioasaph; Martyr Adrian; Commemoration of the Meeting of the Vladimir Icon of the Mother of God; The miraculous renewal of the Vladimir Icon of the Mother of God in Harbin (Manchuria).

THURSDAY   **Fast-free**

AUGUST 27

2 Corinthians 7:1-10
Mark 1:29-35

Self-renunciation is a rarity. Not even we who are monastics have understood that *'good things are acquired through effort.'* And so, we are lenient with ourselves — justifying ourselves and making excuses for everything we do. This is the point at which evil begins. The devil himself also finds justification for each person, and so the years pass. For this reason, let's not be forgetful. We should be a little mindful of death. Since we are to die, let's not be too attentive to the body — not that we won't be careful and cause ourselves harm, but that we should not worship comfort.

St. Paisios the Athonite

MARTYR DJAN DARADA, THE ETHIOPIAN EUNUCH BAPTIZED BY ST. PHILIP THE APOSTLE. Djan Darada was a black man and a potentate under Queen Candace of Ethiopia. He was in charge of all the queen's treasury. On his way home from worshipping in Jerusalem, he was sitting in his chariot reading the Book of Isaiah the prophet. The Holy Spirit said to the Apostle Philip, "Go near and join thyself to this chariot." Philip went up to the chariot and heard the man reading and asked if he understood what he was reading. The eunuch asked Philip to explain it to him, so the apostle began by explaining the prophet's words then taught him about Christ. As they were traveling along the road, they came to some water, and the eunuch asked to receive Baptism. As soon as he was baptized, the Spirit of the Lord carried Philip away, and the eunuch went on his way rejoicing. According to St. Irenaeus of Lyons, the Ethiopian Eunuch preached throughout Ethiopia and was martyred.

COMMEMORATIONS: Poemen the Great of Egypt; Sabbas of Benephali; Hosius (Osia) the Confessor; Martyr Anthusa; Liberius, Pope of Rome; Caesarius, Bishop of Arles; Kuksha, Pimen, and Nicon of the Kiev Caves; Phanurios the Newly-Revealed of Rhodes; Poemen of Palestine; Michael Voskresensky with 28 other martyrs, and Stephen Nemkov with 18 other martyrs; Methodius (Ivanov) of Sukovo; Praulius, Archbishop of Jerusalem.

Friday   **Strict Fast**

AUGUST 28

2 Corinthians 7:10-16
Mark 2:18-22

We must be very careful with everything in our lives. Just as the Fathers have said and as our Geronda has helped us understand, we must become united with God. We have become novices, rasophores, and schema nuns, and God desires abundant love from us. He wants our love to be undivided and completely for Him.

+Gerondissa Makrina of Volos

ST. THEODORE OF THE KIEV CAVES, PRINCE OF OSTROZH. Theodore was descended from the lineage of holy Equal-to-the-Apostles Vladimir. He gained fame himself with the construction of churches and by his defense of Orthodoxy in Volynia against the encroachment of Papism. In 1401 A.D., Theodore participated in the defeat of the Teutonic Knights at the Battle of Gruenwald. Twelve years later he supported the Hussites in their struggle with the German emperor. In 1432, after having gained a series of victories over the Polish forces, Theodore compelled prince Jagiello to protect by law Orthodoxy in Volynia. Later in 1438, he participated in a battle with the Tatars. He received the rights of administration of several cities and became the owner of extended holdings in the best regions. But he left all this behind and entered the Kievo-Pechersk monastery to pursue the salvation of his soul. In extreme old age, St. Theodore died and was buried in the Farther Caves. In the sixteenth century, his body was found intact.

COMMEMORATIONS: Hezekiah, King of Judah; Anna the Prophetess, daughter of Phanuel; Moses the Black of Scetis; Queen Shushaniki (Susanna) of Georgia; Martyrs Diomedes and Laurence; Amphilochius, Bishop of Vladimir; 33 Martyrs of Nicomedia; Theodore, Prince of Ostrog; Sergius Zaytsev of Zilantov Monastery of Kazan, with Laurence, Seraphim, Theodosius, Leontius, Stephen, Gregory, Hylarion, John, and Sergius; Acacius of Miletus; Savva, abbot of Krypetsk; Synaxis of the Venerable Fathers of the Far Caves in Kiev; Uncovering of the relics of St. Job of Pochaev.

SATURDAY

AUGUST 29

Beheading of St. John the Baptist
Strict Fast
Acts 13:25-33; Mark 6:14-30

The truly hungry are the faithful who have already acquired knowledge of the truth. So, too, is the soul of every man who has abandoned the grace of spiritual contemplation and become as slave to the literal and external forms of religion; for he does not nourish his intellect with the splendor of his intellections, but imbues his perception with impassioned fantasies derived from the material aspects of scriptural symbols.

St. Maximos the Confessor

NEW MARTYR ANASTASIUS OF BULGARIA. Anastasius was from eighteenth-century Bulgaria. When he was twenty years old, his teacher of military studies in Thessalonica sent him to sell some Turkish clothes without paying the usual tax. For this reason, he told Anastasius to dress as a Turk, even though he was a Christian, to avoid the customary tax. Anastasius was stopped and questioned. The tax collectors demanded him to recite the Mahometan prayer. When he could not, he was taken to the commander who offered him to become Turkish, but he refused to betray his Christian faith. He was taken to the mullah with five Turks who testified that Anastasius had blasphemed their religion. He was tortured and condemned to hanging. Along the way, they urged him to renounce his faith and save himself, but St. Anastasius died along the way.

COMMEMORATIONS: Beheading of St. John the Baptist; Arcadius, Bishop of Arsinoe, Cyprus; Basil I the Macedonian; Candida and Gelasia of Constantinople; Peter of Russia; Alexander, abbot of Voche of Galich; Anastasius of Bulgaria; Theodora, nun of Thessalonica; Sebbi, King of the East Saxons; Theodora Ivanov of Tobolsk; Translation of the relics of St. Joseph the Sanctified of Samaka; Commemoration of all Orthodox soldiers killed on the field of battle.

SUNDAY

AUGUST 30

Twelfth Sunday of Matthew
Fast-free
1 Corinthians 15:1-11
Matthew 19:16-26

*E*ven worldly persons desire to be associated with the glory of an earthly king. How much more true is this of those whom the finger of the divine Spirit of Life has touched. Divine love has wounded their hearts with the longing for Christ, the true and heavenly King. His beauty and ineffable glory, his unfailing graciousness, and his incomprehensible majesty have conspired to hold them captive with desire and longing. Their whole being is fixed upon him.

St. Makarios the Great

MARTYRS FELIX, FORTUNATUS, SEPTIMINUS, AND JANUARIUS. Bishop Felix and his three companions Januarius the priest, Fortunatus, and Septiminus fought against the deceit of idolatry during the third-century reign of Diocletian and Maximian. These saints were interrogated and put into prison. Then they were bound together and taken to the eparch of the Praetorium, who tried to frighten them, but they would not deny their faith. Again, they were cast into prison. After fourteen days, they were brought out of jail, tied to horses, and taken by boat to various cities. For four days, they did not have food or drink. When they refused one final time to offer sacrifice to the idols, they were beheaded.

COMMEMORATIONS: Alexander, John, and Paul the New, Patriarchs of Constantinople; Felix of Thibiuca; Martyrs Fortunatus, Septiminus, and Januarius; Fantinus of Calabria; 16 Martyrs of Thebes; 6 Martyrs of Melitene; Sarmata of Egypt; Vryaene of Nisibis; Eulalius of Cyprus; Alexander of Svir; Varlaam of Moldavia; John of Rasca and Secu; Alexander of Voch; Christopher of Palestine; Fiacrius of Breuil (Gaul); Ignatius (Lebedev) of Moscow; Peter Cheltsov of Smolensk; Theodore of Tobolsk; Rumon of Tavistock; Synaxis of the Serbian Hierarchs: Sava I, Arsenius, Sava II, Eustathius I, James, Nicodemus, Daniel II, Ioannicius II, Spyridon, Ephraim II, Cyril, Nicon, Macarius, Gabriel I, and Gregory; Translation of the relics of St. Alexander Nevsky.

Monday

August 31

The Venerable Sash of the Mother of God
Fast-free
Hebrews 9:1-7
Luke 10:38-42, 11:27-28

*C*onquer evil men by your gentle kindness, and make zealous men wonder at your goodness.

St. Isaac the Syrian

ST. EANSWYTHE OF KENT. Eanswythe was born in the seventh century, the only daughter of the pagan king Eadbald of Kent. Her mother secretly raised her as a Christian. After some time, the king received holy Baptism. From her childhood, Eanswythe wanted to become a nun, but her father wanted her to marry. She said that she would not have an earthly suitor whose love for her might be mixed with dislike. In those days, there was also a high mortality rate for children, and she did not want to experience those sorrows. She asked her father to build her a cell to pray in. He established for her a monastery in Folkestone in Kent, which was the first women's monastery in England. The duties of the nuns included copying and binding manuscripts, weaving cloth for church vestments and clothes, caring for the sick, the poor, and aged nuns, cooking, cleaning, and reading spiritual books. Miracles are attributed to St. Eanswythe before and after her death. She gave sight to a blind man and cast out a demon from one possessed. St. Eanswythe died in her mid-twenties, and her monastery was later destroyed. Her relics were moved several times. One time they were hidden behind plastered walls to protect them from marauders.

COMMEMORATIONS: The Placing of the Venerable Sash of the Most Holy Theotokos; Cyprian, Bishop of Carthage; 4 Martyrs of Perga; Gennadius Scholarius, Patriarch of Constantinople; Paulinus, Bishop of Trier; 7 Virgin-martyrs of Gaza; 366 Martyrs of Nicomedia; John, Metropolitan of Kiev; Aidan of Lindisfarne; Martyrs Menas, Faustus, Andrew, Heraclius, Phileortus, and Diadochus; Eanswythe of Folkestone; New Martyrs of Jasenovac (Serbia); Commemoration of the Restoration of the Church of the Theotokos in Neorion.

What are Christians? Christians are Christ-bearers, and, by virtue of this, they are bearers and possessors of eternal life.... The Saints are the most perfect Christians, for they have been sanctified to the highest degree with the podvigs of holy faith in the risen and eternally living Christ, and no death has power over them. Their life is entirely Christ's life; and their thought is entirely Christ's thought; and their perception is Christ's perception. All that they have is first Christ's and then theirs.... In them is nothing of themselves but rather wholly and in everything the Lord Christ.

St. Justin Popovich of Chelije

Tuesday

September 1

Ecclesiastical New Year
Fast-free
1 Timothy 2:1-7; Luke 4:16-22

Act in such a way that your humility may not be weakness, nor your authority be severity. Justice must be accompanied by humility, that humility may render justice lovable.

St. Gregory the Great

VENERABLE NICHOLAS KOURTALIOTIS OF CRETE. According to local tradition, Nicholas lived in seventeenth-century Crete. In his youth, he was charitable and would give away his father's grapes and oil to the poor. As a result, the grapes would multiply every harvest, and the oil vessels always remained full. Seeing this, his father gave his blessing to allow Nicholas to devote his life to Christ. He lived in asceticism in Messaras, Heraklion. One day a hunter mistakenly shot Nicholas with an arrow. Nicholas asked to be taken to the place where his chapel is located. When they arrived at the outlet of a gorge, Nicholas spread his five fingers towards the dry mountain and barren slope above, 40 meters high. Immediately five springs emerged to assuage the thirst of his accidental killer. A chapel was built there in the memory of Nicholas where countless miracles happen, and thousands visit his chapel every year. It is said that St. Nicholas is buried near the chapel, but his grave has not been revealed.

COMMEMORATIONS: Church New Year; Symeon the Stylite, and his mother Martha; 40 Virgin Martyrs and Ammon the deacon, at Heraclea; Venerable Evanthia; Nicholas Kourtaliotis of Crete; Joshua the Son of Nun; Callista, Evodus, and Hermogenes at Nicomedia; Angelis of Constantinople; Meletios the Younger; Symeon of Lesvos; Verena of Zurzach (Switzerland); Haido of Stanos; Aegidius (Giles), along the Rhine; Dionysius Exiguous the Humble; Commemoration of the Great Fire at Constantinople about 470 A.D.; Synaxis of the Most Holy Theotokos in Miasena Monastery; Synaxis of Panagia Katapoliani in Tinos; "Chernigov-Gethsemane," "Of Alexandria," "All-blessed One," and "Avgustovskaya" Icons of the Mother of God.

WEDNESDAY   Strict Fast

SEPTEMBER 2

2 Corinthians 9:12-10:7
Mark 3:20-27

How horrible is the emptiness of soul brought on by a sinful life! Unbearable is the torment from passionate, sinful thoughts and feelings, when they roil like worms in the soul, when they tear at the soul that has submitted to them, the soul that has been violated by them! Often a sinner who is tormented by fierce thoughts, dreams, and unfulfilled desires comes to despair. He often tries to take his own life, both temporal and eternal. Blessed is the sinner who comes to his senses during that terrible period and remembers the boundless love of the Heavenly Father, and the measureless spiritual riches overflowing in the house of the Heavenly Father—the holy Church. Blessed is that sinner who, horrified by his own sinfulness, wants to be free of its oppressive weight through repentance.

St. Ignatius Brianchaninov

STS. AEITHALAS AND AMMON THE MARTYRS OF ADRIANOPLE. Aeithalas and Ammon were from Adrianople in Thrace. When Governor Babdos learned that they were Christians, he had them arrested and brought before him. He asked where they were from and what their profession was? Their only response was, "We are Christians!" The governor ordered them to sacrifice to the idols, and when they refused, they were beaten to death with the sinews of oxen.

COMMEMORATIONS: Mamas of Caesarea, and his parents, Theodotus and Rufina; John the Faster, Patriarch of Constantinople; Eleazar, son of Aaron, and Righteous Phineas; Anthony and Theodosius of the Kiev Caves; Holy 10 Martyrs: Diomedes, Julian, Philip, Eutychianos, Hesychios, Leonidas, Eutychios, Philadelphos, Melanippos, and Parthagape; Barsanuphius of Kyrilov, John Ivanov, Seraphima of Therapontov, and Anatole, Nicholas, Michael, and Philip; Damascene, Bishop of Glukhov, Herman, Bishop of Vyaznikov, and Stephen Yaroshevich; Aeithalas and Ammon of Thrace; Hieu of Tadcaster; "Kaluga" Icon of the Mother of God.

Thursday   **Fast-free**

September 3

2 Corinthians 10:7-18
Mark 3:28-35

Cleave to the saints, for they who cleave to them shall be made holy.
St. Clement of Rome

NEW HIEROMARTYR PIMEN, BISHOP OF ALMA-ATA. Pimen was from late-nineteenth-century Novgorod province of Russia, in the family of a priest. Four sons of the priest, including Pimen, were ordained to the priesthood. Pimen's dissertation at the Kiev Theological Academy was "The Relationship of the Ecumenical Councils to the Works of the Church Writers." Pimen was tonsured a monk at the age of twenty-four, and one year later to the priesthood. He was appointed to the Urmia Orthodox Mission in north-west Iran. He mastered ancient and modern Syrian and was able to preach to the Orthodox Syrians. He also translated ancient Syrian patristic works and the Divine services into Syrian. He defended the Orthodox population before Persian authorities. Pimen was appointed the head of several theological academies and would conduct readings for the people. He was elevated to the rank of bishop and was transferred to the see of Alama-Ata. He called people to prayer and repentance, and his talks in the House of Moral Religious Enlightenment attracted many. However, when the Bolsheviks conquered the area, Pimen stood against them and was labeled a counter-revolutionary. He could have fled to the mountains, but he chose to stay with his people in the face of perils. He was arrested and condemned, and persecution of the Church in the whole region began. The body of St. Pimen was found and buried in the park of the Ascension cathedral. The place of his martyrdom has become a place of pilgrimage for the faithful.

COMMEMORATIONS: Anthimus, Bishop of Nicomedia, with Theophilus, Dorotheos, Mardonius, Migdonius, Peter, Indes, Gorgonius, Zeno, Domna, and Euthymius; Aristion of Alexandria; Constantine the New; Ioannicius II of Serbia; Vasilissa of Nicomedia; Theoctistus of Palestine; John "the Hairy" of Rostov; Phoebe, at Cenchreae; Remaclus of Maastricht; Polydoros of Cyprus; Aigulphus of Provence; Pimen of Alma-Ata, and Meletius of Issyk-Kul Holy Trinity Monastery; Neofit and Meletie of Romania; Translation of the relics of St. Nektarios of Aegina in 1953.

FRIDAY   **Strict Fast**

SEPTEMBER 4   2 Corinthians 11:5-21
                                            Mark 4:1-9

Let us submit to God and humble ourselves, and the Lord will cover us, and we will be holy. But until we humble ourselves and accept God's will, until we propitiate God—though we beat our heads against the floor doing prostrations—the passions will not diminish.

St. Anatoly of Optina

MARTYR JERUSALEM AND HER THREE SONS SEKENDOS, SEKENDIKOS, AND KEGOROS. Jerusalem and her three sons were from third-century Alexandria. After the death of her husband, they traveled to many places preaching Christ to the pagans, and this was a time of Christian persecutions. They went to Rome, Athens, Boeotia, Thessaly, and finally Beroia. She became a nun and brought monasticism to the area. She also continued to lead many idolaters to the Christian faith, so she was arrested and sent to the duke of Thessalonica for interrogation. Seeing that she was steadfast in defense of her faith, she was tortured together with her sons. One son was dragged behind horses, one beaten with sticks, and the third was forced to put on a heated helmet. St. Jerusalem was beheaded. Her skull is kept in the Church of St. Anthony in Beroia.

COMMEMORATIONS: Prophet Moses the God-seer, and Aaron the Priest; Babylas of Antioch, and Urban, Prilidian, Epolonius, and Christodoula; Babylas of Nicomedia and 84 children; 3,628 Martyrs at Nicomedia; Sarbelus and Bebaia of Edessa; Hermione, daughter of Apostle Philip the Deacon; Theotimos and Theodoulos the executioners; Charitina of Amisus; Symeon of Garesja; Martyr Sarbelus; Jerusalem of Berroia, and Kegoros, Sekendikos, and Sekendos; Theodore, Ammianus, Julian, Kion, and Centurionus of Nicomedia; Petronius of Egypt; Anthimus the Blind; Peter, Metropolitan of Dabro-Bosnia; Parthenius of Kiziltash Monastery in Crimea; Gregory, Bishop of Shliserburg, Sergius, Bishop of Narva, and Stephen of Nikolskoye; Symeon of Garesja; Gorazd of Prague; Synaxis of the Saints of Voronezh; Finding of the relics of St. Theodore the Hatzis of Mytilene; "The Unburnt Bush" Icon of the Mother of God.

SATURDAY

SEPTEMBER 5

Holy Prophet Zacharias
Fast-free
1 Corinthians 2:6-9
Matthew 23:29-39

Temptations and trials show what hides in the heart of man. Temptation is similar to the medicine called an emetic. An emetic reveals what is hidden in the stomach. So temptations and trials make manifest what is inside a man. … Thus vainglory becomes apparent through the deprivation of glory, avarice through the deprivation of riches, envy through the success of one's neighbor, and anger through disappointment. If, then, you fall into various temptations, O Christian, this all happens by God's permission for your great benefit, that you may thereby know what is hidden in your heart, and so knowing it you may correct yourself.

St. Tikhon of Zadonsk

MARTYRS JUVENTINUS AND MAXIMINUS AT ANTIOCH. In the fourth century, Juventinus and Maximinus were bodyguards of the emperor Julian the Apostate. During a trip to Antioch, Julian decided to defile the Christians by sprinkling all the food in the marketplace with idol-offering blood. Both men openly condemned Julian for this, and they denounced him for his apostasy of the Christian faith. Julian had the saints mercilessly beaten, then put to death.

COMMEMORATIONS: Holy Prophet Zacharias and Righteous Elizabeth, parents of St. John the Forerunner; Urban, Theodore, Medimnus, and 77 companions at Nicomedia; Abdas, Hormizd, and Sunin of Persia; Athanasius of Bretsk; Juventinus and Maximinus at Antioch; Gleb of Russia, in holy Baptism David; Alexis Belkovsky, Archbishop of Great Ustiug; Neophyte and Meletios of Stanisoara Monastery; Appearance of Apostle Peter to Emperor Justinian at Athira, near Constantinople.

SUNDAY

Thirteenth Sunday of Matthew
Fast-free

SEPTEMBER 6

1 Corinthians 16:13-24
Matthew 21:33-42

The reading of the Psalter calms the passions, and the reading of the Gospel consumes the tares of our sins; for the word of God is consuming fire. Once for forty days I read the Gospel for the salvation of a benefactor of mine and I saw in my sleep a field covered by tares. Suddenly there fell down fire from the heavens consumed the tares that covered the field, and the field remained clean. Puzzling over this vision, I heard a voice: the tares covering the field are the sins of the soul that benefited you; the fire that consumed them is the Word of God which you read for it.
+*Elder Parthenius of Kiev Pechersk*

THIRTEEN HOLY MARTYRS BEHEADED IN ALEXANDRIA UNDER DECIUS. These saints lived during the reign and Christian persecutions of the emperor Decius in the year 250 A.D. They were brought before Governor Valerian of Alexandria, who was astounded by their lack of fear and firm faith. This group all died by the sword, and Christians there took their bodies and buried them. These saints included Kalodote who was pregnant, Faustus the presbyter and his disciple Kyriakos, Dionysios the Reader, Bibos the Deacon; Andronikos the Soldier, Pelagia and Thekla, who were virgins and sisters, Theoktistos the Sea Captain, Kyriakos the Commoner, Sarapabon the Councillor, Makarios the Citizen, and Andrew the Hairdresser.

COMMEMORATIONS: Commemoration of the Miracle of the Archangel Michael at Chonae; Romulus and 11,000 Soldiers with him, in Armenia; Eudoxius, Zeno, Macarius, and 1,004 soldiers with them, in Melitene; David of Hermopolis in Egypt; Archippus of Hierapolis; Kalodote, Faustus, Makarios, Andrew, Kyriakos, Dionysios, Andrew, Pelagia, Thekla, Theoktistos, and Sarapabon, in Alexandria; Eleutherius of Spoleto; Lygeri of Chios; Begga, abbess of Landen; Beya, first abbess of Copeland in Cumbria; Magnus of Fussen; "Kiev-Bratsk" Icon of the Mother of God.

MONDAY

Forefeast of the Nativity of the Mother of God
Fast-free

SEPTEMBER 7

2 Corinthians 12:10-19
Mark 4:10-23

All our life is like a day of celebration for us; we are convinced, in fact, that God is always everywhere. We work while singing, we sail while reciting hymns, we accomplish all other occupations of life while praying.

St. Clement of Alexandria

VENERABLE CLOUD (CLODOALD) OF PARIS. Cloud was the son of King Clovis of the Franks, in the early sixth century. When Clovis died in battle, his kingdom was divided between his four sons, who were brought up by their grandmother St. Clotilde in Paris. Their uncles, King Clotaire and King Childebert, killed Cloud's brothers to prevent them from succeeding to the Frankish throne. Cloud, however, escaped to Provence and did not attempt to recover the throne, though he could have. Instead, he embraced the monastic life and became a king of himself, by ruling the passions. He settled as a hermit, then became a disciple of St. Severinus in Paris. Cloud withdrew to Provence again for solitude, where he spent several years and wrought many miracles. Soon many came to him, so he returned to Paris and was made Bishop of Paris. Finally, he retired near Versailles and built a monastery that attracted many pious men who fled the world for fear of losing their souls. Cloud gave his inheritance to churches and the poor, and was tireless in teaching and exhorting the people of Paris. The relics of St. Cloud were destroyed during the French Revolution.

COMMEMORATIONS: Apostles Evodos and Onesiphoros of the Seventy; Sozon of Cilicia; Cassiane the Hymnographer; Eupsychius of Caesarea; Luke and Peter of the Deep Stream; Symeon and Amphilochius of Pangarati; John of Verkhne-Poltavka; Alexander and Andrew, disciples of St. Sergius of Radonezh; Macarius of Kanev; John, Archbishop of Novgorod; Cloud (Cloboald) of Nogent-sur-Seine; Eugene of Nizhni-Novgorod; Leo of St. Alexander Nevsky Lavra; Sozon of Cyprus; Nicholas of Selinginsk; Eugene of Zhitomir; Pachomius of Skanov Monastery; Stephen of Robchik; Repose of St. Macarius of Optina.

TUESDAY

Nativity of the Mother of God
Fast-free

SEPTEMBER 8

Philippians 2:5-11
Luke 1:39-49, 56

The all-virtuous Panagia is always ready: to inspire us toward virtue; to take us by the hand and lead us to Christ.
+Blessed Moses of Mt. Athos

STS. JOHN AND GEORGE-JOHN, CONFESSORS OF GEORGIA. From his youth, John desired to be a monk, so he went to the Iveron Monastery on Mt. Athos. He was simple and obedient and was soon ordained to the priesthood. He stayed on Mt. Athos seventeen years, until 1920 when circumstances became precarious for the Georgian monks. He settled at Armazi Monastery, but Chekists broke in and shot John and another monk, leaving them for dead. A group found them in a gorge and nursed them back to health. John went to live at Betania Monastery and was soon made abbot. He warmly welcomed and fed visitors, especially the children. He had the gift of wonderworking and prophecy and could heal the terminally ill and deaf. Fr. George-John chose to work for the national liberation movement in Georgia. He was tonsured a monk, ordained to the priesthood, and elevated to the rank of archimandrite. The Chekists also beat him, shaved his beard, and cut off his hair. When George-John visited John, he decided to stay. Later, these saints were described as having one soul and two bodies. George-John was often in poor health, but he raised bees and tended the garden, and he would often give away the monastery food to the needy. He also had the gift of healing and prophecy. St. John died at the age of seventy-five and St. George-John at the age of eighty-three. They are buried next to each other at Betania Monastery, in Georgia.

COMMEMORATIONS: Nativity of the Mother of God; Sophronius of Achtaleia; Martyrs Rufus and Rufianus; Martyrs Severus and Artemidorus; Lucian of Alexandrov; Athanasius of Thessalonica; Serapion of Pskov; Arsenius of Konevits; John and George-John of Georgia; Ina of Wessex and Ethelburga; Alexander Jacobson, at Solovki.

WEDNESDAY
SEPTEMBER 9

Synaxis of the Holy Ancestors of God
Abstain from meat and dairy products, and fish.
Galatians 4:22-27; Luke 8:16-21

All the ways of this world are as fickle and unstable as a sudden storm at sea.

St. Bede the Venerable

VENERABLE JOSEPH OF VOLOTSK. At the age of seven, Joseph was sent to a monastery to be educated by the Elder Arsenius. For one whole year, he studied the Psalter, and the following year, the entire Holy Scriptures. He could recite from memory the Psalms, Epistles, and Gospel. At the age of twenty, he became a monk at the monastery of St. Paphnutius. He attended to the sick as if he were attending to Christ. He spent seventeen years there, and when Paphnutius died, Joseph was elected abbot. He transformed the monastic life there to the strict coenobitic principles, where the brethren hold all things in common. Only seven monks agreed with this, so Joseph founded a new monastery in Volokolamsk. A storm whipped up and blew down the trees right before their eyes as if clearing the place for the monastery. The number of monks soon increased to one hundred, and the heart of their monastic rule was detachment from one's own will, total non-covetousness, and constant work. The main task of the monastery was the copying of service books and the writings of the holy fathers, and they created the best Russian monastic library. Joseph compiled the first manual of Russian Orthodox theology to oppose the false teachings of heretics. St. Joseph died peacefully in the year 1515.

COMMEMORATIONS: Holy Ancestors of God Joachim and Anna; Severian of Sebaste; Theophanes of Mt. Diabenos; Martyrs Chariton and Straton; Nicetas the Hidden; Joseph of Volotsk; Joachim of Opochka; Joachim of Suzdal; Onuphrius of Voronsk; Omer of Therouanne; Kieran of Clonmacnois; Bettelin of Crowland; Wulfhilda of Barking; Kyriakos of Tazlau; Onuphrius of Moldavia; Zachariah Lobov, of Voronezh, and Andronicus Surikov of Moscow; Raphail (Raev) of Strazhitsa; Commemoration of the Third Ecumenical Council; Uncovering of the relics of St. Theodosius, Archbishop of Chernigov; Synaxis of the Saints of Glinsk Monastery.

Thursday   **Fast-free**

September 10

Galatians 1:1-3, 20-24, 2:1-5
John 3:16-21

Once men have truly become His sons, our tenderly compassionate Father does not take away their temptations from them when it is His pleasure to 'make a way of escape,' but instead He gives His sons patience in their trials. All these good things are given into the hand of their patience for the perfecting of their souls.

St. Isaac the Syrian

VENERABLE JOASAPH OF KUBENSK, WONDERWORKER OF VOLOGDA. In the world, Joasaph was Prince Andrew, son of Prince Dimitri Vasilievich of Lesser Zaozersk and Princess Maria. They were known for their deep piety. Andrew was orphaned at an early age, but he received a religious education and respected the monastic way of life. At the age of twenty, he entered the Kamenny Monastery at Kubensk. He was tonsured a monk and given the name Joasaph, in honor of St. Joasaph, Prince of India. He kept the fasts, was zealous in prayer, loved books, and was obedient to his elder Gregory, the future bishop of Rostov. Joasaph was meek and sincere and lived an ascetic life there for five years. One day, as he was singing the Psalms of David, the Lord appeared to him, and said, "Do you see this surrounding wilderness? For your sake I will fill all of it with desert-dwellers, glorifying My name." In the final year of his life, Joasaph ate only once a week and received the Holy Mysteries every Sunday. Before his death, he spoke to the brethren, admonishing and consoling them. After praying to the Lord and the Mother of God, St. Joasaph lay down upon his bed and died. Soon after, miracles began to occur at his grave.

COMMEMORATIONS: Menodora, Metrodora, and Nymphodora at Nicomedia; Pulcheria of Greece; Varypsavas in Dalmatia; Salvius of Albi; Joasaph of Kubensk; Theodoritus of Ryazan; Peter and Paul of Nicaea; Paul the Obedient; Cassian of Spaso-Kamenny; Cyril of White Lake; Finian of Ulster; Theodaard of Maastricht; Meletius of Kuzhba, Gabriel of Donskoy, and Warus of Lipetsk; Synaxis of the Holy Apostles Apelles, Lucius, and Clement of the Seventy.

Friday   **Strict Fast**

September 11

Galatians 2:6-10; John 12:19-36

It is not that I want merely to be called a Christian, but actually to be one. Yes, if I prove to be one, then I can have the name.
St. Ignatius of Antioch

VENERABLE EUPHROSYNOS THE COOK OF ALEXANDRIA. Euphrosynos the monk labored in the monastery kitchen, serving the brethren with humility and patience. He never neglected his prayers or fasting. He suffered much abuse from the brothers, but his patience was inexpressible. One night a certain priest who lived at the monastery prayed to the Lord to show him the things which are prepared for those that love the Lord. He had a vision that he was standing in a garden of unimaginable beauty, and he saw Euphrosynos walking by. The priest asked, "Brother Euphrosynos, what is this place? Can this be paradise?" Euphrosynos answered, "It is paradise, Father." When the priest asked what he was doing there, Euphrosynos said that he had made his abode there and distributes to others the gifts of the garden. He then placed three apples in a kerchief and gave them to the priest. At that moment, the semantron was struck for Matins, and the priest awoke and found the three fragrant apples that Euphrosynos had given him in paradise. When he arrived in church, he asked Euphrosynos where he had been that night, and the monk replied, "Forgive me, Father, I have been in that place where we saw one another." The priest asked, "What did you give me, Father, in paradise when I spoke with you?" "The three fragrant apples which you have placed on your bed in your cell; but forgive me, Father, for I am a worm and not a man," answered Euphrosynos. Following the church service, the humble Euphrosynos was nowhere to be found. The apples were divided among the brethren, and whoever ate of them, was healed of their infirmities.

COMMEMORATIONS: Demetrius, Evanthia, and Demetrian at Skepsis; Ia of Persia and 9,000 martyrs; Theodora of Alexandria; Diodorus, Didymus, and Diomedes of Laodicea; Euphrosynos the Cook of Alexandria; Paphnutius the Confessor; Elias the Cave-dweller of Calabria; John of Svyatogorsk; Theodora of Vasta; Joseph of Zaonikieva; Deiniol of Bangor.

Saturday

September 12

Saturday before the Elevation
Fast-free
1 Corinthians 2:6-9
Matthew 10:37-11:1

You detach yourself from the cross to which you have crucified yourself alongside the Savior if you go and hit your brother.
St. Theodore Studite

VENERABLE DANIEL OF THASOS. Daniel was from ninth-century Thasos, during the time of iconoclasm under Leo V the Armenian. Daniel was raised to love virtue, wisdom, temperance, and humility. When he came of age, he withdrew from the world to live in solitude, unceasing prayer, and fasting, in a cave on a small island next to Thasos, called Krambousa. His fame soon spread, and he gathered many disciples seeking guidance, so he established a monastery, creating a city in the wilderness. At this time, St. Ioannikios the Great came to Thasos when there was a plague of snakes, and by his prayers, he drove them into the sea. Daniel went back to Thasos for the opportunity to learn from Ioannikios. They entered a certain haunted cave to live, where there was a fearsome-looking black demon, but the two ascetics ignored it, and this troubled the demon. So he turned himself into a fearsome snake and wrapped itself around Daniel's feet when he was in prayer and caused terrible pain in the side of Ioannikios. By the grace of God, they refused to leave the cave, and the demon disappeared. After a short time, both saints returned to their respective monasteries. St. Daniel reposed in peace at an advanced age and was buried at his monastery.

COMMEMORATIONS: Coronatus, Bishop of Nicomedia (Iconium); Autonomos, bishop in Italy; Julian of Galatia, and 40 martyrs with him; Andronicus of Atroa; Macedonius in Phrygia, and with him Tatian and Theodulus; Daniel of Thasos; Martyr Okeanos; Sacerdos, Bishop of Lyons in Gaul; Dositheus of Tbilisi, Georgia; Bassian of Totemsk; Theodore, Archbishop of Alexandria; Alexis, fool-for-Christ of Elnat and Zharki; Athanasius, disciple of Sergius of Radonezh, and his disciple Athanasius; Kournoutas of Cyprus; Ailbhe (Elvis) of Emly; Translation of the relics of St. Symeon of Verkhoturye.

SUNDAY

SEPTEMBER 13

Sunday before the Elevation
Fast-free
Galatians 6:11-18; John 3:13-17

It is not possible to represent and to think of the Cross without love. Where the Cross is, there is love. In church you see crosses everywhere and on everything, in order that everything should remind you that you are in the temple of the God of love, the Temple of love crucified for us.

St. John of Kronstadt

MARTYRS SELEUCUS, STRATON, CRONIDES, LEONTIUS, AND SERAPION. In the third century, these saints suffered for their faith in Christ during the reign of Licinius. Seleucus was from Galatia. Together with his wife, they were tortured and thrown to wild animals. In Nicomedia, Straton was tortured and bound to two cedar trees, which divided his body in two. Cronides, Leontius, and Serapion were from Egypt. They were bound and thrown into the sea. The waves carried their bodies to shore, and Christians gave them a proper burial.

COMMEMORATIONS: Cornelius the Centurion; Seleucus of Galatia; Straton of Nicomedia; Cronides, Leontius, and Serapion of Alexandria; Theodotus of Alexandria; Hierotheos of Kalamata; Ketevan, Queen of Kakheti, Georgia; Elias, Zoticus, Lucian, Valerian, Macrobius, and Gordian at Tomis in Moesia; Peter of Atroa; John of Prislop (Romania); Meletios Pegas, Patriarch of Alexandria; Litorius of Tours; Cornelius of Padan-Olonets, with Dionysius and Misael; Commemoration of the Founding of the Church of the Resurrection (the Holy Sepulcher) at Jerusalem; (Sunday before the Elevation: Chrysostom, Metropolitan of Smyrna).

MONDAY

Elevation of the Holy Cross
Strict Fast

SEPTEMBER 14

1 Corinthians 1:18-24
John 12:28-36

The Cross is the unconquerable weapon of pious kings in the battle with enemies. Through the apparition of the Cross in the sky, the dominion of Emperor Constantine was confirmed and an end was put to the persecution against the Church. The apparition of the Cross in the sky in Jerusalem in the days of Constantius the Arian proclaimed the victory of Orthodoxy. By the power of the Cross of the Lord, Christian kings reign and will reign until Antichrist, barring his path to power and restraining lawlessness.

St. John Chrysostom

COMMEMORATION OF THE SIXTH ECUMENICAL SYNOD. Emperor Constantine IV Pogonatos convened this Synod at the imperial palace of Constantinople. It was attended by 170 Holy Fathers in 680-681 A.D. to combat the heresies of Monothelitism and Monenergism. These heresies stated that in the one Lord Jesus Christ, there is but one will and one operation, as opposed to the Church doctrine of two wills, divine and human. St. Sophronios, the Patriarch of Jerusalem, and St. Maximos the Confessor were successful in these struggles.

COMMEMORATIONS: Exaltation of the Honorable and Life-Creating Cross; Placilla the Empress, wife of Theodosius the Great; Child-martyr Valerian; Martyr Theokles; Maria of Tarsus; Cyprian, Bishop of Carthage; Makarios of Thessalonica; Papas of Lycaonia; Holy Fathers of the Sixth Ecumenical Council; Repose of St. John Chrysostom; Uncovering of the relics of Sts. Alexandra, Martha, and Helen of Diveyevo; "Lesna" Icon of the Mother of God; Wonderworking Icon of St. Vlasios in Trikala, Corinth.

Tuesday   **Fast-free**

September 15

Colossians 1:24-2:1
Matthew 10:16-22

It is necessary for believers to again gain the way of the Lord. Let us abandon the crowds and their excited shouting; let not their words entice and influence us. The way of the Lord is narrow, uphill, demanding, lonely, but it is also salutary, as he himself has promised us. The believer must at last attach himself with love to what is essential to his personal existence, setting aside decisively and irrevocably the secondary and superfluous.

St. Symeon of Thessalonica

ST. SYMEON, ARCHBISHOP OF THESSALONICA. Symeon was from fourteenth-century Constantinople. He entered monastic life after his education and cultivated the virtues of humility, self-control, and prayer. He was elevated to the see of Thessalonica, and in spite of poor health and frequent illness, he gave his flock the courage to endure the trials that afflicted them. He urged them to place all their hope in God, to be loyal to the emperor, and to have confidence in their patron St. Demetrios. But the city came under siege by the Ottomans, and they fought back for six months before the city fell. Symeon died before this happened. All the inhabitants, Orthodox, Latins, and Jews, mourned his passing for he was a father and shepherd to all. St. Symeon composed hymns and prayers and compiled a vast spiritual commentary on the rites and ceremonies of the Orthodox Church. He was a champion of the Hesychasm of St. Gregory Palamas, and fought against every heresy and falsehood.

COMMEMORATIONS: Nicetas the Goth; Martyr Maximus; Bessarion I and Bessarion II, Metropolitans of Larissa; Symeon of Thessalonica; Gerasimos of Sourvia; Philotheus of Asia Minor; Joseph of Alaverdi; Porphyrios the Mime; Joseph the New; 2 maidens slain; John of Crete; Nicetas, disciple of St. Sergius of Radonezh; Ignatius Biryukov of Aleksievo-Akatov; Dimitry of Melitopol; Mirin of Paisley; Uncovering of the relics of the Holy Protomartyr and Archdeacon Stephen; Uncovering of the relics of St. Acacius the Confessor, Bishop of Melitene; "Novonikita" Icon of the Mother of God.

WEDNESDAY

SEPTEMBER 16

St. Euphemia the Great Martyr
Strict Fast
2 Corinthians 6:1-10
Luke 7:36-50

Silence is a great thing. Being in silence, a person is already praying—even without praying. Silence is a mysterious prayer, and it greatly helps prayer, just as the skin breathing brings man benefit.
St. Paisios the Athonite

ST. CYPRIAN, METROPOLITAN OF KIEV AND ALL RUSSIA. Cyprian was a Serbian monk on fourteenth-century Mt. Athos. Because of his pious life and excellent education, he came to the attention of Patriarch Philotheos of Constantinople. The patriarch consecrated Cyprian Metropolitan of Lithuania and Kiev. Upon the death of St. Alexis, he became Metropolitan of All Russia. The Great-prince brought him many sorrows, so he decided to live away from Moscow in either Constantinople or Lithuania. Cyprian was accepted as primate at Moscow during the time of Great-prince Basil Dimitrievich. St. Cyprian left a collection of pastoral epistles, translations of liturgical literature, corrected Divine-service books, and translated Slavonic manuscripts, witnessing his great scientific work.

COMMEMORATIONS: Euphemia the All-praised of Chalcedon; Victor and Sosthenes at Chalcedon; Dorotheus, hermit of Egypt; Ninian, Bishop of Whithorn; Ludmilla, grandmother of St. Wenceslaus, Prince of the Czechs; Meletina of Marcianopolis; Isaac and Joseph at Karnu, Georgia; Kushka of Odessa; Cyprian of Serbia; Procopius, abbot of Sazava in Bohemia; Cyprian, Metropolitan of Kiev; Edith of Wilton; "Support of the Humble" Icon of the Mother of God.

Thursday

Fast-free

September 17

Galatians 3:23-4:5; Mark 6:30-45

Let's remember my brothers: beggars are biblical characters!
+Elder Arsenius Papacioc of Romania

STS. LUCY THE WIDOW AND GEMINIAN HER SPIRITUAL SON. Lucy was a wealthy seventy-five-year-old Roman Christian, who was a widow for thirty-six years. When the Christian persecutions of Diocletian and Maximian broke out in the early fourth century, Lucy's son, who had converted to idolatry, denounced her as a Christian. She was brought before Diocletian and boldly confessed her faith in Christ but also reproved Diocletian for worshipping idols. He had her placed in a cauldron of burning pitch, which she endured for three days. Then she was dragged around the city with weights loaded on her body, bearing the insults from the crowd that had gathered. When Lucy was taken past the house of Geminian, the statues of the Roman gods in his house shattered. He followed her, asking for instruction in the Christian faith and baptism. For this, he was imprisoned with her. She instructed him, and a priest there baptized him, and the example of Geminian converted seventy-five more people. After three months in prison, an angel of the Lord conveyed Lucy and Geminian to Sicily and Mendilas, where they converted many pagans. St. Lucy died peacefully, and St. Geminian was beheaded.

COMMEMORATIONS: Sophia and her daughters, Faith, Hope, and Love, at Rome; Heraclides and Myron of Cyprus; Maximos, Asclepiodotos, and Theodotos of Marcianopolis; Theodota at Nicaea, and Agathoklea; Lucy and Geminian of Rome; Innocent of Glinsk; Anastasius of Perioteron on Cyprus; Eusipius of Cyprus; Lambert of Maastricht; Joachim I the Pany, Patriarch of Alexandria; 100 Martyrs of Egypt, 50 Martyrs of Palestine, including Peleus, Nilus, Zeno, Patermuthius, and Elias; Paul, Theodosius, Nicodemus, and Seraphim of Koryazha Monastery; Martyrs Haralampus, Panteleon, and others.

FRIDAY   **Strict Fast**

SEPTEMBER 18   Galatians 4:8-21; Mark 6:45-53

An inner cross comes more readily than an outer one. In a state of repentance, you need only direct your thoughts inward to study your soul, and instantly a multitude of crosses will appear. For instance, reflect on how you were created and what is the purpose of your life. Are you living according to Christ's teaching, are you accomplishing something good, are you growing spiritually? Meditate about this in some depth, and soon you will come to realize that you are failing in many important areas. God created you so that with all your works, life, and being you should contribute to the spreading of good and the strengthening of His Kingdom... Reflect on what awaits you beyond the grave and on what side you will find yourself at the Last Judgment: with the righteous or with the evildoers? And if you seriously reflect on all this, you will naturally become distressed and will regret your many words and deeds—and these painful feelings and the desire for repentance will become your inner cross.

St. Innocent of Alaska

VENERABLE EUMENIUS, BISHOP OF GORTYNA. As a young man, Eumenius gave away his possessions, clothed the poor and naked, and gave alms to those that asked. He purified his body and became passionless through the ascetic struggles of vigils, fasting, and abstinence, and so he pleased God by his virtuous life. Because of this, he was made a bishop of the Church of Gortyna in 668. He taught Christianity by example and worked many miracles by his prayers. He put an end to a time of drought and his prayers caused a serpent to perish. In Rome, he vanquished evil spirits and healed sickness and hatred. St. Eumenius gave up his soul in peace, in the Thebaid. He was buried in his homeland of Rhaxos.

COMMEMORATIONS: Ariadne of Phrygia; Eumenius of Gortyna; Sophia and Irene of Egypt; Castor of Alexandria; Arcadius of Novgorod; Bidzina, Shalva, and Elizbar of Ksani; Romulus of Ravanica; Hilarion of Optina; Amphilochius of Krasnoyarsk.

SATURDAY

SEPTEMBER 19

Saturday after the Elevation
Fast-free
1 Corinthians 1:26-2:5
John 8:21-30

*W*hen you are about to begin your prayer, first read a section from the *Holy Bible* or a story from the *Gerontikon*, to get your mind together and your heart warmed up. Then start praying.
St. Paisios the Athonite

HOLY PRINCE IGOR OF KIEV AND CHERNIGOV. In the mid-twelfth century, there was great strife over the principality of Kiev between two princely factions, and they were all close relatives. Igor's older brother Prince Vsevolod ruled Kiev for only a few years, and this time was fraught with wars. Going against tradition, Vsevolod declared that should he die, Igor would inherit Kiev, and this incited anger against the innocent Igor. Eight years later, Vsevolod died, and the Kiev nobles swore fidelity to Igor, but they broke their oath. Igor hid in the marshes, but still, they took him captive. Igor's princely rule lasted two weeks. He became a monk and spent his time weeping and praying, but the Kiev council decided to kill him. In Igor's defense, the metropolitan and clergy attempted to avert the senseless bloodshed, but the mob rushed into the church and seized Igor while he was praying. Prince Vladimir spirited Igor away from the crowd, pushed him behind the palace gates, and locked them. The mob broke down the barriers and murdered Igor, and yet they continued to beat him, then hung him up in the marketplace. That same day the body of St. Igor was taken to the church, and the candles around him lit by themselves.

COMMEMORATIONS: Trophimus, Sabbatius, and Dorymedon of Synnada; Seguanos of Gaul; Theodore, Prince of Smolensk and Yaroslavl, and his sons David and Constantine; Alexis of Zosima Hermitage; Zosimas, hermit of Cilicia; Theodore of Tarsus, Archbishop of Canterbury; Igor-George, Prince of Kiev and Chernigov; Constantine Golubev of Bogorodsk, and 2 martyrs with him; Sequanus of Gaul.

SUNDAY

SEPTEMBER 20

Sunday after the Elevation
Fast-free
Galatians 2:16-20; Mark 8:34-9:1

In preparing your children for life in the world, have you taken care to plant in their hearts faith and the fear of God, which will be their guides in the future? Pray to the Lord that He protect their hearts from the tares which are sown among the wheat by the enemy.

St. Macarius of Optina

ST. EUSTATHIOS KATAPHLOROS, ARCHBISHOP OF THESSALONICA. Eustathios was from twelfth-century Constantinople. In his youth, he entered the monastery of St. Euphemia. He completed his studies with high distinction at the Patriarchal School and later became the head of the school. He was called the most learned man of his age, and public orator. He wrote commentaries on ancient Greek poets, theological treatises, and his widely referred to Commentaries on Homer's Iliad and Odyssey. In his house, students gathered, anxious to learn, including the best minds of the capital. Eustathios was consecrated Metropolitan of Myra and Archbishop of Thessalonica. He lived as an ascetic, gave whatever he had to the poor, and opposed social injustice. When the Normans besieged the city, Eustathios stayed and asked them to put an end to the killing and looting and to respect the faith of the Orthodox. He also struggled to raise the standard of behavior among the clergy, monastics, and the people, as it had become lax. St. Eustathios reposed at about the age of eighty-six, and his tomb became a place of healings and miracles.

COMMEMORATIONS: Eustathius Placidas, his wife Theopistes, and their sons Agapius and Theopistus, of Rome; Theodore, Euprepius, and 2 named Anastasius, disciples of St. Maximos the Confessor; Hilarion the Cretan, of St. Anne's Skete; Michael and Theodore of Chernigov; John of Crete; Eustathius, Archbishop of Thessalonica; Meletios, Bishop of Cyprus; John of Putivl (Ukraine); Martyrs Artemidorus and Thalus; Oleg of Bryansk; John the Confessor of Egypt, and 40 Martyrs; Hypatius and Andrew, Confessors; Synaxis of the Saints of Bryansk.

Monday

Fast-free

September 21

Galatians 4:28-5:10; Luke 3:19-22

*P*eople concern themselves with Christian upbringing, but leave it incomplete. They neglect the most essential and most difficult side of the Christian life and dwell on what is easiest—the visible and external. This imperfect and misdirected upbringing produces people who observe with the utmost correctness all the formal outward rules for devout conduct, but who pay little or no attention to the inward movements of the heart, and to true improvement of the inner spiritual life. They are strangers to mortal sin…they sometimes pass judgments, give way to boastfulness or pride, sometimes get angry…. They are not upset about doing these things, but regard them without any significance. They've been to church, or prayed at home according to the established rule, they carry out their usual business, and so they are quite content and at peace. But they have little concern for what is happening in the heart. In the meantime, it may be forging evil, thereby taking away the whole value of the correct and pious life.

St. Theophan the Recluse

HOLY APOSTLE KODRATOS AT MAGNESIA. Kodratos was one of the Seventy Apostles. He was ordained Bishop of Athens, and taught the Greeks in Athens and Magnesia, bringing many to the faith of Christ. His prayers destroyed pagan temples and the idols within them. Because of this, he was tortured with fire, stones, and other torments. Then he was exiled. During the reign of Hadrian, he was martyred. The relics of St. Kodratos are in Magnesia, and many are healed who approach them with faith.

COMMEMORATIONS: Apostle Kodratos; Jonah the Prophet; Jonah the Sabbaite; Eusebios, Nestabus, Zeno, and Nestor of Gaza; Eusebius of Phoenicia; Priscus of Phrygia; Isaacius and Meletius, bishops; Daniel of Shugh Hill; Theophan of Lipetsk; Joseph of Zaonikiev; Hypatius of Ephesus; 6 Martyrs slain; Platon of Patmos.

TUESDAY   **Fast-free**

SEPTEMBER 22   Galatians 5:11-21; Luke 3:23-4:1

If a man but so desires, he can return to the divine standard and repent anytime, whether early or late.

St. Alonios of Egypt

VENERABLE PARASKEVA (PASHA), THE FOOL-FOR-CHRIST OF DIVEYEVO. Paraskeva came from a peasant family. She was married and remained childless for fifteen years. Her husband died, and she suffered much. She was expelled by the landowners and lived on the street in privation. She decided to devote her life to God and secretly was tonsured in Kiev. For thirty years she lived in the woods of Sarov, in a cave dug with her own hands. At that time, she began to be considered a blessed one and clairvoyant, and the people revered her. But even so, she was cruelly beaten almost to death by robbers, like St. Seraphim of Sarov. She spent nights in prayer, and her glance was exceptionally kind. She took on the task of wandering, going from one place to another. She would cut grass with a sickle while making prostrations and praying. There were so many cases of her clairvoyance that it was impossible to collect and record. She knew the thoughts of those around her and those who visited her. In 1903 the Tsar and Tsaritsa visited her in her cell. If something terrible was going to happen to one of her guests, she would put more sugar in their tea. In the Tsar's cup, she put so much sugar the cup overflowed. Paraskeva foretold the fall of the Russia and the Dynasty, as well as the devastation of the Church and a sea of blood. Later she foresaw the Tsar's holiness. She died at the age of 120, and her relics are at the Diveyevo Monastery.

COMMEMORATIONS: Phocas, Bishop of Sinope; Peter the Tax Collector; 26 Martyrs of Zographou; Phocas the Gardener of Sinope; Macarius of Zhabyn; Theophanes the Silent; Theodosius of Brazsk; Paraskeva (Pasha) of Diveyevo; Emmeram, in Gaul; Jonah of Yashezersk; Benjamin of Romanov; Cosmas of Zographou; Martyrs Isaac and Martin; Maurice and the Theban Legion, including Candidus and Exuperius; Synaxis of the Saints of Tula; "She Who is Quick to Hear" Icon of the Mother of God.

WEDNESDAY

SEPTEMBER 23

Conception of St. John the Baptist
Abstain from meat and dairy products, and fish.
Galatians 4:22-27; Luke 1:5-25

If there were love, people would not deceive us, they would not entice, they would not lie to us: love does not do evil to its neighbor.

St. Tikhon of Zadonsk

NEW MARTYR NICHOLAS PANTOPOLOS FROM KARPENISI. Nicholas was from an Orthodox Christian family in seventeenth-century Karpenesi, Greece. At the age of fifteen, he went to Constantinople to work in his father's grocery store. However, his father wanted Nicholas to better himself, so to that end, he had him tutored in the Turkish language by a well-educated Muslim. Since Nicholas proved to be bright and well mannered, the tutor plotted to make Nicholas a Muslim. One day, as a part of the lesson, the tutor had Nicholas read the Muslim declaration of faith. Then he informed Nicholas that he had just declared himself a Muslim. Surprised by this, Nicholas said that he was an Orthodox Christian. He was taken before their judge with the charge that he had mocked the Muslim faith, but Nicholas denied the allegations. He was offered a high office, riches, and honor, but he said that he did not need honors and would not deny his Christ. The judge had him tied to a post and circumcised, as a sign of their faith. Finally, he was imprisoned with murderers and given minimal food and water for sixty-five days. He returned to the judge with even greater conviction. He was imprisoned again and beaten often. Finally, he was taken to the judge and sentenced to beheading. For three nights, a heavenly light illumined his exposed relics. Christians dipped their handkerchiefs in the martyr's blood for a blessing. St. Nicholas was buried at the Monastery of the Theotokos on the island of Halki. His skull is now at the Monastery of Xeropotamou on Mt. Athos.

COMMEMORATIONS: Conception of St. John the Baptist; Xanthippe and Polyxenia of Spain; Rhais of Alexandria; Andrew, John, Peter, and Antoninus of Syracuse; Nicholas Pantopolos at Constantinople; John of Konitsa; Arsenius of Russia; Adamnan of Iona; Glorification of St. Innocent, enlightener of Alaska; "Slovensk" Icon of the Mother of God.

Thursday

September 24

Commemoration "of the Myrtle Tree" Icon of the Mother of God
Fast-free
2 Timothy 3:10-15
Luke 1:39-49, 56

Even the desire to sin is sinful.

+*Blessed Moses of Mt. Athos*

"OF THE MYRTLE TREE" ICON OF THE MOTHER OF GOD OF KYTHERA. This fourteenth-century icon is on the Greek island of Kythera in the monastery church of Myrtides. On this date, the Mother of God appeared to a shepherd, forty days after her Dormition, telling him to look for her icon that had been brought there many years before. He fell to the ground and prayed to her. When he got up and turned around, he found the icon behind him in the branches of a myrtle bush. He took the icon home, but the next morning, it was gone. Returning to the spot where he had found the icon, he saw it once again in the branches. He took it home, and again, it disappeared. When this happened a third time, he realized that it was there that she wanted to remain. A small church was built to house the icon, and it was called "Of the Myrtle Tree." Several hundred years later, Theodore Koumprianos, a paralytic with strong faith and a descendant of the shepherd, asked to be carried to the icon so that he might venerate it and perhaps be healed. As he was lying before the icon, suddenly there was a loud noise coming from the direction of the sea. The people fled, thinking that pirates were attacking. Theodore was left by himself in the church, and he heard a voice from the icon telling him to get up and flee. He stood, walked, and soon ran to catch up with his relatives. This wonderworking icon has also protected the island from a plague, saved people from death, helped the barren, and many other wonders.

COMMEMORATIONS: Silouan the Athonite; Coprius of Palestine; Thecla of Iconium; Stephen the First-Crowned of Serbia; Dorothea of Kashin; David and Stephen of Serbia; Abraham of Mirozh; Nicander of Pskov; Galacteon of Vologda; Isarnus of Marseilles; Gabriel of Seven Lakes; Leontius of Vilnius; Theodosius of Manyava Skete (Ukraine); Arrival in America of the first Orthodox Mission: Herman, Juvenaly, and Peter the Aleut; "Of Mirozh" and "Of the Myrtle Tree" Icons of the Mother of God.

Friday **Strict Fast**

September 25

Ephesians 1:7-17; Luke 4:22-30

Indeed, our true task is always the same and is always accomplished in the same way: to call upon our Lord Jesus Christ with a burning heart so that His holy name intercedes for us.

St. Hesychius the Priest

COMMEMORATION OF THE GREAT EARTHQUAKE AND THE CHILD WHO HEARD THE TRISAGION. There was a great earthquake in fifth-century Constantinople during the reign of Emperor Theodosios II the Younger. All the people, clergy, the emperor, and Patriarch Proclus left the city and went out to the plain of Hebdomon, and together supplicated God with litanies. Then suddenly, out of their midst, a child was taken up into the air, and with fear, everyone cried out for a long time, "Lord have mercy." Then the child was brought down on a cloud. In a great voice, he reported that an angelic choir told him to tell the bishop and laity that the Trisagion Hymn to God should be sung "Holy God, Holy Mighty, Holy Immortal, have mercy on us." Before this, the heretic Theopaschites had added the words, "Who was crucified for us" to the hymn. After saying this to the people, the child immediately gave up his soul, and the earthquake ceased. After this miracle, St. Pulcheria and Emperor Theodosios issued an edict for the hymn to be chanted in all the churches. Even the Latins chant it in Greek. Holy God refers to God the Father, Holy Mighty is the Son through Whom all things were made, and Holy Immortal is the Holy Spirit, the Giver of Life. The phrase "have mercy upon us" was taken from the Prophets David and Esaias. The place where the child was snatched up is known as Psomatheia, meaning "divine lifting."

COMMEMORATIONS: Paphnutios and 546 companions in Egypt; Euphrosyne of Alexandria and Paphnutius; Euphrosyne of Suzdal; Paul and Tatta, and their children; Dositheos the Recluse; Paraskeva of Kostroma; Arsenius the Great; Finbar of Cork; Cadoc of Llancarfan; Ceolfrith of Wearmouth; Commemoration of the Deliverance from the Great Earthquake in Constantinople in 447, and the child who heard the "Trisagion."

SATURDAY

SEPTEMBER 26

Repose of St. John the Theologian
Fast-free
1 John 4:12-19
John 19:25-27, 21:24-25

The sign of the presence of the Holy Spirit is peace lived, and joy, for God creates joy wherever He is.

St. Seraphim of Sarov

VENERABLE EPHRAIM OF PEREKOP AND WONDERWORKER OF NOVGOROD. Ephraim was born in the city of Kashin during the fifteenth century. At a young age, he desired solitude, so he left home to live at the Kalyazin Monastery. His parents asked him to return, but he persuaded them to become monastics, and they lived the rest of their lives as hermits. Through revelation, Ephraim moved to the monastery of St. Sava of Vishersk, where he was tonsured. Seeking solitude, he moved to Lake Ilmen and built a cell on the river bank. Soon other monks came to Ephraim and settled around him, and a monastery was established. At the request of the other monks, Ephraim was ordained to the priesthood in Novgorod. He built two churches, one in honor of the Theophany of the Lord and the other dedicated to St. Nicholas the Wonderworker. He secured water for the monastery by digging a canal to Lake Ilmen. From this, the monastery received its name "Perekop," meaning "to dig through." Ephraim died peacefully and was buried at the church of St. Nicholas. Due to flooding, his relics were moved to Lake Ilmen, where a chapel was built over his burial site. St. Ephraim revealed the site for a new monastery to the abbot Romanus. Upon completion of the monastery in the sixteenth century, St. Ephraim's relics were transferred there.

COMMEMORATIONS: Repose of the Holy Apostle and Evangelist John the Theologian; Gideon, judge of Israel; Martyr Heras; 5 Virgin-martyrs and Monastrion; Ephraim of Perekop, Wonderworker of Novgorod; Nilos the Younger of Rossano; Neagoe Basarab, Prince of Wallachia; Translation of the Head of the First-Called Apostle Andrew; Glorification of St. Tikhon (Bellavin), Patriarch of Moscow and All Russia; Arrival of the Iveron Icon of the Mother of God in Georgia.

Sunday

September 27

First Sunday of Luke
Fast-free
2 Corinthians 6:1-10
Luke 5:1-11

Nothing is stronger than prayer in its action, nothing more effective in winning God's favor.

St. Mark the Ascetic

VENERABLE SABBATIOS OF SOLOVKI. Sabbatios was humble and gentle and led a rigorous monastic life. Burdened by the crowds, he traveled to the uninhabited island of Solovki for solitude. When people asked him how an elderly gray-haired ascetic could live on that island, he said, "My Master gives the fresh strength of youth to the frail, and nourishes the hungry to satiety." Sabbatios encountered the hermit St. Germanos, and the two set off in a rickety boat for a three-day journey to Solovki Island. They settled there and built cells in the severe weather conditions. When a fisherman and his envious wife settled near the ascetics, two brilliantly clad youths appeared with rods, and the frightened couple departed that place. The accounts of the saints' exploits on Solovki spread. Sabbatios sensed his impending end, and he prayed that he might partake of the Holy Mysteries. He sailed for two days to the mainland and encountered the abbot Nathanael, who had come from a distance to give him Holy Communion. In parting, the two agreed to meet at the church near the Vyg River. Entering the church, Sabbatios gave thanks to God and entered a cell near the church. At that time, a merchant named John arrived at the shore and visited the church, and he went to Sabbatios for a blessing. Sabbatios offered him a place to stay until morning, but John wanted to depart. Suddenly there was an earthquake, and a storm arose on the sea, which frightened John, so he stayed. In the morning, he went back to the cell for the elder's blessing and found St. Sabbatios dead. John and Abbot Nathanael buried him at the chapel.

COMMEMORATIONS: Mark, Aristarchus, and Zenas of the Seventy; Callistratos and 49 Martyrs of Carthage; Sabbatius of Solovki; Flavian I of Antioch; Martyrs Philemon and Fortunatus; Epicharis of Rome; Martyr Gaiana; Aquilina of Thessalonica; Ignatius of the Deep Stream; Anthimos the Georgian; Archippus of Glinsk; Herman of Volsk.

MONDAY

SEPTEMBER 28

Fast-free

2 Corinthians 4:6-15
Luke 6:17-23

You know the first blow the devil gave to Job was through his possessions. He saw that Job had not grieved or separated himself from God. With the second blow, he touched his flesh, but the brave man did not sin by any words from his mouth. In fact, he had within his heart that which is of God, and he drew on this source unceasingly.

St. John the Dwarf

VENERABLE CHARITON OF SYANZHEMA. Chariton was a disciple of St. Euthymius at the River Syanzema at the end of the fifteenth, beginning of the sixteenth centuries. Euthymius had been for a long time a novice at the Spasokamensk Monastery. Then to find solitude, he built a cell amidst impassable swamps that were hidden within a dense forest. However, when the local people discovered Euthymius, he guided them in their spiritual lives, and this was when Chariton met him. Euthymius built a church and monastery, of which he was the abbot. Together they were an example of prayer and humility to the other monks who gathered there. They considered even their food and clothing worthless. In the church, Euthymius would stand in fear and trembling, and with tears. When Euthymius died, Chariton succeeded him as abbot. He continued there for forty years and peacefully died in old age.

COMMEMORATIONS: Prophet Baruch; Chariton the Confessor, abbot of Palestine; Mark the Shepherd of Phrygia, and Alexander, Zosimas, Alphius, Nicon, Neon, Heliodorus, and 24 others in Pisidia and Phrygia; Eustathios the Roman and Kallinikos; Cyril and Maria, parents of Sergius of Radonezh; Chariton of Vologda; Herodion of Iloezersk; Faustus of Riez; Hilarion Gromov of Petushki, and Michaela Ivanova (Moscow); Juliana, Princess of Olshansk; Alkison, Bishop of Nicopolis; Annemund of Lyons; Martyr Alexander; Wenceslaus, Prince of the Czechs; Wenceslaus of Zenkovka; Auxentius the Alaman of Cyprus; Leoba of Bischofsheim; Eustochium, daughter of St. Paula.

Tuesday **Fast-free**

September 29

Ephesians 2:19-3:7
Luke 5:12-16

Flee from people, stay in your prayer room, cry over your sins, do not take pleasure in the conversation of people, and you will be saved.

St. Makarios the Great

VENERABLE THEOPHANES THE MERCIFUL OF GAZA. Theophanes lived in the Syrian city of Gaza. He helped the poor and sick, took in the homeless, and spent all his money on the needy, leaving himself in poverty. Not only did Theophanes give away all his property, but he also lost his health. His body swelled and began to rot, giving off a stench, and he experienced great suffering. While Theophanes was dying, his wife grieved because there was a terrible storm raging, and she feared she would not be able to give him a proper burial. Theophanes told his wife that God would send help at the hour of his death, and the storms would end. As soon as St. Theophanes died, the storm ceased, and the rot, swelling, and stench left him. His relics became fragrant and exuded myrrh that healed the sick.

COMMEMORATIONS: Dada, Gabdelas, and Casdoa of Persia; Theophanes the Merciful of Gaza; Kyriakos the Hermit of Palestine; Gudelia of Persia; Mary of Palestine; 80 Holy Martyrs of Byzantium; Tryphon, Trophimus, and Dorymedon, and 150 Martyrs in Palestine; Onuphrius of Gareji; John of Riga in Latvia; Cyprian of Ustiug; Malachias of Rhodes; Holy Martyrs massacred at Strofades Monastery; Uncovering of the relics of St. John Maximovitch, Archbishop of Shanghai and San Francisco; Translation of the relics of St. Donatos of Euroea; Synaxis of the Saints of Poltava.

WEDNESDAY
SEPTEMBER 30

St. Gregory the Illuminator
Strict Fast
1 Corinthians 16:13-24
Matthew 24:42-47

If we seek God, he will show himself to us, and if we keep him, he will remain close to us.

St. Arsenius the Great

MARTYRS RHIPSIMIA, GAIANA, AND COMPANIONS. Emperor Diocletian decided to marry the beautiful nun Rhipsimia. She secretly fled to Ararat in Armenia with the abbess Gaiana and seventy other nuns, where they hid in a cave. Diocletian asked King Tiridates to find Rhipsimia, but when he heard about her beauty, he wanted her for himself. When soldiers surrounded them, a heavenly voice told the nuns to take courage. The frightened soldiers fled. Abbess Gaiana encouraged Rhipsimia not to give in, and the king gave orders to knock out Gaiana's teeth with rocks, and Rhipsimia fled. However, she was found by the king's men, who cut out her tongue, stretched her on a rack, and burned her with torches. Then they drove spikes into her stomach, and her eyes were removed. Finally, she was cut up into small pieces. When her fellow nuns went to gather the saint's relics, they were captured and beheaded. Gaiana and two other virgins were skinned alive, then beheaded. God's wrath came upon Tiridates, turning him into a wild boar. The soldiers who took part in the killings became mentally ill to the point of eating their own flesh. After some time, Tiridates' sister had a dream that Tiridates would be healed if she removed Bishop Gregory out of a pit. The bishop collected the remains of the martyred nuns, and reverently buried them. Then he commanded Tiridates to pray to the holy martyrs, and he was healed. His entire household accepted holy Baptism, and following his example, all the Armenian people were baptized.

COMMEMORATIONS: Gregory, Bishop of Greater Armenia; Ripsimia, Gaiana, and companions, in Armenia; Michael, Great Prince of Tver; Meletius, Patriarch of Alexandria; Honorius of Canterbury; Seraphim Zagorovsky of Kharkov; Martyr Mardonius; Martyr Stratonicus; 1,000 Martyrs slain by the sword; 2 female Martyrs; 70 male Martyrs; Gregory of Pelshma Monastery; Alexandra Chervyakova of Moscow; Translation of the relics of St. Michael, first Metropolitan of Kiev.

The 2021 Daily Lives, Miracles, and Wisdom of the Saints & Fasting Calendar

Preorder Now at:
www.LivesoftheSaintsCalendar.com

You can also place your order by phone at 412-736-7840
or email OrthodoxCalendarCompany@gmail.com

During prayer always firmly believe and remember that every thought and word of yours may, undoubtedly, become deeds. "Because no word shall be impossible with God."

St. John of Kronstadt

Thursday

October 1

Holy Protection of the Mother of God
Fast-free
Acts 9:10-19; Luke 6:12-19

Let us study the all-powerful and life-giving commandments of our great God, Creator and Redeemer. Let us learn them assiduously — by word and by life. They are read in the Holy Gospels, but they are known only as much as they are done in actual fact. Let us begin the battle against our fallen nature when it rises up against us and begins to fight back — not desiring to submit to the Gospel. Let us not be afraid if this war may be heavy and insistent. Let us rather strive for victory all the more insistently.
St. Ignatius Brianchaninov

VENERABLE JOHN KUKUZELIS THE CHANTER OF MT. ATHOS. John attended the Royal Academy of Music in Constantinople in the twelfth century. He had such a beautiful voice that he would sing for the emperor. He was given the name Kukuzelis, which means beans and peas when he told the royal household those were his favorite foods. Because of his popularity, he secretly fled to Mt. Athos and presented himself as a shepherd at the Sacred Monastery of Great Lavra. However, his talent was soon revealed, and he would sing the hymns beautifully and with great clarity. He had several visions of the Theotokos. One night during a service, he fell asleep near her icon, and she appeared to him, telling him to continue singing and that she would never leave him. Another time, as he was chanting the "Axion Esti" during an all-night vigil, the Panagia appeared before him, thanking him and putting a gold coin in his hand.

COMMEMORATIONS: Apostle Ananias of the Seventy; Romanus the Melodist; John Kukuzelis the Singer; Gregory the Singer of Mt. Athos; Sabbas of Vyshera; Bavo of Haarlem; Domninus of Thessalonica; King Mirian and Queen Nana, and Abiathar of Mtskheta, and Sidonia; Michael of Zovia Monastery, and 36 Fathers; Remigius of Rheims; Bavo of Ghent; Mylor of Brittany; Melchizedek I of Georgia; Alexis of Petrograd; Ismael of Strelna; Joseph and Kyriakos of Bisericani; Miracle of the Pillar with the Robe of the Lord under it at Mtskheta, Georgia.

FRIDAY

Strict Fast

OCTOBER 2

1 Timothy 1:12-17; Luke 6:17-23

The heights of humility are great, and so are the depths of boasting; I advise you to attend to the first and not to fall into the second.
St. Isidore of Pelusium

BLESSED ANDREW, FOOL-FOR-CHRIST AT CONSTANTINOPLE. Andrew lived in tenth-century Constantinople. From his youth, he loved the Holy Scriptures and church. He once had a dream-vision and saw two armies, the one with black menacing devils and the other with men who were radiantly dressed. Then a divine angel showed Andrew beautiful crowns and explained that these were a heavenly treasure that the Lord uses to reward his soldiers who are victorious over the demons. The angel also told Andrew, "Be a fool for My sake and you will receive much in the day of My Kingdom." Then Andrew perceived that it was Jesus Who was asking him to do this work, and from that time he dressed in rags and acted as though he were deranged. Andrew endured beatings, mockery, and insults with indifference. He lived with cold and heat, hunger and thirst, and begged for alms, which he then gave to the poor. For all of these labors, God granted him the gift of prophecy and wisdom, and he saved many spiritually. Once during prayer, St. Andrew saw the Most Holy Mother of God holding her veil over those praying for her protection.

COMMEMORATIONS: Cyprian and Justina of Nicomedia of Antioch, and Martyr Theoctistus, at Nicomedia; Cassian the Greek of Uglich; Theophilus the Confessor; Anna, Princess of Kashin; Theodore Gavras of Atran in Chaldia of Pontus; David and Constantine, princes of Argveti, Georgia; Damaris of Athens; Andrew, fool-for-Christ of Constantinople; Cyprian of Suzdal, fool-for-Christ; Hadji George of Philadelphia in Asia Minor; Theodore Ushakov, admiral of the Russian Navy; Patriarch Paisy Yanevts of Pec.

Saturday   **Fast-free**

October 3

Acts 17:16-34; Luke 5:17-26

Strive to struggle against laziness and drive it away and force yourself to labor in prayer. Remember that you must unfailingly force yourself in order to receive salvation.

St. Joseph of Optina

BLESSED HESYCHIUS THE HOREBITE. Hesychius was a sixth-century monk on Mt. Athos, who passed his life in complete negligence, not paying any attention to his soul. After becoming very ill, he died. But an hour later, he miraculously came back to life. He asked the other monks to leave him, and Hesychius closed himself in his cell, blockading his door. He went into complete solitude for twelve years, without uttering a word and without eating anything but bread and water. The monks could only hear him crying for his sins and singing the Psalms. When he was about to die, the brethren broke down the door and went in, asking him many questions, but all he said was, "Forgive me! No one who has acquired the remembrance of death will ever be able to sin." St. Hesychius was buried, and after some days, the monks could not find his holy relics.

COMMEMORATIONS: Dionysius the Areopagite, with Rusticus and Eleutherius; John the Chozevite, Bishop of Caesarea; Dionysius, Bishop of Alexandria and 8 Martyrs with him; Agathangelus, Metropolitan of Yaroslavl; Damaris of Athens; Dionysius, recluse of the Kiev Caves; Jerome of Aegina; Martyrs Theoctistus, Theogenes, and Theotecnus; Hesychius the Silent of Mt. Horeb; Hewald the White and Hewald the Black, at Cologne; Leodegarius (Leger), Bishop of Autun; Uncovering of the relics of St. Joseph, elder of Optina Monastery.

Sunday
October 4

Second Sunday of Luke
Fast-free
1 Corinthians 6:16-7:1; Luke 6:31-36

*C*lose your eyes to the precious things of the world, that you may deserve to have the peace of God reign in your heart.
St. Isaac the Syrian

MARTYRS ADAUKTOS AND HIS DAUGHTER KALLISTHENE. Adauktos and Kallisthene were from early fourth-century Ephesus. Adauktos was honored with the office of duke and eparch by the Christian-persecuting emperor Maximinus, who sought to marry Kallisthene. Adauktos would not permit this marriage since Maximinus was an enemy of the faith. For this Adauktos was stripped of his wealth and exiled to Melitene, where he was beheaded. Kallisthene disguised herself as a man, cutting her hair and wearing men's clothing. She left Ephesus for Nicomedia, then eight years later moved to Thrace, where she stayed with a woman whose daughter had eye damage. When Kallisthene healed her eyes, the girl asked for permission to marry Kallisthene, who was forced to reveal that she was not a man. When Maximinus died, Licinius took the throne. His wife was Constantia, who was a Christian and the sister of Constantine the Great. Kallisthene visited Constantia, and she helped raise their son. Kallisthene was given back all the property of her father and brought the relics of Adauktos back to Ephesus, where she built a church in his name. Kallisthene died peacefully and was buried near her father.

COMMEMORATIONS: Peter of Capitolias, Bishop of Bostra in Arabia; Hierotheos, Bishop of Athens; Domnina of Syria, with daughters Bernice and Prosdoce; Ammon of Egypt; Theodore of Tamassos, Cyprus; Adauctus and Callisthene of Ephesus; Gaius, Faustus, Eusebius, and Chaeremon of Alexandria; Jonah and Nectarius of Kazan; John Lambadistos of Cyprus; Helladius and Onesimus of the Near Caves; Ammon of the Far Caves; Peter Michurin of Siberia; Vladimir Yaroslavich of Novgorod, and his mother Anna; Evdemoz the Catholicos of Georgia; Stephen Stiljanovic of Serbia, and his wife Helen; Basil Tsvetkov of Ryazan; Barsanuphius Yurchenko of Cherson; Synaxis of the Saints of Kazan.

Monday

Fast-free

October 5

Ephesians 4:25-32; Luke 6:24-30

We have learned from experience that for one who wishes to purify his heart it is truly a great blessing to constantly invoke the name of the Lord Jesus against his intelligible enemies.

St. Hesychius the Priest

HIEROMARTYR HERMOGENES THE WONDERWORKER, BISHOP OF SAMOS. Hermogenes was from fourth-century Asia Minor. When his parents died, he gave his fortune to the poor and became a monk in Egypt. He was later ordained to the priesthood, then consecrated Bishop of Samos, where he worked with zeal and love for the Orthodox people and converted many pagans. But the pagans of Samos denounced him to Governor Saturninus. The saint was suspended and lacerated, his wounds burned, and then was chained in prison. But that night Jesus appeared to him, healing his wounds and encouraging him to persevere until the end. The next day, the bishop was tied to horses and dragged until his flesh ripped. Still, he denounced the idols. Then his teeth were removed, and he was thrown over a cliff. Once again, his wounds were healed, and he was tortured again. Seeing this caused many to convert to the faith of Christ. The enraged Saturninus had St. Hermogenes beheaded.

COMMEMORATIONS: Peter, Alexis, Jonah, Macarius, Philip, Hermogenes, Philaret, Innocent, and Tikhon, hierarchs of Moscow; Charitina of Amisus; Gregory the Archimandrite of Chandzoe, in Klarjeti, Georgia; Methodia, ascetic of Cimola; Damian the Healer, and Jeremiah and Matthew, of the Kiev Caves; Cosmas, abbot in Bithynia; Charitina, Princess of Lithuania; John, Metropolitan of Euchaita; Mamelta of Persia; Varlaam of Chikoysk; Sabbas of Vatopedi, Mt. Athos, Hermogenes, Bishop of Samos; Seraphim Amelin of Glinsk Hermitage; Gabriel Igoshkin of Melekess (Saratov); Daniel and Mishael of Turnu Monastery (Romania); Uncovering of the relics of Basil, Bishop of Kineshma; Uncovering of the relics of St. Eudocimus the Unknown, of Vatopedi, Mt. Athos.

Tuesday

October 6

Holy Apostle Thomas
Fast-free
1 Corinthians 4:9-16; John 20:19-31

He who prays hopes. And he, who hopes, is peaceful.
+Elder Efstratios of Glinsk

VENERABLE CINDEOS THE WONDERWORKER OF CYPRUS. At the age of eighteen, Cindeos became a monk in Jerusalem. Seeking solitude, he went into the Jordan desert. One day a nobleman took his ailing son to a famed ascetic, named Ananias, seeking a cure. Ananias sent the nobleman to Cindeos, who blessed and healed the boy. When word of this miracle spread, Cindeos was elevated to the priesthood. But he fled again into the desert, where he performed other miracles. These miracles angered the demons, so they incited a tribe of barbarians to butcher many desert-dwellers, beheading them and sawing them in two. Thirty-eight ascetics were martyred. Cindeos and many other ascetics sailed to Cyprus, where they built a hut on the edge of a cliff overlooking the sea. One time, the devil took on the form of a man and appeared to Cindeos, asking to be blessed. Cindeos was so startled that he tripped and fell deep into the sea, but the grace of the Lord preserved him. The devil later appeared to Cindeos as a woman, who tearfully begged him to go and bless her house, and he followed. Once there, she promptly disrobed. When Cindeos averted his eyes and prayed, she vanished. Once as he was traveling to visit a certain holy hermit named Jonas, he healed all the sick villagers he passed. Since the people were praising him, he returned to his cave, vowing never to leave again. But an angel of the Lord went to the cell of Jonas and transported him to the cave of Cindeos, and they rejoiced over this meeting. St. Cindeos died peacefully in old age. His hut remains preserved, near Avgoro, Cyprus.

COMMEMORATIONS: Holy and Glorious Apostle Thomas; Virgin-martyr Eroteis; Macarius of St. Anne's Skete, Mt. Athos; Cindeos the Wonderworker of Cyprus; Faith at Agen (Gaul); Glorification of St. Innocent, Metropolitan of Moscow and Missionary to Alaska; "Hawaiian Iveron" and "O All-Hymned Mother" Icons of the Mother of God.

WEDNESDAY	Strict Fast

OCTOBER 7

Ephesians 5:25-33; Luke 6:46-7:1

*T*ry to fill your soul with Christ so as not to have it empty. Your soul is like a cistern full of water. If you channel the water to the flowers, that is, the virtues, you will experience true joy and all the thorns of evil will wither away. But if you channel the water to the weeds, these will grow and choke you and all the flowers will wither.

St. Porphyrios the Kapsokalyvite

VENERABLE SERGIUS THE OBEDIENT OF THE KIEV CAVES. Sergius was a monk on Mt. Athos in the fourteenth century. He went to live at the Monastery of the Life-Giving Trinity in Russia under the spiritual guidance of St. Sergius of Radonezh. Many years later, Sergius entered the Vologda forest to live as a hermit. He built a cross, chapel, and a cell in which to practice his asceticism in silence and patience, enduring the temptations of the demons and unruly people. Later, forty monastics came to live near him, and together, they built a large church and monastic cells. The church was dedicated to the Procession of the Venerable Wood of the Life-Creating Cross of the Lord.

COMMEMORATIONS: Sergius and Bacchus, in Syria; Polychronius of Gamphanitus; Julian, Caesarius, Eusebius, and Felix, at Terracina; Leontius the Proconsul; John the Hermit and 99 Fathers of Crete; Sergius, founder of Nurma Monastery (Vologda); Joseph the Elder of Khevi, Georgia; Sergius the Obedient of the Kiev Caves; Abdon of Persia; Olympiades of Persia; Osyth, Princess of Chich (England); Dubtach, Bishop of Armagh (Ireland); Valentine Sventsitsky of Moscow; Uncovering of the relics of St. John Triantaphyllides of Chaldia in Asia Minor; Uncovering of the relics of St. Martinian of White Lake.

Thursday   **Fast-free**

October 8

Ephesians 5:33-6:9; Luke 7:17-30

The Martyrs earned paradise with their blood; the Monastics, with their ascetic life. Now we, my brethren, who beget children, how shall we earn paradise? With hospitality, by relieving the poor, the blind, the lame, as Joachim (the father of the Theotokos) did.... Almsgiving, love, and fasting sanctify man, enrich him in both soul and body, and bring him to a good end; the body and the soul become holy.

St. Cosmas the Aitolos

ST. IWI OF LINDISFARNE. Iwi was a disciple of St. Cuthbert, Bishop of Lindisfarne, in the seventh century. He longed to become a hermit, so he boarded a ship, trusting God to lead him to where he should settle. When they landed in Brittany, Iwi labored in asceticism for the rest of his days. He was known for his miracles of healing. St. Iwi died peacefully. Two hundred fifty years later, a group of clerics left Brittany with St. Iwi's relics. They stopped at the women's monastery of Wilton in southern England, and the relics were placed on the church altar. When they were about to leave, they found the relics immovable. Abbess Wulftrudis gave them a sum of money to leave the relics behind, and they departed with great sadness.

COMMEMORATIONS: Taisia (Thais) of Egypt; Pelagia the Penitent of the Mount of Olives; Virgin-martyr Pelagia of Antioch; Tryphon of Vyatka; Dositheus, abbot of Verkneostrov (Pskov); Anthony, Archbishop of Novgorod; Ignatius of Bulgaria and Mt. Athos; Jonah Lazarev of Nevel (Pskov); Demetrius Dobroserdov of Mozhaisk, Ambrose Astakhov of Aksinyino, Pachomius Turkevich of Moscow, John Khrenov, and Barlaam, Tatiana, Nicholas, Maria, and Nadezhda; Iwi of Lindisfarne; Triduana of Restalrig; Keyene of Cornwall; Synaxis of the Saints of Vyatka.

Friday

October 9

Holy Apostle James
Strict Fast
1 Corinthians 4:9-16
Matthew 9:36-10:8

The spirit of lukewarmness reigns. There's no manliness at all. We've been spoiled for good. How does God still tolerate us? Today's generation is the generation of indifference. There're no warriors. The great majority are fit for parades and feasts only. … Even people who've got something inside have begun to grow cool saying, 'Can I really do anything to change the situation?' We have to witness our Faith with boldness, because, if we continue to remain silent, we'll have to answer in the end. In these difficult days, each must do what is in their own power. Leave what's out of their power to God. In this way, our conscience will be clear.

St. Paisios the Athonite

VENERABLE PETER THE SOLDIER OF GALATIA. Peter lived in ninth-century Galatia. He was tall, handsome, and powerfully built, so the emperor made him a commander in the military. Peter fought valiantly for many years, then decided to renounce all things to become a monk. He was tonsured a monk at the monastery of Daphnon, then went to a mountain at Olympus. From there he went to Jerusalem to venerate the holy places, then departed for Laodicea and Attaleia. His travels were filled with toil, but his courage sustained him even from attacks by the Ishmaelites. He returned to Olympus, but when the new Emperor Basil the Macedonian heard about the virtuous Peter, he asked him to go live in the Monastery of St. Phokas. There he ended his days peacefully.

COMMEMORATIONS: Holy Apostle James, son of Alphaeus; Andronikos and Athanasia of Egypt; Forefather Abraham and his nephew Righteous Lot; Demetrius, Bishop of Alexandria; Publia the Confessor of Antioch; Peter of Galatia; Maximos of Persia; Stephen the Blind, King of Serbia; Stephen Lazarevic, King of Serbia; Dionysius (Denis) of Paris; Uncovering of the relics of St. Sebastian (Fomin) of Optina and Karaganda; "Korsun" (Cherson) Icon of the Mother of God.

SATURDAY   Fast-free

October 10

1 Corinthians 15:39-45
Luke 5:27-32

*B*e crucified, but do not crucify others.

St. Isaac the Syrian

NEW HIEROMARTYR PETER POLYANSKY, METROPOLITAN OF MOSCOW AND KRUTITSY. Peter graduated from the Moscow Theological Academy in 1892 and was appointed an inspector of all the theological schools of the Russian Orthodox Church. He did not seek ordination and preferred to remain a layman. He visited many theological establishments, made numerous friends, and exercised a beneficial influence on the religious education of future priests. The Patriarch, St. Tikhon, made Peter one of his closest aides and persuaded him to become a bishop. This was becoming one of the darkest hours in many centuries for the Church, as persecution was raging. Finally, Peter was made one of the highest-ranking bishops of the Russian Orthodox Church. The Communist government supported an organization called "The Living Church," which was created to destroy the official Orthodox Church. A significant number of bishops had been imprisoned or exiled. The people were confused and did not know who to believe. Finally, Peter wrote a "Letter to the Russian Church" and stood firm in the truth of Christ. He was arrested and sent to several different prisons. Then he was exiled, even beyond the Arctic Circle, in the frozen tundra. His health suffered. He was offered his freedom if he would stop leading the Church, but he remained firm and refused to compromise. By decision of the Soviet authorities, Peter was shot.

COMMEMORATIONS: Eulampius and Eulampia at Nicomedia and 200 Martyrs; Bassian of Constantinople; Theotecnus of Antioch; Pinytus of Knossos; Theophilus of Bulgaria; Innocent of Penza; Andrew of Totma; Paulinus of York; Ambrose of Optina; 26 Martyrs of Zographou Monastery; Theodore of Volokolamsk; Synaxis of the Saints of Volhynia: Job of Pochaev, Macarius of Kanev, Yaropolk-Peter of Vladimir, Theodore, Prince of Ostrog, Stephen and Amphilocius of Vladimir, and Juliana; "Of the Akathist" Zographou Icon of the Mother of God.

SUNDAY

OCTOBER 11

Sunday of the Seventh Ecumenical Council
Fast-free
Titus 3:8-15; Luke 8:5-15

The church is for us an earthly heaven where God Himself abides and looks upon those standing there. Therefore we must stand orderly in church, with great reverence. Let us love the church and let us be zealous towards it. It is a comfort and consolation for us in time of sorrow and of joys.

St. Hilarion of Optina

SYNAXIS OF THE ELDERS OF OPTINA. The Hermitage of Optina, well known since the sixteenth century, is eighty miles from Moscow. It was the focal point of a movement of spiritual renewal until the Bolshevik persecutions. First, it fell into ruins with the anti-monastic laws, but Metropolitan Platon of Moscow restored it. In 1821 Bishop Philaret of Kaluga built nearby the Skete of the Forerunner as a dependency of the monastery. Here the monks could devote themselves more to prayer. The brothers, Moses and Anthony, directed the life of the skete. The remaining nineteenth-century monastics were Macarius, Hilarion, Leonid, Ambrose, Anatole I the Elder, and Isaac I. The twentieth-century elders were Joseph, Barsanuphius, Anatole II the Younger, Nektary, New Hieroconfessor Nikon, and New Hieromartyr Archimandrite Isaac II.

COMMEMORATIONS: Apostle Philip of the Seventy; Nectarius, Arsakios, and Sisinios, Archbishops of Constantinople; Theophanes Graptus the Confessor; Zenais and Philonilla of Tarsus; Kenneth of Aghaboe (Ireland); Savvas of Vatopedi, fool-for-Christ; Theophanes the Faster of the Kiev Caves; Leonid of Optina; Philotheos of Mt. Athos and Constantinople; Jonah of Pergamos in Cyprus; Germanos Maroulis the Hagiorite; Ethelburga of Barking (England); Cainnech (Kenneth) of Aghaboe (Ireland); Gommar of Lier; Commemoration of the miracle from the Icon of our Lord Jesus Christ in Beirut; Synaxis of the Venerable Elders of Optina: Leonid, Macarius, Moses, Anthony, Hilarion, Ambrose, Anatole I, Isaac I, Joseph, Barsanuphius, Anatole II, Nektary, Nikon, and Isaac II.

Monday

Fast-free

October 12

Philippians 1:1-7; Luke 7:36-50

As a woman knows distinctly that she is pregnant because the babe leaps in her womb and can never be unaware that it is within her, in like manner the person who has Christ formed in himself and knows His movements, that is, His radiance, and His leapings, that is His flashes, is not unaware of the fact that Christ is formed within himself and he does see Christ as the light of the lamp.

St. Symeon the New Theologian

MARTYRS JUVENTINUS AND MAXIMINUS OF ANTIOCH. During the fourth century, Juventinus and Maximoinus were imperial bodyguards in the army of Julian the Apostate. Julian gave orders to pollute all the food in the marketplace with the blood from idol-worship. At a banquet, Juventinus and Maximinus were overheard objecting to this abomination. When the emperor learned this, he questioned them, and the saints refused to recant or give sacrifice to the gods. They were stripped, scourged, then beheaded. Other Christians took the bodies of the martyrs to Antioch, and a tomb was erected for their relics.

COMMEMORATIONS: Martin, Bishop of Tours; Symeon the New Theologian; Domnina of Anazarbus and Anastasia of Rome; Probus, Tarachus, and Andronicus at Tarsus; Maximilian of Noricum; Theodotus of Ephesus; Jason of Damascus; Juventinus and Maximinus of Antioch; Euphrosyne the Faster of Siberia; Amphilochius, Macarius, Tarasius, and Theodosius of Glushitsa Monastery; Theosevios the God-bearer of Arsinoe; Martyrs Andromachos and Diodoros; Arsenius of Svyatogorsk; Juvenal of Ryazan; Lawrence Levchenko of Optina; Martyrs Malfethos and Anthea; 70 Martyrs beheaded; Nicholas Mogilevsky of Alma-Ata; Edwin of Northumbria; Wilfrid of York; Mobhi of Ireland; Synaxis of All Saints of Athens; Translation of the relics of St. Sabbas the Sanctified from Rome to Jerusalem; Transfer of a part of the Life-creating Cross of the Lord from Malta to Gatchina; "Jerusalem," "Rudensk," and "Kaluga" Icons of the Mother of God.

Tuesday

October 13

Fast-free

Philippians 1:8-14; Luke 8:1-3

Subject yourself always to the will of God, and you'll have peace in your soul. Do whatever you're commanded, and don't do anything without a blessing. When you don't know, ask, and when you don't have anyone to ask, pray, and God will show you the good path.

+*Elder Paisius of Zihla*

MARTYRS KARPOS, PAPYLOS, AGATHODOROS, AND AGATHONIKE. Karpos was a bishop, and Papylos was his deacon. They were both physicians. Agathonike was the sister of Papylos. When Karpos and Papylos were arrested during the persecutions of Emperor Decius, they told the proconsul Valerian that they would not forsake Jesus Christ. Immediately, an earthquake knocked down all the idols, and they became dust. Karpos and Papylos were iron collared and tied up behind wild horses and dragged from Thyateira to Sardis. Then they were suspended on posts and clawed, but divine angels healed them at night. Agathodoros was arrested and strengthened by an angel, and he also openly confessed Christ. He was mercilessly beaten with rods and gave up his soul. Valerian told the physicians that they did not appreciate his benevolence, and they must sacrifice to the idols. When they refused, they were stoned, dragged over spikes, thrown to wild beasts to be devoured, and iron shoes nailed to their feet. Then they were thrown into a furnace, where Agathonike joined them confessing her Christian faith. Rain from heaven extinguished the fire in the furnace, and through all these torments, God preserved them unharmed. Finally, Valerian gave orders to behead the saints.

COMMEMORATIONS: Karpos, Papylos, Agathodoros, and Agathonike at Pergamus; Zlata (Chryse) of Meglin; Dioscorus of Egypt; Nicetas of Paphlagonia; Florentius of Thessalonica; Benjamin of Persia; Venantius of Tours; Benjamin of the Kiev Caves; Jacob of Hamatoura; Anthony of Chkondidi and James the Elder; Martyr Antingonus; Luke of Demena; Cogman of Lochaish; Gerald of Aurillac; Translation of the relics of St. Savvas the Sanctified from Venice to Jerusalem.

WEDNESDAY   **Strict Fast**

OCTOBER 14   Philippians 1:12-20; Luke 8:22-25

Sin is a terrible and most lamentable spiritual death that separates us eternally from the joy of the heavenly inhabitants in paradise and buries us in the darkness of hell.
                                    +Archimandrite Seraphim Aleksiev

---

ST. IGNATIOS AGALLIANOS, METROPOLITAN OF MITHYMNA. Ignatios was one of the most important figures in sixteenth-century Lesvos. His father and grandfather were priests. Ignatios desired to live as a monastic, but he obeyed the will of his father and married a pious woman before receiving ordination to the priesthood. They raised children, but not long afterward, his wife and children died during an epidemic, except for one son, Methodios, so Ignatios decided to live as an ascetic. He rebuilt a family-owned church, and together with his father and Methodios, they settled there. They erected new buildings and founded a small monastery. The monastery attracted both men and women, so Ignatios established two communities, close to each other. He also built a school and taught there. Many of these students went on to contribute to the Christian culture in Greece. He wrote the Rule, or Tyikon, under which the monasteries operated. He once traveled to Constantinople on behalf of the monasteries, and while there, he was appointed Metropolitan of Mithymna by the Holy Synod of the Ecumenical Patriarchate. St. Ignatios served thirty-five successful and peaceful years in that capacity. His miracle-working relics are venerated at the Monastery of Panagia Myrsiniotissa.

COMMEMORATIONS: Cosmas the Hymnographer, Bishop of Maiuma; Silvanus of Gaza and with him 40 Martyrs of Egypt and Palestine; Nazarius, Gervasius, Protasius, and Celsius of Milan; Ignatius, Metropolitan of Mithymna; Cosmas, abbot of Yakhromsk; Peter Apselamus of Eleutheropolis in Palestine; Nikola Sviatosha, Prince of Chernigov; Ignatios, Metropolitan of Mithymna; Parasceva (Petka) of Epivato, whose relics are in Iasi, Romania; Pachomios of Chios; Protasius of Milan; Manacca, abbess of Cornwall; Burchard, first bishop of Wurzburg; "Yakhrom" Icon of the Mother of God.

Thursday

Fast-free

October 15

Philippians 1:20-27; Luke 9:7-11

*O*ftentimes, couples tell me of their insecurities regarding the topic of childbearing, and ask for my opinion. Some only want one or two children, while others want to have many. However, it would be to their advantage to leave this matter of childbearing up to God—to entrust their life to Divine providence and not set up their own plan. They must have faith that God, Who cares for the birds in the air, will care much more for their children.

St. Paisios the Athonite

ST. JOHN, BISHOP OF SUZDAL. John became a monk at a young age in one of the monasteries of Suzdal. He was known for his humility and virtues and was consecrated the first bishop of Suzdal and Nizhegorod in the mid-fourteenth century. From this position, he would go before princes to lower the taxes on the poor. John had a love for the sick and destitute. He built poor houses and a hospital. He taught the people in a language they could understand and brought pagans to the Christian faith. Through the grace of God, the sick were healed when they touched the saint. During a Divine Liturgy, Prince Boris saw an angel of God in brilliant vestments serving John. When Suzdal was annexed to Moscow, John lived the rest of his days in seclusion at the Bogoliubov Monastery. He died there peacefully, and many miracles took place at his grave. His holy relics are in the Cathedral of Suzdal where they continue to work wonders.

COMMEMORATIONS: Sabinus, Bishop of Catania; Barses the Confessor, Bishop of Edessa; Lucian, presbyter of Greater Antioch; Lucian, presbyter of the Kiev Caves; John, Bishop of Suzdal; Dionysius, Archbishop of Suzdal; Euthymios the New of Thessalonica; Aurelia of Strasburg; Thecla, abbess of Ochsenfurt (Germany); Valerian Novitsky of Telyadovich; Athanasius, Bishop of Kovrov; Synaxis of the New Hieromartyrs of Belorussia; "Prosperess of Loaves" (Multiplier of Wheat) Icon of the Mother of God.

Friday

October 16

St. Longinos the Centurion
Strict Fast
Philippians 1:27-2:4
Matthew 27:33-54

*W*hatever we do, let us do it because we want to, freely, responsibly and with gladness.

St. Porphyrios the Kapsokalyvite

NEW MARTYR JOHN OF TOURKOLEKA. John was born in 1805 in the village of Tourkoleka in Arcadia. His family was distinguished for their devotion to God, love for Greece, and their heroism. John's father was a famous fighter in the area. Among John's four brothers were Nikitaras, a renowned chieftain, and Nicholas, a well-educated captain and teacher of military tactics. When John was eleven years old, he accompanied his father and another young man, who was a Reader, on a boat trip. The rough seas caused them to land in Neapolis of Lakonia. The aga of that region fraudulently arrested them and sent them to the uppermost ruler of Monemvasia, and they were imprisoned in the castle. The aga ordered the beheading of the three prisoners. The Reader and John's father were beheaded first. John's brother Nikitaras writes, "They suggested to my brother to change his faith. Showing to him his slain father they told him to 'sit down so we can make you a Turk.' The child then did his cross and responded: 'Where my father has gone I am going also.' They said to him again: 'Become a Turk.' The child, however, did his cross again. By his blood, he became a cross. They took their heads to Tripolitsa." This all took place in the courtyard of the Sacred Church of Christ in Chains, in old Monemvasia. On the floor of the courtyard of the church, the blood of St. John formed a cross, and this became a source of strength and pilgrimage for the Christian Greeks. The place of their burial and all their relics remains unknown.

COMMEMORATIONS: Longinos the Centurion, with Isaurus and Aphrodisius; Longinus the Gate-keeper of the Kiev Caves; Martyrs Dometius, Leontios, Terence, and Domninus; Malus the Hermit; John and Longinus of Yaranga; Eupraxia of Pskov; Gall, enlightener of Switzerland; Longinus of Koryazhemka; Domna, fool-for-Christ of Tomsk; John of Tourkoleka.

SATURDAY   Fast-free

OCTOBER 17
Hebrews 11:33-12:2; Luke 6:1-10

*P*eople are divided in this world into good and evil, rich and poor, educated and uneducated, noble and ignoble, intelligent and fools. They do however all have one thing in common. And that is pain. Because all people, without exception, will experience pain during their lifetime. As the saying goes: 'It's a marvel, if someone finds happiness during their life'. Therefore, we all live in the realm of pain. We know that pain is something personal, which one has to deal with alone. It's our cross, which we have a duty to carry, just as the Saviour of the world, Jesus, carried His Cross for our sakes. So find comfort and rest in the paternal hand, which at this time is operating on you with the instrument of pain, and be calm. Accept that it is God who sends it, make peace with it, with pain, so as to be able to deal with it.

Elder Ephraim of Arizona

HOLY PROPHET HOSEA. Hosea lived and prophesied eight hundred years before Jesus Christ. The prophet's writings are in the fourteen chapters of the Book of Hosea, in the Old Testament. He denounced the tribes of Judah and Israel for idol-worship and foretold their punishment. He prophesied how Israel and Samaria would be destroyed for their falling away, of our Lord Jesus Christ Who was to come, and the time when animal sacrifices would be no more. He died peacefully in great old age, which is a sign of a true prophet. False prophets were killed for inaccurate predictions. It is believed that he was buried in the Jewish cemetery of Safed.

COMMEMORATIONS: Hosea the Prophet; Unmercenaries Cosmas and Damian of Arabia, and their brothers Leontios, Anthimos, and Euprepios, in Cilicia; Alexander Shchukin, Archbishop of Semipalatinsk; Anthony of Novgorod; Jacinthus and Callistus of Verkhoturye; Queen Shushanik (Susanna) of Georgia; Andrew of Crete; Joseph, Catholicos of Georgia; Ethelred and Ethelbert, Princes of Kent; Bondarenko the fool-for-Christ; Translation of the relics of St. Lazarus (of the Four Days).

Sunday, October 18

Holy Apostle and Evangelist Luke
Fast-free
Colossians 4:5-11, 14-18
Luke 10:16-21

We are children, and as children of the Heavenly Father we should ask for the support of our Parent. Because we were born of earthly parents, we seek support from them. But they have their cares and their worries; they are beset by all kinds of trouble and difficulties. We look to them for guidance and support, but they do not look after us. "You have a head on your shoulders—use it. You're a grown man," they tell us. The Heavenly Father, however, never avoids helping us. He is always looking after us, always guiding us, if our heart is united with Him. But if we look for support in the world, it will be very difficult to find.

+Elder Thaddeus of Vitovnica

VENERABLE JULIAN THE HERMIT OF THE EUPHRATES RIVER. Julian was an uneducated fourth-century monk from Persia who lived in the desert of Mesopotamia, close to the Euphrates River. He built a church on Mount Sinai, on the rock which Moses stood on when he spoke to God, and it still stands to this day. At that time, Julian prayed that God would end the persecutions of Julian the Apostate. A voice announced to Julian that because of his prayers and tears and the prayers of others, God would slay the apostate, and this happened at that very moment. Julian, who had the gift of insight, saw the spirit of the apostate, and he related this to his disciples. St. Julian had the power to perform miracles, and he died peacefully.

COMMEMORATIONS: Apostle and Evangelist Luke; Marinus the Elder at Anazarbus; Mnason, Bishop of Cyprus; Julian the Hermit of Mesopotamia; Gabriel and Cirmidol of Egypt; David of Serpukhov; Symeon, Theodore, and Euphrosyne, who found the icon of the Mother of God in the Great Cave of the Peloponnese; Peter of Cetinje, Metropolitan of Montenegro; James the Deacon; Isidore, Irene, and George of Crete; 40 Children Martyrs; Gwen and Selevan, Welsh missionaries, in Brittany; Uncovering of the relics of St. Joseph of Volokolamsk.

MONDAY   **Fast-free**

OCTOBER 19   Philippians 2:14-21; Luke 9:18-22

The body, being only the temporal garment of the soul, is perishable, and does not constitute the true life of the man. The true life is the spiritual life.

St. John of Kronstadt

ST. JOHN THE WONDERWORKER OF KRONSTADT. John was born in the far north of Russia to a church reader. From his youth, he would go with his father to their church, where he served in the altar. His favorite book was the Holy Gospel. Learning was difficult for John, so he prayed fervently to God. One day after a night of prayer, he suddenly experienced a lightness and joy in his soul, and from that time, he was able to read easily and memorize everything. After finishing school at the top of his class, he entered the St. Petersburg Religious Academy. He married, was ordained to the priesthood, and was assigned to the St. Andrew Cathedral in Kronstadt. John and his wife Elizabeth dedicated their lives to serving God, and they lived as brother and sister. John worked untiringly serving the poor and destitute, and sinners. Because of this, God granted him the gifts of clairvoyance and miracle-working, for the healing of body and spirit. Such miracles were performed countless times each day through the saint's prayers. These were not only done in person but through letters written to him. Father John's diary, *My Life in Christ*, is written in simple language and is a spiritual treasure that expounds the deepest meanings of Orthodoxy. St. John died in 1908, having foretold his death. Many grace-filled miracles occurred at his tomb. Millions of Orthodox Christians around the world pray to St. John to intercede for them.

COMMEMORATIONS: John, Wonderworker of Kronstadt; Prophet Joel; Warus and 7 others; Sadoc, Bishop of Persia, and 128 Martyrs; Leontius the Philosopher; Gabriel of St. Elias Skete; Demetrius of Moscow; Alexis of Petrograd; Prochorus of Pechenga; Anthony of the Kiev Caves Lavra; Nicholas Dvali of Jerusalem; Cleopatra and John in Egypt; Felix and Eusebius; Frideswide of Oxford; Translation of the relics of St. John of Rila.

Tuesday

October 20

St. Artemius the Great Martyr
Fast-free
Philippians 2:16-23; Luke 9:23-27

*W*hen we approach someone with pain and true love, then this true love of Christ transforms our neighbor. The person who has holiness, no matter where he is, somehow creates an electromagnetic spiritual field around himself, and influences those who come within this field. Of course, we must be careful not to squander our love, and give our heart away too easily, because many times people will exploit our heart and turn it into ground meat; or at other times, they aren't able to understand us and they misinterpret us.

St. Paisios the Athonite

MARTYR ANDRONIKOS OF CRETE. Andronikos was born and raised in Crete. He is known as a champion of the holy icons, along with Nicholas the Studite, during the iconoclast reign of Emperor Leo III the Isaurian. This controversy raged in Asia Minor and Crete for about 117 years in the eighth and ninth centuries. In a study titled, "Dispute Concerning the Recognition of Iconophiles," there were 106 Confessors who suffered by the iconoclasts with Empress Theodora. There was a church dedicated to St. Andronikos in Heraklion, Crete, but the agha had it converted into a public bath.

COMMEMORATIONS: Artemios at Antioch; Aborsam and Senoe of Persia; Zebinas of Caesarea, and Germanos, Nicephorus, Anthony, and Manatho; Gerasimos the New of Cephalonia; Matrona of Chios; Nicholas (Liubomudrov) of Yaroslavl; Artemius of Verkola; Herman Kokel of Alatyr; Theodosius of Svyatogorsk; Acca of Hexham (England); Jonah of Hankou, Manchuria; Andronikos of Crete; Uncovering of the relics of St. Nikodim Kononov, Bishop of Belgorod; Translation of the relics of St. Ignatius of Bulgaria and Mt. Athos; Translation of the relics of St. Gerasimos the New of Kephalonia; Translation of the relics of St. Gregory Kallides of Heracleia.

WEDNESDAY   **Strict Fast**

OCTOBER 21

2 Corinthians 9:6-11
Luke 9:44-50

When I read the lives of the Saints as a child, I felt as though a ray of divine light had entered my heart. It filled my heart with sweetness, joy and jubilation and lit a desire and love for God and heavenly things. Then, whether I was eating, walking or speaking with others, my mind was contemplating heavenly things and my heart was riveted to God.

+Elder Philotheos Zervakos

MARTYRS GAIOS, DASIOS, AND ZOTIKOS OF NICOMEDIA. One day when the pagans were celebrating an imperial festival in Nicomedia in Bithynia, these three saints went into the pagan temples and threw down the idols they found within. They were immediately arrested and taken before the judge for being sacrilegious. They confessed their faith in Christ and faced all manner of tortures. They were hung from poles, and their skin was scraped with goat hair. Then heavy stones were tied to their necks, and they were cast into the sea.

COMMEMORATIONS: Hilarion the Great of Gaza; Dasios, Gaios, and Zotikos at Nicomedia; Hilarion, Metropolitan of Kiev; Hilarion of Pskov; Hilarion of Meglin; Hilarion of the Kiev Caves; Philotheus of Mt. Athos; Socrates and Theodote of Ancyra; John of Monemvasia; Bessarion and Sophronius of Ciorara; Oprea of Salistie; John of Gales and Moses of Sibiel; Theophilus and James of Omutch; Martyrs Azes, Eucratus, Zachariah, Andrew, Stephen, Paul, and Peter; Baruch, monk; Ursula of Cologne and companions; Condedus of Fontenelle; Fintan Munnu of Teac Munnu; Malathgeny of Cluain-Edneach; Paulinus of Mogilev; Alexis of Voronezh; Damian of Kursk; Neophytus of Moscow and Sophronius of Lazeva; Constantine, Sergius, Basil, Theodore, Vladimir, Nicholas, John, Basil, Alexander, Demetrius, Alexis, Sergius, John, and Sophronius, of Tver; Translation of the relics of St. Christodoulos of Patmos; Translation of the relics of St. Hilarion of Meglin.

Thursday

Fast-free

October 22

Philippians 3:1-8; Luke 9:49-56

For a true monk, nothing and no one exist on earth. His joy and delight is unceasing prayer. He loves all people, but is lonely among them because they separate him from God.
+Elder Parthenius of Kiev Pechersk

ST. EULALIOS OF LAMBOUSA. According to tradition, Eulalios was bishop of the city of Edessa in Syria. In this city, the image of the Holy Mandylion, the image of Christ not made with hands, was kept in the royal palace with great reverence. When the king died, his successor, who was a pagan extremist, decided to destroy the sacred relic. When Eulalios heard this, he secretly took the Holy Mandylion, and after walking all night, arrived at the seashore. There he boarded a ship headed for Cyprus. But a great storm arose as they approached their destination, which threatened to sink the boat. Eulalios took out the treasure, which he had kept in his bosom, made the Sign of the Cross, opened it, and stretched it out on the stormy sea and sat on it. Just then, the sea became calm, and the waves brought St. Eulalios to shore at Lambousa. He took the Holy Mandylion to the Monastery of Acheiropoietos.

COMMEMORATIONS: Lot of Egypt; Seven Youths (Seven Sleepers) of Ephesus: Maximilian, Jamblichus, Martinian, Dionysius, Antoninus, Constantine, and John; Abercius, Bishop of Hierapolis; Alexander, Heraclius, Anna, Elizabeth, Theodota, and Glyceria, at Adrianople; Paul and Theodore of Rostov; Rufus of *The Paradise*; Martyr Zachariah; Theodoret at Antioch; Alexander of Cherkassy; Mellon of Rouen; James of Luga and Omutch, disciple of Theophilus of Omutch; Eulalios of Lambousa; Seraphim, Archbishop of Uglich, Menas Shelaev and Herman Polyansky, archimandrites, and Alexander Lebedev, Vladimir Sobolev, Basil Bogoyavlensky, and Alexander Andreyev, priests; "Kazan" Icon of the Mother of God commemorating the deliverance of Moscow from the Poles and Lithuanians; "Andronicus" Icon of the Mother of God.

FRIDAY

OCTOBER 23

St. James the Apostle
Abstain from meat and dairy products, and fish.
Galatians 1:11-19
Matthew 13:54-58

A man full of self-esteem suffers torture when he sees a humble person weeping and being doubly compensated by God, who is moved to pity because of his tears, and by men, who are moved to give him praise that he never sought.
St. Symeon the New Theologian

VENERABLE PETRONIOS, DISCIPLE OF ST. PACHOMIOS THE GREAT. Petronius was the son of wealthy parents. When he decided to leave the world, he built a monastery on their property. He gathered about him "anyone who wanted to live in Christ." This monastery, called Tbow, was located on the west bank of the Nile River. In so doing, Petronius also converted his father and his brother to the monastic life, "with all their household." When he learned about the community of St. Pachomios, he asked him to receive the monks of Tbow. Pachomios came there with his brothers and established the accepted monastic rules. Petronius had purity of heart and was favored by God with revelations. Later St. Pachomios gave Petronius responsibility for several monasteries and appointed him as his successor. However, St. Petronius also died within a few months.

COMMEMORATIONS: Holy Apostle James, the Brother of the Lord; Ignatius, Patriarch of Constantinople; Petronius of Egypt, disciple of St. Pachomius the Great; Nicephorus of Constantinople; Macarius the Roman of Mesopotamia; Elisha of Lavrishevo, Belorussia; Eusebius Rozhdestvensky, Archbishop of Shadrinsk, and Vladimir Ambartsumov of Moscow; Oda of Scotland; Ethelfleda of Romsey; Translation of the relics of St. James of Borovichi, Wonderworker of Novgorod.

SATURDAY   Fast-free

OCTOBER 24

2 Corinthians 1:8-11
Luke 7:1-10

I should say the Jesus Prayer humbly, as if into His ear.
St. Pachomios of Chios

ST. SENOCH OF TOURS THE HEALER. In the sixth century, Senoch found in the area of Tours the walls of an old monstery, and he restored it. He also found an oratory that St. Martin had used, and he repaired it, and placed an altar inside that had a small compartment for relics. When Senoch and the bishop tried to put the small casket of relics in the hollow, they found that the container was too large. They prayed with tears and miraculously the hollow was enlarged, and the casket grew smaller, comfortably fitting into the hollow. Three monks gathered there with Senoch. During Lent, he ate only a little barley bread and a little water. He would attach iron chains to his neck, feet, and hands, and enclose himself in his cell in prayer and vigil, without any pause. The money that the faithful gave him, he offered to relieve the various necessities of the poor, helping more than 200 people. He also cured the sick. But just as his sanctity came from abstinence, so too did vanity emerge from his holiness. He became swollen with pride. However, the brothers corrected him, and he received their words willingly, and he purged himself entirely of his vanity and became so humble. He healed the blind, the disabled, and those bitten by snakes. He also built bridges so that no one would drown during the flood seasons. At the age of forty, he got a small fever and died. Even then, St. Senoch often manifested himself by miracles at his tomb.

COMMEMORATIONS: Arethas of Omir and 4,299 Martyrs; Syncletica and her 2 daughters; Elesbaan, King of Ethiopia; Theophilus, Arethas, and Sisoes of the Kiev Caves; Sebastiana at Heraclea; Acacius of Armenia; John of Pskov; Zosimas of Siberia; Athanasius, Patriarch of Constantinople; Laurence of Balakhna, Alexis Porfiriev, and Alexis Neidhardt; Senoch of Tours; Martyrs Mark, Soterichus, and Valentine; Martyr Nerdon; Arethas Mitrenin of Valaam; Abramius and Abraham in Najran; Maglorius of Dol; "Joy of All Who Sorrow" Icon of the Mother of God.

Sunday

October 25

Sixth Sunday of Luke
Fast-free
Galatians 1:11-19; Luke 8:26-39

"*How* long will God wait for me?" Rest assured that as long as God is allowing you to live, it is a guarantee from Him that He is waiting for you! You cannot deny God the prerogative to wait for your repentance. With this hope and courage in mind, let us approach the majestic throne of God's grace. We have innumerable brilliant examples of people who repented, who were previously living far away from God, but who later returned and were not simply saved but even reached great heights of holiness.

Elder Ephraim of Arizona

MARTYR ANASTASIOS THE FULLER AT SALONA IN DALMATIA. Anastasios was born in Aquileia during the fourth-century reign of Diocletian. He was a fervent Christian and a maker of cloth in the town of Salona. Seeing the tortures that the holy martyrs endured for Christ, he developed a desire for martyrdom. He covered himself with the image of the cross and took himself to the judgment hall, where he declared that he was a Christian. The judge immediately had him disrobed and flogged, then beheaded and cast into the sea. A Christian woman had the saint's body retrieved from the water, and she buried him in her garden. Later, the garden became a Christian cemetery, and a chapel was built there dedicated to St. Anastasios. Many miracles glorified the saint's relics.

COMMEMORATIONS: Tabitha (Dorcas) of Joppa; Anastasius the Fuller at Salona; George of Amastris; Marcian and Martyrius the Notaries; Macarius of Paphos on Cyprus; Crispinus and Crispinianus, martyred under Diocletian; 2 Martyrs of Thrace; Martyrius the Deacon and Martyrius the Recluse of the Kiev Caves; Matrona the Confessor of Diveyevo; Martyrs Vallerios and Chrysaphus; Martyr Savinos; Philadelphus and Polycarp; Martyrs Nikephoros and Stephen; Martyrs Faustus, Basil, and Silouan, at Darion; Martyrs Pappias, Diodorus, and Claudianus, of Pamphylia; Varus of Egypt; Martyr Vallerinos; Front of Perigueux; Miniatus of Florence; Commemoration of the Great Miracle of Panagia Prousiotissa.

Monday

October 26

St. Demetrios the Great Martyr
Fast-free
2 Timothy 2:1-10
John 15:17-27, 16:1-2

Don't rush into anything; the law of God's actions is gradual, slow, and wondrous firmness! The devil is in a hurry, because he has no peace and in haste he inclines to every sin, because in haste there is no wisdom.

St. John of Kronstadt

VENERABLE ATHANASIOS OF MEDIKION MONASTERY. Athanasios was from a noble family in Constantinople. He received a good education, and his father wanted him to enter public service at the Treasury. But Athanasios wished to live as a monk, so he left home secretly and went to a monastery in Bithynia. His father rushed after him, and unable to convince Athanasios to return home, he took him by force. He dressed him in rich clothing and shut him in a room, but Athanasios tore the clothes to pieces. His father then put more expensive garments on him, but he also destroyed those. He beat the young Athanasios, covering him with wounds. Parts of his shoulder and back began to rot, and doctors had to remove part of his flesh. Finally, his father saw his son's resoluteness and sent him off with his blessing. Saints Nikephoros and Niketas later invited him to join their brotherhood in the Monastery of Medikion, and his zeal and piety were widely admired. Before his death, Athanasios told the brethren, "After my death, you will fully make sure whether I will at least get some grace from God." He died peacefully in the year 814. A cypress tree grew on his grave, from which many healings occurred.

COMMEMORATIONS: Demetrios the Myrrh-gusher of Thessalonica, and Lupus; Athanasios of Medikion; Anthony of Vologda; Theophilus of the Kiev Caves; Demetrius of Basarabov; Demetrios of Misti-Konakli; Alexander Okropiridze of Guria; Martyrs Glykon, Leptina, Artemiodorus, and Basil; Joasaph of Mt. Athos; Cedd of Lastingham; Eata of Hexham; Luian and Marcian, former magicians; Translation of the relics of St. George of Ioannina; Commemoration of the transfer of the Icon of St. Demetrios from Thessalonica to Constantinople.

Tuesday   **Fast-free**

October 27

Colossians 1:1-3, 7-11
Luke 11:1-10

Examine your self and strive to adorn it with love, humility, compassion and hope. Seek the regeneration of your soul, enlightened by the voice of the Gospel and helped by God. With fear and love for the Heavenly Father, proceed to sow the seeds of God's word on good soil. Cultivate the talent given by Christ for the salvation of your soul.

St. Raphael of Lesvos

ST. KYRIAKOS I, PATRIARCH OF CONSTANTINOPLE. Kyriakos was known as the Bishop of Argyropolis and Byzantium. The bishop of that area was known as a Patriarch. Kyriakos lived on the shore opposite Byzantium. He became a bishop in the year 214 A.D., which was more than a century before Byzantium was called Constantinople. There was a wealthy pagan senator from Rome, St. Kastinos, who became oppressed by demons and this led him into despair. When he heard about Kyriakos, who had the reputation of being a wonderworker, he went to meet him and fell at his feet begging to be cured. Immediately, Kyriakos freed him of demonic oppression and baptized him. Kyriakos also had the gift of foreknowledge and knowing that Kastinos would one day lead those Christians, he taught him the entire knowledge of the Church and about pastoral care. After sixteen years as bishop, St. Kyriakos died. Before his death, he ordained Kastinos Bishop of Argyropolis and Byzantium. He also gave Kastinos the directive to make an effort to transfer the Church of Argyropolis to Byzantium, which later took place.

COMMEMORATIONS: Alexander, Bishop of Guria and Samegrelo; Nestor of Thessalonica; Mark of the isle of Thasos; Procla, wife of Pontius Pilate; Kyriakos I, Patriarch of Constantinople; Capitolina and Eroteis of Cappadocia; Nestor the Chronicler of the Kiev Caves; Demetrius of Basarbov in Bulgaria; Sergius Chernukhin of Danilov Monastery; Ia, virgin of Cornwall; Uncovering of the relics of St. Andrew, Prince of Smolensk.

Wednesday

October 28

Holy Protection of the Theotokos
Strict Fast
Hebrews 9:1-7
Luke 10:38-42, 11:27-28

*W*atch out for complaining. It only makes situations worse and increases sorrows.

St. Macarius of Optina

NEW MARTYRS ANGELIS, MANUEL, GEORGE, AND NICHOLAS OF CRETE. These four Christian men were cousins in nineteenth-century Crete, which was ruled by the Ottomans. They took on Turkish names and conformed to Islamic customs, but they remained true to the Orthodox faith. However, after 400 years of domination, all Greeks took up arms against their oppressors. These cousins fought in the Greek War of Independence, and when the Turks recaptured Crete, they were no longer afraid to declare their faith. When the tax collectors went to collect the tax imposed on the Christians, the four men, who everyone thought were Muslims, went up to pay. When the governor Mehmet Pasha heard this, he had the cousins brought before him, and they confessed that they had always been Christians. The governor offered them gifts and high social positions, but they said that they were born Christians and would die Christians. They were imprisoned and tortured, to no avail. They were beheaded as they were praying, "Lord have mercy!" Their relics were left unburied for three days, and the guards witnessed a holy light shining on them. Christians gathered the relics and took them to a monastery.

COMMEMORATIONS: Parasceva of Iconium; Kyriakos, Patriarch of Jerusalem, and Anna; Athanasius I, Patriarch of Constantinople; Terence, Africanus, Maximus, Pompeius, and 36 others; Stephen the Hymnographer; Terence and Neonilla of Syria, and their children; Febronia, daughter of Emperor Heraclius; Arsenius I of Srem; Firmilian of Caesarea, and Malchion; Neophytus of Urbnisi; Parasceva of Pirimin; Angelis, Manuel, George, and Nicholas of Crete; Job of Pochaev; Michael Lektorsky of Kuban; Arsenius of Cappadocia; Constantine Dyakov of Kiev; Demetrius, Metropolitan of Rostov; Nestor of the Kiev Caves; Theophilus, fool-for-Christ of Kiev; Hyacinth of Vicina.

Thursday

Fast-free

October 29

Colossians 1:24-2:1
Luke 11:14-23

*O*f all the afflictions that burden the human race, there is not one, whether spiritual or bodily, that cannot be healed by the Holy Scriptures.

St. John Chrysostom

VENERABLE MARTYR ANASTASIA THE ROMAN. The infant Anastasia was orphaned in third-century Rome. She was taken to a women's monastery, where she was raised by a nun named Sophia, who instilled in Anastasia a strong faith, the fear of God, and obedience. When the governor Probus was told that Anastasia did not venerate their gods and proclaimed Christ as the true God, he commanded she be arrested and brought to him. When he saw her, he was impressed by how young and beautiful she was, and desired to marry her. He tried to reason with her to worship their gods and to live with honor, but she responded that her spouse, wealth, life, and happiness were Jesus Christ. She was horribly tortured but continued to glorify God, prompting her executioners to cut out her tongue. Probus became angry when he heard this, so to end the violence quickly, he ordered the saint's beheading. St. Anastasia's relics remained on the ground for several days, and no bird or animal touched her. The nun Sophia and two others collected her relics and transferred them to the city of Rome, where they were honorably buried.

COMMEMORATIONS: Anastasia of Rome; Abramius the Recluse and his niece Mary, of Mesopotamia; Anna (Ephemianos) of Mt. Olympus in Bithynia; Melitena of Marcianopolis; Athanasius of Sparta; Timothy of Esphigmenou Monastery; Abramius, archimandrite of Rostov; Sabbas the Commander; Serapion of Zarzma, Georgia; Martyrs Cyril, Menas, and Menaeus; Abramius, recluse of the Near Caves in Kiev; Ermelinidis, hermitess; Colman of Kilmacduaagh (Ireland); Glorification of St. Rostislav, Prince of Greater Moravia.

Friday   **Strict Fast**

October 30

Colossians 2:1-7; Luke 11:23-26

Be dead in life, then you will not live in death. Let yourself die in integrity, but not live in guiltiness. Not only those who suffer death for the sake of the faith of Christ are martyrs, but also those who die for the sake of keeping his commandments.

St. Isaac the Syrian

VENERABLE STEPHEN MILUTIN OF SERBIA. When King Milutin was crowned in the thirteenth century, he promised to build one church for every year that he was king. He reigned for forty-two years and built forty-two churches, not only for his people but also in Jerusalem, Constantinople, Thessalonica, and Mt. Athos. He also built hospitals where the poor could receive treatment at no cost. Stephen always prayed and entrusted himself to God; therefore, he was successful in each of his endeavors. He defended his country against the Bulgarians and Tatars and defended Orthodoxy in Serbia and on Mt. Athos by not accepting a relationship with Rome and the pope's rule. As king, Stephen always gave alms to the poor. He dressed simply and lived an ordinary family life. St. Stephen died peacefully, and God preserved his wonderworking relics.

COMMEMORATIONS: Apostles Tertius, Mark, Justus, and Artemas of the Seventy; Apostle Cleopas of the Seventy; Zenobios and Zenobia of Aegae, Cilicia; Alexander, Cronion, Julian, Macarios, and 30 companions at Alexandria; Eutropia of Alexandria; Asterius, Claudius, Neon, and Neonilla of Cilicia; Asterius, Metropolitan of Amasea; Joseph I Galesiotes, Patriarch of Constantinople; Marcian, Bishop of Syracuse; Dometius of Phrygia; Martyr Manuel; Stephen Milutin, King of Serbia, his brother Dragutin, and their mother Helen; Therapon of Lythrodontas; 9 martyred by fire; Jotham Zedghinidze, near Lake Paravani (Georgia); Varnava (Nastic), Bishop of Hvosno; Finding of the relics of St. Stephen-Urosh III of Decani, Serbia; Uncovering of the relics of St. Eutropia of Cherson; "Ozeryansk" Icon of the Mother of God.

SATURDAY   Fast-free

OCTOBER 31
Romans 16:1-16; Luke 8:16-21

Be like a king in your heart, seated high in humility.
St. John Climacus

NEW MARTYR NICHOLAS OF CHIOS. Nicholas was born into a pious family in the town of Karyes on the island of Chios. In his youth, he grew in the virtues. He became a stone-mason in Magnesia, and his profession took him to various cities. One day, Nicholas awoke in a mentally-disturbed state of mind, possibly due to an illness or accident. He remained so for an extended period. While in this state, some local Turks saw this as an opportunity to turn Nicholas into a Muslim. They took him to the religious authorities and presented him as a young man who desired to abandon Christianity. When he was questioned, however, Nicholas was incapable of answering, so they sent him unharmed to his sister in Chios. He resorted to tending sheep, and over time and with the patient help of a monk, Nicholas was finally brought back to his right mind. He began to live a life of prayer and fasting. In the meantime, in Magnesia, a rumor spread that Nicholas had changed his name and embraced Islam. Sometime later, Nicholas was seized by some Turks and taken to the judge. He said that he had never denied Christ, nor would he do so now. They attempted to change his mind through flattery, force, torture, and imprisonment. He was put on a bed of nails with a chain wrapped around his neck. Also, a large weight was put on his chest. Two attempts were made to behead the saint, but finally, his throat was slit.

SAINTS COMMEMORATED: Apostles Stachys, Apelles, Amplias, Urbanus, Aristovoulos, and Narcissus; Spyridon and Nicodemus the Prosphora-bakers; Maura of Constantinople; Epimachus of Pelusium; James of Mygdonia; Epimachus the Roman and Gordian; Anatolius of the Kiev Caves; Nicholas the New of Chios; Foillan of Burgh Castle; John (Kochurov) of Chicago; Seleucius and Stratonica; Martyr Pais; Leonid of Vologda, Euphrosynus of Kazan, Anatole of Tver, and Innocent of Volokolamsk; Stephen, Barnabas, Trophimus, Dorymedon, Cosmas, Damian, Sabbas, Bassa, Abraham, and others; 3 Martyrs of Melitene; 12 Virgin-martyrs; Martyr Abramius; Quentin of Rome; 100,000 Martyrs of Tbilisi.

Life is a precious and unique gift, and we squander it foolishly and carelessly, forgetful of its brevity. Either we look back with yearning on the past or else we live in the expectation of a future in which, it seems to us, life will really begin; whereas the present—that is, our life as it actually is—is wasted in these fruitless dreams and regrets.

+Fr. Alexander Elchaninov of Russia

Sunday

November 1

Fifth Sunday of Luke
Fast-free
1 Corinthians 12:27-13:8
Luke 16:19-31

We need to live the mysteries, especially the mystery of Holy Communion. It's in these that Orthodoxy is found. Christ is offered to the Church through the mysteries and primarily through Holy Communion.

St. Porphyrios the Kapsokalyvite

NEW MARTYR DAVID THE GREAT KOMNENOS, LAST EMPEROR OF TREBIZOND, WITH HIS SONS BASIL, GEORGE, AND MANUEL, AND HIS NEWPHEW ALEXIOS. In 1461 Mehmed the Conqueror occupied the capital in Trebizond. The final strong bastion of Orthodoxy and Hellenism in the East ceased to illuminate. David was made a hostage together with his three children and nephew, the successor of Alexios V. They were held prisoners and chained in the Tower of Adrianople. Mehmed gave David two choices: to stay alive as long as he renounced his faith or for him and his family to be killed. David chose the second option, saying, "No torture is going to bring me to the point of renouncing the faith of my fathers." David saw the slaughter of his sons and nephew; then, he was executed by the sword. The Greeks boast two emperors: one who died in battle bravely fighting for his Hellenism, Constantine Paleologos, and St. David who was martyred for the faith. St. John Chrysostom said, "Just as the sun will not embarrassingly extinguish, the same goes for the memory of the martyrs."

COMMEMORATIONS: Holy Unmercenaries Cosmas and Damian of Mesopotamia, and their mother Theodota; Cyrenia and Juliana in Cilicia; Helen of Sinope; David of Evia (Euboea); John the Bishop and James the Presbyter, in Persia; Caesarius, Dacius, Sabbas, Sabinian, Agrippa, Adrian, and Thomas at Damascus; Hermeningilda the Goth of Spain; James of Mt. Athos and his 2 disciples James and Dionysius; Martyrs Cyprian and Juliana; Marcellus, Bishop of Paris; Sergius Zverev of Elets and Melitopol; Benignus of Dijon and Burgundy; Stremonius, first bishop of Clermont and apostle of the Auvergne.

Monday

Fast-free

November 2

Colossians 2:13-20; Luke 11:29-33

*T*he people of today's generation, aside from the other sins which they have, also have pride, and being prideful they neither receive counsel, nor correction nor repentance. The teacher, if he is a priest and spiritual father, must be careful to invent medicines and appropriate ways, to correct them. Neither should he be silent, nor should he censure them harshly and abruptly, because strict censures are bruises to prideful and impious ones, and if he abruptly censures them, he will lose them completely.

+Elder Philotheos Zervakos

HOLY SENATORS OF SEBASTE, WITH STS. EUDOXIOS, AGAPIOS, AND EIGHT OTHER MARTYRS. When Emperor Licinius (308-324) was at war with Constantine the Great, he proclaimed persecution against the Christian faith in the year 315. These senators whose names have not all been preserved had the courage to tell the emperor that his decree was unjust, and in return, God would show him divine justice if he did not stop his persecution. For their boldness, Licinius ordered them to be tortured and killed. The martyrs encouraged and blessed each other before they were thrown into a fiery furnace.

COMMEMORATIONS: Acindynus, Pegasius, Anempodistus, Elpithephorus, Aphthonius, and those with them, of Persia; Anthony the Confessor, Archbishop of Thessalonica; Attikos, Eudoxios, Agapios, Karterios, Eustratios, Pactobios (Tobias), Nikopolitianos, Styrax, and companions, at Sebaste; Marcian of Cyrrhus in Syria; Martyrs Domna, Domnina, and Cyriaca; Cyprian of Storozhev, former outlaw; Bishop Victorin and Basil Luzgin, of Glazomicha; Erc, Bishop of Slane, Ireland; Gabriel Urgebadze of Georgia; Justus of Trieste; Lambros, Theodore, and one who is anonymous, in Vrachori; Martyrs of senatorial rank beheaded under Marcus Aurelius; "Shuisk-Smolensk" Icon of the Mother of God.

TUESDAY   **Fast-free**

NOVEMBER 3   Colossians 2:20-3:3; Luke 11:34-41

*B*efore you begin your daily work, think about the condition of your soul and where it will go when it leaves this corruptible and temporary body; and be not remiss even for one day with regard to our soul. Take care continually to remember unceasingly the end of your life and to have before your eyes both that end and eternal Hell, as well as those who are tormented and suffer there. Think not of your self as one alive but as one of those burning in the flames of eternal Hell.

St. Isaiah the Solitary

VENERABLE NICHOLAS, RADIANT STAR OF THE GEORGIANS. Nicholas was known as one of the greatest hymnographers of thirteenth- and fourteenth-century Georgia. He composed numerous canons and services, including a "Canon of Supplication for Rain." He also enriched the spiritual literature of Georgia, translating many services and prayers from Greek to Georgian, including the "Canon for the Blessing of Holy Water." Though many of his works were lost, some manuscripts were preserved at Iveron Monastery on Mt. Athos. St. Nicholas gave up his spirit peacefully.

COMMEMORATIONS: Achaemonides (Hormisdas) of Persia; Theodore of Ancyra; Snandulia of Persia; Pimen of Zographou; Acepsimas, Joseph, and Aeithalas of Persia; Elias of Egypt; Hubert of Liege; George the Younger of Neapolis; Nicholas, Radiant Star of Georgia; Acepsimas of Cyrrhus; Pirminius of Germany; Anna, Princess of Kiev; 9 Martyrs slain by the sword; 28 Martyrs slain by fire; Martyrs Dasius, Severus, Andronas, Theodotus, and Theodota; Winifred of Wales; Rumwold of Buckingham; Translation of the relics of St. Apostolos the New; The Meeting of St. Sava and St. Symeon the Myrrh-gusher of Serbia at Vatopedi; Dedication of the Church of Great Martyr St. George in Lydda.

WEDNESDAY

Strict Fast

NOVEMBER 4

Colossians 3:17-4:1; Luke 1:42-46

*M*others, teach your young children to cross themselves. If they cannot make the Sign of the Cross by themselves, sign them yourselves with your own hands.

St. John Chrysostom

JOHN DOUKAS VATATZES THE MERCIFUL, EMPEROR. John was from twelfth-century Adrianopolis. His grandfather was commander-in-chief of the emperor's army. When John's parents died, he distributed their wealth to the poor and donated money to churches and shrines. Later he went to visit his uncle, a clergyman in the emperor's court, and John befriended the king. Rather than being proud of this, John conducted himself with humility and modesty. He was serene and spoke with a gentle countenance, and he also had cheerful eyes. John married the king's daughter, but first, he had to fight a duel with the Latin prince Coradus. After defeating him, John prayed, "Lord Jesus Christ help me." John became emperor after the death of his father-in-law. He was just, merciful, and defended the victims of wrongdoing. He was a pious Orthodox Christian, and for this reason, many Jews were baptized into Orthodoxy. John also tried to bring about the union between the Eastern and Western Churches through a dialogue chaired by Patriarch Germanos the New of Constantinople. It would have happened if the West had agreed to renounce their belief that the Holy Spirit proceeds from the Son. John fought and won another duel against Sultan Azeddin, who had pillaged cities along the Meander River. Seven years after St. John's death, his relics were found incorrupt and fragrant, and healed the sick and cast out demons.

COMMEMORATIONS: Ioannicios the Great of Bithynia; Nicander of Myra, and Hermas; Sylvia, mother of Gregory the Dialogist; Porphyrios the Mime; Mercurius the Faster; Luke of Novgorod; Nicander of Gorodnoezersk Monastery; Paul of Tobolsk; Simon of Yurievets and Zharki; John III Doukas Vatatzes the Merciful; George Karslides of Drama, and his sister Anna; John, Stephen, and Isaiah the Georgians; Clether of Cornwall; Birnstan of Winchester; Agricola and Vitalis of Bologna.

Thursday   **Fast-free**

November 5

Colossians 4:2-9; Luke 11:47-12:1

*W*e don't have to fight with people but with rulers and powers, in effect the evil spirits. But do not be afraid, take power from the name of Jesus.

St. Luke of Simferopol

ST. JONAH, ARCHBISHOP OF NOVGOROD. Jonah was orphaned at a young age and was adopted and educated by a pious widow in fifteenth-century Novgorod. One day a certain clairvoyant monk, St. Michael of Klops, chanced to meet young Jonah and foretold that he would one day become Archbishop of Novgorod. Jonah was tonsured a monk at the Otnya Wilderness Monastery and later became abbot. After the death of the archbishop, St. Euthymius, the people chose Jonah to replace him. During his tenure, the princes of Moscow never infringed upon the independence of Novgorod, out of respect for Jonah. Even the Metropolitan of Moscow wanted Jonah to one day replace him. In an effort to imbue the Novgorod of his day with the reverence of the past, Jonah enlisted the support of a famous hagiographer to write and bring to life the lives of the well-known saints of his city, and to write services to them. Jonah also helped to establish two new monasteries through much assistance and a land grant. God granted Jonah the gift to work miracles. Sensing the end of his days, he wrote instructions to bury him at the Otnya Monastery.

COMMEMORATIONS: Galacteon and his wife Epistimia, at Emesa; Apostles Hermas, Patrobus, Linus, Gaius, and Philologus of the Seventy; Gregory, Patriarch of Alexandria; Domninus, Timothy, Theotimos, Theophilus, Dorotheus, Carterius, Eupsychius, and Pamphilus, of Palestine, and the 3 virgins of Palestine; Jonah, Archbishop of Novgorod; Hilarion, recluse of Troekurovo; Silvanus, Bishop of Gaza; Odrada, virgin of Balen; Martyr Kastor and Agathangelos; Gregory of Cassano, Calabria; Cybi, abbot in Cornwall and Wales; Kea, Bishop of Devon and Cornwall; Dositheus of Glinsk Hermitage; Commemoration of the Consecration of the Church of St. Theodore the Tyro in the Sphorakion.

Friday
November 6

**St. Paul the Confessor,
Patriarch of Constantinople**
Strict Fast
Hebrews 8:1-6; Luke 12:8-12

Remain in our Lord God until He shows compassion on us. Ask for nothing else other than mercy from the Lord of Glory. When you seek mercy, do so with a humble and contrite heart, and cry out from morning until evening, and if possible all night long.
St. John Chrysostom

ST. DEMETRIANOS, BISHOP OF KETHERIA IN CYPRUS. Demetrianos was close to the church from a young age since his father was a priest. His parents convinced him to marry, but after only three months, he became a widower. He was tonsured a monk at the Monastery of St. Anthony near Ketheria and devoted himself to obedience, vigils, strict fasting, and prayer, and was a model to all the monks. He was also a source of spiritual gifts to the faithful who came to see him. Bishop Eustathios appointed him Bishop of Ketheria. During his time as bishop, and for centuries, the island was subject to numerous invasions. Many of his flock were captured and taken to Egypt in the years 911-912. But Demetrianos followed them into captivity and secured their release. It is said that St. Demetrianos died around the year 915 in Cyprus, at the age of eighty-one. He is considered the patron saint of refugees.

COMMEMORATIONS: Paul the Confessor of Constantinople; Herman of Kazan; Gregory the Cross-bearer of Russia; Luke of Taormina (Sicily); Winnoc of Flanders; Luke of the Kiev Caves; Demetrianos of Cytheria on Cyprus; Barlaam of Keret (Karelia); Barlaam of Khutyn Monastery; Paul of Corinth; Martyr Nicander; Nicetas Delektorsky of Orekhovo-Zuevsk; Barlaam Nikolsky of Andreyevskoe (Moscow); Gabriel Vladimirov of St. Michael Skovorodsky Monastery; Gabriel (Gur) of Lytkarino (Moscow); Illtyd of Wales; Leonard of Noblac (Gaul); Agapios the Presbyter, in Argos; Cowey of Portaferry; Elias Fondaminsky of Paris; Synaxis of the New Martyrs of Sarov: Anatole, Basil, Hierotheus, Isaac, and Rufinus; Commemoration of the falling of ash from the sky in 472 A.D.

SATURDAY   **Fast-free**

November 7

Colossians 5:1-10; Luke 9:1-6

*T*ruly lamentable is that person who does not have humility. He who is not able to humble himself will later on be humbled by other people. And he whom other people cannot humble, God will humble.

St. Anthony of Optina

MARTYR ATHENODOROS, BROTHER OF ST. GREGORY THE WONDERWORKER. Athenodoros and his brother St. Gregory the Wonderworker were from a wealthy pagan family in early third-century Neocaesarea. They were afforded an excellent education. After their father died, they intended to study in modern-day Beirut, where there was one of the most prestigious schools in the Hellenic world. However, they stopped in Caesarea in Palestine, where they heard about the celebrated scholar Origen. After talking with Origen, they decided to study under him, in the year 233. Origen taught them a love for philosophy, then led them into the study of divinity, and converted them to Christianity. For five years they studied at the Catechetical School of Alexandria. When the brothers returned home, Gregory became the first bishop of Neocaesarea, and Athenodoros also became a bishop in Pontus. Gregory preached the Gospel with such zeal that he converted almost all the pagans of Pontus. He was venerated as the founder of the Church of Cappadocia. Gregory and Athenodoros were among the most eminent and illustrious bishops of the time. St. Gregory died in peace, and St. Athenodoros is said to have died a martyr.

COMMEMORATIONS: 33 Martyrs of Melitene; Auctus, Taurion, and Thessalonica, at Amphipolis in Macedonia; Cassina and Melasippus, their son Antoninus, and 40 children converted and martyred, at Ancyra; Theodotus of Ancyra; Alexander of Thessalonica; Athenodoros, brother of St. Gregory the Wonderworker; Herculanus of Perugia; Lazarus of Mt. Galesion near Ephesus; Zosimas of the Annunciation Monastery at Lake Vorbozoma; Willibrord of Utrecht; Cyril Smirnov of Kazan; Michael Gusev of Diveyevo; Joseph Petrovykh of Petrograd; "The Joyful" Icon of the Mother of God.

SUNDAY

NOVEMBER 8

Seventh Sunday of Luke
Fast-free
Hebrews 2:2-10; Luke 8:41-56

*G*od the Word, the God-Man, our Lord Jesus Christ, compares our life with the market, and the work of our life on earth He calls trading. He says to us all: *"Trade till I come"* (Lk. 19:13), *"buying up every opportunity, because the days are evil"* (Ephesians 5:16). In other words, make the most of your time getting heavenly blessings through earthly goods. Earthly goods are good works done for Christ's sake that confer the grace of the All-Holy Spirit, on us.

St. Seraphim of Sarov

ST. WILLIHAD, BISHOP OF BREMEN. Willihad was from eighth-century Northumbria. After his ordination, he went to Frisia to continue the missionary work of St. Boniface who had been martyred by the Frisians. Charlemagne commissioned Willihad to preach in the region of the Weser River, but he barely escaped with his life when the Frisians wanted to kill him. Then he went to Utrecht with fellow missionaries, but pagans tried to kill them for destroying some temples. Finally, Charlemagne sent Willihad to evangelize the Saxons. He did so for several years until the Saxons rebelled against Charlemagne. After the conquest of the Saxons, Willihad returned and was consecrated bishop. The city of Bremen was his see. He built a cathedral there, which was praised for its beauty. St. Willihad is buried within the cathedral.

COMMEMORATIONS: Synaxis of the Archangels Michael, Gabriel, Raphael, Uriel, Salaphiel, Jegudiel, Barachiel, and Jeremiel and the other Bodiless Powers; Maria (Martha), Princess of Pskov; Michael the Blessed of Chernigov; Willihad, Bishop of Bremen (Germany); Tyssilio, abbot of Meifod; 70 Monk Martyrs on the Island of Flowers.

Monday   **Fast-free**

November 9

1 Thessalonians 1:1-5
Luke 12:13-15, 22-31

Quietude in solitude is no small teacher of virtue.
St. John Chrysostom

VENERABLE THEOKTISTE OF LESVOS. In the ninth century, a hunter on the island of Paros went to the church of Panagia Ekatontaphyliani. He noticed some movement at the holy table, and as he approached, he heard a woman's voice commanding him to throw her a garment since she was naked. He was terrified by her appearance. She had white hair, a dark complexion, and was skin and bones. She told him that God brought him to the church to learn about her life. Theoktiste was orphaned at a very young age and was raised in a convent, where she became a nun. When she was eighteen years old, she went to visit her sister in a nearby village. That night Arabs from Crete attacked the island of Lesvos, taking Theoktiste and her sister. They were taken to the island of Paros to be sold as slaves in the market place. She escaped and hid herself in the wilderness, living on seeds, herbs, and vegetables, and the word of God, for thirty-five years. She asked him to bring a portion of the Holy Mysteries in a clean vessel the following year when he returned to hunt, and not to tell anyone about her. The man returned and found Theoktiste in the church, at which point she received the Holy Mysteries. After a few days, he desired to see the saint again. When he went into the church, he found St. Theoktiste lying dead where he had last seen her. One thousand years later, the holy relics of St. Theoktiste were taken to Lesvos.

COMMEMORATIONS: Nektarios of Pentapolis; Onesiphoros and Porphyrios of Ephesus; Eustolia and Sosipatra of Constantinople; John the Short of Egypt; Matrona of Constantinople; Symeon Metaphrastes of Constantinople; Onesiphorus the Confessor; Anthony of Apamea; Theoktiste of Lesvos; Claudius, Castor, Sempronian, and Nicostratus of Pannonia; Parthenius of Ananyevsk; Alexis of Yaroslavl; Martyrs Christopher and Maura; Euphymios and Neophytos the Serbians; Martyrs Narses and Artemonos; Helladius, monk; Benignus of Armagh; "The Quick Hearer of Mt. Athos" Icon of the Mother of God.

TUESDAY

Fast-free

NOVEMBER 10

1 Corinthians 4:9-16
Luke 12:42-48

If some quarrel in your presence and you hear words of wrath, close your ears and flee from that place, lest your soul perish from life. A wrathful heart is entirely devoid of the mysteries of God, but the meek and humble man is a well-spring of the mysteries of the new age.

St. Isaac the Syrian

APOSTLES ERASTUS, OLYMPAS, HERODION, SOSIPATROS, QUARTUS, AND TERTIUS OF THE SEVENTY. Apostles Olympas and Herodion are mentioned in Romans 16:15. They accompanied Apostle Paul to Rome to spread the faith. Herodion became bishop of Patras, where he suffered many tortures. Olympas and Herodion were beheaded under the emperor Nero in the year 54, on the same day Apostle Peter was crucified. Erastus served as deacon and steward of the Church at Jerusalem and later became Bishop of Paneas in Palestine. Sosipatros was Bishop in Iconium. He traveled with Apostle Jason to the island of Kerkyra, where they converted many pagans to the Christian faith. Tertius succeeded him in Iconium. Through his words and deeds, and the power of the Holy Spirit, many pagans were converted to Christ. Quartus became Bishop of Beirut. He suffered many trials and converted many pagans. Apostles Erastus, Sosipatros, Quartus, and Tertius died peacefully.

COMMEMORATIONS: Apostles of the Seventy Erastus, Olympas, Herodion, Sosipater, Quartus, and Tertius (Terence); Arsenios of Cappadocia; Orestes of Cappadocia; Nonnus of Heliopolis; Milos (Miles), bishop in Persia, and his disciples, Aborsam and Senoe; Eucharius, first bishop of Trier; Constantine-Kakhi, Prince of Kartli, Georgia; Theocteristus of Symbola on Mt. Olympus; Justus of Canterbury; 10 Martyrs of Gaza, at Jerusalem; Martyrs Orion, Niros, and Calliopios; Augustine Belyaev of Kaluga, and Ioannicius, Niphon, John, Alexis, Apolloius, and Michael; Procopius of Cherson, and Seraphim Gushchin of Optina; Glorification of St. Matthew, monk of Yaransk.

WEDNESDAY

NOVEMBER 11

Strict Fast

2 Corinthians 4:6-15
Luke 12:42-48

For it is a commandment of the LORD not to be silent at a time when the Faith is in jeopardy. Speak, Scripture says, and hold not thy peace.

St. Theodore the Studite

MARTYR STEPHEN OF DECANI, KING OF SERBIA. The Greeks considered the Slavs barbarians, but they were amazed at the beauty of St. Stephen's soul as one of the rarest wonders of the time. When King Stephen was blinded, St. Nicholas appeared to him and said, "Stephen, be not afraid; behold your eyes in my palm. In due time I will return them to you." The Byzantine emperor acted very cruelly towards the blind king Stephen and forbade anyone access to him. He then sent Stephen to a monastery, hoping that the strict asceticism would weaken and kill him. However, Stephen endured like the best of monks, and his wisdom became known throughout Constantinople, and the emperor began seeking his advice. Along with St. Gregory Palamas, Stephen helped defeat the heresy of Barlaam, who called monastics men with souls in their navels. He also accused them of Messalianism, a claim that God can be perceived by the carnal senses, and that this perception is necessary to reach perfection. Heeding Stephen's advice, the emperor drove Barlaam from the capital with dishonor. After five years, St. Nicholas appeared to Stephen again in a vision and restored his eyesight by tracing the Sign of the Cross on him. In gratitude, Stephen built the Church of Decani, one of the most famous Byzantine monuments. St. Stephen died as a martyr in 1336. He was strangled in his old age.

COMMEMORATIONS: Menas of Egypt; Theodore the Confessor of the Studion; Stephen-Urosh III of Decani; Euthymius and Nestor of Decani; Maximus of Moscow; Vincent of Spain; Martyrius of Zelenets; Neophytus and Stephen of Serbia; Victor and Stephanida, at Damascus; Nicodemus the Younger of Beroea; Bartholomew the Younger of Rossano; Drakonas of Arauraka; Milica (Eugenia) of Serbia; Synaxis of the Saints of Decani; Myrrh-streaming "Montreal" Iveron Icon of the Mother of God.

Thursday

November 12

St. John the Merciful
Fast-free
2 Corinthians 9:6-11
Matthew 5:14-19

God looks down from the heavens with attentiveness upon that which springs from love, for love is in its entirety the sum of His commandments.

+Elder Cleopa of Romania

ST. VARNAVA NASTIC, BISHOP OF HVOSNO. Varnava is the first American-born Serbian to be proclaimed an Orthodox saint. He was born in 1914 in Gary, Indiana. He grew up in a very spiritual family and served as an altar boy. At the age of nine, the family moved to Yugoslavia, and with the bishop's blessing, he studied theology. As Varnava would say, "Theology is the science of sciences." He was ordained a priest, and in 1947 the Serbian Church elected him bishop. Varnava began to preach against the Communist way of life, and he was arrested on charges of treason and sentenced to eleven years at one of the worst prisons at that time in Yugoslavia. After three years, the government transferred him to another prison with the intent of killing him along the way. They arranged for a train wreck, but he survived, though his legs were broken, and he suffered from this the rest of his life. Because of health problems, he was released from prison in 1951 but was always under guard by the Communist government. He died in 1964 under suspicious circumstances, and many believed that he was poisoned. Just before his death, St. Varnava wrote letters to his family about his good health.

COMMEMORATIONS: Martin the Merciful; Prophet Achias (Ahijah) of Silom; John the Merciful; Martin of Terracina; Nilus the Faster; Nilus the Myrrh-gusher of Mt. Athos; Leontius (Leo) Styppes, Patriarch; Emilian of Vergegio; John "the Hairy," of Rostov; Nicholas of Marmaran; Sabbas Samoladas of Nigdi; Varnava the New Confessor; Martyr Arsakius; Zebinas, Anthony, Germanos, Nikephoros, and Manatho, in Caesarea; Sinell of Cleenish; Machar of Aberdeen; Cadwaladr, king of the Welsh; Lubuinus, missionary to Friesland; New Martyrs and Confessors of Nasaud, Romania: Athanasius Todoran of Bichigiu, Basil of Mocod, Gregory of Zagra, and Basil of Telciu.

FRIDAY
NOVEMBER 13

St. John Chrysostom
Abstain from meat and dairy products, and fish.
Hebrews 7:26-8:2; John 10:9-16

You are a man, and yet you spit the venom of a poisonous serpent. You are a man and yet you become like a raging beast. You have been given a mouth not to wound but to heal.

St. John Chrysostom

ST. QUINTIANUS, BISHOP OF RODEZ. According to tradition, Quintianus was a sixth-century priest of Carthage in Africa. He fled to France due to the persecutions of the Vandals, and to Rodez because of the Arian Visigoths. King Theodoric I appointed him Bishop of Rodez. Later he went to Clermont and was given all the power over the Church, and was given houses, fields, and vineyards. Once when an enemy had the town under siege, Quintianus toured the walls of the city all night singing psalms, fasting, and keeping vigil. The attacking King Theuderic was seized with terror, leaped from his bed, and tried to flee down the main road. He had lost his senses. The attack was thwarted when the king's duke told him not to attack because churches surround the walls of the town, and the bishop is great in the eyes of God. Quintianus was also magnificent in his almsgiving. When he heard poor men cry out, he would say, "Run, I beg you, run to this poor man and give him the food that he needs. Why are you so indifferent? How do you know that this is not the very one who had ordained in His Gospel that one should feed Him in the person of the poorest?" The prayers of the saint would drive out demons, heal households of terrible illness with holy water, and cause rain to fall during a great drought. St. Quintianus died in old age. Today many people who are sunk in melancholy pray at his tomb for relief.

COMMEMORATIONS: John Chrysostom, Archbishop of Constantinople; Euphrasius, Bishop of Clermont (Gaul); Quintianus, Bishop of Clermont (Gaul); Bricius, Bishop of Tours; Damascene of the Great Lavra, Mt. Athos; Leonardo of Vienne (Gaul).

SATURDAY

NOVEMBER 14

Holy Apostle Philip
Fast-free
1 Corinthians 4:9-16
John 1:43-51

To parents who asked what to do when their children don't listen: Pray with faith, counsel them as much as possible with love, in a gentle way. For, forgive me, nothing good comes of being strict. This is because they will up and leave…and today we live in Sodom and Gomorrah and worse.

+Elder Iakovos of Evia

ST. EUPHEMIANOS THE WONDERWORKER. Euphemianos was one of 300 Palestinian Christian refugees who fled to Cyprus in the mid-twelfth century during the Arab persecutions against the Christians. Once in Cyprus, they decided to live as ascetics, and each person went his own way to a remote location. Euphemianos settled in a cave and drank water from a nearby river. He was granted the gift to work miracles that benefited Christians, and his fame spread. Many came to hear his words, to receive his blessing, and to be comforted and strengthened. He died in old age, beloved by the people, and was buried where he lived. Later a picturesque Byzantine chapel was built there in his honor. Before the Turkish invasion of Cyprus in 1974, thousands would visit the chapel on his feastday.

COMMEMORATIONS: Holy and All-Praised Apostle Philip; Gregory Palamas, Archbishop of Thessalonica; Philip, founder of Irap Monastery; Fantinus the Younger, of Calabria; Alberik of Utrecht; Virgin-martyrs of Emesa (Syria); Euphemianos of Cyprus; Constantine of Hydra, at Rhodes; Aristarchus of St. Nicholas Peshnosha Monastery (Moscow); Malo (Machulus) of Brittany; Dyfrig, bishop in Hereford; Gwent of Bardsey Island; Repose of St. Alexander Nevsky of Novgorod.

SUNDAY

NOVEMBER 15

Eighth Sunday of Luke
Nativity Fast Begins
Abstain from meat
and dairy products.
Ephesians 2:4-10; Luke 10:25-37

The emotions, the doors through which the soul communicates with the outside world, are constantly led by the devil into fleshly pleasures and their inextricable bonds. In famous concert calls, loud music expresses and arouses various passions. These passions are depicted on the stages of theatres. People are led in all possible ways to these pleasures of deathly evil. When drunk with these pleasures, a person forgets the divine goodness that saves him—the blood of the God-Man that redeems him.

St. Ignatius Brianchaninov

MARTYR DEMETRIOS OF THRACE. Demetrios was from the third- and the fourth-century village of Davoudio during the Christian persecutions of Emperor Maximian. He was taken before the pagan governor Pomplius. Not only did he boldly profess his faith, but through the Holy Spirit, he taught everyone who stood around about the incarnation of Jesus Christ. He also taught them about the deceptiveness of idolatry and how the idols are deaf and dumb together with those who worship them. This enraged the governor, and he gave orders to have St. Demetrios beheaded. Christians took his body and buried him with honor. Shortly after that, his grave became a source of miracles.

COMMEMORATIONS: Gurias, Samonas, and Habibus of Edessa; Herman, wonderworker of Alaska; Elpidios, Markellos, and Efstochios, who suffered under Julian the Apostate; Justinian the Emperor, and his wife Theodora; Kyntion, Bishop of Seleucia; Malo of Aleth; Philip, founder of Rabang Monastery (Vologda); Paisius Velichkovsky of Moldavia and Mt. Athos; Thomas the New, Patriarch of Constantinople; Demetrios of Thrace; Quinctian, Bishop of Seleucia; "Kupyatich" Icon of the Mother of God.

MONDAY

Holy Apostle & Evangelist Matthew
Abstain from meat and dairy products.

NOVEMBER 16

Romans 10:11-11:2
Matthew 9:9-13

Our profit comes not from the quantity of words, but from the quality. Sometimes much is said, but nothing is heard, and at another time you hear only one word and it remains in your memory for your whole life.

St. Anthony of Optina

\ST. EUCHERIUS, BISHOP OF LYON. After the death of his wife, Eucherius withdrew for a time to the Lerins Monastery in Gaul. This was a common practice during the fifth century. He took with him his sons Veranius and Salonius and devoted himself to their education. Later Eucherius withdrew from the world to a neighboring island with the thought to perhaps join the anchorites in the desert of the Egyptian Thebaid, and he consulted with men of that time renowned for learning and piety. He wrote many essays, such as "On the Contempt of the World" and "Formulas of Spiritual Intelligence." His fame spread in southwestern Gaul, and he was chosen Bishop of Lyon in the year 434. Both of his sons also became bishops. In his essay, "In Praise of the Desert," Eucherius writes, "When Moses....saw from afar in fire that did not consume the splendor of God; and not only did he see, he even heard speech. Clearly then the Lord when he would remind us to rid our feet of our chains, tells us of the sacred land of the desert, saying, 'The place in which you stand is holy earth.' ...It is confirmed by God to be a place of sanctity, by which sacred testimony, I think, He also secretly announces that coming to the desert one may cast off the cares of life for one's original obligations, advancing free of one's prior chains lest one pollute the place. There Moses was first admitted to familiarity with Divine converse; there he received the words and in his turn he answered, speaking and doing and questioning and learning."

COMMEMORATIONS: Holy Apostle and Evangelist Matthew; Fulvianus, Prince of Ethiopia; Sergius, abbot of Malopinega; Otmar, abbot and monastic founder in Switzerland; Eucherius, Bishop of Lyon; Panteleimon Arzhanykh, abbot of Optina Monastery.

TUESDAY

Abstain from meat and dairy products.

NOVEMBER 17

1 Corinthians 12:7-11
Luke 14:25-35

It was my desire to be silent, and not to make a public display of the rustic rudeness of my tongue. For silence is a matter of great consequence when one's speech is mean. And to refrain from utterance is indeed an admirable thing, where there is lack of training; and verily he is the highest philosopher who knows how to cover his ignorance by abstinence from public address.
St. Gregory the Wonderworker of Neocaesarea

VENERABLE GENNADIOS OF VATOPEDI MONASTERY. Gennadios was in charge of acquiring, storing, and distributing the provisions of Vatopedi Monastery on Mt. Athos. It happened one year that there was only one large jar of oil left in the monastery. Gennadios decided to save this for the church lamps and not to serve the brethren oil at mealtime. The abbot, however, trusted that the Theotokos would provide for the monastery's needs. He directed Gennadios to give oil to the monks at mealtime freely. One day, Gennadios went to the storeroom expecting to find the last of the oil. Instead, he found the jar overflowing, even covering the floor as far as the door. The monks gave thanks to the Theotokos, and to her icon named "Elaiovrytissa," which stood in the storeroom. Since that time, the icon has hung in the storeroom, and it emits a beautiful fragrance. This icon is commemorated on Bright Friday. St. Gennadios died peacefully.

COMMEMORATIONS: Gennadios I and Maximos III, Patriarchs of Constantinople; Gregory, Wonderworker of Neocaesarea; Gregory, Victor, and Geminus of Heracleon; Basil, Bishop of Hamah; Longinus of Egypt; 150 philosophers converted by St. Catherine and martyred at Alexandria; Zacharias and John at Constantinople; Gregory, Bishop of Tours; Gennadios of Vatopedi; Vulfolaic, Stylite of Trier; John the Cobbler of Olumba, Cairo, and Sinai; Zachariah the Cobbler and his wife Mary; Nicon of Radonezh; Righteous Justin; Lazarus the Iconographer of Constantinople; Michael-Gobron and 133 soldiers of Georgia; Hilda of Whitby; Sebastian Dabovich, missionary in America.

WEDNESDAY

Strict Fast

NOVEMBER 18

1 Thessalonians 4:1-12
Luke 15:1-10

If you fast regularly, do not be inflated with pride, but if you think highly of yourself because of it, then you had better eat meat. It is better for a man to eat meat than to be inflated with pride and to glorify himself.

St. Isidore the Priest

MARTYR ROMANUS THE DEACON OF CAESAREA AND CHILD-MARTYR BARULAS OF ANTIOCH. During the persecutions of Emperor Maximian, the prefect of the city, Asclepios, was about to enter the pagan temple when Romanus stopped him and said that the idols were not gods. For this, Romanus was suspended, beaten, and his sides torn. St. John Chrysostom writes that Romanus did this so that the prefect would not worship demons. Then Romanus asked that a child be brought forth. When Barulas arrived, Romanus asked him whether it was better to worship God or images that people called gods. The child answered that people should worship the God of the Christians. Thus, Romanus made the child a critic of the prefect and showed him wiser as well. The two were suspended from a post, and Romanus' tongue was cut out. The child was beaten while his mother watched, and she urged him to endure and enjoy the everlasting water of blessedness. The child continued to reprimand the prefect even though he was beaten a second time. St. Barulas was finally beheaded. St. Romanus, who could still speak clearly by the grace of God, was strangled to death in prison.

COMMEMORATIONS: Platon of Ancyra; Zacchaeus the Deacon and Alphaeus the Reader, of Caesarea; Romanus of Caesarea in Palestine, with Child Martyr Barulas of Antioch; Romanus, who suffered under Maximian at Antioch; Daniel of Corfu; Anastasios of Paramythia in Epirus; Odo of Cluny; Mabyn of Cornwall; Mawes, bishop in Cornwall and Brittany; Helen of Novodevichy Convent (Moscow); Synaxis of All Saints of Estonia; Translation of the relics of St. Kosmas the Protos of Vatopedi.

THURSDAY — **Abstain from meat and dairy products.**

NOVEMBER 19

1 Thessalonians 4:18-5:10
Luke 16:1-9

*W*hen a man walks the straight path, he does not have a cross. But when he begins to step away from one side to another, then various circumstances arise that push him back unto the right path. These pushes comprise a man's cross. They vary, of course, according to what each individual needs.

St. Ambrose of Optina

ST. SIMON THE WONDERWORKER OF CALABRIA. Simon was a monk from tenth-century Calabria. One day the Saracens attacked the saint's monastery, taking three monks as prisoners to North Africa, and these three endured many tribulations there. Simon was sent to free them, but when he arrived, he found that they had been sold into slavery. When a Saracen approached Simon, he raised his hand to hit him, but the culprit's hand withered. Simon was accused before the authorities of being a magician, but then he prayed and made the Sign of the Cross over the Saracen, and he was healed. After this, the Saracens proclaimed that Simon was indeed a servant of God. They released him and the other three monks, as well as all the other Christian prisoners, and gave them a boat for their journey home. But along the way, they ran out of drinking water. Gathering water from the sea, Simon blessed the containers of water, and it became drinkable. St. Simon continued to perform miracles throughout his life. He died peacefully.

COMMEMORATIONS: Obadiah the Prophet; Azes of Isauria and 150 soldiers; Heliodorus in Pamphylia; Barlaam and Ioasaph of India, and Abenner the King; Patroclus of Bourges; Barlaam of Caesarea; Simon of Calabria; Barlaam of the Kiev Caves; Philaret of Moscow; Agapius of Gaza; 12 soldiers beheaded; Hilarion of Georgia; Martyrs Anthimus, Thalalaeus, Christopher, Euphemia and her children, and Pancharios; Egbert of York; Porphyrius of Simferopol, with Ioasaph, Gregory, and Gerasim; Ioasaph and Peter of Guslitsky Monastery; Alexis Kabaliuk of Khust; Ioannicius of Glinsk; Uncovering of the relics of St. Adrian of Poshekhonye Monastery; "Consolation in Grief and Sorrows" Icon of the Mother of God.

Friday **Forefeast of the Entry of the Mother of God**
                                              Strict Fast

November 20

1 Thessalonians 5:9-13, 24-28
Luke 16:15-18, 17:1-4

For us Christians, life on this earth is a school in which we learn how to secure for ourselves immortality and eternal life. For of what benefit is this life, if we cannot attain to eternity within it?
                                                    St. Justin Popovic of Serbia

---

ST. SOZOMONOS THE WONDERWORKER OF KARPASIA. Sozomonos lived as a hermit in a cave on the Karpas peninsula in Cyprus. According to the tradition of the residents, the hermit St. Auxentios would go to the cave of Sozomonos every Saturday evening, and they would pray and chant together until Sunday evening. Then Auxentios would return to his own hermitage. A church was built over the cave of St. Sozomonos, and some of his relics are still in the cave, and they emit a delightful scent. Many miracles occur to the faithful Christians, and to unbelievers, who go there and are quickly healed if they have a longing for God and St. Sozomonos. The last known miracle attributed to St. Sozomonos happened before the invasion of Cyprus. A man had a wound on his leg caused by infection. After seeing many doctors in many countries, they were not able to cure him, and they wanted to cut off his leg. In desperation, the bedridden man called out to St. Sozomonos to save him. When he fell into a light sleep, the saint came to him, telling him not to have the leg removed. After making the Sign of the Cross on the man's leg, he was immediately healed. St. Sozomonos only asked of him to make a celebration of the saint's feastday, and he disappeared.

COMMEMORATIONS: Gregory Decapolites; Proclus, Archbishop of Constantinople; Dasius of Dorostolum; Azades the Eunuch; Sozomonos of Cyprus; Eustace, Thespesius, and Anatolius of Nicaea; Diodorus of Yuriev; Nirses of Shahrqart, with Joseph and others: John, Isaac, and Shapur of Seit Selok; Guhshtazad, Mari, Sasan, Tima, Noah, and Zaun, of Lashom, and Bautha, Denachis, Thecla, Dinaq, Tatun, Mama, Mazakya, Ana, Abyat, and Hatay; Isaac of Armenia; Theoctistus the Confessor; Edmund of East Anglia; Macarius of Dnepropetrovsk, Arsenius, Eutychius, and Hilarion; Ioannikia of the Convent of the Entry of the Theotokos (Tikhvin).

SATURDAY

NOVEMBER 21

The Entry of the Theotokos into the Temple
Abstain from meat and dairy products.
Hebrews 9:1-7
Luke 10:38-42, 11:27-28

The Feast of the Entrance of the Theotokos into the Temple is of great significance. First of all, it is a most moving and remarkable and amazing fact that the elderly parents did not keep the gift of God, the elect daughter acquired at the setting of their life… Rather, having a presentiment of her future sublime and salutary service to the Benevolent God's plan for the redemption of the entire human race, they offered her without reservations to the Temple of God: to the Holy of Holies.

+Blessed Moses of Mt. Athos

THE ENTRY OF THE MOST HOLY THEOTOKOS INTO THE TEMPLE. There are four days on the Church calendar dedicated to the Theotokos: Her birth, Presentation into the Temple, Annunciation, and Dormition. Righteous Joachim and Anna were childless for many years, and they prayed fervently for a child whom they would dedicate to God. When the Virgin Mary was three years old, she was taken in procession to the temple. With lighted candles and the singing of sacred songs, Joachim and Anna, together with their relatives, carried Mary to the first step of the Jerusalem Temple, and from there she ran up the remaining fourteen steps. Prophet Zachariah, the father of St. John the Baptist, took her by the hand into the temple. He was instructed by divine inspiration to take her into the Holy of Holies, where only the high priest enters once a year. Joachim and Anna visited Mary often until their death. Mary read Holy Scripture, made handcrafts, and prayed always. She desired to remain a virgin and to live in the temple her entire life, but Jewish law would not permit this. To protect Mary's virginity, Zachariah chose an elderly relative, Joseph, to whom she was betrothed. The feast of the Entry into the Temple of the Theotokos signifies her total dedication to God and the promise of the coming of Christ.

COMMEMORATIONS: Entrance of the Theotokos into the Temple; Columbanus of Bobbio; Alexander Khotovitsky of New York and Alexis of Tver.

Sunday

November 22

Ninth Sunday of Luke
Abstain from meat and dairy products.
Ephesians 2:14-22; Luke 12:16-21

These unseen enemies of God have made their sole purpose, day and night to seek our destruction.

St. Luke of Simferopol

VENERABLE IAKOVOS TSALIKES OF EVIA. Iakovos was born to pious parents in Asia Minor. After the catastrophe of Asia Minor, the family settled in Evia. At the age of seven, Iakovos, who was still illiterate, memorized the Divine Liturgy. St. Paraskevi once appeared to him, revealing his ecclesiastical future, and this stimulated his faith. He would read prayers for the sick with such devotion that he healed them. He completed elementary school and worked manual labor with his father. Still, he maintained his prayerful disposition, strict observance of the fast, love for work, and lack of sleep. During his time in the army, his fellow soldiers would call him Father Iakovos. He entered the Monastery of St. David near Rovies and was tonsured a monk and ordained to the priesthood. He ascetized in the cave of St. David, with divine visions and miracles, and still suffered many attacks from the demons. Iakovos often saw angels serving him in the altar during the Divine Liturgy. In 1963, in a wonderous way, he fed seventy-five laborers with three kilos of noodles. In 1975 he became the abbot of the monastery, but his body suffered terribly from his ascetic labors. He died in 1991. When news of his death spread, thousands of people from all over Greece flocked there the next day. During the procession, many of the faithful saw St. Iakovos get up from his coffin and bless the crowd. There have been dozens of posthumous miracles.

COMMEMORATIONS: Archippos, Philemon, Onesimus, and Apphia, Apostles of the Seventy; Menignos the Fuller; Cecilia, Valerian, Tiburtius, and Maximus, at Rome; Procopius the Reader; Stephen, Mark, and Mark at Antioch; Callistus II, Patriarch of Constantinople; Agabbas of Syria; Agapion of Greece, with Sisinius and Agapius; Germanus of Eikoiphinissa; Martyrs Thaddeus, Christopher, Euphemia, Thallelaius and Anthimus; Anthony of Izeru; Yaropolk-Peter of Vladimir; Michael, Great Prince of Tver; Clement of Ochrid; Michael the Soldier of Bulgaria; Iakovos (Tsalikis) of Evia.

MONDAY — Abstain from meat and dairy products.

NOVEMBER 23

2 Thessalonians 1:1-10
Luke 17:20-25

Pre-eminent among all the evils is ignorance; next comes lack of faith.

St. Mark the Ascetic

ST. METROPHANES, BISHOP OF VORONEZH. Until the age of forty, Metrophanes was a married parish priest with children. After the death of his wife, he became a monk. He served as the abbot of his monastery for ten years. When Patriarch Joachim learned of his piety, he was made an archimandrite, and seven years later was consecrated Bishop of Voronezh. His first act was a letter to all the priests in his diocese, saying that they should pursue moral improvement. He wrote, "pastors care for their flock in three ways: by the words of teaching, by prayer and the power of the Holy Mysteries, and by their way of life. You must also act by all three methods… above all enlighten the unbelievers by holy Baptism, and try to lead sinners to repentance. Take care of the sick, so that they do not depart from this life without receiving Holy Communion and Holy Unction." In the twenty years that Metrophanes was a bishop, fifty-seven churches were built, and two monasteries were founded in his diocese. He consoled the poor and the rich, defended the wronged, and his house was a hospice for the sick and a hostel for strangers. He prayed for the living and departed, especially for fallen soldiers. St. Metrophanes once wrote, "For everyone the rule of wise men is: do work, preserve a balance, and you will be rich. Drink temperately, eat little, and you will be healthy. Do good, shun evil, and you will be saved." He died peacefully in extreme old age, in the year 1703.

COMMEMORATIONS: Gregory, Bishop of Agrigentum; Sisinios the Confessor; Amphilochius of Iconium; Ischyrion, bishop in Egypt; Metrophanes, Bishop of Voronezh; Trudo of Zirkingen; Dionysius I, Patriarch of Constantinople; Amphilochius of the Kiev Caves; Gregory of Georgia; Helenus of Tarsus; Anthony of Iezeru-Vilcea; Seraphim of Moscow; Boris of Ivanovo; Eleazar of Eupatoria; Alexander, in Perm; Burial of St. Alexander Nevsky, Great Prince of Novgorod.

TUESDAY — **Abstain from meat and dairy products.**

NOVEMBER 24

2 Thessalonians 1:10-2:2
Luke 17:26-18:8

*W*hy does the Lord command us to love our enemies and to pray for them? Not for their sake, but for ours! For as long as we bear grudges, as long as we dwell on how someone offended us, we will have no peace.

+Elder Thaddeus of Vitovnica

MARTYR CHRYSYGONOS AT AQUILEIA. During his persecution of Christians, the emperor Diocletian learned that the prisons of Rome were overcrowded with Christians who resisted torture. So he ordered them all to be killed in a single night. He had Chrysygonos, who was the teacher of Great Martyr St. Anastasia, brought to him. Anastasia followed her teacher from a distance. Diocletian personally interrogated Chrysygonos, but when he could not get him to renounce his faith, he had him beheaded and thrown into the sea. The saint's body and severed head were carried to shore by the waves and were recovered by a Father Zoilos who put them in a coffer and hid them in his home. Chrysygonos appeared to Father Zoilos and told him that three sisters who lived nearby, Sts. Agape, Chione, and Irene would soon be martyred and to send Anastasia to encourage them. He also told him that he would even die that same day. Nine days later, this all came to pass. St. Anastasia buried the three sisters whom she had strengthened.

COMMEMORATIONS: Hermogenes, Bishop of Agrigentum; Clement, Pope of Rome; Peter, Archbishop of Alexandria; Gregory, founder of the monastery of the Golden Rock in Pontus; Alexander at Corinth; Theodore of Antioch; Mastridia of Alexandria; Mercurius of Smolensk; Mercurius of the Kiev Caves; Mercurius the Faster of the Far Caves; Luke, steward of the Kiev Caves; Simon of Soiga Monastery; Chrysogonos at Aquileia; Mark of Trigleia; Malchus of Chalcis; Martyrs Philoumenos, Christopher, Eugene, Procopius, and Christopher; Righteous Carion; Nicodemus the Younger of Philokalos Monastery in Thessalonica; Protasius of Auvergne (Gaul); Romanus of Bordeaux; Portianus of Arthone (Gaul).

WEDNESDAY
NOVEMBER 25

St. Catherine the Great Martyr
Abstain from meat and dairy products, and fish.
Galatians 3:23-4:5; Mark 5:24-34

If we do not confess our involuntary sins as we should, we shall discover an ill-defined fear in ourselves at the hour of our death. We who love the Lord should pray that we may be without fear at that time; for if we are afraid then, we will not be able freely to pass by the rulers of the nether world. They will have as their advocate to plead against us the fear which our soul experiences because of its own wickedness. But the soul which rejoices in the love of God, at the hour of its departure, is lifted with the angels of peace above all the hosts of darkness.

St. Diadochos of Photike

HIEROMARTYR MOSES, PRESBYTER OF ROME. Moses was a third-century presbyter of Rome, who fiercely opposed the Novatian schism and heresy. Novatian was the second anti-pope in papal history, whose schism persisted for several centuries. He refused readmission into the Church of baptized Christians who had denied their faith and who had under pressure sacrificed to pagan idols. Novatian even tried to become the Pope of Rome himself. Moses refused to commune with Novatian and the five presbyters with him who had separated themselves from the Church. For his unbending courage, St. Moses was one of the first martyrs under Emperor Decius. Moses and his companions were in prison for over eleven months. St. Moses was consoled by the letters of St. Cyprian of Carthage.

COMMEMORATIONS: Mercurios of Caesarea in Cappadocia; Catherine of Alexandria, and 150 rhetoricians; Augusta (Faustina) the Empress, Porphyrius Stratelates, and 200 soldiers, at Alexandria with Great Martyr Catherine; Moses, presbyter of Rome; Peter, Archbishop of Alexandria; Peter the Silent of Galatia, Syria; Seraphim Ostroumov, Archbishop of Smolensk, and Gregory, John, Basil, Cosmas, John, Simeon, Hilarion, Iaroslav, Alexander, John, Victor, Andrew, and Paul; 670 Martyrs beheaded; Clement of Ochrid, Bishop of Greater Macedonia (Bulgarian).

THURSDAY   **Abstain from meat and dairy products.**

NOVEMBER 26

2 Thessalonians 2:13-3:5
Luke 18:31-34

*C*onsider with me that there are twelve passions that lead to sin. If you willingly cherish one of them, that one passion will come to occupy the place of the other eleven.

St. Mark the Ascetic

NEW MARTYR GEORGE OF CHIOS. When George was eighteen months old, his mother died. At the age of ten, he apprenticed with a cabinetmaker who took him from Chios to the island of Psara to build an icon screen in a church. The young boy was caught stealing a watermelon from a garden and was handed over to the judge, who frightened him into accepting Islam, and George was circumcised. He began working as a seaman, and one day arrived in Chios. His family, who had lost all track of him, were overjoyed to see him, but George was heartbroken. He confessed his conversion, and after a few days, his father took him to a Christian home in Asia Minor to be raised, out of fear of the Turks. When George was twenty, he was betrothed to a Christian girl, but her cruel brother reported George to the authorities as an apostate from Islam. George was arrested, and before the judge, he declared that he was a Christian. George refused all offers to deny his faith. He was put in prison and asked for a priest to come to him, and he confessed his sins and received Holy Communion. On the way to his execution, George asked for forgiveness from the Christians he passed. The executioner cruelly ended George's life by first shooting him in the back, then striking George's neck twice before finally severing his head, in the year 1807. He was twenty-two years old. Faithful Christians buried St. George on the island of Nisopoula.

COMMEMORATIONS: Innocent, first bishop of Irkutsk; James the Solitary of Syria; Stylianos of Paphlagonia; Alypius the Stylite of Adrianople; Peter, Patriarch of Jerusalem; Silas of Persidos; Acacius of Mt. Latros, who is mentioned in *The Ladder*; George of Chios; Sophianos of Dryinoupolis; Athanasius and Theodosius of Cherepovets Monastery (Vologda); Nicon Metanoeite of Armenia; Tikhon Buzov of Donskoy Monastery (Moscow).

FRIDAY   **Strict Fast**

NOVEMBER 27
2 Thessalonians 3:6-18
Luke 19:12-28

*C*hrist gave us the commandment to love others but did not make it a condition of salvation that they should love us. Indeed, we may positively be disliked for independence of spirit. It is essential in these days to be able to protect ourselves from the influence of those with whom we come in contact. Otherwise we risk losing both faith and prayer. Let the whole world dismiss us as unworthy of attention, trust or respect—it will not matter provided that the Lord accepts us.

+Elder Sophrony of Essex

VENERABLE NATHANAEL OF EGYPT. The monastics have a saying when a new monk enters his cell for the first time, "From here to eternity." It means that the monk should pray and eventually subdue his passions and his imagination. Nathanael was a sixth-century monk from Nitria. Within the confines of his cell and through constant prayer, he came to a mystical understanding of the works of God. He did not leave his cell once in thirty-eight years.

COMMEMORATIONS: Pinuphrius of Egypt; James the Persian; James, wonderworker of Rostov; 17 Monk-martyrs in India; Theodosius of Turnovo; Diodorus of George Hill; Palladius of Thessalonica; Palladius of Elenopolis; Nathaniel of Nitria; Akakios and Damaskinos the Studite, Bishops of Liti and Rendini; Maurice of Rome, and his 6 sons; Andrew Ogorodnikov, fool-for-Christ; Nicholas Dobronravov of Vladimir; Nikon Belyaev of the Staro-Golutvin; Ioasaph Boyev of Nikolskoye; Nicholas Saltykov of St. Nicholas-Peshnosha Monastery; Apollos Fedoseyev of Moscow; Cronides, Seraphim, and Xenophont of St. Sergius Lavra; Virgil of Salzburg; Congar of Somerset; Fergus of Glamis; Maximus of Riez; Uncovering of the relics of St. Vsevolod of Pskov; Synaxis of the New Martyrs and Confessors of Radonezh; Commemoration of the Miracle of the Weeping Icon "Of the Sign" at Novgorod; "Kursk-Root," "Of Abalak," "Of Tsarskoe Selo," and "Of Seraphimo-Ponetaev" Icons of the Mother of God.

SATURDAY   **Abstain from meat and dairy products.**

NOVEMBER 28

Galatians 1:3-10; Luke 10:19-21

"Take away temptations and no one would be saved." This does not mean, however, that we should lead ourselves into temptation on purpose, but as we struggle according to God and look out for ourselves, we shall encounter temptations coming from His fatherly endearment, from the demons' envy, from our carelessness and inexperience, from the cunning of men, etc. But the goal is one: to struggle with patience and perseverance, reflecting that nothing happens without the will of God. Therefore, we need patience and gratitude.

Elder Ephraim of Arizona

ST. ANNA, MARTYR FOR THE HOLY ICONS. Anna was from a noble family in eighth-century Constantinople. When her husband died, she was tonsured a nun by her spiritual father, St. Stephen the New, who is also commemorated on this day. Emperor Copronymos was one of several iconoclast emperors to persecute Stephen for his vigorous defense of the icons. The emperor urged Anna to slander her spiritual father, saying that she had physical relations with him. When she refused, Copronymos had her flogged and thrown into prison, where she gave up her soul.

COMMEMORATIONS: Stephen the New of Mt. St. Auxentius; Martyrs Basil, Stephen, Gregory, Gregory, John, Andrew, Peter, Anna, and others, who suffered with St. Stephen the New; Irenarchos and 7 Women-martyrs, at Sebaste; Timothy and Theodore, Peter, John, Sergius, Theodore, Nicephorus, Basil, Thomas, Hierotheus, Daniel, Chariton, Socrates, Comasius, Eusebius, and Etymasius, at Tiberiopolis; Christos of Constantinople; Anna, Martyr for the Holy Icons; Oda of Brabant; Theodore of Rostov; Juthwara of Cornwall; Seraphim Chichagov of St. Petersburg; Raphael Tyupin of Zlatoustov Monastery and Vincent Nikolsky of Optina.

SUNDAY

NOVEMBER 29

Thirteenth Sunday of Luke
Abstain from meat and dairy products.
Ephesians 4:1-7; Luke 18:18-27

Nothing burdens the soul and draws it down as the consciousness of sin.

St. Gregory of Nyssa

NEW HIEROMARTYR PHILOUMENOS OF JACOB'S WELL. Philoumenos was born in 1913 and lived on the island of Cyprus. From his youth, his grandmother taught him about Christ, the Lives of the Saints, and hymns of the Church. At the age of fourteen, he entered the Monastery of Stavrovouni and stayed there for five years, then went to Jerusalem. He was appointed the caretaker of the Monastery of Jacob's Well. Every Friday, many Jewish people would come to Jacob's Well to pray. Some would tell Philoumenos to take all the Orthodox icons and leave, or he would regret it bitterly. On November 29, 1979, it rained very hard all day, with lightning and thunder, and no one visited the shrine. While Father Philoumenos was serving Vespers, a group broke into the monastery, killing Philoumenos with an ax and chopping off his three fingers with which he made the Sign of the Cross. Not only did the group take the icons, candleholders, and vessels, but they also defiled the church. When the guard arrived the next morning, Philoumenos was found in a pool of blood. He was taken to the morgue, and after six days, his relics were handed over to the priests for burial. They found the saint's body still flexible, and he was buried on Mount Zion. Christians, Muslims, Hodjas, and others from various religions attended his funeral and mourned Father Philoumenos with great sadness. After four years, the grave of St. Philoumenos was opened, and his relics were found mostly incorrupt and exuding a beautiful fragrance.

COMMEMORATIONS: Nicholas, Archbishop of Thessalonica; Philoumenos of Ancyra, with Valerian and Phaedrus; Philoumenos of Jacob's Well; Dionysius of Corinth; Tiridates of Armenia; Abibus of Nekresi; Paramon and 370 Martyrs; John of Persia; Urban of Macedonia; Saturninus of Toulouse; Pitirim of Egypt; Radboud of Utrecht; Nectarius the Obedient; Brendan of Birr; Mardarije Uskokovic, bishop in America; Pankosmios the Ascetic; 6 Martyrs who entered a rock.

MONDAY

NOVEMBER 30

Holy Apostle Andrew, the First-Called
Abstain from meat and dairy products.
1 Corinthians 4:9-16
John 1:35-52

It is impossible to live at peace with God without continual repentance.

St. Theophan the Recluse

STS. PETER AND SAMUEL, FIRST AND SECOND CATHOLICOS OF GEORGIA. Peter was a disciple of St. Gregory the Theologian in the fifth century. During a visit to Byzantium, he met King Vakhtang, and they developed a close spiritual bond. At this time, he also met Samuel. This bond contributed significantly to friendly political relations between Georgia and Constantinople and the autocephaly of the Georgian Church. King Vakhtang sent a request to Constantinople to elevate Peter to the highest rank of Catholicos and consecrate Samuel a bishop. The Georgian Church had been under the authority of Antioch, but when Peter was elevated, the Georgian Church became autocephalous. Peter established a form of self-rule that helped solidify the power of the Georgian Church. His efforts also helped develop good relations between the Church and secular authorities and a national love and respect for the king. Peter accompanied King Vakhtang to war with the Persians. When the king was mortally wounded, Peter gave him his last confession, conducted his funeral service, and blessed the prince to succeed him. St. Peter led the Church with great wisdom and died peacefully. Samuel was from Constantinople, and he succeeded Peter after his repose. He led the Church during the reigns of two kings. St. Samuel showed great foresight and cared deeply for the people, strengthening them in the Christian faith until the end of his days.

COMMEMORATIONS: Holy and All-Praised Apostle Andrew the First-Called; Alexander, Bishop of Methymna; Frumentios, Archbishop of Abyssinia; Peter I and Samuel I, Catholicoses of Georgia; Vakhtang Gorgasali, King of Georgia; Tudwal, bishop in Wales; Andrew Saguna, Metropolitan of Transylvania; Simeon (Stefan), Metropolitan of Belgrade; Elias of Valaam; Sebastian Dabovich of San Francisco and Jackson.

TUESDAY — **Abstain from meat and dairy products.**

DECEMBER 1

1 Timothy 1:8-14; Luke 19:45-48

*L*et us fast, my children. Do not listen to those who say that fasting is nothing, and that this is something from monks. This is not from monks, my children, forgive me, God says this. The first commandment of God is fasting, and our Christ fasted.

St. Iakovos Tsalikes of Evia

ST. THEOKLETOS THE WONDERWORKER, ARCHBISHOP OF LACEDAEMON. Theokletos was from early ninth-century Lacedaemon. From a young age, he preferred to spend time with monastics and ascetics, to learn from them and acquire their virtues, so he became a monk. He was elevated to the Archiepiscopal throne of Lacedaemon. He was a defender of the wronged, fed the poor, and protected widows and orphans. He led the youth on the right path with advice and admonitions. He also taught the elderly to be respectable and wise, and an example to the youth. Theokletos was granted the gift of wonderworking. Once when locusts threatened to destroy the crops, he lifted his rod and dissolved the cloud of insects. When a woman went to the saint weeping that her hand was destroyed, the saint restored it with the touch of his hand. St. Theokletos died peacefully.

COMMEMORATIONS: Prophet Nahum; Onesimus of Ephesus; Ananias and Solochonus of Ephesus; Philaretos the Merciful of Amnea; Anthony the New of Kios; Ananias of Persia; Theokletos, Archbishop of Lacedaemon; Eligius of Noyon; Tudwal of Lan Pabu; Botolph of Ikanhoe, England; Innocent Letyaev of Kharkov and Akhtyra; Leontius, Bishop of Frejus; Translation of the relics of St. Botolph of Ikanhoe, England.

WEDNESDAY — Strict Fast

DECEMBER 2

1 Timothy 1:18-2:15; Luke 20:1-8

We should ask for the will of God to be done. That is what is in our best interest and the safest thing for us and for those for whom we pray.

St. Porphyrios the Kapsokalyvite

ST. JESSE, BISHOP OF TSILKAN IN GEORGIA. Jesse was from a pious family in sixth-century Syria. With the blessing of his parents, he became a monk in Antioch. Jesse was one of the Thirteen Cappadocian Fathers, and these were chosen by lot to establish monasticism in the country of Georgia. By his word and example, Jesse taught the people how to lead a pious life, and he healed the sick with his prayers. Archbishop Eulabios decided to fill the vacant cathedra seats from these thirteen ascetics. Jesse was appointed to the See of Tsilkan. When he arrived there, he found his diocese overrun by pagan rites and superstitions. He celebrated frequent divine services and continuously preached to the people about Orthodox Christianity, and he restored piety. Jesse gained the gifts of prayer and wonderworking. Through prayer, he separated a part from the Xana River into a stream, causing it to form a canal that ran past the church of the Mother of God. Next Jesse turned his efforts to reach the people in the surrounding mountains, with Gospel and cross in hand. Learning of his impending death through revelation, Jesse gathered the faithful around him. And giving them spiritual instruction, he received the Holy Mysteries, raised his arms to heaven, and commended his soul to the Lord. Even at the time of his burial, miraculous healings took place. He was buried in the Church of the Most Holy Mother of God in Tsilkan.

COMMEMORATIONS: Prophet Habakkuk (Abbacum); John, Heracleon, Andrew, and Theophilus, of Egypt; Solomon of Ephesus; Cyril of Phileotes; Stephen-Urosh V, King of Serbia and his mother Helen; Jesse of Tsilkani; Athanasius "the Resurrected," recluse; Athanasius, recluse of the Kiev Caves; Myrope of Chios; Abibus the New; Abbaum of Cyprus; Joannicius of Devic (Serbia); Viviana of Rome; Chromatius of Aquileia; Danax of Arkhangelskoye and Cosmas of Milyatino; Porphyrios of Kapsokalyvia.

THURSDAY

Abstain from meat and dairy products.

December 3

1 Timothy 3:1-13; Luke 20:9-18

I advise you not to stop reading spiritual books, for it happens sometimes that one line, read at the right time, becomes more dear than a year of publications and remains in your memory for always.

St. Anthony of Optina

VENERABLE GEORGE OF CERNICA. From his youth in Romania, George aspired to the monastic life. The rulers of Transylvania suppressed both Orthodoxy and Orthodox monasticism, so George found a spiritual father in Metropolitan Rosca in Bucharest. He followed him to Vatopedi Monastery on Mt. Athos, where he received monastic tonsure and ordination to the priesthood. It was there that he comprehended the joy of living in Christ. Over the next thirty-odd years, George followed his elder, along with many others, to live in several different monasteries. But George had a vision of St. Nicholas, who convinced him to revive a monastery named after him that had been in ruins for more than thirty years. With the help of the local ruler and other Christians, they created a hotbed of spiritual life in Cernica Monastery, where 103 monks gathered. Because of this success, George was entrusted with yet another monastery. These two monasteries followed the Athonite rule of worship, which included seven times of daily worship, frequent confession, obedience, constant prayer, and a shared meal. St. George died peacefully in 1806.

COMMEMORATIONS: Prophet Zephaniah; John the Silent of St. Sava's Monastery; Theodore of Alexandria; Theodulus of Constantinople; Theodoulos of Cyprus; Angelis of Chios; Cosmas of St. Anne's Skete; Martyrs Mamas, Seleucus, and Agapius; Gabriel II, Patriarch of Constantinople; Sabbas Storozhevsky of Zvenigorod; Gregory of Cherniksk; Nicetius of Lyons; George of Cernica and Caldarusani; Birinus of Dorchester; Sola, Anglo-Saxon missionary; Lucius, King of Britain; Hilarion Grigorovich of Krutitsa.

Friday	St. Barbara the Great Martyr
	Abstain from meat and dairy products, and fish.
# DECEMBER 4	Galatians 3:23-4:5; Mark 5:24-34

A hidden and unknown enemy is more dangerous than a visible enemy.

St. Luke of Simferopol

GREAT MARTYR BARBARA AND MARTYR JULIANA, AT HELIAPOLIS IN SYRIA. Barbara was the daughter of a pagan in the third century. She grew up shielded from the world by her father, who had her housed in a high tower due to her physical beauty. He had given her a life of ease, with servants, a bath with two windows, and idols to worship. However, through divine revelation, she began to question the validity of the pagan beliefs. Once, she left the tower and met a few Christians who taught her their faith. When she returned to the tower, she had a third window placed in the bath to represent the Holy Trinity. When she traced the Sign of the Cross on the wall, it was as if etched by a chisel. A holy spring came out of the floor that later healed the sick. When her father heard this, he was so angry that he beat her and threatened her with a sword. Barbara fled and found refuge in a rock that miraculously split open. Informants told her father where she was, and she was captured and taken to the ruler Marcian. The saint confessed Christ, and for this, endured many torments. Jesus appeared to her in prison and healed her. Another woman, Juliana, witnessed the healing by Jesus, and she marveled and desired to suffer for the faith. The next morning, Barbara suffered more torments. Juliana cried out that she was a Christian, so the governor tortured her together with Barbara. St. Barbara was beheaded by her father, and it is said that on that day, lightning struck and killed him. St. Juliana was also beheaded.

COMMEMORATIONS: Barbara and Juliana, at Heliopolis in Syria; John Damascene of St. Sabbas Monastery; Gennadius, Archbishop of Novgorod; Seraphim, Archbishop of Phanarion and Neochorion; John of Polybotos; Damascene of Glukhov, and his father Nicholas; Martyrs Christodulus and Christodula.

SATURDAY

DECEMBER 5

St. Sabbas the Sanctified
Abstain from meat and dairy products.
Galatians 5:22-6:2; Matthew 11:27-30

*P*erhaps if you do not call yourself a sinner, you do not have the devil as an accuser? Anticipate this and snatch the honor away from him, because it is his purpose to accuse. Therefore, why do you not prevent him, and why do you not tell your sin and wipe it out, since you know that you have such an accuser who cannot remain silent? Have you sinned? Come to Church. Tell God, 'I have sinned.' I do not demand anything else of you than this.

St. John Chrysostom

VENERABLE NEKTARIOS OF KARYES. Nektarios was from fifteenth-century Bitola, in Macedonia, and godly parents raised him. Before a raid by the Hagarenes, his mother had a vision of the Mother of God, telling her to flee to avoid capture. After this, his father took the young Nektarios and his brother to the Monastery of the Holy Unmercenaries. Later, the monk Dionysios Iagaris took Nektarios to Mt. Athos, where he was tonsured a monk. He became a disciple of St. Philotheos, who had the gift of clairvoyance. Nektarios led an ascetic life, and attained the virtues, making him well known throughout Mt. Athos. This caused envy among his fellow ascetics, so he was sent to Karyes. Dionysios joined Nektarios there, and they founded a monastery. Any money they made from their handicraft was given to those in need. The humble Dionysios lived a long life and died peacefully. St. Nektarios bore many grave bodily illnesses with great humility. He died peacefully in the year 1500. Four years later, his relics were uncovered, and they exuded a beautiful fragrance. Those who venerate his icon with faith benefit in body and soul.

COMMEMORATIONS: Sabbas the Sanctified; Nicetius, Bishp of Trier; Gurias of Kazan; Kosmas the Protos of Vatopedi and the monks of Karyes; Philotheos and Nektarios of Bitol, of Karyes; Martyrs Gratos, Diogenes, Abercius, Nonnos, and Crispina; Martyr Anastasias; Carion and Zachariah of Egypt; Justinian of Ramsey Island (Wales); Elias Chetverukhin of Moscow and Gennadius Petlyuk of Yaroslavl; Sergius Pravdolyubov of Ryazan.

SUNDAY

December 6

Tenth Sunday of Luke
Abstain from meat and dairy products.
Hebrews 13:17-21; Luke 13:10-17

In the Church, which has the mysteries that save, there is no desperation. We may be extremely sinful. However, we confess, the priest reads the prayer over us and so we are forgiven and we move towards immortality, without any anxiety, without any fear. Whoever lives in Christ, becomes one with Him, with His Church. He lives something crazy! This life is different to human life. It's joy, light, gladness, an uplift. This is the Church's life, the Gospel's life, God's Kingdom. "The Kingdom of God is within you" (Luke 17:21). Christ comes in us and we are in Him.

St. Porphyrios the Kapsokalyvite

MARTYRS DIONYSIA, DATIVA, EMILIANUS, BONIFACE, LEONTIA, TERTIUS, AND MAJORICUS. There is a work titled, "A History of the African Province Persecution, in the Times of Genseric and Huneric, the Kings of the Vandals." Cruel tortures were sent throughout all the lands of Africa so that there did not remain a single home or place that was free of wailing and lamentations. Orthodox Christians were beaten, hung, burned, and women were stripped and tortured. Dionysia was one of these women. While she was beaten with rods and streams of blood flowed over her whole body, her words strengthened others for martyrdom. She also strengthened her young son, Majoricus, and turned him into a person who was ready for martyrdom, far stronger than herself. Many people in that town were gained for God through Dionysia, including her sister Dativa, Emilianus her relative, Leontia the daughter of the bishop, Tertius a religious man, and Boniface of Sibida. Many were the sufferings that the others endured as well.

COMMEMORATIONS: Nicholas the Wonderworker of Myra; Theophilus of Antioch; Maximus, Metropolitan of Kiev; Nicholas of Patara; Nicholas of Tobolsk; Nicholas of Moscow; Dionysia, Dativa, Emilianus, Boniface, Leontia, Tertius, and Majoricus, in Africa; Nicholas of Novo-Nikolskaya; Nicholas Karamanos of Smyrna; "Seafaring" Icon of the Mother of God.

MONDAY — **Abstain from meat and dairy products.**

December 7

1 Timothy 5:1-10; Luke 20:27-44

Love for God can be kindled in the heart only by ceaseless prayer.
+Elder Parthenius of Kiev Pechersk

VENERABLE AMMOUN OF NITRIA. Ammoun was orphaned and raised by his uncle, who forced him to marry. On the wedding day, he persuaded his bride to take a vow of celibacy. He read to her many passages from Scripture about virginity and purity, and at length, she was persuaded. They lived together as brother and sister for eighteen years. One day she told him, "It is not good that, for my sake, you who dwell with me in purity for our Lord's sake should hide the spiritual excellence of your philosophy; for it is not seemly that your good deeds should be hidden, and should not be known. Let your dwelling be apart from me and thus you shall benefit many." When Ammoun went to Mt. Nitria in the Egyptian desert, there were no monasteries there, so he built himself a place to live and labored there for twenty-two years in the fourth century. Once when the family of a certain young man who had been seized with madness and was bound with chains was brought to Ammoun for healing, in humility Ammoun said, "You are seeking from me what is greater than my power." Because of his clairvoyance, he said, "…it lies in your own hands to help and to heal the young man. Be gone, and restore (the value of) the widow's bull which you slew secretly, and your son shall be given back to you healed." After fulfilling what Ammoun asked, he prayed, and their son was healed. Many other miracles were worked through him. St. Ammoun was one of the most venerated ascetics of the Nitrian Desert.

COMMEMORATIONS: Ambrose of Milan; Athenodoros of Mesopotamia; 362 Martyrs of Africa; Philothea of Turnovo; Paul the Obedient; John the Faster; Ignatius, near Blachernae; Nilus of Stolben Island; Ammoun of Nitria; Anthony of Siya; Holy woman martyr of Rome; Bassa of Jerusalem; Acepsimas, Isidore, and Leo; Gaius and Gainus; Gerasimos of Euripos; John of St. Sabbas; Gregory the Silent; Ambrose of Cyprus; Neophytus, Dometius, Priscus, Martin, and Nicholas; Sergius and Andronicus of Tambov; Ambrose of Kamenets; Gurias of Optina; Galacteon of Valaam.

TUESDAY — **Abstain from meat and dairy products.**

DECEMBER 8

1 Timothy 5:11-21; Luke 21:12-19

*W*hen we are immersed in sins, and our mind is occupied solely with worldly cares, we do not notice the state of our soul.
St. John Maximovitch

VENERABLE PARTHENIOS OF CHIOS. When Parthenios was a young man in Chios, he got engaged, and worked at a trade that took him to Constantinople and Smyrna. While he was away, he was notified that his fiancé became very sick, and before he could return, she died. But Parthenios desired to see her, so he dug up her grave. As it is written in the hymns of the funeral service, "We went out and saw in the tombs that the naked bones of man are worms and filth and stench." Parthenios left the world and went to the Nea Moni Monastery on Chios and became a monk. He would go up the mountain to the abandoned church of the Holy Apostle and Evangelist Mark, light the vigil lamp, and in general care for the place. He discovered a cave on the side of the mountain, where he decided to live in asceticism. Seeing his spiritual feats, the Lord gave him many spiritual gifts, including foresight. Hence, he foresaw the terrible earthquake of Chios. Soon his fame grew, and the abandoned church of St. Mark became a skete, where disciples gathered with him. People from around the island came for his prayers, blessing, and spiritual guidance. St. Parthenios performed many miracles during his life.

COMMEMORATIONS: Apostles of the Seventy: Sosthenes, Apollos, Cephas, Tychicus, Epaphroditus, Caesarius, and Onesiphorus; Patapius of Thebes; Cyril, founder of Chelmogorsk Monastery (Karelia); Sophronius I, Bishop of Cyprus; Parthenios of Chios; Budoc, Bishop of Dol; Valerius, Bishop of Trier.

WEDNESDAY

DECEMBER 9

Conception by St. Anna of the Most Holy Mother of God
Abstain from meat and dairy products, and fish.
Galatians 4:22-27; Luke 8:16-21

In the Orthodox Church, the place of our All-Holy Lady, the Theotokos and Ever-virgin Mary, is especially sublime. According to St. John of Damaskos, she holds the second place after the Holy Trinity…The person of the Theotokos is presented in the Gospels as a model and example of a faithful woman, called to salvation in the faith and grace of God. She holds an exceptional position within the Church. She is the beautiful, modest, humble maiden who totally accepted the divine Word with complete faith. In contrast to the first Eve, Mary is obedient to the divine will — to the divine calling in its most perfect form.

+*Elder Moses of Mt. Athos*

THE CONCEPTION BY SAINT ANNA OF THE MOST HOLY MOTHER OF GOD. St. Anna was descended from the tribe of Levi, the youngest daughter of the priest Nathan from Bethlehem. She married St. Joachim, a native of Galilee. For a long time, they remained childless. After twenty years of fervent prayer by Anna and Joachim, the Archangel Gabriel, the messenger of God, appeared separately to them, announcing that God had heard their prayers and they would give birth to a daughter, Mary, who would bring blessings to the whole human race. St. Anna conceived at Jerusalem, and after nine months, the Most Holy Virgin Mary was born.

COMMEMORATIONS: The Conception by St. Anna of the Most Holy Theotokos; Prophetess Anna (Hannah), mother of the Prophet Samuel; Stephen "the New Light" of Constantinople; Narses of Persia; New Martyr Priest Sergius Mechev of Moscow; Sositheus of Persia; Martyr Isaac; Valeria of Aquitaine; Mardarije of Libertyville, Illinois; Commemoration of the Founding of the Church of the Resurrection at Jerusalem; "Unexpected Joy" Icon of the Mother of God.

THURSDAY — **Abstain from meat and dairy products.**

DECEMBER 10   1 Timothy 6:17-21; Luke 21:28-33

*W*e remain all the time against one another, grinding one another down. Because each considers himself right and excuses himself, as I was saying, all the while keeping none of the commandments yet expecting his neighbor to keep the lot! This is why we do not acquire habits of virtue, because if we light on any little thing we tax our neighbor with it and blame him saying he ought not to do such a thing and why did he do it—whereas ought we not rather to examine ourselves about the commandments and blame ourselves for not keeping them?

St. Dorotheos of Gaza

ST. ATHANASIOS, BITHOP OF METHONI. When Arabs attacked ninth-century Sicily, the parents of Athanasios moved to Old Patras, in the Peloponnese. While yet young, Athanasios became a monk at a local monastery. He quickly attained the virtues. Even though he repeatedly refused, the Metropolitan of Patras made him abbot of the monastery, and shortly after that, he became Bishop of Methoni. With eagerness, he responded to the material and spiritual needs of the people, while still living a virtuous life. He advised his disciples to love and always have the remembrance of the Lord's Second Coming. St. Athanasios died peacefully, in the year 880. His grave became a source of miracles that people ran to for healing.

COMMEMORATIONS: Menas the Melodius, Hermogenes, and Eugraphus, of Alexandria; Hieromartyr Theoteknos; John, King of Serbia, and his parents Stephen the Blind and Angelina Brancovich; Gemellos of Paphlagonia; Martyrs Marianos and Eugenios; Athanasios of Methoni; Thomas Defourkinos of Mt. Kyminas in Bithynia; Joasaph, Bishop of Belgorod; Sergius Sorokin and Anna, nun-confessor, of Sreznevo (Ryazan); Translation of the relics of St. Nicholas of Vounenis.

Friday   **Strict Fast**

December 11

2 Timothy 1:1-2, 8-18
Luke 21:37-22:8

A novice monk at the Monastery of St. Panteleimon grew accustomed to praying ceaselessly...And, behold, one day during the vespers service, this disciple looked at the icon of the Savior and said the prayer: 'Lord Jesus Christ, have mercy on me the sinner.' At that moment, he saw the icon turn into the living Savior; the soul and body of this disciple were filled with ineffable sweetness, and his soul came to know our Lord Jesus Christ and that the Lord has ineffable beauty and meekness...Ever since then, his soul burns with the flame of love for the Lord.

St. Silouan the Athonite

VENERABLE LUKE THE NEW STYLITE. The practice of living on a pillar in asceticism continued into the tenth century. When war with the Bulgarians raged, Luke was ordered to go to war. He witnessed the carnage of the many thousands who had died, and he rejected the world as he saw it. Luke became a monk and was ordained to the priesthood. As a labor of asceticism, he wore heavy chains to subdue his body, and fasted six days out of the week, eating nothing but prosphoron that was brought to him. Then for three years, he lived on a pillar near the city of Chalcedon. A divine voice told him to go to Olympus, where he did not speak because he put a stone in his mouth. The saint later returned to Chalcedon and ascended another pillar. He lived there forty-five years, working many miracles, and praying for his soul.

COMMEMORATIONS: Daniel the Stylite of Constantinople; Mirax of Egypt; Barsabas of Ishtar, and 10 companions in Persia; Aeithalas and Acepsius at Arbela; Nicon "the Dry" of the Kiev Caves; Theophanes Ilminsky of Perm and Solikamsk, and 2 priests and 5 laymen; Nomon of Cyprus; Martyrs Terence, Vincent, Emilian, and Bebaia; Leontios of Monemvasia; Luke the New Stylite of Chalcedon; Synaxis of All Saints of Georgia; Repose of St. Kuksha of Odessa.

Saturday

December 12

St. Spyridon the Wonderworker
Abstain from meat and dairy products, and fish.
Ephesians 5:8-19; John 10:9-16

Here, in this world, many are living for the sake of the first seats of honor, the applause, the accolades, the rewards and the prestige, as they marvel at themselves and are glad seeing themselves in first place. When these people are mocked, they in turn mock others. They live to be applauded and praised, provoking others, seeking and begging for honors. And while imagining themselves in first place, they are indeed in last.

+Elder Moses of Mt. Athos

VENERABLE AMONATHAS OF PELUSIUM. Amonathas was the abbot of the Monastery of Pelusium. One day a magistrate went there to levy the poll-tax on the monks, so they gathered to decide a course of action to be taken. Some suggested they could go to the emperor, but Amonathas said, "So much trouble is not necessary." He told the monks to remain quietly in their cells for two weeks and to fast, and with the grace of God, he would deal with the matter. He also stayed in his cell. At the end of that time, the brothers were disgruntled because they had not seen Amonathas stir from his cell. They assembled once more, and Amonathas showed them a favorable document bearing the emperor's seal and the magistrate's signature. He said that he had accomplished it the night when they first met, and the brothers were filled with fear.

COMMEMORATIONS: Spyridon the Wonderworker, Bishop of Trimythus; Alexander, Archbishop of Jerusalem; John, Metropolitan of Zichne; Therapon, abbot of Monza Monastery; John of Zedazeni Monastery, Georgia; Anthus of Palestine and Amonathas of Pelusium; Abra of Poitiers; Synesius of Rome; Finian of Clonard and Skellig Michael, teacher of Ireland; Corentin, Bishop of Quimper; Colman of Glendalough; Mardarije Uskokovic of Libertyville; Synaxis of the First Martyrs of the American land: Juvenal the Protomartyr, Peter the Aleut, Seraphim of Uglich; John Kochurov of Chicago, Alexander Khotovitsky of New York.

SUNDAY

December 13

Eleventh Sunday of Luke
Abstain from meat and dairy products, and fish.
Colossians 3:4-11; Luke 14:16-24

As soon as children begin to comprehend, the parents should teach them the Symbol of Faith, how to pray and chant, and the order of the Divine Services.

St. John Chrysostom

VENERABLE ARCADIUS OF VYAZMA AND NOVY TORG. From his childhood, Arcadius was taught prayer and obedience by his pious parents. When he was in church, he would often weep tears of spiritual joy. Even though he seldom spoke, his advice was always right, and his predictions would come to fruition. Arcadius found an experienced guide in St. Ephraim the Wonderworker of Novy Torg, who taught him to avoid spiritual dangers and how to navigate the difficult path of being a fool-for-Christ. The people of Vyazma would witness his miracles, but Arcadius fled fame. Ephraim and Arcadius founded a church and monastery in honor of Sts. Boris and Gleb the Passion-bearers. Arcadius received monastic tonsure there, and he never missed a divine service and was always the first to arrive for Matins. St. Ephraim died in 1053, and St. Arsenius died twenty-four years later. About 500 years later, a chapel dedicated to St. Arcadius was built in Vyazma. His relics that had been glorified by miracles were uncovered and placed in a stone crypt in the Sts. Boris and Gleb Cathedral in Novy Torg.

COMMEMORATIONS: Lucia (Lucy) of Syracuse; Eustratius, Auxentius, Eugene, Mardarius, and Orestes, at Sebaste; Arsenios of Mt. Latros; Ares, monk; Auberius, bishop; Columba on Lough Derg (Ireland); Odilia of Alsace (Gaul); Innocent of Cherson; Mardarius of the Kiev Caves; Gabriel, Patriarch of Serbia; Arcadius of Vyazma and Novy Torg; Dositheus, Metropolitan of Moldavia; Repose of St. Herman, Wonderworker of Alaska; Commemoration of the miracle by the Holy Five Martyrs.

MONDAY   **Strict Fast**

DECEMBER 14

2 Timothy 2:20-26
Mark 8:11-21

Unfortunately nothing, nothing at all scares or intimidates us; we have become worse than the irrational beasts because they know their protector and master. Man, however, not only does not know Him, but even blasphemes against Him.

+Elder Philotheos Zervakos

COMMEMORATION OF THE TERRIBLE THREAT OF THE EARTHQUAKE IN 557. The terrible earthquake of 557 lasted ten days, and the walls of Constantinople suffered damage so that the enemy could pass through. The dome of Aghia Sophia weakened and then collapsed five months later. Many churches also fell. People left their homes, and a shower of sleet soaked them so that they suffered greatly from the cold. They mingled freely without regard for social rank. Still, large numbers of ordinary people perished. The short-term result of all this was that the wealthy were motivated to charity, the doubters to pray, the vicious to virtue and even Emperor Justinian went around without his crown for forty days. However, the lessons in humility, charity, and virtue that were learned from this catastrophe were short-lived, and everyone lapsed into their former selves.

COMMEMORATIONS: Philemon, Apollonius, Arianus, Theoctychus, and 4 guards converted by St. Arianus, martyred at Alexandria; Thyrsus, Leucius, Callinicus, with others, in Bithynia; Folciunus, Bishop of Tervas; Hilarion, Metropolitan of Suzdal and Yuriev; Nicasius of Rheims; Venantius Fortunatus, Bishop of Poitiers; Hygbald, abbot in Lincolnshire; Bassian Pyatnitsky, Archbishop of Tambov; Miraculous deliverance from an earthquake in the year 557.

TUESDAY

DECEMBER 15

St. Eleutherios the Hieromartyr
Abstain from meat and dairy products, and fish.
2 Timothy 1:8-18; Mark 2:23-3:5

*I*f you continue attentively to study yourself, you will find many… inner crosses. For instance, hell, which you have so carelessly avoided considering until now, will suddenly appear to you as a very real threat. Paradise, which the Lord has prepared for you and which has barely crossed your mind, will vividly present itself to you as it really is: a place of eternal and pure joy from which you have deprived yourself by your careless way of life. If, in spite of the inner turmoil brought about by such reflections, you firmly resolve to repent and amend your ways and… you diligently pray to the Lord to save you and you decide to surrender yourself totally to His will, then the Lord will reveal to you more clearly the state of your soul so that you may be totally healed.

St. Innocent of Alaska

MARTYR BACCHUS THE NEW OF PALESTINE. Bacchus was one of seven children from eighth-century Palestine. His mother remained a Christian, but his father apostatized from the Christian faith and raised his children as Muslims. When his father died, Bacchus received Baptism and monastic tonsure at the Monastery of St. Savvas near Jerusalem. He adorned himself with the virtues of prayer, fasting, vigil, and labor. However, fearing that harm would come to the monastery, the abbot sent Bacchus back home. He told his mother everything that had happened to him, and she told her other sons. They decided to receive holy Baptism, except for one, who reported Bacchus to the authorities. Bacchus was arrested, and he confessed his faith in Christ and was beheaded.

COMMEMORATIONS: Susanna the Deaconess; Eleutherius of Illyricum, and Anthia, Coremonus, and 2 executioners; Paul the New; Eleutherius of Byzantium; Pardus of Palestine; Stephen the Confessor; Joseph of Petrograd; Bacchus the New; Hilarion of Vereya; Tryphon of Pechenga, and Jonah; Aubertus, bishop; Nectarios of Bitol; Synaxis of the Saints of Kola.

WEDNESDAY   **Strict Fast**

DECEMBER 16
2 Timothy 4:9-22
Mark 8:30-34

*W*hen you don't live with Christ, you live in melancholy, in sadness, in stress, in grief. You don't live correctly. So then many anomalies appear also in the body. The body gets affected, the endocrinous glands, the liver, the spleen, the pancreas, the stomach. You are told: "In order to be healthy, you must have some milk in the morning, an egg, butter and a couple of rusks." And yet, if you live correctly, if you love Christ, you are just fine with an apple and an orange. The greatest of all medicine is to offer oneself in devotion to Christ. Everything gets healed. Everything functions properly. God's love transforms all; it alters, it sanctifies, it corrects, it changes, it modifies everything.

St. Porphyrios the Kapsokalyvite

HOLY PROPHET HAGGAI. In Hebrew, Haggai means "feast." He was born in Babylon of the priestly tribe of Levi. At a young age, he returned to Jerusalem. He prophesied with the Prophet Zachariah for thirty-six years. He was famous for his virtue and honorable manner. Haggai prophesied the return of the Jews to Jerusalem from Babylon and the rebuilding of the Temple of Solomon. He died peacefully in old age and was buried in the area where the most esteemed priests were laid to rest.

COMMEMORATIONS: Prophet Haggai (Aggaeus); Modestos, Archbishop of Jerusalem; Theophano, wife of Byzantine Emperor Leo the Wise; Memnon, Archbishop of Ephesus; Sophia (Solomonia), nun, wife of Grand Duke Basil III of Moscow; Nicholas Chrysoberges, Patriarch of Constantinople; Martyrs Promus and Hilarion; Marinos of Rome; Vladimir Alexeyev of Okhansk; Parasceva Rodimtseva, abbess of Toplovsky Convent (Simferopol); Arcadius Ostalsky, Bishop of Bezhetsk.

THURSDAY

DECEMBER 17

Holy Prophet Daniel
Abstain from meat and dairy products, and fish.
Hebrews 11:33-12:2
Mark 9:10-15

*C*lear conscience is acquired with fasting, vigil, with patience and courage.

+Elder Efstratios of Glinsk

ST. DIONYSIOS THE NEW OF ZAKYNTHOS. Dionysios was born to wealthy and noble parents on the island of Zakynthos. His godfather was St. Gerasimos of Cephalonia. He was bright and well educated and recognized the vanity of the world. After the death of his parents, he gave up wealth and glory and went to the Monastery of Strophades, about forty miles away. He received monastic tonsure and gave himself over to fasting, prayer, vigils, the pursuit of the virtues, and humility. Later, he was ordained Reader, Subdeacon, Deacon, and Presbyter. During a pilgrimage to Jerusalem, by way of Athens, the Archbishop of Athens selected him to become the Bishop of Aegina. Many pilgrims sought after him for his prayers, blessings, and spiritual instructions. Frightened that the praises of men would make him fall into arrogance, he chose a successor and returned to Zakynthos. He founded the Monastery of the Theotokos, called Anafonitria, where he settled in solitude and Hesychasm. Dionysios had mercy on the poor. The income that the monastery earned, he gave to the poor and helped them to prosper. For his virtuous life, God granted him the gift to work miracles. St. Dionysios died peacefully at the age of seventy-five. His holy body remains incorrupt and can be seen on the island of Zakynthos.

COMMEMORATIONS: Holy Prophet Daniel and the Three Holy Youths: Ananias, Azarias, and Misael; Dionysius the New of Zakynthos; Daniel (Stephen) the Confessor of Spain and Egypt; Patermuthius, Coprius, and Alexander the Soldier, of Egypt; Athanasius, Nicholas, and Anthony, founders of Vatopedi Monastery; Nicetas of Nyssa; Iacchus of Triglia; Paisius of Trnava Monastery, Cacak, and Abbacum the Deacon, at Belgrade; Misael of Abalak Monastery (Irkutsk); Sturm of Fulda Monastery (Germany); Sergius Florinsky of Rakvere, Estonia.

Friday   **Strict Fast**

December 18

Titus 1:15-2:10; Mark 9:33-41

Even the slightest thought that is not founded on love destroys peace.

+Elder Thaddeus of Vitovnica

HOLY LIVING-MARTYR EUBOTIOS. Eubotios lived during the fourth-century persecutions of Emperor Galerius. Because of his virtuous and God-pleasing life, he was arrested, placed in chains, and taken from place to place to be beaten. Even as he suffered, his prayers caused miracles that inspired many pagans to convert to Christ. Once, after he had been beaten with sticks and stones, he was thrown into a fire. However, God preserved him unharmed. Many people who saw this were amazed, believed in Christ and were baptized. When the governor Leontios of Cyzicus was informed of this, he had Eubotios bound, suspended, stoned, and whipped until his flesh fell apart. Then he was thrown to wild animals to be devoured, but when they did not harm him, the saint was locked up in prison. Many Greeks witnessed these miracles and continued to join the Christian faith. The governor sentenced Eubotios to be killed by gladiators, but instead, they killed each other. Twenty-two days later, while Eubotios sat in prison, Maximian received a message that Constantine was coming from western Europe to fight him. He was so scared that he gave orders to release all the Christians from prison. St. Eubotios was set free, and he returned to his cell, living five more years and performing many miracles. He peacefully gave up his spirit.

COMMEMORATIONS: Sebastian at Rome, and his companions; Modestus I, Archbishop of Jerusalem; Zacchaeus the Deacon and of Amisus; Daniel the Hesychast of Voronet (Romania); Sebastian, founder of Sokhotsk Monastery; Martyrs Phocas and Hermylus; Michael the Confessor at Constantinople; Living-martyr Eubotios at Cyzicus; Gatianus, first Bishop of Tours; Symeon, wonderworker of Verkhoturye; Sophia the Wonderworker; Winebald, abbot and missionary of England and Heidenheim; Thaddeus Uspensky, Archbishop of Tver, and Nicholas Klementiev, Archbishop of Great Ustiug.

SATURDAY

DECEMBER 19

**Saturday before the Nativity
Abstain from meat and
dairy products, and fish.**
Ephesians 1:16-23; Luke 13:19-29

We must always say the Jesus Prayer, wherever we may be.
St. Pachomios of Chios

ST. AGLAIS OF ROME. Aglais lived during the reign of Emperor Diocletian and was the daughter of the proconsul of Rome. She was merciful and loved the Martyrs of Christ. However, she was having an affair with Boniface her servant, who was hospitable and compassionate to those in need. Their conscience accused them, and they desired to cleanse their sin. One day, she instructed Boniface to travel to an area where there was great persecution and to return with the relics of a Christian martyr, who would protect and help them. Boniface responded, "If I bring back my own relic, will you accept it?" Aglais admonished Boniface to take the task seriously, as it was a sacred quest. Boniface went to Cilicia with twelve servants, where he saw tortured martyrs, and his heart was changed. He stood before the governor and confessed his Christian faith. He was arrested, and after many tortures, he was beheaded. When the servants learned that Boniface was martyred, they purchased his relics from the soldiers and took them back to Aglais. The evening before they arrived, she received a revelation from an angel of God, telling her that the relics of Martyr Boniface were coming. Together with the clergy, Aglais received the holy relics with reverence and buried them outside the city of Rome. Later she built a church dedicated to St. Boniface. Many miracles happened there every day. From that time, Aglais distributed her wealth to the poor, lived in repentance and harsh asceticism, and God granted her the grace to work miracles. St. Aglais died peacefully.

COMMEMORATIONS: Boniface at Tarsus, and Aglais of Rome; Boniface the Merciful of Ferentino; Gregory of Omirits; Elias, Ares, and Probus, in Cilicia; Polyeuctus at Caesarea and Timothy the Deacon; Martyr Tryphon; George the Scribe and Sava of Khakhuli Monastery; Amphilochius of Pochaev; Eutyches and Thessalonica, with 200 men and 70 women; Capito of Cherson; Elias of Murom; Martyr Tryphon; Seraphim of Sukhumi.

SUNDAY

DECEMBER 20

Sunday before the Nativity
Genealogy Sunday
Abstain from meat and dairy products, and fish.
Colossians 1:12-18; Matthew 1:1-25

Men forsook God, and made carved images of men. Since therefore an image of man was falsely worshipped as God, God became truly Man, that the falsehood might be done away.
St. Cyril of Jerusalem

PHILOGONIOS, PATRIARCH OF ANTIOCH. Philogonios was an accomplished academician with an in-depth knowledge of each science, as well as all areas of learning. He was well versed in sacred writings and had a love for God. He had a well-ordered mind and became a lawyer. He also had a wife and family. He became famous for his eloquent and masterful defense of the oppressed and those unjustly harmed. He was a man of integrity and led an impeccable life. He was imprisoned for a time during the fourth-century persecutions. St. John Chrysostom says that Philogonios was elevated to the episcopal throne of Antioch in a surprising manner. The people physically took him from the marketplace to the episcopal throne and made him their bishop. He used his considerable legal skills in defense of Orthodox unity against the heretical Arians, who denied the divinity of Christ. Philogonios was one of their primary opponents. He was an expert administrator, and the Church prospered under his guidance. St. Philogonios died peacefully in about the year 323. St. John Chrysostom wrote a eulogy to St. Philogonios in the year 386.

COMMEMORATIONS: All the Ancestors of Christ according to the flesh: including, Adam, Abel, first martyr in the history of mankind, Abraham, Isaac and Jacob, Moses, Joshua, David the King, Solomon; Prophets Elias and Daniel, Zechariah, Joachim and Anna, Joseph the Betrothed, Sarah, Rebecca, Ruth, Deborah, and others; Ignatius the God-bearer, Bishop of Antioch; Philogonios, Patriarch of Antioch; Daniel II, Archbishop of Serbia; Ignatius, archimandrite of the Kiev Caves; John of the isle of Thasos, at Constantinople; Anthony, Archbishop of Voronezh; Repose of St. John of Kronstadt; "Rescuer of the Drowning" Icon of the Mother of God.

Monday   **Strict Fast**

December 21

Hebrews 3:5-11, 17-19
Mark 9:42-10:1

*D*o not grumble, little one, do not; if the Lord had forgotten you or was not merciful to you, then you would not be alive. Only you do not see His mercies because you want your ways and pray for your ways, and the Lord knows that you are better and more useful. Pray always for deliverance from sorrow and from sins, but at the end of the prayer always say to the Lord: "O Lord, O Lord, Thy will be done."

+Elder Alexy Zosimovsky of Russia

ST. PROCOPIUS OF VYATKA, FOOL-FOR-CHRIST. At the age of twenty, Procopius feigned foolishness to escape a marriage that was being forced upon him. He secretly fled to the city of Khlynov where he became a fool-for-Christ. He lived in the streets half-naked and slept wherever night found him, never accepting the shelter of a house. He never spoke, and he used signs to make himself understood, except with his spiritual father he conversed normally. Whenever Procopius was given clothing, he would wear it for a while and then give it away to someone in need. God granted him the gifts of clairvoyance and prophecy. Whenever he visited the sick and knew they were going to get better, he would set fire to their bed. If they were going to die, Procopius rolled them up in their sheets. When St. Procopius made a prediction, he did it disconcertingly, so his meaning would not be apparent until the event came to pass. He lived thirty years in this manner. St. Procopius foretold his death at the age of forty-nine, in the year 1627.

COMMEMORATIONS: Abel, son of Adam and first Martyr in history of mankind; Juliana of Nicomedia, and with her 500 men and 130 women; Themistocles of Myra in Lycia; Macarius the Faster, abbot of the Khakhuli Monastery; Juliana, Princess of Vyazma; Procopius of Vyatka, fool-for-Christ; Philaret (Theodosius), Metropolitan of Kiev; Nicetas Pribytkov, Bishop of Belev; Repose of Peter, Metropolitan of Kiev and Moscow; Finding of the relics of New Monk-martyr St. Ephraim of Nea Makri.

Tuesday   **Strict Fast**

December 22

Hebrews 4:1-13
Mark 10:2-12

If you want your child to be healthy, I will teach you what you need to do. Sewing or buying a child's outfit, do the same to the poor child: for his sake, God will keep your child. If you only care about your child eating and drinking sweetly and wearing beautifully, and the fate of a poor child will not worry you, your child will die and your heart will be torn to pieces. When you cut a tree, its branches dry out immediately, and if you water its root, the branches are filled with force. Similarly, you, parents, can be likened to a tree: you are the root of your children, and when you "water" yourself with fasting, prayer, alms and good deeds, God also keeps your children. And if you "dry up" from sins, God will kill your children by sending you to hell with them. If an apple tree gives sour apples, who is to blame: an apple tree or apples? Apple tree. So, do the right thing, you parents, so that your apples become sweet.

St. Cosmas Aitolios

MARTYR FLAVIAN, FORMER PREFECT OF ROME. In the fourth century, Emperor Julian the Apostate replaced Flavian as the Prefect of Rome because it was discovered that he was a Christian. He was branded on the forehead as a slave and exiled to Tuscany, Italy. They tortured him, and he died from his wounds while in prayer. Flavian's widow, Dafrosa, was later pursued in marriage by a certain Faustus, but she refused and converted him to Christ. He was baptized and later executed. His body was thrown to the dogs, but Dafrosa recovered it and secretly buried him. St. Flavian appeared to Dafrosa in a dream, calling her to join him in heaven. After five days, while engaged in prayer, she also died.

COMMEMORATIONS: Anastasia of Rome, the Deliverer from Bonds, and her teacher Chrysogonus, and with them: Theodota, Evodias, Eutychianus, Zoilus, and others, who suffered under Diocletian; Flavian, former Prefect of Rome; Boris Talantov of Kostroma.

WEDNESDAY   **Strict Fast**

December 23
Hebrews 5:11-6:8
Mark 10:11-16

*N*ow may the God and Father of our Lord Jesus Christ, and the eternal high priest himself, the Son of God Jesus Christ, build you up in faith and truth and in all gentleness and in all freedom from anger and forbearance and steadfastness and patient endurance and purity.

St. Polycarp of Smyrna

HOLY TEN MARTYRS OF CRETE. These ten martyrs were distinguished citizens and Christians from the island of Crete. Greek pagans captured them during the third-century persecutions of Emperor Decius. The prefect of Crete ordered torments for them because they would not willingly sacrifice to the idols. For thirty days, they were beaten, stoned, and mocked. They remained steadfast in their faith, so the prefect gave orders to behead them. Their last prayer was, "O Lord, forgive Thy servants and accept our outpoured blood that all may be released from the darkness of ignorance and come to know Thee, the true light, O eternal King!" Sixty years later, the relics were uncovered and found incorrupt. Their names are Theodulus, Saturninus, Euporus, Gelasius, Eunician, Zoticus, Pompeius, Agathopus, Basilides, and Evaristus.

COMMEMORATIONS: Paul, Bishop of Neo-Caesarea; Theoctistus, Archbishop of Novgorod; Niphon, Bishop of Constantia on Cyprus; Holy 10 Martyrs of Crete: Theodulus, Saturninus, Euporus, Gelasius, Eunician, Zoticus, Pompeius, Agathopus, Basilides, and Evaristus; Nahum of Ochrid, enlightener of the Bulgarians; David of Echmiadzin in Armenia; Egbert of Rathmelsigi; Martyr Schinon; Paul Kratirov, Bishop of Starobelsk; Macarius Mironov of Zavidovskaya Gorka (Tver); John Smirnov of Bolshoye Mikhailovskoye (Tver); Consecration of the Church of Holy Wisdom in Constantinople.

Thursday

December 24

Eve of the Nativity of Christ
Strict Fast
Hebrews 1:1-12; Luke 2:1-20

*B*lessed are those who have Christ as their hearts' axis and joyfully revolve around His Holy Name.

St. Paisios the Athonite

VENERABLE APHRODISIOS THE SABAITE. Aphrodisios was by birth Asian. He was a monk that worked with mules and was able unassisted to lift from the ground a load of a mule and place it on his shoulders. He once lost his temper with a mule and hit it in the face with his hand. The animal instantly fell to the ground and died. His abbot, the great Theodosios, expelled him from the monastery for killing the mule. Aphrodisios was advised that if he wanted to be saved, he should go to Abba Savvas and do what he said. Savvas told him to go into a cell and be content there, to not visit any other cells or go outside the monastery, and to control his tongue and belly, and he will be saved. For thirty years, Aphrodisios followed this obedience. He slept in straw on a rush-mat, wore a patchwork cloak, and made ninety baskets each month. He would put his food, whether greens, pulses or roughage, in a single bowl and eat a little from it each day. If the dish began to smell or produce worms, he would not throw it away but added more leftovers. His wailing accompanied his prayers every night. Aphrodisios received foreknowledge of his death a week in advance. He went to visit Theodosios with a note from Abba Savvas, which said that he had received Aphrodisios as a man and was sending him now as an angel. After a short illness, St. Aphrodisios died.

COMMEMORATIONS: Eugenia of Rome, and with her, Philip her father, Protus, Hyacinth, Basilla, and Claudia; Aphrodisios and Antiochus, monks of Palestine; Bitimius of Scetis; Achmed (Ahmet) the Calligrapher, at Constantinople; Nicholas the Monk of Bulgaria; Martyr Achaikos; Innocent Beda of Voronezh; Sergius Mechev of Moscow.

FRIDAY

DECEMBER 25

The Nativity of Jesus Christ
Fast-free period until January 5
Galatians 4:4-7; Matthew 2:1-12

*W*hat shall I say! And how shall I describe this Birth to you? For this wonder fills me with astonishment. The Ancient of Days has become an infant. He Who sits upon the sublime and heavenly Throne, now lies in a manger. And He Who cannot be touched, Who is simple, without complexity, and incorporeal, now lies subject to the hands of men. He Who has broken the bonds of sinners, is now bound by an infant's bands. But He has decreed that ignominy shall become honor, infamy be clothed with glory, and total humiliation the measure of His Goodness.

St. John Chrysostom

MARTYR JONAH OF PECHENGA, WITH 50 MONKS AND 65 LAYMEN. Jonah was a parish priest in Russia's Murmansk district. After the death of his wife, he entered the Pechenga Monastery as a disciple of St. Tryphon. The Russian monastery of Pechenga was for centuries the northernmost monastery in the world. St. Tryphon, a monk from Novgorod, wanted to convert the local Skolts to Christianity. Many other Russian monks eagerly joined him in this effort, so that fifty monks and two hundred laypeople were living there. However, in 1583, six years after St. Tryphon died, the wooden monastery was raided and burned down by the Swedes in revenge. St. Jonah was martyred during the celebration of the Divine Liturgy. Fifty monks and sixty-five laymen also perished.

COMMEMORATIONS: The Adoration of the Magi: Melchior, Caspar, and Balthazar; Commemoration of the shepherds in Bethlehem who were watching their flocks; Massacre of St. Jonah, with 50 monks and 65 laymen, at St. Tryphon of Pechenga Monastery.

SATURDAY

DECEMBER 26

Saturday after the Nativity
Synaxis of the Mother of God
Fast-free
Ephesians 2:11-13
Matthew 12:15-21

Let us be satisfied simply with what sustains our present life, not with what pampers it.

St. Maximos the Confessor

VENERABLE NICODEMUS OF TISMANA. Nicodemus was from fourteenth-century Serbia, and he was related to Prince Basarab of Wallachia and Prince Lazar of Serbia. He learned to read Holy Scripture from his childhood. Even though his parents wished to see him hold a high position, Nicodemus gave up their wealth and fled to Mt. Athos, to the Monastery of Hilander. After three years, he received monastic tonsure and later ordination to the priesthood. He returned to Serbia and set up two monasteries according to the regulations of the Holy Mountain of Athos. He had a great enthusiasm for the Hesychast renaissance initiated by St. Gregory the Sinaite of Mt. Athos, and Nicodemus brought the practice of this prayerful state to Romania. Through divine revelation, he founded the monastery of Tismana, which had the vital task of opposing the Catholic proselytism. Over time his monasteries benefited from the help of ruling princes, including Radu I, Dan I, and Mircea the Old, who called Nicodemus "my prayerful father Nicodemus." Nicodemus also impressed King Sigismund of Hungary with his gift of working miracles. When Nicodemus died, his relics were buried at Tismana Monastery. Later they were hidden due to the hostilities of the time. St. Nicodemus worked miracles both during his life and after death.

COMMEMORATIONS: Synaxis of the Most Holy Theotokos; Commemoration of the flight into Egypt; Euthymius of Sardis; Zeno of Maiuma; Nicodemus of Tismana; Andrew of Ufa and Valentina of Russia; Archelaus of Haran; Constantine of Synnada; Constantius the Russian; Evarestus of the Studion Monastery; Tathai of Llantathan; Jarlath, first bishop of Tuam (Ireland); Leonid of Mariisk, Isaac II of Optina Monastery, Basil, hieromonk, and Augusta, schema nun; "Bethlehem," "The Blessed Womb," "Merciful," "The Three Joys," and "Vilensk-Ostrobramsk" Icons of the Mother of God.

Sunday

December 27

Sunday after the Nativity
Fast-free
Acts 6:8-7:5, 47-60
Matthew 2:13-23

No one single virtue alone can open our physical door unless all of them follow as interrelated. If you acquire all of the virtues your soul will rejoice, and your mind will be delighted with this spiritual gain. You will be imitating God and you will possess the virtues and will seek to rise up to the likeness of God.

St. Mark the Ascetic

NEW HIEROMARTYR TIKHON, ARCHBISHOP OF VORONEZH, WITH 160 MARTYRED PRIESTS. Tikhon was from mid-nineteenth-century Novgorod. He graduated from Novgorod Theological Seminary and the St. Petersburg Theological Academy. At twenty-nine years of age, he was tonsured a monk and ordained to the priesthood. At the age of thirty-three, he was made the rector of both the Novgorod monastery and the theological seminary. Tikhon was a very kind man who gave simple and easily understandable sermons. Over a period of years, he was made bishop in several different cities, and in 1913 he became Archbishop of Voronezh and Zadonsk. With the Russian upheaval, the White Army retreated from that area, but Tikhon and 160 priests did not want to leave their flocks, so they were martyred.

COMMEMORATIONS: Holy Apostle and Archdeacon Stephen the Protomartyr6; Theodore Graptus "the Branded" of Palestine and Bithynia, brother of St. Theophanes the Confessor; Maximus, Bishop of Alexandria; Theodore, Patriarch of Constantinople; Barlaam, Metropolitan of Tobolsk and All Siberia; Maurice and his son Photinos, with 70 soldiers, of Apamea; Luke, monk of Tryglia; Fabiola of Rome; Boniface, founder of Panteleimon Monastery (Kiev); Tikhon, Archbishop of Voronezh, and with him 160 martyred priests; Uncovering of the relics of St. Therapont of Belozersk and Mozhaisk; (Sunday after the Nativity: Joseph the Betrothed, David the King, and James the Brother of the Lord).

Monday

December 28

20,000 Martyrs of Nicomedia
Fast-free

Hebrews 8:7-13
Luke 14:25-35

All…possessions do not really belong to the one who has them or to the one who has acquired them for they are exchanged back and forth like a game of dice. Only virtue among our possessions cannot be taken away, but remains with us when we live and when we die.

St. Basil the Great

VENERABLE BABYLAS THE MIME OF TARSUS. This account was written by St. John Moschos, in his book "The Spiritual Meadow." Babylas was a mime in the city of Tarsus, and with him were his two concubines, Cometa and Nicosa. They lived in a very self-indulgent style, doing whatever the demons might put into their minds. One day, they went into a church and heard, "Repent for the kingdom of heaven is at hand." Babylas wept with horror against his miserable self and for his sins. He called Cometa and Nicosa and said, "You know how self-indulgently I have lived with you…everything I have belongs to both of you…for as of now I renounce the world to be a monk." The two women burst into tears, saying, "We have shared with you this life of pleasure to the endangering of our souls. …We shall share with you in the good things as well." So Babylas enclosed himself in one of the towers of the city, and the two women gave all the money to the poor, took the monastic habit, and lived in a little cell near the tower. St. John Moschos writes, "I met this man myself, and was greatly edified by him. He is exceptionally gentle, humble, and merciful. Let those who read profit from what I have written."

COMMEMORATIONS: 20,000 Martyrs of Nicomedia, including: Glycerius, Zeno, Theophilus, Dorotheus, Mardonius, Migdonius, Index, Gorgonius, Peter, Euthymius, Agape, Domna, Theophila, and others; Apostle Nicanor the Deacon; Simon the Myrrh-gusher; Babylas of Tarsus; Ignatius of Lomsk; Cornelius of Krypetsk (Pskov); Nikodim Kononov of Belgorod, and Arcadius Reshetnikov; Martyr Secundus; Wunibald of Heidenheim; Nephon the New Cenobiarch; Repose of St. Hilarion Troitsky of Verey.

Tuesday

December 29

14,000 Holy Innocents
Fast-free
Hebrews 2:11-18
Matthew 2:13-23

If you observe the following, you can be saved: Be joyful at all times, pray without ceasing, and give thanks for all things.
— St. Benjamin of Nitria

VENERABLE BENJAMIN OF NITRIA. Benjamin was an ascetic and physician from Nitria in the fourth century. He persevered and fasted for eighty years, perfecting the ascetic life. God granted him the gift of healing, and whenever he laid his hand on any wound, it was healed immediately. Eight months before Benjamin's death, his body began to swell as it continued to retain water. His fingers became so large that a man could not encircle one of the saint's fingers with his whole hand. Benjamin continued to glorify God, saying, "Even when this my body was in health it in no wise helped me, and now that it is sick it in no wise hinders me." Because of his suffering, Benjamin was called a second Job. His friends built him a large chair for rest, since lying down was too painful. He continued to heal those who came to him but would not ask healing for himself. When St. Benjamin died, the doorway to his room was removed because he was so swollen.

COMMEMORATIONS: 14,000 Infants (Holy Innocents) slain by Herod at Bethlehem; Mark the Grave-digger of the Kiev Caves; Thaddeus, Confessor of the Studion; Athenodorus, disciple of St. Pachomius the Great; George, Bishop of Nicomedia; Benjamin of Nitria in Egypt; Marcellus, abbot of the monastery of the Unsleeping Ones, Constantinople; Lawrence of Chernigov; Basiliscus of Turinsk (Siberia); Theophilus and John of the Kiev Caves; Trophimus, first Bishop of Arles; Theophilus, abbot of Luga and Omutch; Evroult, abbot of Ouche in Normandy; Job Knyaginitsky, founder of Manyava Skete (Ukraine); Commemoration of all Orthodox Christians who have died from hunger, thirst, the sword, and freezing; Consecration of the Church of the Holy Forty Martyrs near the Bronze Tetrapylon.

WEDNESDAY   **Fast-free**

DECEMBER 30

Hebrews 10:1-18
Mark 11:22-26

Pride is when we trust in ourselves, in our mind, our strength, when we think we are more capable than someone else, better, more beautiful, more virtuous, more pleasing to God. Then it is certain that we are overcome by the ugly sin of pride, from which may God, who humbled Himself for our salvation, preserve us. Let us humble ourselves, brethren, because a proud man cannot be saved. Let us weep for our sins here, so we can rejoice forever in the next life, for after we leave this world everyone will forget us. Let us not hope in men, but only in God.

+Elder Paisius of Sihla

VENERABLE MARTYR ANYSIA OF THESSALONICA. Anysia was a Christian maiden in late third-century Thessalonica. When her wealthy parents died, she sold her inheritance and distributed it to the poor. Girlhood was a vexation to her because of its scandals. She fasted strictly and prayed with tears in her home and church. She regretted the length of life, as this kept her from heaven. She slept little, remembering that the demons did not sleep at all. On her way to church one day, as was her daily custom, a Roman soldier arrested her. Since the emperor Maximian decreed that it was permissible for anyone to kill a Christian, for whatever reason, he compelled her to offer sacrifice to the idols. She spat on his face, and he immediately killed her with his sword. Christians buried St. Anysia and had a chapel built at the site of her grave.

COMMEMORATIONS: Anysia at Thessalonica; Theodora, nun of Caesarea; Philoterus of Nicomedia, and with him, 6 soldiers and 1 count; Magistrianus, Paulinus, Umbrius, Verus, Severus, Callistratus, Florentius, Arianus, Anthimus, Ubricius, Isidore, Euculus, Sampson, Studius, and Thespesius, under Julian the Apostate; Apostle Timon the Deacon; Macarius, Metropolitan of Moscow; Tryphon, Bishop of Rostov; Leo the Archimandrite; Gideon of Karakallou Monastery; Egwin of Worcester; Uncovering of the relics of St. Daniel of Pereyaslavl.

Thursday

Fast-free

December 31

Hebrews 10:35-11:7
Mark 11:27-33

If we love someone, we always think of him, strive to please him, day and night our heart is occupied with this subject. Is it thus that you…love God? Do you often turn to Him, do you always think of Him, do you always pray to Him and fulfill His holy commandments? For our good, for our happiness, at least let us make a promise to ourselves, that from this day, from this hour, from this minute we shall strive to love God above all, and fulfill His holy will!

St. Herman of Alaska

ST. GEORGE THE MACHEROMENOS, AND WONDERWORKER. Macheromenos means "the Stabbed." Today near the abandoned village of Kataliontas in Cyprus are the ruins of the ancient Church of St. George. The Cypriot folklore scientist Nearchos Clerides writes that during the Frankish rule and also the Byzantine period, this church and the village of Analiontas were famous for the many miracles that St. George performed. For many years the miraculous icon of St. George adorned St. Marina, the main village church of Analiontas. Today the icon is kept at the Archdiocese in Nicosia. It is likely that St. George was an ascetic hermit in that region, as there are two caves where the saint would have lived.

COMMEMORATIONS: Theophylactus, Archbishop of Ochrid; Gelasius, monk of Palestine; Dositheus, Metropolitan of Zagreb; 10 Virgins of Nicomedia; Zoticus the Priest of Constantinople, feeder of orphans; Melania the Younger, nun of Rome; Peter Mogila, Metropolitan of Kiev; Gaius, monk; Sabiana, abbess of Samtskhe Convent; Anysius, Bishop of Thessalonica; Cyriacus of Bisericani Monastery (Romania); Cyriacus of Tazlau Monastery (Romania); Gaius, monk; Martyr Olympiodora; Martyr Nemi; Martyrs Busiris, Gaudentius, and Nemo; George (Macheromenos) the Wonderworker.

2021 Daily Lives, Miracles, and Wisdom of the Saints & Fasting Calendar

Place your order at
www.LivesoftheSaintsCalendar.com

Orthodox Calendar Company
P. O. Box 11331
Pittsburgh, PA 15238
Email: OrthodoxCalendarCompany@gmail.com
Facebook.com/OrthodoxCalendarCompany
Tel. 412-736-7840